D0504227

EDENDERRY

2 9 OCT 2021

WITHDRAWN

Beyond Faith and Adventure

*Irish Missionaries in Nigeria
tell their extraordinary story*

Irene Christina Lynch

ICDL

First published 2006 by

ICDL

First edition.

Copyright © 2006 Irene Christina Lynch

The moral right of Irene Christina Lynch to be identified
as the author of this work has been asserted
by her under the Copyright, Designs and Patents Act 1988.

Every effort has been made by the author to identify all copyright holders.

The author would be happy to rectify any omissions at the earliest opportunity.

All rights reserved. No part of this publication may be reproduced, stored in or
introduced into a retrieval system, or transmitted in any form or by any means
(electronic, mechanical, photocopying, recording or otherwise) without the prior
written permission of the publisher, or in accordance with the provisions of the
Copyright Act 1956 (as amended). Any person who does any unauthorised act in
relation to this publication may be liable to criminal prosecution and civil claims
for damages.

A catalogue record for this book is available from the British Library.

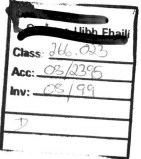

Class: 266.023
Acc: 08/2395
Inv: 08/99

ISBN 0-9553047-0-9

ISBN 978-0-9553047-0-5

Produced by Ross Print Services, Greystones, Co. Wicklow, Ireland.

Acknowledgements

It is a tremendous honour to have the President of Ireland, Mrs. Mary McAleese, contribute the foreword to this book. I wish to acknowledge this with gratitude.

I am immensely grateful to the principal sponsor of the production costs of the book, Irish Entrepreneur, Denis O'Brien, Chairman of Digicel Ltd. When he understood the importance of the book, he not only decided to sponsor it but also agreed to personally launch it. I am very proud that he has associated himself with my book in this way.

I am also grateful to Irish Life & Permanent plc for part-sponsorship of the book.

Warm thanks also go to Novartis AG for their assistance.

For his great interest and support, I should like to thank the Minister of State at the Department of Foreign Affairs, Mr. Conor Lenihan TD.

The generosity of all the sponsors is a great encouragement to St. Mary's Hospital, Eleta, Ibadan, Nigeria which will receive all the profits from the launch and sales of the book.

Thank You

I wish to thank sincerely all the people who agreed to be interviewed for this book.

I thank also Fr. Christopher Clarke OCD, Mrs Elizabeth Ekechi Okaro and Ms. Breda Collins for reading the manuscript.

A very special word of thanks to my husband, His Excellency, Joseph Lynch, Ambassador of Ireland to Switzerland, for his unstinting encouragement.

I dedicate this book to the late Sister Regina Diamond, RJM
whose radiance illuminated all our lives in Nigeria.

Taken seriously ill in Ekpoma in Edo State,
she was brought home to her native Ballina in the west of Ireland
where she died in January 2003.

'Unless a wheat grain falls on the ground and dies,
it remains only a single grain;
but if it dies, it yields a rich harvest.'

John 12:24

ÁRAS AN UACHTARÁIN

DUBLIN 8

Foreword

President Mary McAleese

Irish missionaries have made an enormous contribution to the physical, spiritual and economic well-being of so many people in the Third World. Nowhere is this more evident than in Nigeria. Since the arrival in West Africa of the first Irish missionaries one hundred years ago, many thousands of Irish men and women have devoted their entire adult lives working in every part of what was to become the Federal Republic of Nigeria in 1960. They brought not only material benefits in the form of education and health care, but also a deep love for the talented and generous people of this vast country.

At its peak in the early 1960s, over 2,000 Irish priests and nuns worked in often difficult and dangerous conditions in all parts of the country. Today those numbers have dwindled considerably. It is timely, therefore, that Irene Lynch should bring out a book which captures, in such a vivid way, the spirit, commitment and enthusiasm of these missionaries. It is a story worth celebrating. Irene came to know many Irish missionaries while her husband was Irish Ambassador to Nigeria from 1998 to 2003. Realising that we will probably never see such Irish missionaries again, she determined to bring at least some of their extraordinary stories to a wider audience.

She has done so in an engaging and insightful manner. She brings to life people with different personalities, backgrounds and aptitudes, each telling their stories in a simple yet gripping fashion. United in a desire to preach the gospel in its fullest sense, they continue to reach out to all, while working to build a new and better future for the people of Nigeria. They freely admit that they have often received more than they gave and have become better people, and better Christians, as a result.

Irish people have traditionally been supportive of their missionaries but that is now changing. It is my hope that, as a result of this book, many Irish people will re-discover the enormous contribution of these truly remarkable men and women.

MARY McALEESE
PRESIDENT OF IRELAND

Contents

Nigeria's 36 States

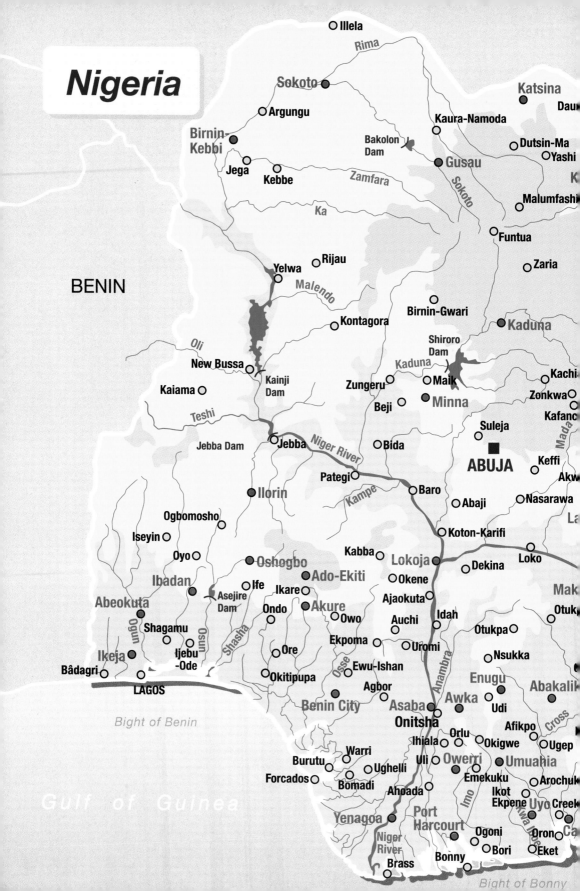

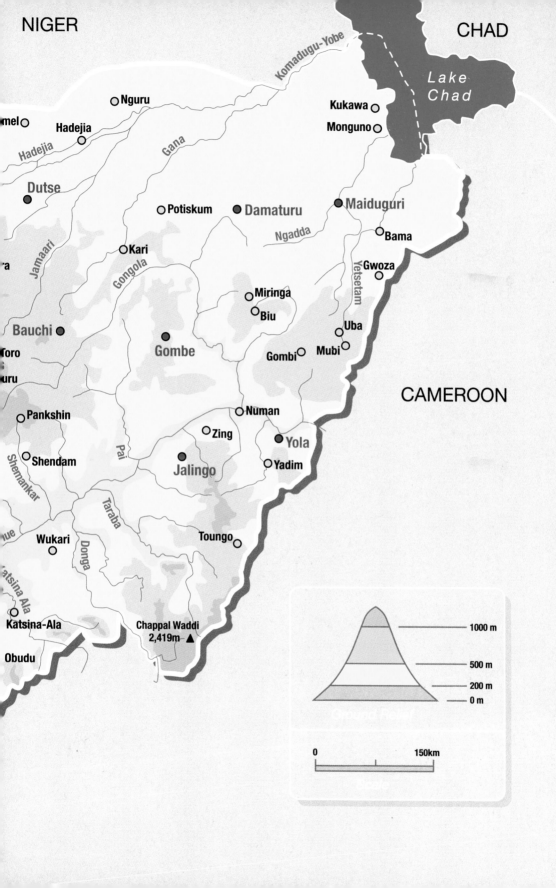

Nigeria

An Introduction

Nigeria is an enormous country of almost 1 million square kilometres. Composed of 250 pure ethnic groups, its population today is about 140 million, or one quarter of the total population of Africa. Situated wholly within the tropics, forest and woodland are to be found in the southern part of the country, which has an 800 kilometre coastline. As one progresses northwards, the land becomes drier and the vegetation more savannah. The northern part of the country forms part of the semi-arid sahel region on the fringes of the Sahara. In most of the country, the rainy season lasts from April to October and the dry season from November to March although there have been some remarkable changes to this pattern recently. The further north you go, the shorter that rainy season becomes.

The country is naturally divided into three by the Niger and Benue rivers, which flow from the north-west and north-east to meet just below the new capital of Abuja in the centre of the country. The enlarged Niger then flows south to the sea at the Niger Delta.

The three principal ethnic groups – the Hausa, Yoruba and Igbo – which make up about 40% of the population inhabit the northern, western and eastern regions respectively, although large minorities of these groups and other ethnic groups can be found all over the country. Hausa, Yoruba and Igbo are the three national languages and English is the official language.

The northern part of the country is largely Muslim while the southern part is mainly Christian. Traditional and animist religions are also to be found in pockets all over the country. The first traces of Islam in northern Nigeria can be traced as far back as the 11th century, while the earliest Christian missionary activity (Portuguese) in the south, dates from the 16th century.

In recent history, Nigeria was a British colonial territory administered on the basis of three administrative provinces, northern, eastern, western and the colony of Lagos. The British annexed Lagos in 1861 and it became the base from which, through traders and missionaries, its influence in the area continued to grow. Following the Berlin Conference of 1885 at which the western powers sealed the Partition of Africa, the territory of Nigeria came under British colonial rule. The British created the Protectorate of Southern Nigeria under Sir Frederick Lugard, who then conquered Northern Nigeria. For administrative/financial reasons, Lugard decided in 1914 to amalgamate the two parts into a single country called Nigeria.

During the decades following the amalgamation and indirect rule there was little rapprochement between the northern and southern parts of the country, and there was no great effort to make progress on the central or national question: how to establish a framework to encourage peaceful co-existence and equitable sharing of resources and responsibilities in the country. A movement for Independence arose from the educated elite in the south and this led to the granting of Independence to a very unready Nigeria on 1 October, 1960. The country became a Federal Republic in 1963. Nigeria adopted federalism to manage the country's ethnic and religious diversity.

After Independence, because of mistrust between the three regions and considerable instability, the first of many military coups and attempted coups took place in 1966. This signalled the beginning of military involvement in government and led to the control by the North over the army and the affairs of the country continuously from 1966 to 1999 with the exception of the years between 1979 and 1983 when a civilian northern president was in place. The secession of Biafra from Nigeria led to a civil war from 1967 to 1970 which resulted in over a million deaths and ended with the defeat of the secessionist regime of the Igbos.

The period of military rule was overall one of considerable corruption, destruction and hardship for the Nigerian people. It was not until 1998 that elections were held in a successful attempt to restore democratic rule to Nigeria. In May 1999, Olusegun Obasanjo was elected as President of the Fourth Republic. He was re-elected for a second four year term in 2003.

Nigeria is a Federal Republic with a vertical three-tier administrative structure comprising the Federal Government, 36 State Governments and 774 Local Government Councils. The constitution of 1999 distributes power among the three tiers. The Federal Government comprises three branches: the executive, legislative and judicial branches. The President, who is also Commander-in-Chief of the Armed Forces, is directly elected by the people. Administration of each of the 36 states is vested in an elected Governor, and each State has its own Assembly with elected members. There are now six registered political parties.

Nigeria is a country with enormous potential, and has huge resources of oil and gas. Its agriculture provides employment for almost 70% of the population. The Nigerian people are intelligent, talented, generous and welcoming. Their ardent hope for changes that will greatly improve their lives and realize the potential of their country lies in the restoration of democratic government. While much may have been done to restore the reputation of the country since 1999, much certainly remains to be done.

The leadership role of Nigeria in the future of Africa is of very great importance.

Irish Missionary Achievement in Nigeria

Irish missionaries have left an indelible mark on generations of Nigerians before and throughout the 20th century, and up to today. By their often heroic work, they have created an enduring bond of good will between the Irish and Nigerian peoples. The Irish people have at all times generously supported their missionary sons and daughters as they went to this distant and unknown African country.

In their work, they faced great difficulties and many dangerous situations in territory that was at one time known as 'the white man's grave' on account of its harsh climatic conditions. In addition to bringing Christianity to millions of Nigerians, they also provided education and health services which have educated generations of Nigerians and improved the quality of their lives.

The huge number of Catholics in Nigeria today is primarily due to the Irish missionary effort. The extraordinary Irish missionary impulse in Nigeria attained its greatest strength in the 1950's and 1960's, when there were more than 2,000 missionary priests and sisters in the country. That impulse is now coming to an end in its present form, due to a dearth of vocations in Ireland, but the work of the Irish is now being carried forward and developed by a strong local Church which is blessed with a very involved laity and a great number of Nigerian priests and reverend sisters who belong to indigenous religious congregations or congregations founded by the Irish.

What the Irish missionary men and women have accomplished may not be as well known or appreciated in Ireland as it deserves to be. It is because of this that I have compiled this book of interviews which allows the missionaries to talk freely about their lives and work in Nigeria. There are a number of interviews with the Nigerian priests and sisters.

I lived in Nigeria from 1998 to 2003 and during the course of my stay there, I met and got to know a great number of the remaining 280 or so Irish missionaries. I saw their work at first hand – work in the tradition of that done by their predecessors for well over 100 years. I visited many of them in their various locations which are spread over the vast and populous country of Nigeria.

I thought it would be very worthwhile to record some of the experiences of as many of them as was possible because their contribution to Nigeria has been a major achievement of the Irish Church. The set of circumstances which produced this unique flowering of missionary activity in Ireland may never be repeated.

I wish to thank all the missionaries who agreed to give me interviews and who offered me generous hospitality which I always enjoyed and appreciated. I ask pardon of those, many of whom I met, who are not interviewed in these pages. It would have been my wish to have included each and every one of them but this simply was not possible. I take this opportunity to recall with appreciation the visits of the six Irish Bishops who came to our residence annually for dinner and whose company we very much enjoyed – Bishop E. J. Fitzgibbon of Port Harcourt (Emeritus), Bishop Patrick F. Sheehan of Kano, Bishop Senan O'Donnell of Maiduguri (Emeritus), Bishop John Moore of Bauchi, Bishop Richard Burke of Warri and Bishop Timothy J. Carroll of Kontagora. I recall also the visit my husband and I made to *Sacred Heart Hospital*, Abeokuta which is run with outstanding efficiency and care by Sr. Helena O'Connell, OLA. I remember with joy the 7:30 a.m. walk I took in Enugu with the dedicated and talented Fr. Máirtín Conroy. I thank Fr. P.J. Sexton, former parish priest of St. Matthew's Parish, Amukoko, Lagos for the welcome I always received in St. Matthew's. Fr. P.J., I will not forget our céilí dancing at *The Small World Festival* in Lagos especially the year that you danced, despite suffering from the last vestiges of a bout of malaria! I thank Fr. Charles O'Reilly, OSA, for taking care of me when I visited Maiduguri. Thank you also to Sr. (Dr.) Deirdre Twomey and Sr. Joanne Kelly of the MMM hospital and leprosy village in Abakaliki for sharing a great morning with me at their compound. Thanks too to Sr. Cecilia Azuh, MMM, Abuja who took time out to tell me about the impressive HIV/AIDS prevention programme which she was co-ordinating for Archbishop John Onaiyekan of the Abuja Archdiocese.

I say to all the sisters and priests who came annually to our residences in Lagos and Abuja for our Christmas dinner party that I regarded those evenings of good food, song, dance, story and conversation as one of the highlights of the year. I remember with fondness and mirth one such Christmas party in Lagos when Fr. Dan Murphy, SMA, took two OLA sisters in blue habits by the arms and gave a sweet and delightful rendition of *Two Little Girls in Blue*. Last but not least, let me mention Fr. John Sheehan, an Irish American Jesuit whose fine operatic voice and enthusiasm for many events and projects added a special ingredient to our evenings and to our life in Nigeria.

To all, I offer sincere thanks for friendship and generosity. Their presence and their extraordinary work in this foreign land was always a huge source of pride and inspiration to me, as well as to countless numbers of Nigerians.

Cardinal Anthony Olubunmi Okogie

Archbishop of Lagos

His Eminence, Cardinal Anthony O. Okogie
Archbishop of Lagos

His Eminence Cardinal Anthony Olubunmi Okogie, Archbishop of Lagos, was educated by Irish missionaries in Nigeria from a very young age. During a recent visit to the mother-house of the Society of African Missions (SMA) in Blackrock Road, Cork, I was fortunate to meet with his Eminence who was having a few days rest and relaxation. Being tired, he had no wish to give interviews but did, at the request of SMA Provincial Father Fachtna O'Driscoll, agree to speak to me for a short while.

He enters the room in which I am waiting quietly and without ceremony. I feel very honoured to be in the company of a man whom I had come to know from my earliest days in Lagos as a holy man who was also fearless and relentless in his crusade for good governance, human rights, and social justice for the people of Nigeria. He was and continues to be one of the most outspoken of Christian leaders. Ever since he was appointed Archbishop of Lagos in 1973, at the age of thirty six, he has been unsparing in his criticism of military dictators and has not hesitated in recent years to criticise President Olusegun Obasanjo's administration for moving too slowly to implement reforms to improve the lives of Nigeria's poverty-stricken millions. Recent headlines in some of the country's reputable newspapers attest to this: *Okogie and Others Task Leaders on Service; Okogie Warns against Religious Politics; Okogie Condemns Police Siege on 1004 Estate, Victoria Island, Lagos; Riches at the Expense of the Soul lead to Eternal Damnation.*

Though Anthony Okogie was born and raised in Lagos and has for more than three decades played a prominent role in the Church and in his country's affairs, his ancestral background lies elsewhere. I ask him to tell me a little about that.

"Well, my father was from Benin in present-day Edo State and my mother came from Oyo. Both were born into princely families. My father had a very big royal history and though I grew up at a distance from all that – my father often sat us down as children and familiarized us with family history. I am now," he says simply and modestly, "a triple prince – from my mother's side, from my father's side and a prince of the Church.

"I was brought up in a Catholic home and eight days after I came out of my mother's womb, I was baptized by Fr. Dan Daly, SMA who is still alive and living in this house. I visited with him this morning. Unfortunately, he has lost his hearing.

"My first school was *St. Mary's Convent* in Broad Street, right in the centre of Lagos Island, run by Irish Sisters of Our Lady of Apostles (OLA) since the late 1870's. After that I attended the SMA-run *St. Gregory's College, Lagos* for a period.

"The idea of becoming a priest was not with me from a very early age. At a certain time, I became an altar server and so I got used to the Church – being around the priests, helping out and generally being introduced to their way of life which I gradually grew to admire and respect. There was one reverend father in particular who had a great way with children, so from him, a few of my friends and I learned a great deal. Gradually, a few of us began to develop the idea of becoming priests.

"In 1953, when I had already spent two years in *St. Gregory's College*, I became afraid that I was losing my vocation. I'm not exactly clear about what was going on in my mind but something pushed me to move out of the college and into the junior seminary in Ibadan. Among the Irish priests I met there were Fr. Jennings and Fr. McKay both of whom now live in this house here in Cork.

"There were many reasons for my becoming a priest. Firstly I just liked and respected the type of life they led. Secondly, when I was at *St. Gregory's*, there was a particular priest who was very rough with the students and I happened to be one of the ones who suffered from his harshness. One day a few of us said, 'let's become priests and show this man what a priest should really be.' Three of us moved out of the college after that and headed for Ibadan. Among the people I met there was the now Archbishop of Ibadan, Felix Alaba Job. He was just two years younger than me. We became enduring friends.

"In 1966, I was ordained a priest of Lagos and after ordination, I and others went back to Ibadan to finish our doctorates. All that was interrupted when the civil war – the so called Biafran War – broke out in 1967. I was asked in 1968 by Monsignor Pedro Martins who was a commissioned officer with the Nigerian Federal army and first Roman Catholic Chaplain to the Nigerian army, to go to the war front as an assistant chaplain. I was not a commissioned officer myself; all I had for protection was a scapular and a large crucifix. It was a tough and hard time."

When you reflect back on that war your Eminence, do you think that it was good that the Federal Republic of Nigeria remained intact by putting an end to the secessionist aspirations of the Biafrans – who were largely Igbo?

"Yes, I think that it is good that Nigeria has remained intact. The good Lord has placed each and every one of us within certain groups and settings, so for some of us to want to break out of those groupings is like wanting to undo the Lord's work. I observed many things during the war years. On one occasion at Christmas time 1968, there was a proclamation of peace for about an hour. During that hour, I saw that Nigerians and Biafrans were acting like brothers in friendship. When the hour was up, they went back to war!"

When I arrived in Lagos in 1998, I quickly became aware that you were a fearless and courageous man who was not afraid to speak out against all forms of injustice. Have you always been a forthright person?

"I think that fearlessness has a lot to do with my family background. My father was a very outspoken man, so was his father and his grandfather. All of them in their day confronted the British and that is why they were frequently exiled from their kingdom in Benin. My father came to Lagos at the age of seventeen and got a job as a custom's officer. When a number of years later, the British authorities brought in an expatriate – and a junior officer and placed him above my father in rank, my father resigned in protest, forewent his gratuity and walked away from everything."

Your Eminence, you have a huge task being Archbishop of Lagos – a teeming, sprawling city with its millions of Catholics in its 60 or more parishes. You told me earlier that you were feeling quite exhausted. Now that you have been elevated to Cardinal, has your schedule and workload become even more demanding?

"It hasn't been easy. Nigeria has two cardinals – Cardinal Francis Arinze and myself. Since I am the only one living in the country, naturally everyone is expecting to see me – to visit me. There are also so many events to which people want to invite me to and then I have to mind my own archdiocese which as you said is a huge one and it demands exacting attention. Apart from all of that, I have to attend a large number of conferences both in Nigeria and outside."

I understand that the number of Catholics in the country is close to 20 million. To the outsider, many aspects of the Church are beautiful to observe. The celebratory and joyful atmosphere at the Sunday mass – the singing, the offertory 'dance' – the sheer conviction of the participants and in general, the profound involvement of the laity. How would you rate the health of the Catholic Church in Nigeria today?

"Well now – ! In the first place, we thank God that the Church in Nigeria is growing and doing quite well but my fear is that the spirituality is not firm. It could be regarded as being only skin-deep in certain respects. This provides a challenge for the clergy. From them we need more action than preaching. If you see a man of God, you need to see him act as a man of God. The age of preaching that the good Lord said this and said that is over. People need to see more of the action as actions speak louder than words. As for the laity in the Church, they are now realizing that the Church belongs to them as well and they do not see themselves just as the icing on the cake. As I see it, in Nigeria, and in other places, they want very much to play an active part in the Church and they are beginning to tell us what they want to do and what they do not want to do. In Nigeria, we try to encourage this and we want to avoid the problem that not involving the laity sufficiently has caused in other parts of the world. For the Church to have a strong future, the laity and the clergy must collaborate and we still have much to do in Nigeria in this regard. Some of our priests coming out of the seminary want to style themselves as 'modern priests' and they will tell you that it is 'in fashion' to do things in a certain way or to dress in a certain style. As far as I'm concerned this sort of thing called 'fashion' has no place in the Church. A number of the priests for example do not want to wear vestments and it is my experience that the laity frowns on this sort of thing – they do not like it. I try to make my young priests aware of all of this. Take for example something as simple as kissing the altar before and at the end of mass! A very disturbed parishioner phoned me recently to ask when I had cancelled the 'kissing of the altar'. Now this is a layman and he is very upset saying – 'Your Grace, on the three occasions that I attended mass read by Fr. X, he never kissed the altar. Are there no more relics on the altar?' I think that priests cannot be careless about these important liturgical details and rituals because the laity notice and they care."

Your Eminence, what are your hopes for this great country – Nigeria – a country that has been blessed with phenomenal natural resources and whose people are so abundantly talented in so many ways?

"Well, I see a very bright future for the country. Presently, we are going through very rough waters but they will calm down. The present generation of politicians will go and a new generation will come up who will be more God-fearing, more honest, more down to earth, more caring and more in solidarity with the people. This sort of thing is taking place in Ghana now. Things are settling down very well there. The people may not always notice the changes but an outsider can see them. I think that is the kind of thing that is going to happen here. What is killing us at the moment is that many of those in power are there without the necessary qualifications, talent or ability. A country has a greater chance of prospering if the most qualified and talented individuals are running affairs. These individuals must also be imbued with integrity and have a commitment to social justice and human rights.

"Right now in Nigeria, I'm sorry to say that we have a government which is quite dictatorial. Our President seems to take pride in the fact that his party has a majority and that all he needs to do is send legislation to the House to be passed. This in not democracy in action. Time is showing that this way of governing is throwing up many problems. Look at the trouble they are having in the oil regions! I have found that before you say anything to the President, he feels he has the answer. He feels that he has the monopoly of wisdom.

"In Nigeria today, we should be worried about many aspects of our life. Take for example our educational system. The education I myself was lucky enough to receive was modelled on that established by the missionaries. They set good standards and laid solid foundations. They were extraordinarily dedicated. When our own people began to take over, many tried to improve on the missionary model and for a time, there was a certain amount of healthy competition. Gradually however things began to decline and when the government took over all the schools from the missionaries and voluntary agencies in the 1970's, they thought that they could manage education alone. They have since learned that it is not so easy. That is why they offered, some five or more years ago, to return some of the schools to the voluntary agencies. The Archdiocese of Lagos accepted to take back five. One of these is the OLA-run Maryland Comprehensive Secondary School in Ikeja. The school has made impressive progress.

"But we cannot leave all the blame at the door of the government. There is a kind of apathy right now so it is up to each and every one of us to play our part in this important area of the life of our country and in many other areas such as the fight against corruption and indiscipline. Now we need leadership and Nigerians are always asking for leadership but we must all – each and every one of us – play our part, be that big or small."

Cardinal Okogie has on many occasions spoken about this topic and has at times pointed out that the lawmakers are often the first to break the law, thereby giving the people the excuse to follow suit. In a recent interview with the 'Chinua Achebe Foundation' in Lagos, he spoke about how unfortunate Nigeria has been with its leadership and claimed that many of the leaders suffered from a lack in their upbringing. "Many of them came from incredibly impoverished backgrounds from an economic, spiritual and moral point of view. At the sight of public money, they just went crazy." He agreed that some of the present governors seemed up to the task of governing but is critical of the desperation displayed by some to be re-elected. He feels that if the conscience of the person in power is clear and in the right place, then that person should be confident that his good work will speak for itself in relation to re-election. He regrets that many of the people in power – once they find themselves there never want to leave and wonders if this is something peculiar to Africa. He admitted that he was ready to be removed from his position at any time if such became the desire of the Pope.

Your Eminence, when you were ordained a priest at the age of 30 in 1936, did you have an ambition to rise in the Church hierarchy?

"To be totally sincere and honest with you, the only thing I ever prayed for was to be a good priest. When I was appointed Auxiliary Bishop of Oyo at the age of 35, I was in shock and when at the age of 36, I was appointed Archbishop of Lagos, I was even more shocked."

How do you envisage your future?

"I don't know what the good Lord has in store for me or where He will lead me."

In your conferences with your fellow cardinals around the world, what is your sense of the health or state of the Catholic Church worldwide?

"The Church is both human and divine. The human element is what most people see and we forget that to be human is to err. The 'divine' is less to the fore. The late Holy Father, John Paul II made the divine element more evident by his own example and style of life. He was troubled and worried about the many things that were happening and that should not be happening. He was a true man of God and that message reached the people beneath and around him. He reached out in a very special way to the young people and they responded. We have only to remember the outpouring of sorrow at his passing to understand and realize the affect he had on both Catholics and non-Catholics. The new Holy Father will use his own remarkable talents and holiness for the good of the Church and the world."

Your Eminence, I thank you for giving me the privilege of speaking with you.

"Thank you."

Cardinal Okogie lives in a simple house adjacent the architecturally beautiful *Holy Cross Cathedral* in Lagos Island where he says, he is available to anybody who wishes to see him.

Society of African Missions
(SMA)

An Introduction

The Society of African Missions was founded in France in 1856 by Bishop Melchior de Marion de Brésillac to evangelize Africa. Less than three years later, in January 1859, the first SMA missionaries arrived in Freetown, Sierra Leone. In May of the same year, the founder himself arrived. Yellow fever, a deadly tropical disease, was raging, and by the end of June, the whole party with the exception of one had died of the disease.

Back in Lyon, this devastating news reached the tiny group of founding members. Father Augustine Planque succeeded Bishop de Brésillac as superior general. During his years as superior (1859-1907), mission territories were opened in what is now Nigeria, Algeria, Ghana, Egypt, South Africa, Liberia and the Ivory Coast.

The SMA was established in Ireland in 1878 and the Irish Province was established in 1912. Its main objectives have always been to establish full-fledged African Churches. Most of the 51 African dioceses in which they work have their own African bishops.

The SMA feels itself called to the service of the most abandoned, not only those who have not had the Gospel preached to them but also to those who are most in need of liberation from poverty, hunger and oppression.

The 944 members of the SMA come from Africa, America, Asia and Europe.

Most Reverend Dr. John Moore

Society of African Missions (SMA)
Bishop of Bauchi, Bauchi State

Most Rev. Dr. John Moore, SMA
Bishop of Bauchi

"I am very clear about my reason for becoming a missionary priest. My becoming one was a huge surprise to everybody else. Growing up, I wasn't in the least bit pious, in fact I was quite the opposite. When I told my father of my decision, he just couldn't believe it. He thought that if anyone was going to make a mess of the priesthood, it would be me! Right up to my ordination and maybe beyond, my family couldn't convince themselves that I was serious. As far as I was concerned, I felt that I was being reasonably honest with myself. I think I knew that if I didn't decide to do something which presented a religious challenge, I'd end up a millionaire maybe, but maybe also a proper gangster who might not pass through the pearly gates at the end of it all. There were sterling priests in my parish at home but I knew their type of life was not for me. I felt that the more rugged life of a missionary priest engaged in primary evangelization might suit me better. I felt that Christ would speak to me in that type of environment. I was a voracious reader as a boy and I used to enjoy books on foreign countries and different peoples. Characters like Stanley and Livingstone and all these types fascinated me. I had a very special interest in Africa so when I decided to join a missionary society, it had to be one that only sent men to Africa. I had no interest in finding myself among the Eskimos in the Arctic or anything like that."

This was Bishop John Moore speaking to me in Abuja. At that time, he was Vicar Apostolic of the Vicariate of Bauchi in Northern Nigeria. Since then, the Vicariate has become a fully fledged diocese.

Bishop Moore was born in Dublin on January 12th, 1942. After his secondary education in Synge Street Christian Brothers' School, he went straight to the SMA seminary in Cloughballymore, Kilcolgan, Co. Galway.

"I have been in Nigeria for more than thirty six years and they have been absolutely fantastic. They have measured up to all my expectations. I always expected them to be rugged, tough and unrelenting and they were. Clambering around mountains, crossing rivers, out in the beating rain, under the scorching sun, never having the best transport, trekking for hours, blood, sweat, tears, dust – I have experienced it all but nothing ever surprised me and I always managed. I was very naive when I came out and I was very, very thin. At the 25th anniversary of my ordination, the superior of my class in the seminary said to me: 'Out of all the students in your class, we thought you would never make it. You came from the city and you were used to the comforts and niceties of life there and then you went to Northern Nigeria'.

"I came to Nigeria in 1966 and in the '60's, Southern Nigeria had a certain amount of polish. There were some amenities. I went up to the North where there was nothing. We were frequently trekking for six weeks with the carriers of our loads. We'd arrive at an out-station in a little village – set down, cook on stones, wonder where we would put our beds – in the mud – in the pouring rain – in the middle of the night. But all of that was fantastic to me. I enjoyed every bit of it – the harder it was, the less it mattered – the more rugged the place, the more I thrived. I think God fits the back to the burden. Here in Nigeria, God has spoken to me through the people. My definition of a missionary would be a person to whom God speaks from a culture that is not his own. I believe that is why I am in Nigeria today. It's not that I had anything to give but I can tell you that I have been given a lot and I have learned a lot since coming here. I have become a better person. I have seen goodness. I have seen kindness. I have seen sacrifices here that would astound you and all that has touched me. They say that you think with your heart and that you go where you think you will find yourself and the truth. I knew I wasn't pious but I knew that by working among the people of Nigeria, I would become a better person, a more rounded person and a better Christian. Hopefully, that is what I have become over the years.

"In 1966, Northern Nigeria was forty years behind the rest of the country. The Catholic Church came there in 1907 so there was a basic structure on the ground. We inherited that which was forged by good men with the strong character that was perhaps bred out of loneliness and hardship. When we went into a place, we were expected to be like these men. We were expected to be upright and honest and to be people to whom children could be entrusted. Nowadays, when you hear all these stories of child abuse, you think of how innocent we were when we came out here! We never thought of anything nefarious. The children were very free with us. They were in our houses – playing under the table and over the table; they were like family. They came and threw their arms around us. They gave affection. Now that this whole scandal has happened, confidence and trust has been destroyed. It has not reached here, but if it does, it will unfortunately change that carefree and trusting relationship. At home, you are so conscious of your every movement – even with your own nieces and nephews when they come running to say *Hello Uncle John*. You don't want to lift them up and be affectionate because you feel eyes are upon you and you feel they are thinking – *what is he up to now?*

"Like every other human being, priests need affection. They need it from people and if they don't get it, the need will go underground and perhaps emerge in some irregular form. We need the people and the people have got to be educated to this fact and they have got to be encouraged not to leave the priests on their own – not to isolate them. We keep telling them here that they have an obligation to the priest who became a priest and a celibate for them. For God's sake we tell them, give him affection, give him affirmation, be amenable, invite him into your home. Don't leave him on his own. You find where people in communities do this, the priest lives a good life. If the priest himself isolates himself from the community, then that priest may move towards trouble.

"Now I have been very fortunate in Nigeria. Early on in my years here, I moved into the parish of Kwa in Plateau State for one year. I was with a Fr. Brendan Murphy, a terrific priest from Limerick. His house was always full of people from the community. He sat with them, ate with them and talked with them. In the beginning, I resented it and felt that they should not always be around the place. Then as the barriers broke down, I began to see the people for what they really were and I began to see their needs and that experience affected me for my whole mission life.

"After that, I was sent to Kwande, a very isolated place, for six years. It's in the Shendam region of Plateau State. The pattern of interacting with people kept me sane because for six to eight months of every year, I was cut off from everything because there was no way of crossing the flooded river. Today there is a bridge and road but in my time, there was nothing. I came to know every single person in that town. During the rainy season, if you got sick or anything, the people came around, looked after you and cared for you. When the dry season came and when the waters receded, other priests came in to visit. They'd come in and say, ' John, we have come to see you, can you not get rid of all these people for a while!' My response was always: 'Listen, my friend, when you are not around and when I am down and out and maybe at my lowest ebb, these people are around to lift my spirits and keep me focused, together and human. Now if you don't like it, you don't have to come here. They are with me for eight months and they too are looking forward to meeting some other expatriates so I will not deprive them.'

"Don't have any doubt about it but that you have your low days on the missions – days when you are depressed and feeling down and out. Sometimes this is brought about by bouts of malaria or it could be that things are not working out or that you are not getting the response you were expecting from certain quarters or not getting the backing from the Bishop for something that you think is worthwhile. You might see an opportunity pass you by – a building that you could have used for a school or a piece of land suitable for a church. You could find yourself putting your heart, your mind and your strength into a project only to see it disintegrate before your eyes. I don't mind the constant struggle; in a way, many of us thrive on that but if after the struggle, you find yourself back at square one, it can be very hard to start all over again.

"In my diocese of Bauchi, there is an estimated population of 1.5 million. Approximately eighty-five thousand are Catholic. We spend much time looking after settled parishes and engaging in the ongoing formation of those who have already been evangelized. There are so many places around that need support and encouragement. There are places that have not got the basic structures like proper churches and we also have very few priests available. We have vast areas comprising of over sixty villages with one priest to serve them. We need to divide these areas into new parishes and we need vocations to the priesthood. Right now we have eight indigenous priests and about twenty seminarians so the future looks quite good.

"If the Apostolic Vicariate is made into a Diocese, it is my ambition to be able to hand it over to a local Bishop. In that event, I'd retire and go off to be a parish priest somewhere. It has been done before so it can be done again. They may want me to stay on but certainly it is not a matter of will I hand over, it's a matter of choosing the right time. Before a hand-over could happen, Rome might have to look at a few things from an economic point of view. It might be a question of what contacts and what access to funding I might have that a Nigerian Bishop might not have. It would not necessarily be fair to put in prematurely a man who might not have the tools to accomplish what is expected. That could create a situation where the trust of the people could be lost from the beginning. There have been examples of this in the past. However, when the structures of the diocese are up and going, that will be the time for me to bow out.

"New bishops get some training. They are about to have a young bishops' meeting in Rome. What form it will take, I don't know but at least they will be given some idea of structures – how the Vatican works and how they can go about getting things done in a diocese.

"Most of the local clergy are excellent. You will always find one or two who are not great. The youngsters are very apostolic. Some of the older men may have had mixed motivation for joining the priesthood. They may have seen it as a nice way of life – status, a car, a house, electricity, a generator, a good meal or a way of life far above that of their contemporaries at school. It's possible that some looked at the comfort zone! Now the young priests are very focussed. The opportunities for them today outside the priesthood are many, so by choosing the priesthood, they are perhaps conscious of giving up a lot and making a pure and clear choice. The Nigerian priests will not do things the same way as we did them. There may be a slide down in some areas but in other areas, it will be the opposite and they will even do better than us. They know their own people and the people's response to them will be fantastic. That response will endure if the people are respected and not embarrassed by the behaviour or the lifestyle of the priest. Many wonder if the Nigerian priest will get caught up in obligations to the extended family, the ethnic group and so on. I would say that he cannot be expected to turn a total blind eye on his family and people who may be struggling but I think that most priests and bishops will try to make sure that all that is kept to a minimum.

"Here in Bauchi, we are in an area where there are non-Christians and a big Muslim population so it is very important that we are seen to be Christians, who are honest and upright, kind and forgiving and who stand up for what we believe in. There are people who are never going to read the Bible, the only Bible they will read is us, so we have to live the Christian message because only as it is lived, will it make an impression. I have many Muslim friends and my interpersonal relationships with them have always been good. When I was inside in Kwande, there were Muslims and Christians. My cook was Muslim. His Muslim children played around my house. His wife was wonderful. I know so many excellent Muslims and the vast majority here in the North are moderate. There are the fundamentalists however who feel that they are fighting for survival. They think that what they have is going to be taken away from them so some of them respond by being belligerent.

"Islam, especially here in the North is very much linked to politics and to the Hausa people. When you think 'Hausa', you think Muslim but this is not always true. There are large numbers of pagan Hausas who since British times, have been dominated and ruled by the Muslim Emirs. These people now want to be self-ruling and they are beginning to flex their muscles. This is interpreted by the Muslim Hausa as a threat to their control so jihadists from outside can often be brought in, in an effort to consolidate control.

"Because of recent worldwide terrorism, Islam has become associated with terror. A huge public relations job needs to be done. It is not sufficient to insist that Islam means peace when all you see on your television screen are signs of the opposite. Many peace-loving Muslims are working behind the scenes urging peace and tolerance but sometimes, it is an uphill battle. Here in Nigeria, it is alleged that people are being paid big money by outsiders in Saudi Arabia and Libya to build mosques and big houses. Once that sort of thing happens, the recipients have got to show some gratitude by implementing some of the ideas of the outsider. It is also alleged that poor and uneducated people are frequently manipulated by crookish 'Big People' who present themselves as good Muslims but who have other agendas.

"The enormous poverty in the country unfortunately plays into the hands of the manipulators. Nigeria is a wealthy country. It is rich in natural resources, yet the vast majority of the people are poor. In my years here over three and a half decades, I have always been hearing about the huge potential of this country. Sadly, I have seen standards fall. Education standards have gone way down. The brain drain is serious and there is a mad scramble for money and wealth at any cost. If all this was coming from the bottom up, there might be something that could be done. The country desperately needs good leaders who will be principled enough to resist the bribe. We seem to be in an age of thuggery, violence and assassination. People are often terrorized and it's very difficult to see how the country can extricate itself from its present situation. The people deserve better. Most of them live on a shoestring, making sacrifices for their children and suffering huge deprivations. Perhaps the hope lies with the ordinary person because out of their common struggle for survival, goodness, love and kindness are being born with an intensity that would never be found in an affluent society. There is a richness being generated that cannot be put on the market or the stock exchange. My hope is that all of that will not come to nothing.

"Being a bishop can remove you somewhat from the grass roots and I do admit that I miss the easy come and go of the ordinary people. I try to compensate for this as much as I can. People tend to put their bishop on a pedestal so it is important to remind yourself that you are a bishop not necessarily because you deserve to be one, or that you have extraordinary qualities or that it is your destiny. You are a bishop for the people and you are there as a symbol of their faith and of their efforts to be good and loyal over many years. When you go out, you have to live up to their expectations. They don't want to see their bishop go around on a bike or frequent public houses and bars. There are lots of little freedoms – harmless in themselves – that you have to do without because you know your people want it that way. There are certain functions you have to attend and there are certain things they like you to do. They want to see you on television at Christmas being interviewed about this and that. When you come out on formal occasions with your mitre and crozier, you shouldn't fool yourself that you are important. You are there because they are important and you are dressed up for them.

"Another aspect of being a bishop is the great sense of care that you develop for your priests. As a priest, you were not overly concerned about the priest in the next parish. You might even have been inclined to criticize him but now that he is one of your priests, you feel responsible for him. You will want to make sure that he is leading a reasonably fulfilled life and that he is not sad or depressed. You will not be in the business of criticism. You will want to defend him and help him as you know that he has put himself forward to dedicate his life to the priesthood. If he is having problems, you will want to help him and give him a chance. You will say to your people: 'be patient, give this man a chance to get back on the right track. Show mercy and charity.'

"Now I am a brash sort of fellow and I blast off, hit the roof or say something I shouldn't say but when people get to know me, they learn that I don't hold anything in or over a person – bringing it up again and again. I'll hit the person with it when it happens and then it's over. As a non-Nigerian bishop, there is a limit of course to the amount of blasting off you can do about many things. In many ways, it is good that the days of the expatriate bishop are nearly over. We had our day and we had our tasks and assignments. It's now time for the Nigerian to take over and many have done that already. The Nigerian knows his people and he is entitled to stand up in his church and make criticisms that are true and constructive. I cannot do that. If I do, I will have my marching orders. I was down in Jalingo recently and the Archbishop of Jos, Most Rev. Dr. Kaigama was openly talking about the Government and being brutally honest and critical. The Governor was sitting there in the church listening to all. What the Bishop didn't say was not worth saying but he was absolutely right and correct in all he said. I could never put myself in that position and it is a limitation. It means that I do not always feel empowered to speak on behalf of my people about injustices.

"Once the structures are on the ground for Nigerian Bishops to take over in every diocese, that is what will happen. I hope to remain here in another capacity. I like it here and as I said, this where God has spoken to me. This country is my burning bush. People sometimes say to me that I should take a sabbatical. 'For what?' I ask. I have seen people coming back from sabbaticals feeling very unsettled. I don't feel the need for sabbaticals. I read voraciously and I listen to loads of tapes to bring myself up to date. I see my indefinite future here. Of course, I could get a heart attack in the morning and go sooner than I think. I hope that will not happen. This is very much my country now."

Reverend Father Tom Walsh

Society of African Missions (SMA)
Abuja

Fr. Tom Walsh SMA, with two parishioners
- Chief and Mrs. Emmanuel Nwoye Okongwu
- at the Irish Embassy, Abuja on 17 March, 2003

"I came to Nigeria in 1982 and the initial two years were perhaps the most painful of my life. I was deeply culture-shocked, home-sick and I felt the absence of everything that was familiar. I was dispatched along with three others to a remote place in Ondo State where the SMA had a house which we nicknamed h-block. There, we were meant to learn the Yoruba language and become absorbed in the culture of the people. We had no water, no electricity and no news from home. We were living with a man who was warm and deeply spiritual but who had no awareness of any type of human need.

While there, I picked up almost every known illness and was constantly in and out of hospital. It is true that when the spirit is low, the body is weak. Many advised me to leave Africa. Two things kept me from doing so – the memory of the warm farewell of the people of my home parish and the haunting lines from Pádraig Pearse's poem which I had put on my ordination card: 'I have set my face to this road before me – to the deed that must be done and to the death that I must die.'

"I was born in 1953, the first of nine children and the older of twin boys. My mother was from Tipperary and my father from Athlone. I grew up on a council estate in Ballyphehane on the south side of Cork city. It was a wonderful parish and neighbourhood. Young and old, rich and poor lived side by side in harmony and friendship. Communities intermingled and our parish was the first in Ireland to establish a credit union. The Gaelic ethos was strong and roads were named after Irish patriots. We were sandwiched between the two great hurling teams of the day – St. Finbar's and Nemo Rangers. It was the dream of every boy to wear the jersey of one of these teams. Glen Rovers were to the north of the city but that was a world we southerners never ventured into. We had wonderful freedom as our homes were within one mile of the city centre and the countryside was just out the road.

"At fourteen, my twin and I went to the local technical school but I left at age sixteen to take what was regarded in those days a secure and well-paid job in Carroll's Cigarettes. During the three years that I worked there, I became greatly moved by the political events in Northern Ireland. The black and white television images of protesters being beaten off the streets and the shooting dead of nationalists on *Bloody Sunday* had a deep and lasting effect on my life. Nationalism and Catholicism became the driving forces in my life. I turned to Catholicism though many would argue that I left neither.

"When priesthood began to loom in my mind, I thought only of becoming a missionary. Ballyphehane had many missionary priests coming and going. They captivated our minds with heroic tales of courage and adventure. The SMA headquarters was just about two miles from my home so naturally I turned to them for advice. They were very welcoming. After a long period of discernment, I was accepted by them but since I hadn't studied for my *Leaving Certificate*, I was sent to Campion House, a Jesuit College in London which prepared men like me to get the qualifications necessary for entry into the seminary. It was a tough place and discipline was severe – sometimes cruel. It was also a difficult time to be in England and attitudes did little to improve race relations.

"I returned to Ireland in 1975 to do my novitiate year with twenty-two others who were fresh from secondary school. Only four out of that group reached ordination. In 1976, we went to Maynooth to study philosophy and theology. The college at that time had begun to open itself to the world. Clerical and lay students sat side by side. There was a host of activities to get involved in and I started a number of groups which offered support to republican prisoners in the North. Despite the new openness in the college, such *subversive activities* were not tolerated so I frequently found myself in conflict with the authorities. Nevertheless, my years in Maynooth were very happy ones.

"I was ordained in 1982 and it is still the most memorable event in my life. It was a huge community celebration in Ballyphehane and it lasted for more than two days. I set out for Nigeria in October of the same year and entered as I said the most painful period of my life. I managed to pull through and when my first leave came in summer 1984, Nigeria didn't seem such a bad place at all. After a glorious three-month vacation, I returned – this time to Lagos, a city which a British journalist described as having no parallel on earth. I was to spend the next ten years there – in Agege – a sprawling and dangerous shanty town in the western outskirts of the city. There you found huge numbers of people from many other West African countries. It was where they camped down after entering Nigeria. Some never managed to leave or improve their circumstances. I was the only white man and no matter how little I had, it was much, much more than they had.

"Crime was rampant and I was robbed many times. Since those days, no matter how hot it gets during the night, I never put on an air-conditioning unit as I never again want to be woken up with a fellow pointing a knife at my throat. Some of these people were really evil because they had grown up accustomed to a certain level of living and they were not able to change. Most of the people however were horrified and outraged when this sort of thing happened to me and I always believed in the innate good of the vast majority. Many white fellows walked away from this environment but I was intent on staying and bit by bit, we developed a church, a clinic, a school and credit unions. We also got big numbers of the people doing courses on development and leadership skills.

"The area was completely congested and you lived with constant and horrendous noise which came from the streets and the aeroplanes flying directly overhead. Looking back, I wonder how I ever stuck it for a day never mind ten years. In Lagos, which is said to have a population of thirteen million, one somehow becomes immune to huge pressure. The human body and the psyche seem to have a great capacity to absorb and adjust.

"We had a missionary network of course but frequently you became so absorbed in the work that the thought of driving out in dangerous traffic in the evenings became too much. We did make great efforts to meet on Thursdays at Badagry beach up the coast from Lagos. We brought cold boxes full of sandwiches, beer and things and that sort of thing really saved you. The waters at Badagry were lethal and some of us bought life jackets and took turns at dipping in the breakers.

"Fr. Cathal McKenna an SMA from Omagh was with me there for about six years. I think he was rather more nervous than I was! Cathal took a great interest in the cultural aspects of the great variety of ethnic groups we had in the area. He is now with me in Abuja and has got very involved in the parish action group for creating HIV/AIDS awareness. It's a very good group and they, among other things, go into schools educating the youth on the implications of the disease and urging specific life style changes. There is still huge ignorance and stigma attached to AIDS so a robust and ongoing education programme is an absolute must.

"In March 1993, I was asked to go to Abuja, the new capital of Nigeria which was then in the very early stages of development. The Archbishop there – Most Rev. Dr. Onaiyekan asked the SMA for a priest for his diocese. We had never been to the region before so when I arrived, there was absolutely no infrastructure. I was sent to a house once occupied by a Nigerian priest. It was an appalling place which was infested with rats. I began to think that I had made a shocking mistake in coming to Abuja and furthermore, I felt that I was wasting my life as a priest. In Lagos, you had teeming throngs of people at every mass on a Sunday whereas in Abuja, you had just a few scattered groups. For the first six months, I was hanging around with no support from any corner. The Archbishop was too busy with the African Synod which was taking place at the time and the SMA in Ireland were stingy enough about giving help. Finally, I had a showdown with the Archbishop and asked if I could take over three out-stations from a priest from another parish who was managing them. He gave permission so I went ahead.

"At this time also, I was mercifully rescued from my awful living conditions by Mr. Hugo Flynn – owner and managing director of P.W., an Irish construction company in Nigeria which has always been very helpful to the missionaries. He came to visit my house and instantly decided that I could absolutely not continue to live there. He moved me into one of his modern and fully equipped houses on the P.W. life camp. I felt as though I had moved from hell to heaven. In Nigeria, life camps are housing compounds built by employers for their expatriate workers. They are usually operated to very high standards and frequently have swimming pools, social clubs and clinics attached.

"The SMA idea for me in Abuja was that I should negotiate with the Archbishop to get a piece of land which we could develop. The potential for a mission was there though it was hard to see at the time. After much difficulty, I got a piece of land. I didn't have the money to put up a sign so one day I arrived to find that it had been taken over by the Anglicans. I was ready for a big-time fight as I was not about to let go of something I had struggled so hard to get. The people (from the out-stations I had taken over) urged me to let it go and convinced me that we would find a better place. Soon after, they brought me to a site in a bush area which I first thought was useless as it had no access from any main road. Despite drawbacks, the site which is in the Qwarimpa area was adopted and as you can see today, it has turned out to be a prime location and a far better site than the one appropriated by the Anglicans.

"My church and parish committee had about four million naira which had been collected from enthusiastic people – many of whom were civil servants who had been moved from Lagos to Abuja and who were living in the Qwarimpa area. When they first arrived, they refused to worship in the existing church buildings which were wretched so they were driving into the city until I persuaded them to throw in their lot with myself and my committee. Abuja was very small in those days and I got to know many of them through having to go through the official procedures of land buying and so on at the FCDA. Most ultimately decided to work with me and they turned out to be very generous. Many of them had already contributed to the building of two churches in Abuja, so to ask them to start building a third time was kind of testing their generosity.

"We hired an Italian contractor and started building with our four million naira and about a similar amount which we got from Rome. Before phase one was quite finished, the builder ran into difficulty and disappeared with some of our money – though not very much. We were feeling quite stranded until Mr. Flynn stepped in again, this time giving us gravel, shuttering, scaffolding and vibrators as well as two of his senior expatriate men to show us what to do. We were then able to work with gusto. Energy and enthusiasm were released from every corner. We got the building to the stage where the pillars were off the ground. Since then, we have been moving through the different phases of the project and we make sure that all work is of a very high standard. Though I say so myself, I think that the finished product will be something to be proud of.

"The Nigerians are probably the most generous people in the world particularly if they see that their money is being well used. They also respond very well to good leadership. Identifying with their church and parish comes natural to them and they are willing to make tremendous sacrifices towards ongoing development. We called our Church and parish after the *Holy Family* because we purchased the land in 1994, the year dedicated to the family by the United Nations. It was also a time when many families were being torn apart by the big civil service move to Abuja and in the early years, Abuja did not have family accommodation so fathers and in some case mothers who worked here often had to sleep in their offices during the week and return to Lagos at the weekend. There was great uncertainty about transfers and a great many were hoping to be re-transferred to Lagos.

"Things have greatly improved since those days but conditions can still be harsh. The population in the city is increasing rapidly so growing demand for almost everything pushes up prices. The Muslim-Christian violence in the northern cities of Kaduna, Kano and Jos in recent years has meant that many people have moved to Abuja for security. This migration has caused the growth of many shanty towns all around the outskirts. In the nineties, vast amounts of public money were being spent on construction and many families were living off the wages of the one man who was being paid good money by a construction company. In recent times however, public works and development has slowed down greatly and as a consequence, many families are living in very straitened circumstances.

"Part of our parish is very shanty – with no decent facilities, no water and no electricity. People with huge needs have come and set up little mud-block houses with zinc roofs. They are helped by our very powerful St.Vincent de Paul Society which is run by a woman who was trained as a radiographer in Ireland. She can really mobilize the people and the Society manages to extend its help into areas beyond our parish where nothing is being done for poverty.

"We have many other parish groups; in fact the number is mind-boggling. There are the lay readers, the Eucharistic ministers, the church wardens and the Legion of Mary which is very strong even though it is almost defunct in Europe. There are also tribal societies which could be compared to the Corkman's Association in London or the Cavanman's Association in New York. They meet in the church and they try to integrate newcomers who might otherwise end up badly. There is the charismatic renewal group and there are a number of pious societies such as the Sacred Heart Society. Every evening the church is a hive of activity with the different societies going through their programmes. They are facilitated by the electricity we can provide from our generator. Young people coming up to their exams also come to the church and take a bench outside to study.

"In addition to all of this, we run a little clinic in the church grounds and the poor especially turn to it. It's small but decent by lots of standards around here. I take a great interest in this and if I weren't a priest, I think that I would probably have made a fairly good doctor. I have found that to date, I have not made a wrong diagnosis!

"Fr. Aodhgan Mac Criostail who has come to the parish recently and who spent years in Zambia was quite astonished at the level of activity and commitment that he found here. All the groups support each other and they have developed a deep sense of community which is something they would not be able to do in big city parishes. People often wonder how I keep an eye on everything. From day one, I tried to train good leaders and I normally let them move ahead on their own. If there is big money involved, I pay special attention and make sure that it comes through me. I then release it as it is needed. It's a big workload but I am a fairly well organized person and I have developed good systems.

"There are now about four thousand parishioners and we have two masses on Sundays which are joyful and vibrant. There is a kind of boisterousness and generosity about the singing and the responses. The style has a lot to do with the Nigerian character which can sometimes seem loud and aggressive to an outsider. Their commitment and approach to Church and parish have a lot to do with the way the Church was established by the Irish missionaries. From the beginning, they insisted that the Nigerians be financial supporters. This often enraged the French SMA who felt that the Irish were too mercenary. The older missionaries will tell you today that their strictness in this regard meant that they left behind them a totally self-supporting Church. This is something that did not happen in French speaking West African countries. There, the Church to this very day is a kind of receiving Church depending on handouts.

"Sometimes when arthritic pain strikes and you begin to feel that this is no country for you anymore, you have only to go over to the Church and be confronted with people who are making desperate efforts to live good Christian lives. You are then revived and you feel that your work is somehow affirmed. I have been an incredibly happy priest in this country. There are adjustments and frustrations by the score and you need patience and a lot of tolerance. Never to be able to assume that you are going to have water or electricity or fuel is not easy. Petrol queues can waste days and when things go wrong, the amount of time it takes to rectify them is enormous. Incorrect phone and electricity bills can take weeks to sort out.

"Our SMA House here in Abuja is a sort of a transit house for our Fathers passing through or going on leave. I have the task of handling their emigration papers. A new system that was introduced recently to simplify things has had the opposite effect. Some of the men live in very remote and isolated conditions – conditions that I think I could no longer endure myself. When they come, I like to be kind and generous and help out in whatever way I can. I also enjoy the company and they certainly liven up the place!

"In Kontagora, to the north west of Abuja by many hours, I have a good friend called Fr. Dónal Ó Catháin. He lives hours and hours down a dirt-road deep inside the bush. He works with the Kamberries – a tribe of people who are not Christian at all and who are very primitive. Dónal is there and he has lots and lots of health projects and development programmes like digging dams and wells. During the dry season, he holds courses in literacy which are quite spectacular really. Whole families come in for three months and spend mornings learning to read and write Kamberi, a language for which Bishop Tim Carroll, SMA of Kontogora invented an alphabet. In the afternoons, they learn how to read and write Hausa and then in the evenings, they are introduced to Christianity. If they do the latter for three years and then want to be baptized, Dónal will baptize them. It's heroic work really and you could write an epic on Dónal. His work and way of life require a certain temperament. He is very concerned that the good aspects of the Kamberi culture are preserved – language, music, art, customs and even food and drink items. He sent me a bottle of local gin recently to see if I could have the ingredients analyzed. Luckily, I have almost every type of person that I need over there in the church. A professor who is in research and development has become very interested in the gin as he thinks that it contains chloroform. Dónal tells me that the minute a person drinks it, he becomes comatose and if he wakes up and drinks more, he immediately falls asleep again!

"Bishop Tim Carroll is another fascinating man. He was working with the Kamberries for twenty-five years. He is a quiet and self-contained man and one of his hobbies is birdwatching. He became absorbed in the sounds of the Kamberi language and developed a written version. He is now living in Kontogora town, a typical Nigerian town with lots of Igbo traders, a bank and a post-office. The wider Kontogora region is a remote and forgotten place and it is about twice the size of Ireland. Its people are neglected really. Here and there you can be shown sites where a town-hall or a hospital is supposed to be but the buildings only exist on paper. The millions of naira which were apportioned for the projects simply disappeared into people's pockets.

"It's hard to come to terms with the rampant corruption in Nigeria. You know the country is wealthy and yet you see such little progress. The corruption is pervasive because everyone believes that everyone else is engaged in it. The small man is corrupt in a small way and the big man is corrupt in a really big way. Developmental theory suggests that all change must come from the bottom up. I think Nigeria will prove to be the opposite. If ever there is going to be meaningful and long-lasting change, it will have to come from the top down in the form of good leadership. Nigeria desperately needs leaders who will outwardly and strenuously live lives of integrity and by so doing, persuade and urge their people to follow. If this kind of leadership emerges and Nigerians pray fervently for it, I think the people will respond magnificently.

"The other evening somebody came to me in the church after a discussion we had about saints. He said, 'Father, it is very hard to be a saint in Nigeria.' He meant that it was hard to avoid all corruption because despite good intentions, there will be, from time to time, pressures from different sources that will lead a person into petty or big crime or corruption. I told this man that I had met more saints in Nigeria than anywhere else. On another occasion, we did a human rights course with a number of young people. When it was over, one of them cried and said: 'it will now be even harder to live in Nigeria.'

"In the Catholic Church, we do challenge them to try to relate religion to life. We try to lead them away from corruption, so even if they do become involved, they will have a conscience about it and try to consider better ways of handling the temptation next time around. Some of what we call these mushroom churches which spring up by the wayside under the broad umbrella of Christianity try to convince the people that it is a curse from God if they are not successful with big houses and motor cars. The Cross and suffering don't feature at all in their preaching.

"My hope now lies in the young people coming up. Previously, graduates were absorbed into the system and often became corrupt themselves. Today huge numbers of them are wandering around with no work and they are beginning to ask all kinds of questions because they know that Nigeria, with all its wealth, should be able to look after its people. We may begin to see a change.

"In this country, we live with faith, hope and hard work but there is also joy and enthusiasm. Unlike many priests working in Ireland right now, we feel our work is appreciated and that is life giving. Here the people need you; they are coming at you all the time so you have no choice but to become inextricably bound up in their lives. In Ireland now, the priest tends to get cut off and in that context, he tends to retreat rather than go on the offensive. Of course with all the child abuse scandals, many natural outlets for being with young people in leadership roles have been closed off. Here still, you can be very affectionate with children and life is much more natural.

"I find myself being a little critical of the performance and defeatist attitudes of some priests in Ireland. Every now and then however, you can encounter gems. I know one incredibly shy man who came to my own parish from the islands off West Cork. He was not a great preacher but he worked terribly hard to get to know the young people. When I go home and see them all around him, I have to conclude that if you make an effort, you will tap into the latent needs and religiosity of young people.

"I detect a despondency and lack of enthusiasm in many priests. Sometimes you feel that there must be a lack of faith. Pope John Paul himself, while recognizing the crisis in vocations, admitted that there was a far greater crisis of faith. If we look at biblical history, we learn that affluence is the one thing that no civilization has coped with. We can cope with war and disaster because they bring out the best in us but affluence turns people in on themselves. Now, we here in Africa try to bring the downtrodden to some level of affluence because extreme poverty can be demeaning and destructive. I often think of De Valera's famous line – 'people living with frugal comforts'. A great English developmental theorist – a man called Douthwaite, is very taken with that phrase. In fact he has gone to live in Co. Mayo in the west of Ireland.

"It seems to me that there is a great spiritual illiteracy in Ireland now. The catechism that you got as a child served you well as a child but it is not sufficient for the adult living in an increasingly secular society. Further education in scripture and spirituality for example, would help people in their faith. Even people who have left the Catholic Church or who have no religion will tell you that they can learn a lot from reading the scriptures. They were only opened up to myself in the seminary. It was so uplifting and faith-giving to learn about the early Church – the pain it went through to come to terms with itself – the persecutions – how they lived in a world with a light as it were.

"Now I was always interested in politics and revolution but at the back of my mind, I knew that they were not sufficient and that Christianity was the only way of life that produced the perfect altruistic person. No ideology has come anywhere near it and this would be accepted by many scholars. J.S. Mills, an Englishman and one of the great atheistic philosophers came to the conclusion before he died in his 70's, that Christianity was the only way of life that liberated and uplifted human beings in all their dimensions.

"If I were to return to Ireland, I would be very keen to work with young people. When on holiday, I sometimes give retreats in my parish and I introduce young people, often for the first time, to prayer and the scriptures and really, you can see the light coming into their eyes. Later, you could find them praying quietly and you realize that though the faith may be dormant, something innately good is there. That is why I sometimes feel myself getting upset with priests and bishops as I feel they are not tapping into this. I often feel a great need to be in Ireland doing this kind of work. That being said, I know that Nigeria is where I want to be for the moment.

"When I came out first, I thought that I was going to change the face of the world or at least the face of Nigeria. It was a presumptuous way of thinking and of course, I thought that I had all the answers. Why you come and why you stay are very different. Today I meet many people in the parish who have a far deeper level of spirituality than I would have myself. I have no great illusions anymore but I would like to think that I have touched the lives of a few people. I thank God for his goodness to me and from my past experiences, I feel that I can be more trusting in the future."

Fr. Cathal McKenna, SMA

Father Damian Bresnihan

Society of African Missions (SMA)
Blackrock Road, Cork

Fr. Damian Bresnihan, SMA

Father Damian whom I had known in Nigeria was having a very busy day when I met him at SMA House where he is currently house superior. In addition to preparing for a trip to Medugorje the following day, he had a number of important house visitors to welcome and attend to. One of those was Cardinal Anthony Okogie from Lagos. It was after 10:00 p.m. when we sat down to talk.

"I leave at six in the morning" he tells me, "to lead a group on pilgrimage to Medugorje. Six months ago, when Fr. Éamon Finnegan whom you met earlier was asked to go and was unable to do so, I volunteered to take his place. The group is from Tyrone, my own county, but I don't know any of them. I was in Medugorje once before in 1988. At the time there was all this talk of Our Lady having appeared there. It didn't seem important whether there was proof of that or not. To me, it was a place of pilgrimage and the experience of Medugorje for many people who go there from all over the world is that it is a place of new beginnings and indeed conversion for many. I suppose what I carry with me from that first visit is a sense of prayer from the heart and the purity of the Christian message. They say that nobody goes to Medugorje without being invited to do so. It's perhaps true. The scriptures are full of God calling or inviting us to do things.

After spending more than fifteen years in Nigeria, Father Damian returned to Cork to be house superior at SMA House in Blackrock Road.

"I came back because I was invited to do so by our newly elected Provincial, Father Fachtna O'Driscoll. This house was our first in Ireland and because of that; it is looked upon as the mother-house. About fifty of our members from the Irish Province live here. Because we have round the clock nursing care in a beautiful unit, some of our older members, who have become disabled or who have medical problems feel it is a natural place to come to. It is also a very beautiful house and it has always been very well maintained.

"Managing this community in this house involves lots of different kinds of work. It's a wonderful community and coming here, I wondered if I was presumptuous in saying Yes to the request. Many of the men are twice my age. Most of them have lived their lives simply in many parts of Africa for forty, fifty or more years and they continue to do so here. They are not at all demanding. Some find it easier to settle back into Ireland than others. The atmosphere here is happy and the spirit is good. Every group or community has some kind of leader. I perform that role here. I don't regard it as some kind of a maintenance job. I try to be creative so that life here for everybody will be life-giving. I try hard to create a sense of *Home* though it is a very big home. We have sixty-nine bedrooms. For most of the year we are not full as people come and go.

"My appointment to my position is for three years but I am reminded that it is a three-year term that is renewable! I have finished two years and after one more, it will be important for me to look and see if this ministry is life-giving for me and for the people who are here. If I found myself getting annoyed with older or sick men, then I think that it would be better for me to pack my bags. I don't believe in holding down a job just because of an expectation that I should do so. The people living here or those who appointed me might also feel that it is time for me to move on. It's important that both sides do not take things for granted.

"I am enjoying being back in Ireland. It gives me an opportunity to catch up with family and friends and activities I enjoy. I was born in Omagh. Both my parents were from Co. Tyrone. We were eight in family – three boys and five girls. I am the third son and the third child. My father died at fifty-five, the week I was ordained. I convinced myself the day of my ordination that he knew what was happening. I believe that he did. He had stopped talking at that stage. He was a mechanic by trade but also kept a small piggery outside the town as a pastime. My mother died in 1987. She was just sixty-two.

"One of my great interests growing up in Omagh was Irish step-dancing. We were blessed with a Mr. Seamus Kerrigan who ran *The Kerrigan School of Dancing*. Every Saturday, there were boys from my housing estate going off to a boy's only dancing class. It has been found that boys frequently leave mixed gender classes because they are afraid of being called sissy or whatever. We came together with the girls for feiseanna and céilithe. Five or six times at different levels, I won the provincial championships and at an all Ireland level, I was in a three-way tie. In the end, I came second. I enjoyed the dancing and, like sport, you have to have a lot of discipline to do the hard work that is involved. We developed discipline in the art of dancing but we also had a very disciplined class. We had opportunities to go to festivals in different parts of Europe and we had the sense of being ambassadors for our country at a time when Irish dancing was often scorned. *Riverdance* and Michael Flatley have changed all that. I continued dancing until I joined the seminary but before that, I had qualified as a dancing teacher just so that I would have more than cups and medals. Later in 1995, I qualified as an adjudicator. I still adjudicate from time to time and I am very happy to do so.

"The idea of becoming a priest came to me towards the end of my secondary school years. I had attended the Christian Brothers Schools in Omagh – just down the road from where we lived. They influenced me a lot and my experience with them was very positive – not just from the point of teaching and the sense of discipline which they instilled but also the fact that they were prayerful and spiritual men who had dedicated their lives to God. In fifth year, I got an invitation to go to a vocations' weekend in Donegal. The fact that I got it at all was pure chance as there was a postal strike all over Ireland at the time. During the weekend, I spoke briefly to Fr. Cathal McKenna, SMA who was working on vocation recruitment at the time. A few months later, I got an invitation to visit the SMA house in Dromantine, Co. Down. I went along with my mother who acted as my sponsor. My becoming a priest took off from there I suppose.

"I had thought of doing other things like teaching or nursing and I used to dream of running a big hotel. Maybe this present job is that dream come true! When I first became aware that I might have a vocation, I tried to push it out of my mind but it kept coming back. In September 1980, I travelled to Cork to do my novitiate. Our whole formation encouraged reflection and discernment. We were twenty-two young men from sixteen counties in Ireland. Over the years before ordination, different fellows left or were advised to leave for one reason or another. I used to wonder what was keeping me there as many of the fellows who left seemed so fine. I self-questioned a lot. Is this what I want? Is God inviting me? I was always trying to clarify. I don't think that there is ever complete clarity for anyone who follows a religious vocation. Living with uncertainty, trust and openness to the possibility of not continuing was very much part of the process. Only two from the original class of twenty-two were ordained.

"The idea of becoming a missionary priest was not to the fore of my thinking initially. I thought that it might be nice to be a secular priest in the Derry diocese and then maybe spend some time in Africa at a later stage. After a few vocation weekends, when I found out that things didn't work in that way, I opted for a missionary order. From 1980 to 1988, my sense of going on mission changed a lot. When I joined up, I was focused on the idea of evangelization. Later the whole humanitarian aspect of mission became a real interest.

"Three months after ordination, I came to southern Nigeria and was appointed to the village of Imomo, thirty minutes from the town of Ijebu-Ode in present-day Ogun State. There I was to learn the Yoruba language and become immersed in the culture of the people. After that I was appointed by Archbishop Job to Odo-Ona in his diocese of Ibadan.

I was meant to assist Fr. Frank McCabe but eight weeks after my arrival, Fr. Frank had to go home sick and I became acting parish-priest! Much help was available however. The Irish OLA Sisters had a school and a convent nearby. They were wonderful women and I recall Sister Hilda Spain, a Galway-woman who died a few years ago in Castlemacgarrett Nursing Home in Co. Mayo, and Sister Imelda Hurley of Cork who is now retired here in Cork in the OLA mother-house in Ardfoyle. Both of these sisters were made traditional chiefs as a mark of appreciation for their contribution to education. There was great life and a lot of hard work all around me during those early days in Ibadan. It had all started long before I came. The SMA founded all the missions in that particular area of western Nigeria.

"In my parish, I was given great opportunities but I was always conscious of the need for fraternity and fellowship with other missionaries. Fortunately I was able to get into my car and visit fairly often. In those days in Nigeria, it was easy to travel, even at night. You never dreamed of anyone stopping you or trying to harm you in any way. I had an old banger of a car which I used to say had air-conditioning on account of all the holes in its floor. It got me from A to B and if it didn't start, there were always willing hands in the compound to give it a push. I have always had a great awareness of the personal needs of a missionary priest. Others older than me would say that as long as you were able to do the work, that was all that counted. I wouldn't share that opinion. Work is important but if the life is not right for you, the work will not yield fruit.

"I was very happy working in the diocese of Archbishop Job. He is a native of a town called Esure in Ogun State. He had previously been a priest in Lagos. He and I share the birthday (though not the same year) of June 24, the feast of John the Baptist. At thirty-three, he may have been one of the youngest bishops ever to have been consecrated. He took over in Ibadan when Bishop Finn, an Irish SMA, retired. He is a big Yoruba man with a wonderfully colourful character and he is always ready to encourage and acknowledge efforts. He is a great man of the people and to stand back and watch him after confirmation or canonical visitation, standing for hours with the people, being photographed with them or just having a kind word, is very impressive. He is about sixty-six now I think, a few years younger than Cardinal Okogie.

"Ibadan is a city of hills. When I arrived first, I was struck by the vast expanse of tin roofs. I was soon to become aware that it was among the worst cities in the world from the point of view of poor housing. Large and destitute families share one-room homes. The city however has a sense of being a very friendly, sprawling village. I grew to love it and to feel at home in it. When returning from appointments in Lagos, I always had this feeling of coming home to a nice place. I remember on occasion stopping the car and saying 'Damian, slow down, you are no longer in Lagos, relax.' The Irish OLA and MMM Sisters run two very good hospitals in Ibadan and the sisters of St. Louis were there during my time running a very good school. The place was very blessed with good people. Ibadan has also been the location for a long time of a major seminary and students from all over Nigeria studied there until such time as the major seminary in Jos was established to cater for students from the north. Archbishop Job often refers to Ibadan as *Little Rome*. Not far away is the town of Ife which is regarded as the cradle of Yoruba civilization.

"I was very happy with my work in the parishes. It was missionary life as I had expected it to be. The SMA objective from the very beginning was to establish a local Church in Nigeria with an indigenous clergy. This often meant that many of our men had to move out of parishes and become lecturers and professors in seminaries. This work is still very important and is ongoing but in the late 1980's, it was decided to recruit Africans to be missionaries themselves as a Church that is not missionary is not Christian. A need arose then to provide a programme for the formation of African SMA priests. I was invited to work with the formation team in our house in New Bodija also in Ibadan. This work brought me all around Nigeria. To prepare for it, I did a course on religious formation in Loreto House in Carysfort, Dublin. A good formation has nothing to do with training. Someone once said that you can only train dogs! In formation, you accompany people on their way and this is a great privilege and a great responsibility. You share in a student's life at a level that involves a discerning process and a broadening of horizons. In the end, you may have to make a decision on the life of a young person who wishes to give generously but who is struggling. The student discerns for himself but there is also a team which discerns. You trust that the two together will be God's will. You work very hard to be objective and to be for the good of the student, the Church and the mission.

"In 2000, I was elected vice-regional superior in Nigeria with Fr. Martin Farrell as regional superior. I moved to our house in Challenge on the other side of Ibadan. From then until I left, my work was a mixture of pastoral, formation and leadership work.

"It was a bit of a wrench to leave when I was asked to but I managed it fairly well I think. I remember writing to the Provincial to tell him that I thought that the position of house superior would be onerous. At the same time, I felt that I should give support and felt if everyone said no to invitations from him, his life as Provincial would be very difficult. I felt young enough – I wasn't even forty at the time – to be able to give a few years to the role and then prepare to go on mission again and fill whatever need that might exist at that time in some place in Africa.

"If that need happens to be in Nigeria, I will be very happy to return as there is so much to be done there. The years before I left were difficult as conditions in the country were deteriorating on many levels. Corruption of all kinds was rampant. I do believe however, that things will change again for the good. I date the serious decline to the year 1996. Lack of security and personal security became a dominant feature of my own last four or five years there. I had two very bad experiences. I was shot at and I was robbed and I would be a liar to pretend that I was not affected. It had a serious effect on my life but it gave me a better understanding of the great suffering and lack of security which ordinary Nigerians endure every day of their lives. During my early years, I lived in a house with an open verandah and a door made of plywood and it never occurred to me that someone would try to break in.

"Here in Ireland, people seem very aware of the corruption that is in Nigeria. We forget that we here have a more subtle level of corruption. I believe that people are the same the world over. The colour of our skin, the shape of our nose or the texture of our hair may be different but we are the same in essentials. We all need the same things in life – some happiness and some peace and comfort. Much stress and lack of basic needs lead to crime in Nigeria."

SMA vocations in Ireland have been declining for many years. In Africa however, the numbers are substantial. I ask Fr. Damian if this gives a certain consolation to the congregation.

"I wouldn't use the word consolation. I have from time to time heard some of the older men say that they were glad that there were younger ones coming through the ranks who might be able to push wheelchairs! The fact that we have young African SMA Fathers would be more of a hope for the Church than a consolation for us. I certainly wouldn't be in favour of bringing Africans here just to preserve our Irish institutions and buildings. If they come for the sake of the Church in Ireland, that would be a different proposition. If the Irish SMA Province dies out from lack of vocations, my own feeling would be that it should be allowed to die out gracefully."

Father Liam Burke

Society of African Missions (SMA)
Blackrock Road, Cork

*Fr. Liam Burke SMA, in Kaduna on the occasion of the blessing
and opening of the Queen of the Apostles Parish multipurpose hall which was
built by the Christian mothers*

The soft spoken Father Liam was settling into a contented retirement after his long sojourn in Africa when I spoke to him at SMA House in Blackrock Road in Cork. He was nevertheless anxious to keep himself up to date with everything that was happening at home and abroad. His comfortable and spacious room was packed with books, publications, newspapers and the many letters he continues to receive from friends and contacts connected with his former mission life.

"I retired in 2001 after spending 47 years in Northern Nigeria. It took a while to settle at home but I have managed fairly well. They take great care of us in this house and we are not short of company. It is a very lively place with people coming and going all the time. We have many visitors because visitors are encouraged. At the moment, Cardinal Okogie from Lagos is with us. I try to keep alert and in touch with what's happening. I have always been a good student and the scriptures are my number one interest. At the moment, I am reading Seán Freyne's recent book. It's tough going but I enjoy the challenge. Unfortunately I am not doing much writing as I have arthritis in my hands.

"There is much I could write about because I have been a witness to many events and many changes in my time as an active missionary. When I arrived in Northern Nigeria in 1952, there was no Catholic Bishop, no black African priest, just a handful of missionaries – mostly SMA, a few Augustinians and some Holy Ghost priests from the English Province. I was first appointed to the Prefecture Apostolic of Kaduna. The Prefect who was later to become Bishop and Archbishop was Monsignor John McCarthy, SMA from Skibbereen in West Cork. During my years in Northern Nigeria, the Church grew very quickly and the Prefecture of Kaduna was, over time, divided six times in order to create new dioceses.

"I spent my first four years in the old Niger Province of which Kaduna at the time was part. Abuja, the present Federal Capital of Nigeria was one of my parishes. I was in charge of a mission called Gawu and under Gawu came Abuja. We had four or five small schools in the area and the tribes who were mostly Gwari and Gbagu were reasonably friendly.

"Very few people know how Abuja got its name. About 200 years ago when the Fulanis came from the Niger basin into the Sokoto region, they began to subdue all the Hausa kingdoms which were seven in number and Muslim at the centre but not Muslim enough for the Fulanis. As they conquered each kingdom, they appointed an Emir, a word which comes from the Arabic word *Amir* which means military governor. When they reached Zaria which was a very strong Hausa kingdom, there was a big struggle which went on intermittently for many years and which spread down into the area where Abuja is today. Eventually there was a big showdown and the Fulanis suffered badly. They departed and never came back. Hausa people began to settle in the Abuja area and they intermarried with the local tribes. A little town grew and they chose a chief to rule them who was called Abubaker Ja. Ja means *light complexioned* in Hausa and Abubaker, a very common Hausa name is always shortened to Abu. Out of these two words was born the name Abuja.

"When my four years and first term in Nigeria were complete, I had a holiday for six months and after that, two of us were sent to Ghana for a year to observe the relationship between the Church and State in the first black African country to gain independence. When we were introduced to President Kwame Nkrumah, who was Catholic and a product of a mission school, he remarked that 'it was nice to see missionaries now coming to learn from Africans.' We were attached to the Department of Community Development which dealt with literacy, water supplies and rural hygiene. We found that the Church was not too involved with post independence development apart from having some schools, teacher training colleges and hospitals. Nkrumah did not take over schools and hospitals in the beginning. It may have been done later. He saw things a little differently to that of post-independence Nigerians. He spoke of Africanization while Nigerians spoke of indigenization. He saw a bigger picture. He saw himself as an African leader and not just a Ghanaian. He had idealistic ideas on the role Ghana could play on the African continent.

"When I returned to Nigeria, I was sent to Southern Zaria to a place called Zonkwa in the south of what is now Kaduna State. We had a mission there but very soon I was brought back to the city of Kaduna as secretary to Bishop McCarthy. I lived with him in a little house in the central market area until we built the present bishop's house. At the time, the northern territory of Nigeria was being divided up by the missionaries and Saint Patrick's Society, for example, took over the old Niger Province which ultimately became the Diocese of Minna. Others went to the many other new dioceses which were being created – Sokoto, Kano, Kafanchan and Zaria.

"In 1964, I was sent back to Zonkwa by the Archbishop as he wanted me to work on a five-year development plan for the whole of the area. It was in the Zonkwa region that development had started and once it got off the ground, great progress was made. When I had completed this task, I presented it to the Secretary of the Government in Kaduna who was Fulani and a graduate of Imperial

College, London. After he read it, he said 'Father, you are about ten years ahead of Government which means you are always going to be in trouble. Why not break it down into different sections!' I took his advice. We had the feeling at that time that the Government was with us and that they were happy to let us deal with our own people when it came to education and some other aspects of development. That was later to change.

"The Church was growing all the time and eventually it established itself with regional offices in the capitals of the three administrative regions which were formed in Nigeria at the time of Independence. A Secretariat was located in Lagos and the Archbishoprics of Lagos, Kaduna and Ibadan were created. The Church was then well placed to deal with regional governments over issues concerning its work. During this time also, the Church decided they needed a major seminary for the north of Nigeria as prior to that, seminarians from all over the country had to go to Ibadan. One was established in Jos and the Augustinian Fathers were asked to run it. When it later got too big, sections of it were moved to Makurdi in present-day Benue State. Things were moving very fast and it was not long before archbishops were appointed in Abuja and Jos.

"Being in the Archbishop's office, meant that I was the person dealing with the various government ministries with regard to schools and hospitals in particular. Gradually most of the people appointed at the senior levels of these ministries were Muslim. There were very many negotiations between the Government and the voluntary agencies such as ourselves over schools and teacher training colleges prior to the government take-over of all of them. The take-over took a lot of time. Initially we thought that we might have been able to keep some but it became impossible to achieve that wish. The Sisters of Saint Louis in Kano managed to keep their school but the Government controlled admissions.

"In the wider area of the north of Nigeria, religious and ethnic strife has sadly become a feature of life over the last few decades. It is said that there are politically motivated people behind this as politics is very mixed up with religion. A Professor of African history at London University once told me that there was bound to be a clash between Muslims and Christians as the former have been pushing southwards from North Africa for centuries and young Christian communities have been pushing northwards. He predicted this clash would happen around the year 2000. As we now know, it happened before that.

"Efforts are being made to have Muslim/Christian dialogue but it is very difficult. Archbishop Jatau took over from Archbishop McCarthy in Kaduna and he was the person who attended all the meetings on this issue. He found it very hard to dialogue with individuals who had sway and power. Around 1998, he sent me to Rome to the Congregation of Evangelization to become updated on the whole issue. The Nigerian Cardinal Arinze was in charge of the secretariat which dealt with Muslim/Christian dialogue at the time. He told me about the reports on tensions coming in from Malaysia, Pakistan and the Middle-East but of course it was a very delicate matter and nothing much could be said publicly. Now there is this very powerful man called Michael Fitzgerald who is a White Father from Scotland (with Irish origins) and a fluent Arabic speaker in charge of this secretariat. He is finding it very challenging as some of the cardinals don't wish to have inter-faith dialogue. In the past, when Pope John Paul II held annual meetings in Assisi with the leaders of different faiths, many of the cardinals stayed away.

"Irrespective of dialogue difficulties, it's essential that the lines of communication between Islam and Christianity be kept open. I was on many committees in Nigeria dealing with this subject. The Emir of Kano was with me on one. When the work of the committee wound up, he gave me his private phone number and invited me to call on him any time. He is under a lot of pressure. The youth were his big concern the last time I saw him. Only about 30% of them come to the mosque on Fridays.

"Another man I was friendly with in Nigeria was the Grand Khadi – the Muslim Chief Justice for Northern Nigeria. He presided over the quasi-sharia law which was established after Independence. He was raised in the Sokoto area and was educated at the University of Khartoum and at El Azar in Cairo. After the slaughter of the Igbos in the counter-coup in the 1960's, I called him and went to his house.

"Probably the man I could talk most to was Liman Ciroma from the small emirate of Ficca close to the Borno border. Liman means priest. His brother was the Emir of Ficca. I was on a committee with him in Kaduna when he was called to Lagos in the late 1970's during the military regime of Olusegen Obasanjo to be head of the Civil Service. We kept up our friendship and when he retired to Kaduna, I had good contact with him. He died suddenly in May, 2004. I wrote to the family and got a very nice letter back from the eldest son. Some people thought him to be a very zealous Muslim who had a big input into many of the things that were done but I think myself that he was greatly misunderstood.

"Religious and ethnic tensions persist in Nigeria. The Plateau State riots of recent years have been very distressing as much progress was wiped out overnight. I am told that Jos is de facto two cities now – a Muslim city and a Christian city and that the army is present to keep the peace. Kaduna is the same. Christians are gradually moving towards the south of the city and the north is largely Muslim. Not a whole lot of communication between the two sides is going on. It is much harder for the native Catholic priest to build communication and to have contacts with high level Muslims than it is for the outsider. I was always free to call on Muslim leaders."

Reverend Father James Higgins

Society of African Missions (SMA)
Uromi, Edo State

Fr. James Higgins, SMA

Eighty-year-old Father James Higgins was holidaying at SMA House, Blackrock Road, Cork when I spoke with him. He has spent more than fifty four years in Nigeria. "I am very happy there and when you enjoy good health in Africa, as I do, you want to stay for as long as you can. I am now in a retired position in my post at Uromi in Edo State and my life is very pleasant. I look after our house, say mass at the local convent and stroll to meet my friends in the village each evening. Many are past pupils from my earlier teaching days.

"I was born in Collooney, a small town of three hundred inhabitants, seven miles south of Sligo city. It's a very picturesque place. The scenery is breathtaking. If you stand at the River Brae in Main Street and look across the rocks of the Owenmore River, you can see the Ox Mountains. A little to the right, you can see the exquisite round-shaped Knocknarea with Queen Maeve's cairn prominent on top. Further again to the right looms Ireland's own Table Mountain – the beautiful blue Ben Bulben. Today, after spending more than fifty years in Africa, I am still haunted by that view.

"There were three in my family but my mother died when I was six months old. Dad worked in the Station House in the town so he got a local woman whom we called Nan Nan to look after us. When she died some years later, he brought us into town to live with him. The only time that I remember shedding tears in my life was when Nan Nan died. She was the only mother I ever knew.

"I went to the local school in Camphill beside the town. The headmaster was a Mr. Rooney. He had a son who became a well-known author and one of his books *Captain Boycott* was made into a film. Mr. Rooney was very interested in local history so he probably instilled that interest in his son.

"I had never given a thought to the priesthood but one day when I was about thirteen, I met the local curate as I was out strolling. He told me that there were priests from SMA House, Ballinafad, Co. Mayo coming to the town to interview a lad called Aloysius Davey. He asked if I would like to go along to the interview. I replied that 'I wouldn't mind.' He was not so keen on my attitude and I remember him telling me to be more positive if I did go along. I went to the interview and the two of us were accepted to go to Ballinafad which was a secondary school and a junior seminary. Going there did not mean you had to commit to priesthood so for the first couple of years I drifted along. As the time for entry into the novitiate approached, I had developed something of a vocation. This was largely due to a priest called Fr. Michael O'Mahony. He was a very practical man and related well with the students. He had been to Liberia and was later to become Bishop of Ilorin in Nigeria.

"I was ordained in June 1949 and towards the end of 1950, I was sent to Nigeria. I was not really shocked when I arrived as I was prepared for it mentally. When I touched down in Lagos, a priest from Asaba who had just purchased a car gave me a lift to Benin City where I was supposed to meet Bishop Kelly SMA. I was fortunate in my mode of transport as the usual one was a mammy wagon – so called because of all the mammies going to the market with their big baskets. When I arrived in Benin, I was told that the Bishop was in Enugu at a meeting and that I should head out to nearby Ibusa where the Bishop would visit me on his return from Enugu. I followed instructions and duly met the Bishop who told me to stay in Ibusa. I was to remain there for seven years teaching English, religion and education in the teacher training college which was set up by Bishop Broderick, SMA – a Kerryman in 1928. It gave our Society a great advantage over others as we were able to train teachers for the schools we were setting up all over the place.

"As a young missionary, I often felt that teaching was not really mission work and I would have preferred to have been at a mission house, going out to the out-stations in the bush. That was the ideal and the men before us had done all that. When my time came, the need for education was being constantly stressed so many of us had to go into schools from the beginning.

"Ibusa is a fairly big town which is located about seven miles from Asaba on the western banks of the Niger. I suppose it grew up around the markets. There you had the western Igbos as opposed to the Igbos from the eastern side of the river. The general area was part of the Mid-West region and its inhabitants were made up of many minority ethnic groups.

"Apart from four white priests all the staff in the Training College was African. The students were very serious as they realized how privileged they were and how many sacrifices their parents had to make to have them there. Being in the college, it was not possible to be involved in the full flow of parish and village life and that in a way was a disadvantage. After seven years, I was moved up to Uzairue near Auchi in present-day Edo State. A Fr. Michael Grace, SMA, had opened Assumpta Training College there in 1955. I was appointed principal. By this time, Nigeria was preparing for Independence and they had begun to take control of local and regional bodies. There was also a great push for universal primary education so more and more training colleges were being opened.

The SMA were leading the way in this regard if you like. At this point, the British were supportive but in the early days, they tended to be suspicious and cautious. They regarded the Igbos who were largely Catholic and who were the most educated of Nigerians at the time as provocative. The northerners were the least educated and the last to be ready for or even interested in the idea of independence.

"I spent ten years as principal in Uzairie and I suppose from a human point of view at least, they were the most rewarding years of my life. The pupils there were very mature, some in fact were married and they were there to gain higher qualifications. By 1966, the Government decided that they had reached saturation point with regard to training colleges so they began to convert many of them into secondary schools which had become the big need at the time. Ibusa remained a training college as it was one of the oldest. Uzairie became a grammar school.

"My next post was in Ubiaja (also in Edo State) where I became principal of St. John Bosco College, a training college turned secondary school. Fr. Paddy McGrath, my predecessor there had been a strict disciplinarian and it was my job to continue what he had begun. I could never have laid down the rigid rules and regulations which he had but I was able to keep them in place! It was a boarding school and of course from time to time there were problems. Feeding often became an explosive issue and if food was scarce, the students tended to make an unmerciful racket with their enamel plates. Whenever I saw that there was a serious grievance, I promised double portions for the next day. I always kept my promise!

"In the early days the French SMA in particular were against opening schools. Fr. Carlo Zappa who was in Asaba during the first decade of the twentieth century delayed establishing schools as he was against imposing western education on Africans. He believed that his mandate was to preach the Gospel and nothing but the Gospel. The Holy Ghost Fathers however had already established many schools in eastern Nigeria and they were regarded as being successful. With time, the SMA thinking changed and schools were established. They realized that if they didn't establish them, others would. In the 1970's, the Government took over all mission schools so the generations that we educated and who were very appreciative have almost passed away and the younger ones are more or less unaware of our contribution. It's a pity!

"I was in Ubiaja during the Biafran war. The Biafrans managed to occupy the Mid-West for about two months until the Federal forces made them withdraw. We certainly had sympathy for them as before the war, there had been many pogroms and much slaughter of Igbos. One problem that they had was the fact that the many minority tribes within Biafra did not trust the Igbos. They were fearful of being dominated by them in the event of an Igbo victory. It was a great relief when the war ended fairly peacefully and when the military Head of State, General Gowon acted in a very moderate and mature way. He welcomed the Biafrans back into Nigeria. Colonel Ojukwu of Biafra had great support during the war but the whole thing ended very badly and the Igbos were left in a desolate state after a truly horrific war. It is believed that Ojukwu was not originally in favour of breaking up Nigeria and that he may have had ambitions to be in charge of the whole country. People of that way of thinking were not surprised when he put himself forward in the Presidential elections of 2003.

"I spent the years between 1973 and 1981 in Ozoro in the Diocese of Warri in the now Delta State. I was persuaded to take the principalship of a government-run training college. I was reluctant as I felt the time had come for Nigerians to hold those positions. Initially I enjoyed the post as I was a classroom teacher at heart and I loved communicating with the young people. Gradually however, standards fell and we were often pressurized by politicians and influential people to take in candidates who were unsuitable. One thing that helped at that time was the opportunity I had to 'go bush' at the weekends helping out with parish work in a few out-stations. This was a great freedom and it satisfied the need to be out in the field and in the thick of it.

"It was while I was in Ozoro that I began to feel the reduction in the number of our SMA priests. We were at our peak in the 1950's but from the 1960's onwards, numbers started to decline. This had a slightly depressing effect on morale and style of life. As the years rolled by, the big happy social gatherings of the early days became less frequent and the older men in particular were not inclined to travel and stay overnight in the different mission houses. While I was in Ozoro, there were only ten of us in the diocese.

"I began a sabbatical year in Maynooth in 1981 and in the middle of a very good course, I was recalled to Nigeria to become parish priest in Sapele again in Delta State and not far from the big oil town of Warri. At the time there was trouble between the different ethnic groups and they couldn't agree to have a priest from any particular group. They were however happy to have an expatriate priest and that is why I was asked by the Bishop to fill the position. I arrived before Christmas as I felt it would be a good time to introduce a note of peace and calm. Following a cautious start, things settled down and I remained there for the next thirteen years during which time I got enough evangelical and pastoral experience to satisfy the most avid of missionaries! Sapele was once a very important town and there was a time when it was the most advanced in the country from the point of view of industry. The port was booming and the timber business was thriving. ATP (Africa Timber and Plywood Industry) employed thousands and there were rubber factories, flour mills and grain stores. That has all changed due to harsh economic circumstances. Sapele is now a ghost town. The rise of Warri as the big oil capital and Benin as a nearby flourishing city means that Sapele which was once king is now the poor relation.

"By April 1994, I felt my workload was getting too much for me so I asked the Bishop for a change. He agreed but the SMA had other plans and I was asked to come to Uromi in Edo State to help out Fr. Dick Wall who was trying to manage his large parish of Irrua from there. The SMA house in Uromi was built as a tyrocinium where young priests coming from Ireland could reside for six months or so to get acclimatized and to immerse themselves in language and culture. It's a lovely house with an upstairs verandah from which you can view wonderful gardens which are packed with glorious trees, shrubs and bushes such as the flame of the forest, the purple, violet and pink bougainvillea and the soft red hibiscus. The whole compound which comprises six acres is a beautiful and peaceful place.

"I went from having a very busy life in Sapele to an extremely quiet one in Uromi as my main task was to look after the premises. Within six months however, I was on the move again as I was asked to resume parish work at Asaba as Fr. Jack Casey who was there with Fr. Seán Ryan was not enjoying good health. I had known Seán since my Ozoro days so I took up residence with him at Cable Point in Asaba. I was back on familiar territory as I was within a few miles of Ibusa – my first mission post. I threw myself into the work. It was gratifying to see the progress that had been made over the years. The big numbers attending church, the many catechumens and the increase in vocations were all signs of a vibrant Church. The nearby cemetery of St. Joseph's, where many SMA Fathers and OLA sisters who died very young, are buried, bears testimony to the sacrifices that were made to bring Christ to that part of Nigeria.

"I returned to Uromi in May 2000 where I have since been enjoying retirement. Other than caring for the house and grounds, I have no responsibility. Most of my friends in the surrounding area speak Ishan but we communicate through English. Many as I said are former pupils. I go to the nearby convent twice a week to say mass. Other days, I say it at my house and a number of people from the village attend. On Saturdays, I go to an out-station. Most mornings are quiet so that is when I do my writing. I have already written two books *Kindling the Fire* and *The Pilgrim Soul in Me*.

"When the time comes for me to permanently return to Ireland, I will be happy to come to this very fine mother-house in Cork. I don't think that anyone could be lonely here as there is talk, fun and argument going on all the time. I will miss Nigeria: who wouldn't after more than fifty years? Despite the bad publicity the country gets, I have to say that I have really seen great progress in my time. Pessimists forget how bad things used to be. If there is now a power failure for a few hours, there is an outcry but it is not so long ago since we were using candles and bush lamps. People cry out about the crime and corruption, but if we study history, we will find that unfortunately, it is often the price of progress and development. The sudden increase in wealth that came with the discovery of oil and gas was accompanied by a level of corruption that was previously unknown. In time, I believe that Nigeria will adjust in a good way. It has the potential to be a great country because its people are enormously talented and the vast majority of them have a great desire to realize that potential at every level. Despite setbacks and disappointments, coups and counter-coups, exploitation of religious and ethnic differences by unscrupulous leaders, the spirit of the people has not been crushed."

In 1982, Fr. Higgins was honoured by the then Nigerian President, Shehu Shagari with the honour of MFR (Member of the Federal Republic of Nigeria) for his services to education.

Sisters of Our Lady of Apostles
(OLA)

An Introduction

The Missionary Sisters of Our Lady of Apostles were founded in Lyons in 1876 by the Superior General of the Society of African Missions (SMA) Father Augustine Planque to enable the missionary priests to reach out to the women of Africa with the Gospel of Jesus Christ.

The first OLA convent was set up in Ireland in Blackrock Road, Cork in 1877. From that year forward, Irish OLA Sisters were among the first female missionary pioneers along the West African coast. They responded to the most pressing needs of the people usually by setting up schools and hospitals, and faced with courage the harsh living conditions and dangers of living in one of the world's most deadly climates. The large number of graves of very young sisters in the cemetery in Topo Island near Badagry in south-western Nigeria is a poignant testimony to their missionary zeal.

Today, 900 OLA Sisters from twenty countries work throughout Africa, the Middle-East, Argentina and Canada spreading the Gospel and working to improve the lot of their fellow human beings especially women and children.

The Sisters also live and work in England, France, Holland, Italy and Ireland.

Sister Mary Crowley

Sisters of Our Lady of Apostles (OLA)
Ardfoyle, Cork

*Sr. Eileen Cummins (left) Superior General, OLA
and Sr. Mary Crowley, Provincial Superior (photo: OLA)*

Sr. Mary Crowley was the Chief Administrator of Maryland Comprehensive Secondary School in Ikeja on the western outskirts of Lagos when I first visited her. The school was one of the five former mission schools which had been returned by the Government of Lagos to the Archdiocese of Lagos in the late 1990's. Some months after my visit, she was transferred by her congregation to Ireland to assume the position of Provincial of the Irish Province of the OLA. I met her again at the OLA mother-house in Ardfoyle, Cork.

Returning to Ireland, I reminded her, was not on her mind when I spoke with her in Lagos. Then she was thinking more of a mission posting to another African country once her Lagos assignment came to an end. "It's true" she replies, "but in our life, you have to be ready to do whatever you are called to do. I was not expecting to be back in Ireland but now that I am here, there is a job

59

to be done and I am happy to give it my best effort. It is a great honour to be asked to take on the role of Provincial and I feel privileged to be able to serve my congregation in this way.

"We have 118 sisters in the Irish OLA Province. Many of these are retired here in this house and some have reached an advanced age. It's an important aspect of my work now to cater for the needs of these senior sisters who have spent many decades on the missions. Most of the others from the Irish Province are still on mission in Argentina, Tanzania, Nigeria, Ghana and Algeria. My provincial team and I keep in close contact with them and try to assist with their work and their needs in whatever way we can. A small number of our sisters are engaged in different apostolates here in Ireland. A number are caring for the elderly in Castlemacgarrett Nursing Home in Claremorris, Co. Mayo and some more are working with refugees and asylum seekers. Sr. Julie Doran, who spent many years in Nigeria, is now doing a certain amount of mission awareness in Irish dioceses. Prior to that, she worked with Nigerians who were trying to settle in Dublin."

Sr. Mary spent thirteen years in Nigeria. She tells me about her last assignment in Lagos. "Maryland Comprehensive Secondary School has a long history. It was set up by the OLA in 1969 as a co-educational secondary school. The late Sr. Kathleen O'Regan was the founding Principal. In the late 1970's, the Federal Government of Nigeria took over the ownership and administration of what were known as mission schools or schools run by voluntary agencies. The history of education in Nigeria since those years has demonstrated that the outcome of that takeover was not always good. Many schools which flourished under the voluntary agencies slowly but surely deteriorated in standards. In the late 1990's, the Government of Lagos in an effort to cope with declining standards made an offer to return a number of the schools to the voluntary agencies such as the missionaries from different denominations. Cardinal Okogie of Lagos decided to take back five. His objective was to raise academic performance and provide an education founded on sound moral principles.

"The Maryland school caters for all denominations. Christian religious knowledge and Islam are taught. The OLA were happy to return to the administration of the school for the diocese because we believe our input will help bring about the objectives of the Cardinal. It was a daunting task in many ways as apart from the totally run-down state of the buildings, we commenced the new era with sixty new teachers and 2,000 pupils. There was quite a bit of tension in the beginning as both pupils and teachers were fearful and suspicious of change. It took three or four months for relationships to form and stabilize. They are now very good and we are all happy with the way things have progressed.

"From the beginning, we worked as a team and I met a lot with the head teacher, the two vice-principals and the class tutors. Parent-teacher meetings were arranged on a monthly basis. The code of discipline in the school is quite strict and pupils understand clearly that they must adhere to it. It is a fee-paying school that does not get any government funding even for teachers' salaries. Teachers don't earn quite as much as they would in government-run schools but they have the security of knowing that they will be paid every month and they also benefit from the higher standards of discipline. In recent years, there have been times when teachers in state schools could not be sure of getting their salaries though that situation is now greatly improved.

"During my time in Maryland, I dealt with day to day administration and all financial matters. I was also a figure-head who could deal with specific problems. Coping with huge renovations and constant maintenance created an additional workload but I found the work very satisfying and did not miss being in the classroom."

Mary Crowley was born in Macroom Co. Cork in 1959 and was educated in Coláiste Íosagáin, Ballyvourney. "Growing up, I was aware of a strong desire to help people. I was quite fascinated by the whole concept of Africa and the idea of being able to help people in need there took hold early on in my life. I was always reading mission magazines which gave good insights into the lives of the missionaries.

"I think I made up my mind to become a missionary after a retreat given by an SMA Father during my final year at secondary school. I spoke to him afterwards and he encouraged me to visit the OLA Sisters in Cork. After my eighteenth birthday, I made that visit and was invited to spend a weekend with them. I liked everything I saw and experienced during my visit so shortly afterwards in 1978, I joined up. A nine-month postulancy was followed by two years in the novitiate. I then went to Maynooth University to study for a B.A. in theology. After that I took a Higher Diploma in Education in UCC.

"When I arrived in Lagos in 1989, I started teaching in St. Mary's primary school in Broad St. in the heart of the city. Irish OLA Sisters have been in that school since 1877. Within three months, I developed kidney stones and had to be sent home. They had been turbulent months as I was just flabbergasted by the conditions that I found around me in the city – no sanitation, dirt everywhere and massive poverty. After a number of months in Ireland, I returned to Nigeria – this time to the rural area of Ijebu Ode in present-day Ogun State. There, families did not suffer the same hardship as the population was not dense and there was adequate food from farming. I taught in a government-run school for three years, enjoyed the work and had no problems with climate, food or illness. It would have been easy to find things to complain about of course but you tended to do your day's work and put discomforts to the back of your mind.

"In 1992, I moved to Kaduna where I was put in charge of a primary school with up to sixty teachers and 2,000 children. I was there for three years and I absolutely loved it. The little children who were so eager to learn and so innocent were wonderful to work with. The school was within the Archdiocese of Kaduna and there were two other OLA Sisters on the teaching staff. I loved the city, particularly the climate as it was not as humid as the south. The people were largely Hausa and they were very gentle and courteous. I related well with them. This very modern city which has few points of historical interest used to be the old colonial capital of Northern Nigeria. In Hausa, Kaduna means *crocodiles* and many of these mammals can be found in the Kaduna river which divides the town. Today, the city is the capital of Kaduna State but it ranks second to Kano in Northern Nigeria in terms of population, industrial and commercial activities and of course historical interest.

"While in Kaduna, I personally never experienced a period of Muslim/Christian clashes though there had been riots shortly before

I arrived and many since I left. It was during one of these clashes that the Irish Holy Rosary Convent which was located in a predominantly Muslim area of the city was burned down. The sisters were evacuated in time by the army. It was very traumatic for them. Today Kaduna is divided into Christian and Muslim areas and the city frequently experiences tense and dangerous times which can erupt very quickly.

"In 1995, I was asked to come home to do a year of formation studies in Loreto House in Carysfort, Blackrock, Dublin. I took courses in psychology, human and self-development, counselling and spiritual direction. My teachers were mostly lay. Following the course, I was sent to our formation house in Agbor in Delta State which is about one and a half hours from the oil city of Warri. Our Nigerian postulants spend a year there before moving to the novitiate in Ibadan. I regarded my assignment with the young women as one which had serious responsibility attached to it. Handling it badly could have meant turning young postulants against the religious life. I quickly learned that it was very necessary to be sure of my own beliefs and standards.

"After two years there, I was asked to be available and present to our young Nigerian sisters during the five-year period between their novitiate years and final profession. In formation, we call this 'accompanying the sisters'. These sisters were located in different convents all over Nigeria so it meant that I travelled a lot, sometimes on risky public transport. The work was demanding on many levels as the young sisters relied on you to help them through any personal or spiritual problem they had.

"Today, we have up to eighty Nigerian OLA Sisters who are involved in medical work, education, social and pastoral work. We try to accommodate everyone's choice of apostolate. I had the opportunity to get to know a great many of them between 1995 and 2001 and that was a very good experience for me. We continue to get a number of vocations in Africa. The fact that we are not getting any in Ireland is not something that worries me unduly. If we believe that vocations come from God, then I think we should trust in God for the future. I believe however, that we should encourage the Irish lay person to have an interest in mission as lay volunteers who might become involved in such areas as development, aiding refugees, environment and justice and peace issues. Young people have their own spirituality today; they may not be going to the sacraments but they are looking for worthwhile and fulfilling activities.

"Since returning home, I have noticed that many of them are looking for an alternative way of life. On my last two trips to Tanzania, I was accompanied by two young doctors who worked with our sisters in Tanzania for a month. A young teacher also went out from Galway to give her services for a period. This sort of voluntary work can create an awareness of other options for life and commitment."

Sr. Mary Crowley with some bright young students
from St. Theresa's Secondary School, Ole Ado, Ibadan (photo: OLA)

Sister Marciana O'Keefe

Sisters of Our Lady of Apostles (OLA)
Ardfoyle, Cork

Sr. Marciana O'Keefe
Archivist, OLA Convent, Ardfoyle

"I was born in 1926 so I'm eighty years old. I keep fairly well. I get tired of course but my mind is active."

I am talking to Sr. Marciana O'Keeffe at the OLA mother house in Ardfoyle, Ballintemple, Cork. The sisters have inhabited this beautiful building with its fabulous views of the River Lee and the beautiful houses of Montenotte on the heights beyond, since 1913. It's a well-ordered place with the aura of a tradition that has been carefully built up over a period of almost ten decades. The provincial council of the order has its offices there but it is also home to a great number of retired sisters who have spent as many as forty, fifty or even sixty years on the missions. Other visitors to the place come and go. Sisters still on the missions come to pass a peaceful vacation. Young OLA Sisters from Africa and other parts of the world who take courses in Ireland also make it their home for a period.

The tall and poised Sister Marciana is charismatic and eloquent. Her life with the congregation has been divided between the mission fields of Nigeria and administrative positions with the OLA in Ireland and Rome. She grew up in Middleton, Co. Cork where her grandfather on her mother's side was in charge of all the buildings on the Middleton Estate, which was then the property of Lord Middleton. "My mother, Ellen Foley grew up on the Estate and became well known as a woman who had an interest in everybody and everything. She was also a great camogie player. My father was a carpenter on the buildings.

"I was raised in a happy family with brothers and sisters. I think that I realized from a young age that I wanted to be an African missionary. I had heard about OLA in school – mostly from the SMA priests who came regularly to visit. I was also aware of the existence of the Medical Missionaries of Mary and the Holy Rosary Sisters but I was not anxious to join a congregation who was exclusively working in the medical field. I do remember, however, having a great desire to care for poor children. We used to hear of the Little Sisters of the Assumption who went into broken homes to help mothers cope with raising children. That appealed to me greatly as a youngster.

"The summer after my Leaving Certificate, I was shopping in a shoe shop with my mother in Middleton. The shop was owned by the then manager of the GPO in Cork which was a very big job in those days. He happened to walk in when we were there and he starting chatting with my mother whom he knew. He wanted to know what I intended to do for a career. When he heard of my desire to be an African missionary, he advised me to visit the OLA in Cork saying that I could not find a better congregation! When we left the shop, I said to my mother that I would like to follow his advice. My mother, who was always available to help and to follow up on tasks, suggested that we take the next train to Cork and make a visit. When we arrived at the OLA door, the porter announced that he thought it would be difficult to meet anybody as the sisters he said, were all out at a funeral. It was much later and after I had chosen the name Marciana that I learned that the sister who was being buried on that day was called Sr. Marciana O'Brien. Despite the funeral, my mother and I did manage to speak to somebody before we returned to Middleton. That first visit sparked off the chain of events which ended in my entering the OLA in 1944 at the age of eighteen.

"After a few years in the novitiate, I went to UCC and studied for a science degree. I then did a Higher Diploma in Education in Cambridge as it was believed at the time that the diploma offered by UCC was not very good. The OLA policy was to give anybody who was capable the opportunity to get third level education because there was a great need in Nigeria in the 1950's for qualified people to run schools and teacher training colleges. It was no longer acceptable to have unqualified people staffing these institutions.

"I went to Nigeria in 1951 and started working in Queen of Apostles College, Kakuri – one of the first big secondary schools in the north of the country. It was four miles outside the city of Kaduna, which was at the time the colonial capital of Northern Nigeria. We no longer run the school and today it is known as Queen Amina College. I taught there for fifteen years and loved it so much that I could have stayed there for the rest of my life. At the time, we also had a primary school and a teacher training college in Kaduna. Up the road from the secondary school, we had our St. Gerard's Hospital which became quite a big hospital and nursing school. It is still there but we have no involvement with it.

"During my time in Kaduna, I did not experience any great tension between Muslims and Christians. We had children of both denominations in our schools with girls coming from as far away as Ilorin and Benue. All the parents were very anxious to have their girls educated and they were not concerned with religious differences. The tensions that emerged in subsequent years and that have continued right up to the present time may have something to do with a developing link with Saudi Arabia. I know that the Sardauna of Sokoto, Ahmadu Bello who was a very important leader in the north of Nigeria prior to his assassination during the first military coup in 1966, was becoming more and more convinced of the need to promote Islam. When Queen's College, Ilorin was set up by some prominent Muslims, Muslim parents at our school came under pressure to send their children there. Most refused, saying that they would not move their children from where they were happy and doing well. These kinds of developments gave us an indication of what was beginning to happen and we began to understand how things might develop in the future.

"Tafawa Balewa, Nigeria's first Prime Minister and a Muslim sent his sons to St. John's College in Kaduna which was run by the SMA. He was a most reasonable man in every way and he was very adamant that his sons would not be given any kind of preferential treatment. When one of them wanted a bicycle, he telephoned to see if other boys had bicycles and when he was told that they hadn't, he said that his boys wouldn't have any either. The Muslim parents of our own girls were just the same. They were very sensible and had great skills in solving problems. If you had a large number of children from a particular area, the parents appointed a guardian in Kaduna. In the event of trouble, palaver or arguments, that person was called in to listen to both sides of the story. The problem usually ended there.

"I was in Nigeria for the handing over to self-government and subsequent Independence in October 1960. The feeling was good. It was a progressive concept in the minds of the Nigerians to take on self-rule but there were certain apprehensions. Many had secure jobs in the colonial administration and the future held some uncertainty. They were of course instinctively delighted with the idea of Independence. There was "Nigeria, we hail thee, our own dear native land . . ." and all that. That was good. We experienced the same emotions in Ireland in 1922. When Independence celebrations were held in Lugard Hall in Kaduna, all the missionaries were there in the background. Nobody was quite sure how things would develop as many of the Europeans had been told to take their 'lump' (lump-sum) and go. During the ceremonies a big *Oga* came down to us and said: '**you** are all staying, **you** belong to us' and he brought us all forward to the top of the hall.

"Life in the North was very colourful. There were the great Sallah festivals with their spectacular durbars for the two most important Islamic holidays: *Id-el-Fitri* to mark the end of Ramadan and *Id-el-Kabir*, a thanksgiving ceremony commemorating the substitution of Isaac with the sacrificial ram. The sight of spectacularly ornate horsemen wearing breastplates and coats of flexible armour, scarlet turbans and exotically coloured plumes charging on gaily bedecked horses in the Emir's honour is a memorable experience. The Emir himself, draped in white and protected by a heavily embroidered brocade parasol, rides in the middle of the cavalry to a position from where he can observe the charge of honour. We always had good seats at these events.

"After Independence, Kaduna remained an important place as it was the seat of the regional government for Northern Nigeria. I often visited the Assembly for meetings. I didn't ever get to know the northern city of Kano very well though I was in and out of it several times. Unlike Kaduna which is a very modern city, Kano is more than a thousand years old. It's the oldest city in West Africa and has always been one of the most active commercial centres of the region and one of the important cities on the age old trans-Saharan trade route. The Emir of Kano is a very senior Emir and one of the most important of the traditional rulers in the North. He is much respected and to this day influences the people considerably.

"While in Kaduna, I travelled quite a lot around Nigeria. I was Regional Superior for a time so I had to visit our missions all over the country. We also took the girls from the school on trips – south to Lagos and the sea, to Ibadan to visit our big school there and to many other places. We tried to broaden their perspectives as we knew they would play an important part in the future of their country. We either travelled by train or hired a bus. Distances as you know, mean nothing in Nigeria. You somehow manage long journeys in the heat and dust without too much discomfort. I never had fear and I must say that in all my travels in Africa – right up to the late '90's, I never once had an ugly experience or anything close to it.

"In 1965, I was brought home to help with the formation of all the young sisters we had in Ireland at the time. I also went out on the road promoting the missions. After all of that I was elected onto our Provincial Council for two seven-year terms. I worked with Sr. Colombiere O'Driscoll, a former Provincial Superior and a very fine woman, for the first seven-year term. She lives here now but was formerly working in Ghana. When my two terms on the Provincial Council were over, I was elected onto the General Council in Rome for two terms of five years. We established our headquarters in Rome after we moved from Lyons in France where we were founded. The move was planned during our General Chapter of 1978. Geneva, London and Rome were considered as places that would reflect the international aspect of our congregation but in the end, Rome won out.

"Within a month or two of finishing in Rome in 1988, I was asked by the Congregation for the Propagation for the Faith in Rome to go to Nigeria for a year or two to help the young African congregations who were at various stages of forming their constitutions and organizing their chapters. I was sent to Lagos and was supposed to be under the Apostolic Nunciature if I needed money or anything. Once there, I organized a meeting of the superiors of the different indigenous congregations to explain what Rome had asked me to do. These women were very open and I had a huge number of requests for assistance and advice over a period of eighteen months. I moved around the country and it was all very absorbing and interesting as prior to that time, I had only known the Africans in our own congregation. Now I was meeting all these indigenous congregations who had different charisms and different outlooks. I found them to be very courageous. Often their biggest problems were related to the large numbers who wanted to join. We advised them to cut down on the numbers until such time as they had the personnel to train them. These Nigerian sisters were open to working all hours of the day and night. I have always found that the Nigerians have a great capacity for work when the work is there and when there is guidance. I grew to admire greatly many of these congregations. One such was the DDL (Daughters of Divine Love). Many of their members were past pupils of our own. You also had the DMM (Daughters of Mary, Mother of the Church). They had very big numbers and were very brave in the way they took on the management of big buildings, extensions and so on. We founded one indigenous congregation ourselves – the Eucharistic Heart Sisters. We trained them until such time as they were able to move out on their own. It was part of what we did early on in our history as it was an important component of establishing the local Nigerian

Church. It was not until 1957 that we decided to found a Nigerian congregation of OLA. I think that we have now between seventy and eighty in that congregation. They are very impressive on every level. A few of them come here from time to time to visit or to take courses. You will probably meet Margaret Uhwache who is studying in Dublin at the moment. I knew her as a little girl when she joined OLA.

"After that period in Nigeria, I returned home and took a sabbatical. Then I went back in 1996 for a further three years as I was asked to help with the young professed and the growing number of young Nigerian OLA Sisters who were scattered throughout the country studying at universities and so on. That was my last opportunity to travel around meeting people and offering advice. I could have stayed on but in 1999, I was asked to come to Cork to work on the archives.

"Working on the archives is very interesting as we have been keeping records and photographs since the beginning. We have log books going back to the 1880's. I have just been given log books from Ghana which were written in French. One of our sisters who is older than I am works every day on translation. My own French is fairly good and I speak some Italian and Spanish.

"I spent twenty-four years of my life on the Regional and General Councils. The former opened up Ghana and all parts of Nigeria to me and the latter gave me an opportunity to experience places like Morocco, Algeria, Ivory Coast, Lebanon, Egypt, Palestine and all the other countries that we were in. We were in twelve countries at that time. Towards the end of my ten-year term on the General Council, we opened in Sudan and Ireland gave personnel for the foundation. We remained there for a number of years with a lovely international community of Egyptians, Ghanaians, Irish and Lebanese. I have always loved the international aspect of a foundation.

"The future of OLA is, I suppose, a kind of a mystery but the congregation will continue to develop I hope. A lot will depend on the young Africans. We certainly have fine young people amongst them and also amongst the Italians and the French. Our Canadian sisters are getting old. They are now in their fifties and sixties. At one time, we were counting a lot on Canada for vocations. In Ireland, there are none. It's all in the plan of God but the work will go on – I hope.

"The approach to mission has changed over the years – especially since Vatican II. Now there is a much more open and tolerant approach to every aspect of our work. I was never one who believed that there was no salvation outside the Church. In Northern Nigeria, we had great respect for pagans and Muslims. You were happy of course if they were baptized but you would not encourage it too soon or be forceful in any way because they had to profoundly understand what obligations they had to take on. We were very open-minded with regard to ecumenism and we had good relations with the CMS (Church Mission Society), the Methodists and others. I know that it wasn't until 1949 that the Catholic Church dropped the teaching about no salvation outside the Church but you know, this sort of belief is always part of conviction long before it is stated in a formal way. I think if you are reared in a family as I was, where there was respect for other denominations and different points of view, you brought that respect into your adult life.

"One of the many things we did when I was on the General Council was to invite to Rome on an annual basis, for a month or so, an international group of OLA Sisters to expose them to the best lecturers, speakers and discussions on topics such as ecumenism and Islam. The purpose of this was to broaden their perspectives and to prepare them indirectly for a time when communications between different countries would be easier. That time has arrived and nowadays, you can have sisters from any of our missions spending time in another mission in a completely different part of the world. In Africa, the sisters move from one African country to another and I think that is very important. We also have a good handful of our African sisters in Argentina. It was at the request of the Argentinian Cardinal that we established a foundation there. He wanted to introduce the missionary dimension to the Church in Argentina.

"Looking back on my life, I must say that I loved the apostolate of the OLA. I especially loved dealing with the work at an international level. It allowed me to come face to face with the fears and hopes and indeed the great courage of peoples of different cultures all over the world. I think that I should consider writing something about my life. If I get somebody to help with the archives, I may be able to do that in the near future. Seven of us recently took part in oral interviews with a man who is working for the centre of oral history which they are setting up in Maynooth. The interviews lasted for about four hours and they were totally spontaneous and began at the beginning of each person's life story. I'm glad we did that."

Left to right:
Mallam Isa Kaita, Minister of Education, Northern Nigeria
Sr. Marciana O'Keeffe, principal of Queen of Apostles College,
Sardauna of Sokota - Sir Ahamadu Bello
(Photograph from the 1960's)

Sister M. Ethelbert Coleman

Sisters of Our Lady of Apostles (OLA)
Castlemacgarrett, Claremorris, Co. Mayo

Sr. Ethelbert, OLA, with Cardinal Montini - later Pope Paul VI

"Africa was to me the most wonderful place. The Irish missionaries got on very well with the people and we were all entirely devoted to the work in hand. During my time there, primary schools, grammar schools, training colleges, clinics and hospitals were founded and staffed by OLA Sisters and reverend fathers from many other Irish congregations. I found the Nigerians and the Ghanaians to be very welcoming and appreciative of whatever help we were able to give. I fear that times have changed and today, while much good mission work continues, there are many sad stories and we frequently hear of Catholic churches and other institutions being looted and destroyed. In Nigeria in particular, there seems to be quite a lot of tension between Muslims and Christians. This is a pity as the country always prided itself on religious tolerance."

Sister Ethelbert, now in her late 80's, has for many years been a friendly and concerned presence at the OLA-run nursing home for the elderly in Castlemacgarrett. She came there following a missionary career in Ghana and Nigeria and a period of administrative work at the OLA Houses in Ireland and England. "I presume" she says to me when we sit down in the sitting room in Castlemacgarrett to talk, "that I will end my days here. The work is rewarding. The care of the old and infirm is so necessary especially for those who have been living alone and who have no one to care for them.

"I come from a family of four – two boys and two girls. My parents died when we were young but we were fortunate to have had wonderful relatives on both sides of the family to care for us. My first significant experience happened when I went to school to the local convent. On day one, I decided that I wanted to be a nun. My only fear concerned the wearing of the headdress as I had the impression that once it was put on, it never came off! During my secondary education in boarding school, I found the nuns to be approachable, understanding, caring and kind. That nurtured my desire for a future in religious life.

"It was customary for many religious orders to come to our school to speak to the senior classes about their work on the missions. I suppose that you could call it 'canvassing'. They came from Rome, England, China, Australia, and Africa. I was very impressed by the Columban Sisters so I gave much thought to China as that is where they worked.

"At the time, my brother who was studying medicine was not keen on my going on the missions and kept urging me to consider the many religious congregations that existed in Ireland. One day, he happened to pick up a copy of the *African Missionary* and was so impressed by what he read that he decided to withdraw from the university and join the SMA missionary Fathers. This was a significant decision as the study of medicine was very much in the family; three of my mother's brothers were doctors and two of her sisters were nurses. My grandfather had also been a G.P. in Milltown Malbay in Co. Clare.

"I wrote to the OLA in Ardfoyle and requested an interview. I was not too impressed with how things went but as I was leaving the convent, I happened to meet the Provincial Superior who was also novice mistress. I introduced myself and explained the purpose of my visit. It was her unreserved welcome and encouragement at that moment that caused me to change my initial impressions and to ultimately join the congregation. It had always been my intention to join a congregation that was demanding and challenging. In the OLA, I got just that and I recall that the novice mistress was not slow to remind us regularly that she did not want 'tissue paper' missionaries.

"We had many vocations in those days. It was the golden age of generosity when young men and women wanted to give their lives for the salvation of souls in Africa. This continued into the 1960's and then there was a terrific drop in numbers joining. During those years also, the numbers leaving religious congregations reached an all time high. Those of us who remained continued to train and work for the missions with total conviction.

"1939 was a bad year. World War II engulfed many lands. This raised a big problem for our sisters who were due to return to Africa after vacation and for those of us who were preparing to travel there for the first time. A bright light shone for seven of us in 1943, when our provincial superior told us that we would travel to Africa in July of that year. She had been advised by the shipping company that there would be vacancies on a troop ship. It was a risky way to travel but given the absence of alternative ways, she was prepared to take some risks. Preparation got underway and we set forth on 7 July. We travelled to Larne in Co. Antrim, crossed to Stranraer and then went to Glasgow where I remember the weather being extremely cold and misty and the streets being alive with troops preparing to travel to their theatres of war. Our ship, *The California* was to travel in convoy with *The Duchess of York* and a third which was a South American oil tanker.

"Among the passengers on board were thirteen SMA Fathers, two White Fathers, two Augustinians and one Father from St. Patrick's Society, Kiltegan. We OLA Sisters were joined by two sisters of St. Joseph of Cluny. In all there were twenty-seven missionaries and it was frightening to think of the possibility of being sent to *Eternity* before we reached our destination and the goal of our lives! We must have come close to such an outcome on 11 July as we all sat on deck after dinner wondering how we might celebrate the *12th of July*. 'Would it not be terrible if the bombs were now to come' were the words I heard from one priest who was sitting alone. As soon as the words were uttered, the reality was upon us. Sirens sounded and the order *to the cabins* boomed loudly. From a height of 30,000 feet, a solitary German plane dropped bombs on *The California* and *The Duchess*. Miraculously the tanker was saved.

"There were few lifeboats at the ready. While we sisters were standing together on deck, one of us called on one of the priests to give us absolution! My own belief was that God would never let twenty-seven of us go to heaven at the same time! Our work in Africa awaited us and I believed that we would reach our destination. Soon we were in a lifeboat facing the deep but having problems with the suspension ropes which would not function. Finally adjustments were made and the boat slid down to sea. It was then a question of having all hands on deck. Anyone who could row was asked to take an oar. One of our sisters who never got sea-sick volunteered and she did a mighty job. We were rowing about for almost five hours. If the Germans had returned that would have been the end for all of us. Finally in the distance, a corvette escort vessel was spotted. We headed in its direction with joy and relief and were very fortunate that it was within its capacity to pick us up. What a lucky omen it was for us OLA Sisters to see that its name was *MOYOLA!* We climbed on board via rope ladders and though the boat became packed to bursting point, we somehow managed. The following night, an enemy plane flew overhead again but this time failed to harm us.

"We reached Casablanca on 14 July. We were welcomed by the British Consul and the American Ambassador, who had received before our arrival, a radio message advising them to prepare for 1,800 survivors. One hundred and twenty had lost their lives on *The*

California and forty were believed to have died on *The Duchess of York*. Military lorries quickly fetched the men and brought them to the military camps. The women – diplomats' wives, teachers, doctors, nurses and the sisters were given tents which were deftly fitted out by the efficient soldiers, with camp beds, blankets and mosquito nets. Ladies working for the Red Cross brought us some necessary requisites and at 2:00 p.m. on the same day, I remember that the military chaplain offered holy mass in thanksgiving. That evening, the officers' quarters was turned into a ladies' dining room and we were served our food by the soldiers.

"The landscape around Casablanca was sandy and nondescript. Always there were camels laden with heavy loads on the move. Two days after our arrival, 230 nurses from the United States, many of them Catholic and of Irish ancestry arrived to help out. They were capable and wonderful workers. Our OLA Sisters from Marrakech also arrived and brought us veils and other essential items of clothing. The American chaplains were intrigued by our costumes as they had never seen anything like them before.

"On 19 July, we left Casablanca on *The Neahellas*, a sister ship to *The California* and headed for Freetown in Sierra Leone. Despite having travelled through submarine infested waters, we arrived safely on 25 July. We remained in the harbour for a full week but made many excursions on to dry land. These gave a good feeling after the long days at sea. As Freetown was the destination for the two Cluny Sisters, we bade them a fond farewell. Neither of them remained in religious life. They settled instead for secular lives in the United States. I had the pleasure of meeting one of them many years later when she was a patient suffering from arthritis in Castlebar Hospital here in Co. Mayo.

"Those of the passengers who were travelling to Lagos from Freetown changed to the *S.S. Tasmania* while *The Neahellas* continued to the Gold Coast (now Ghana) with the rest of us. Our arrival there was without incident. We had little or nothing to declare at the customs as our huge cargo was at the bottom of the Atlantic. When we reached our regional house however, our Superior seemed anxious about the luggage! We ourselves didn't give it a second thought. We had reached our goal and all we could do was weep with happiness.

"I lived and taught for seventeen years in Ghana and was then transferred to Nigeria because our regional provincial wanted me to help her establish an African foundation of OLA Sisters. That was begun on 2 February, 1958 and over the years has achieved remarkable success. There is now a substantial number of Nigerian and Ghanaian OLA Sisters. Some are currently on mission in Tanzania and Argentina. They have taken our place in a big way with this work. We continue to get vocations in Africa and it is encouraging to know that at present, there are eleven novices and about fourteen postulants in our formation houses. The number of vocations to the priesthood in Africa is equally encouraging.

"It was a big disappointment to me when I was recalled from the missions. I had always hoped that I would spend my life in Africa but like the soldiers, we are an army and when we get orders to move, we move."

Sister Margaret Anave Uhuache

Our Lady of Apostles (OLA)
Ibadan

Sr. Margaret Anave Uhuache, OLA

"*Anave*, my traditional name means *the one who comes*. I am not sure why my late father gave it to me but I like it."

Margaret Anave Uhuache, a delightful Nigerian OLA Sister in her early thirties was studying in Dublin when I met her at the convent of the Sisters of St. Louis in Rathmines. She was participating in a year long course on religious formation which was being run by the IMU (Irish Missionary Union) and she was very enthusiastic about all aspects of her studies. "The participants who are male and female are made up of eighteen nationalities from four continents. We are all greatly motivated by our lecturers who are both lay and religious and who are very skilled and conscientious. Our studies explore human development, human sexuality, our experience of God, the cosmos and much more. We have group dynamic sessions which are very insightful and which lead to very good discussions. We all feel that we are being intellectually challenged."

Margaret was born into a family of nine – five sisters and three brothers. Both her parents came from the Ebira ethnic group in Kogi State. "Ebira is the family language and our mother tongue. We also speak Yoruba and Hausa and some members of the family speak Igbo. Hausa is easier to learn than Yoruba because in Hausa words are pronounced as they are written. In Yoruba, you have all sorts of stresses and intonations and a large number of words can mean different things depending on the stress or intonation. I started learning English in primary school. When my father died in 1980, my senior sister who was working as secretary to the Vice-Chancellor of Maiduguri University took over the training of the eldest four. Then my senior brother, as soon as he had established himself in NNPC (Nigerian National Petroleum Corporation), took responsibility for the rest of us. My father worked with the Nigerian Airport Authority in different locations in Nigeria. This meant that the family had to relocate many times when we were growing up. We were first in Maiduguri then in Yola, Ilorin and Zaria. It was in Zaria that my father died. He was suffering from very high blood pressure. Our mother is still well and living in Zaria.

"I have some memory of most of the places I lived in. Maiduguri is the capital of Borno State in the far north-east. Most of the inhabitants are Kanuri and they speak Kanuri. They came to Nigeria from the central Sahara as Muslim conquerors in the 15th century. They became very powerful over a wide area after that. You also have many Hausa Fulani people in Maiduguri and they speak Hausa. The groups get on well. Maiduguri is very hot in the dry season and temperatures can be as high as the mid-forties. Fortunately the city is full of evergreen neem trees which were brought from India by the British and they provide shade. The city has a very good university and some faculties like medicine are of high standard. The town has great markets which sell products from many different cultures.

"Yola, where I also spent some years is the capital of Adamawa State. It is situated on the upper reaches of the Benue and is close to many beautiful areas near the mountainous border with Cameroon. It is possible to visit some beautiful valleys in the Mandara Mountains from there.

"Ilorin in Kwara is clearer in my memory as I was not so young when we were there. It's an ancient city and is capital of the State. It is often regarded as the gateway between northern and southern Nigeria both economically and culturally. The huge blue-domed mosque with its many minarets dominates the city. Nearby you have the sparkling white Emir's palace. I have lovely memories of visiting the huge market of Ilorin. The city got its name from a local stone which was used for sharpening metal tools. In the past the stone was worshipped with sacrificial offerings but that ritual has died out.

"I was fifteen years old and living in Zaria when my father died. Outside the convent, Zaria is my home. It is one of the original walled Hausa cities which were founded in the 16th century. It has still an ancient appearance because most of the industry and modern development is in Kaduna, a modern city, not very far from Zaria which was established during colonial times. There was once a fourteen-kilometre mud wall surrounding the old city of Zaria and though much of that is now gone, the narrow streets of the old town still have great examples of traditional Hausa homes with decorated mud walls. The Emir's palace is the best example of this kind of building. In the market, you can find lots of interesting things like the traditional *kaptani* which are knee-length embroidered shirts for men. Food is also interesting and you can taste a local dish called *kunu* which is a typical Hausa meal made from millet, water, sugar and peanuts. It is served warm and most people find it delicious. Zaria is the seat of the Ahmadu Bello University which was the first university in Northern Nigeria. The youngest member of my family is studying there now.

"Many tensions have developed in Zaria in recent years because of Muslim/Christian clashes. For those reasons, the Christians who no longer feel safe in the old city have nearly all moved to the outskirts. It is said that Zaria is the brewing area for the Muslim/Christian tensions which then spread to cities like Kano and Kaduna. Many believe that the trouble is often sparked off by idle young people who are paid by unscrupulous political individuals. The habit of fighting and killing has begun to take root and now any little thing can spark off trouble."

From a young age, Sr. Margaret had considered joining a religious order. She had three congregations in mind but when a Sr. Elizabeth, OLA came to her school in Zaria for a vocation rally, she began to focus on the OLA. Shortly afterwards, she visited the sisters in Kaduna. "I was beautifully received by Sr. Mary Taylor who is now in the north of Ireland. Her personality made a strong impression on me. I became drawn to the idea of mission – the idea of leaving my own country to offer my services to people in need. That was a great pull for me. I was also attracted to the idea of being part of an international congregation with people of different cultures coming together with the common goal of bringing the Christian message to others. The day-to-day way of life of the sisters also impressed me as there was a simplicity attached to their communal living and sharing. All of that was wonderful to me.

"I come from a close-knit family. The females especially are very caring and work for unity. The boys are more independent. When I made my decision to be in religious life, my mother and sisters gave me great support. It took my senior brother some time to come to terms with it and initially he wanted my senior sister to forbid me from entering. Her preference was for me to make my own choices. By the time I was finally professed, my brother had come to accept my choice.

"After I joined, I was sent to Kaduna College of Education for three years to study English and religion. I then worked as a teacher and administrator for a number of years in our convents in Benin and Ibadan. After that I was asked to come to Dublin to do the formation course which would prepare me to work on the formation team with our young novices at our novitiate in Ibadan. I'm maybe a little scared of this work as I will be dealing with people's vocations and will have a say in decisions made about their lives. This is a serious responsibility. When I finish my course, I will return to Ibadan to our training house. There we have Sr. (Dr.) Josephine Cox and Sr. Eithne McDevitt, who are Irish and very experienced and will be there to give advice and support.

"I look forward to going back to my own country even though we have many problems. Poverty is the root cause of much of the crime we experience. Our country's resources and wealth are not channelled to the people. Money is in the hands of the few. I am hoping and praying that someday we will get a leader who will be interested in justice and human rights. Nigerians are suffering very badly now and the vast majority of our people find it difficult to make ends meet."

Though Sister Margaret had only spent a short time in Ireland at the time of our interview, she had become conscious of some of the controversies involving Nigerians. She recalled how annoyed she was with a Nigerian woman who was calling into a radio show broadcast by RTE some weeks previously claiming that she would be stoned to death were she to return to Nigeria. "It was obvious that she was not telling the truth and yet there seemed to be nobody attached to the radio show making any effort to check out the authenticity of the woman's story. This woman didn't even come from an area where anything like stoning is even talked about.

"I was also sad when I was told that a number of Nigerians are regularly deported from Ireland. It's painful to think that these are my own brothers and sisters who maybe have run away from home in order to better themselves. Back home, the greed of the few prevents people from having decent lives.

"Despite the difficult things about life in Nigeria, there are so many things that we cherish. The value of caring for each other is strong. We also have a great respect for the elders and this you will find in every part of the country. We show warmth and hospitality and this is something that I am proud of. You will also find that people can smile in the midst of suffering and poverty and are willing to share what little they have with the person who has less."

The Spiritans – Holy Ghost Fathers
(CSSp.)

An Introduction

The Spiritans were founded in Paris in 1703. They now work in fifty countries all over the world. Their work ranges from working with the poor in developing countries to education at all levels in the developed ones.

By 1765, the Holy See had begun to entrust the Congregation with the direct care of mission territories. By 1845, it was entrusted with the pastoral care of a vast area in West and East Africa which included regions under British rule. To provide English speaking personnel for these missions, it was decided to open a house in Ireland in 1859.

The Irish Spiritan Province came into being during the tumultuous years that lead to Irish Independence in 1921. The missionary history of the Province can be said to centre on the towering figure of Bishop Joseph Shanahan who, after completing his secondary studies and formation in France was appointed to Nigeria in 1903.

His thirty years in Nigeria were full of pioneering missionary activity. Early on in his mission life, he became convinced of the crucial place of education in his work. Schools were his chosen means to communicate the Christian message to children and to adults.

The Spiritan foundation which was established by the French in Nigeria and developed by the Irish is now the Province of Nigeria and one of the fastest growing Provinces in the congregation. It has 320 members and their work includes pastoral work, education, working with the youth and spiritual animation.

Father Tim Buckley

Spiritans – Holy Ghost Fathers (CSSp.)
St. Joseph's Parish, Emene, Enugu State

Fr. Tim Buckley with one of his Nigerian parishioners

My very short meeting with octogenarian Father Tim Buckley took place one morning over a cup of tea after his 7:30 a.m. mass in his parish church. This tall and lean missionary, who retains a laser sharp memory, came to Nigeria in 1952, one year after his ordination. Most of the following fifty-three years have been spent working in parishes, in schools and helping the Igbo people pick up the pieces of their shattered lives after the civil war. He was born in Tarbert on the river Shannon in County Kerry and those who know him well credit him with the keen sense of humour and the shrewdness that is not uncommon among the people of that county!

"I arrived in Port Harcourt all those years ago" he tells me, "in a chartered plane which carried a large number of us who were arriving for the first time. The same plane took home an equally large number who were returning to Ireland after their first five-year tour of mission service. Archbishop Heerey, CSSp. of Onitsha Archdiocese was there to meet us and we travelled with him to Onitsha. Almost immediately, I was given an assignment at Awgu parish, as assistant to the parish priest who was also Irish. Our predecessors were two Nigerian priests who later became Bishops of Enugu – Bishops Eneje and Okoye. I took to things quite easily but in the beginning, I got a lot of malaria. Despite being on medication, I was in and out of the hospital every few weeks. I finally got the better of it and since then, I have had very little sickness.

"The fact that I didn't have any great difficulty settling into Nigeria was due to the fact that I was expecting things to be a lot more difficult than they turned out to be. The priest's house was very basic but in fairly good condition. When I went to the out-stations during the midweek, I usually slept in schools. I got quite used to setting up my camp-bed and putting together a rudimentary meal with the young boy who travelled with me to do the cooking and other chores. Most schools were quite open. Sometimes the local people fenced me in with palm branches. I was only disturbed once when I was awakened by a goat feeding on the branches. The people in those days were very poor but extremely generous. The colonial period was coming to an end and Nigerians were preparing for 1960 and Independence. Despite these great political changes, conditions remained very peaceful in the country until the military coups of the mid 1960's and the civil war. Everything changed in Nigeria after those events. The country was never again to enjoy any real peace or security. The discovery of oil in the 1970's brought about further far reaching changes. Millions of people moved from the land into the cities in search of jobs and money. The enormous wealth which poured into the country was not always put to good use. Many would say that the corruption we hear so much about nowadays started during those years.

"When the civil war started, I was brought out of Nigeria by my superiors in Dublin. We all thought that it would be over in a matter of months but that was not to be. As time passed, I made it known that I would be willing to go back with either the permission of the Federal Government or the Biafrans. I was in the United States when I finally got word that I was to be given permission to re-enter by the former. That permission ultimately made it possible for me to remain when the war ended.

"I came back to the Onitsha Diocese which was a major war area within Biafra. It was a heart-breaking and dangerous time. Huge numbers of people were not there as they had fled into hiding in different locations or into the bush. Many others were dead. When the war finally came to an end, we all tried to help the people pick up the pieces of their shattered lives. A huge population started to return to their villages and towns. Thousands and thousands were walking – pushing wheelbarrows and old bicycles which sometimes had no tyres. Children trailed along after their parents. Old cars barely able to chug along were weighed down with the elderly and the sick. Most were returning to nothing so the poverty was awful. I remember having a little money and distributing it among a few. One woman bought so many oranges with what I gave her she was able to set up a little business! Streets were overflowing with beggars and destitutes. Devastation, penury and disease were the order of the day and the life.

"Despite the emphasis put on reconciliation by the Nigerian Head of State, General Yakubu Gowan at the end of the war, and following his famous speech in which he declared that there were 'no victors or no vanquished', the road to recovery and reconciliation took a very long time. It is in fact a work in progress – up to this present day. Efforts to establish the 3R's (Reconciliation, Rehabilitation and Reconstruction) so much proclaimed and advocated by General Gowan became hard to actualize. To the Igbos – the main war victims – efforts in these areas were regarded as feeble. Undoubtedly, the huge war damage made reconstruction difficult but more than seven years later when Nigeria was said to be awash with money from the oil boom and when the country played host to other African nations in FESTAC – the second world black and African festival of arts and culture – little reconstruction had taken place within the Igbo territories.

"Gradually people settled down and life started to build slowly. The concepts of survival and re-growth came to be eulogized and respected. My memory is that the children were brave and very good. Schools reopened, businesses were restarted and the people reached out to each other in whatever way they could and with whatever resilience they could find. One interesting development that took place in the post-war years was the emergence of many new towns in Igboland which became flooded with the business activities of the thousands of Igbo business people who had to flee other areas in Nigeria, especially Northern Nigeria. Nevertheless, it was not an easy time and it is believed that certain socio-economic conditions which were imposed on the Igbos by the Federal Government at the time acerbated matters.

"In late 1972, I took a break – first in Ireland and then in Ghana where my brother Martin, also a Holy Ghost priest, went when he was not allowed to stay in Nigeria after the war. I found him to be in great form. All he wanted was plenty of work. Those missionaries who went to Ghana from Nigeria grew to love it. The Ghanaians are a very gentle people. They are not as pushy as the Nigerians who sometimes can be aggressive and materialistic.

"I have got very used to the life here now and have no wish to return home for another while. I am enjoying very good health thank God, so as long as that continues, I would like to keep doing what I am doing. All the priests in the parish are Nigerian. Some are teaching in the university. Most of the Irish missionaries who came out with me have either passed away or have returned to Ireland."

As I leave Father's house, a sunny and fresh April morning has come into full glory. The wide-open spaces of the church compound which were relatively empty at 8:00 a.m. when I arrived are now filling up. Daily routines have begun. Outside Father Buckley's front door, a line of parishioners wait for him to finish his breakfast and start the morning consultations.

St. Joseph's Parish is reputed to be among the best run parishes in the Enugu diocese.

The anguish of war: a disturbing
reminder of the Nigerian Civil
War.   (photo: Associated Press)

The anguish of war; a disturbing reminder of the Nigerian Civil War (photo: Associated Press)

Father Breifne Walker

Spiritans - Holy Ghost Fathers (CSSp.)
Spiritan International School of Theology
Enugu

Fr. Breifne Walker CSSp. opening the 300th anniversary celebrations
of the foundation of the Holy Ghost Congregation in 1703,
at the Spiritan International School of Theology (SIST) in Enugu.
Seated (L to R) Fr. G. Odigbo CSSp. Rector of SIST and
Fr. G. Ezewudo CSSp. Provincial Superior

Although I had first met Father Breifne Walker at the Spiritan International School of Theology (SIST) in Enugu, my interview with him took place in Holy Ghost College, Kimmage Manor, Dublin where he was engaged in a research project called *Christian Ethics and Warfare and other uses of Military Force*. This subject has always interested him because of its relevance to the lives of missionaries, many of whom work in countries which are often torn apart by warfare and conflict.

He first went to Nigeria in 1990 and apart from a year's sabbatical leave in 1997, remained until 2003. His only experience of Africa prior to that was a two-year mission post in Ghana. "There I was in the interior of the country, rather close to the Ivory Coast and about two and a half hours from the Ashanti capital of Kumasi. I was engaged in straightforward parish work and the parish I served in had 33 very rural out-stations. In some places, we were starting off the Church, and in others, we were building on what was already there. Because I did a very good language course in one of the Ashanti languages before starting, I was able to communicate with the people fairly well and I found them to be calm, gentle and sincere. The two years I spent in Ghana were a great introduction to Africa and my experiences there brought home to me that we have much to learn as Europeans from the Africans. This has a lot to do with the value placed on respecting every human being. For the Ghanaian, it is very important to give the person you are with your full attention and if you are a few minutes late for your next appointment, you will be forgiven and respected for having been fully present to the person you were with. How we carry this into the frantic lives of people in the developed world is something we should try to work out. Efficiency and the market seem so important to most of us now. Ireland has become enmeshed in this ethos and I find that young people are driven by it. It's all about getting things done and making money and it is very self-centred. I don't want to sound self-righteous but it does take some getting used to. An interest in a religion of any sort is marginal and I sense indifference more than any level of hostility. I am puzzled as to where people are getting their values. They are certainly not getting them exclusively from the Gospel which directs us to love and do good to our neighbour and to extend that love of neighbour to all people in need. The Church, to its credit, has been trying hard in recent times to spread the message of the social gospel which urges us to think in a global way about love of neighbour because the world is divided and there are huge populations of wretchedly poor people who are trapped in poverty for all sorts of unjust reasons.

"When I first came to Nigeria my work involved training young African Spiritan (Holy Ghost) clerical students. These were the students of SIST and they were senior seminarians who came to us from other institutions to study the theology that would prepare them to be future missionaries to other countries in Africa and beyond. The students came from many parts of Africa but especially from the West-African countries of Sierra Leone, Ghana, Gambia, Senegal, Congo Brazzaville and Cameroon. At any given time, we had up to ten nationalities represented in our student body. There was a great diversity of cultures and the students were very much strangers to each other. The cultural richness that existed manifested itself on many occasions such as on national days. These were days which were celebrated very solemnly.

"The Spiritan congregation is essentially a missionary one, so those who join can expect to be sent outside their own culture to preach the Gospel to people who have never heard of it or to help a local church already established. They could also be sent to a place like Ethiopia to work with a nomadic tribe or perhaps even to a place where they would co-operate with the Orthodox Church. We are now in many different countries worldwide. In recent years, the congregation has gone into Asia – into the Philippines, Taiwan and Papua New Guinea and students from SIST are working in all these places in a variety of ministries.

"The early missionaries, who were involved in primary evangelization, attached a lot of importance to preaching the Gospel through education. Nowadays the methods of preaching would be less structured and there would be a consciousness of the need to spend a lot of time learning the language and becoming immersed in the culture of the people. Preaching by example – Christianity being portrayed by the way one lives one's life has always been part of the way the missionary did his work and that continues to be the same.

"In SIST, they take a very intensive four year course in theology and particular attention is paid to how their studies relate to other African cultures. They also learn computer skills and self-sufficiency skills in agriculture and medicine. When I first came to SIST, I was teaching moral theology along with a completely African staff. It was a very enriching experience and I found that I had much to learn and understand. At a later period, when I was moved to the non-academic role of Director of Students, I found myself coming face to face with a set of new insights. My role involved accompanying the students during their formation, training them at an individual level and paying attention to their human and spiritual development. This included urging people to be conscious of the nature of relationships, personal behaviour and the use of power. Today the Pope and many others are emphasizing the huge importance that should be attached to the formation of the priest as a human being who can be a credible witness to the Gospel. That was something that was neglected in the past.

"The issue of celibacy in priesthood and religious life is now also being addressed more openly and constructively. In most countries in the world, celibacy is not a value. It's a contradictory sign. Africans find the concept very hard to understand so it's extremely important to prepare the students there in a way that will enable them to live a life of celibacy which will be life-giving to themselves and to others. Ideally, the celibate religious person is a source of life and energy and all going well, he should be able to channel those energies into the service of other people, and into having mature, loving and free from strain relationships with both men and women. This whole area was one of neglect for a long time and there were few guidelines. Much was covered up and not spoken about or spoken about in very precious language – language that was spiritualized out of all existence. This resulted in many issues and anxieties being put to one side in a way that was not healthy. From my own experience as a celibate priest, I know that if I want to be life-giving to others, I have to be able to integrate my celibacy into my whole being and as a sexual being I have to be happy as a celibate. To my mind celibacy is a very valid way of living out one's sexuality. You are not just negating something – not just depriving yourself; you are choosing a valid option and rightly understood, it is a very positive way of coping with and living out one's own sexuality.

"Celibacy and its relation to human sexuality will continue to be a difficult subject from the point of view of explanation and communication. Students and others find it a threatening and invasive topic. It's threatening as it is seen as an area of darkness. If somebody in authority enters into discussion about sexuality, it sometimes can be perceived as a threat. Many seminarians open up on the subject; others find it very difficult to do so. In SIST, the staff tries to help students in this area by organizing group work which explores different emotions.

"For people in religious orders such as ourselves, the Benedictines or the Augustinians, the celibate life is not an option and won't be in the future because we freely take the vows of poverty, chastity and obedience. The celibacy rules for diocesan clergy could change because there is no essential connection between priesthood as a ministry of the Church and celibacy. It's part of the current discipline of the Western Latin Church but it is not essential to priesthood."

Following his period as Director of Students, Fr. Walker took a one-year sabbatical in Ireland. When he returned to Nigeria, he resumed a teaching role in SIST but was also appointed Community Superior.

"One of the things that I was asked to do during that period was to organize a programme of pastoral work for the students. This involved sending them to local hospitals, prisons and to a nearby village for former lepers which is organized in a wonderful way by the Marist Brothers. The students were then encouraged to reflect on their experiences and relate these reflections to their theology studies. Some students were quite scared going into prisons in the beginning – scared of the criminals and repelled by their alleged crimes. As they got to know the circumstances of the individual prisoners, they became more compassionate. They also learned that the prisons in Nigeria are full of people who are awaiting trial. In extreme cases, that wait can be as long as twenty years. Those who are fortunate enough to have their cases promoted and brought to trial by influential people, by church leaders, by priests or by other benevolent organizations have very frequently been proved innocent.

"As Community Superior, I was very involved in the day to day life of a community that is made up of seventy students and ten members of staff. Sustaining a good community spirit can be challenging because where you have many young people, you tend to have a great deal of activity and that can sometimes militate against a sense of unity. At times, I found that certain tensions made my role demanding. Overall though, my years in the position were very happy ones."

Back in Dublin, immersed in his research project, Fr. Breifne cannot help thinking of the ongoing war in Iraq and the present dangerous situation in the world.

"I think that war has a very strong grip on the universal imagination. Immediately after the terrible events of 11 September, 2001, George Bush's first words were: 'we are at war'. The words were meant to encourage and console his people but to my mind, they were badly chosen and they put the United States and much of the rest of the world on a war footing. By using them, he handed over a huge moral advantage to Bin Laden and the perpetrators of the atrocities, and he re-enforced Bin Laden's self-image as a warrior. We know that the language of war is very sacred to people of his way of thinking. If the destruction of the twin towers and the death of three thousand persons had been described as mass murder, then a note of morality would have been introduced and the appropriate response would have been a policing one.

"What I hope to produce from my research is some form of document or treatise that will be a Christian theological reflection on the realities of war. If we are promoting war, we really need to allow ourselves to be confronted with God's revelations in the scriptures and with the whole Christian tradition because if we talk about war and use of military force as a way of achieving justice or some other moral good, we have then to ask ourselves the question: *What God do we believe in?* I believe the gospel of Christ really requires us to be pacifists. The fullness of God's revelation is on the Cross where Jesus the son of God is revealed and displayed in terms of complete powerlessness. What appears to the world as total powerlessness and ineffectiveness is actually the fullness of God's revelation, because the Cross is not complete without the Resurrection. Good Friday and Easter Sunday go together as one event. I think that all this has to be highly relevant to the way we think about war.

"On what grounds then do we authorize young men and women to go out in armies to kill and maim in a hugely efficient way on our behalf? Today we should be looking at the traditional 'just war' criteria very critically. These criteria which were worked out by thinkers and theorists over a period of time were based on the belief in the rationality of human beings. In the light of modern scientific knowledge into the levels of aggression and violence in human beings, we can no longer consider these criteria in the same way. Furthermore, the nature of war has changed and it is not now a straightforward taking of life. Today we know that war is extended to include sexual abuse of prisoners and all kinds of humiliating, aggressive and violent interrogations. These are integral to the nature of war now and they are not simply aberrations.

"There is an ambiguity in the way people are thinking right now. We are not sure of our convictions or our beliefs and it's why so many people don't speak out. One of the alarming features of the discussion surrounding the war in Iraq is its hugely utilitarian perspective. The discourse is all connected to consequences – 'Iraq is on its way to Democracy' or 'Saddam is in custody'. There is a studied silence about the thousands of Iraqi civilians who have been killed. The number is far in excess of the 9/11 figures. Unfortunately, we are being urged to accept that the orthodox view is the utilitarian one and that what really matters are the consequences. If the consequences are good, we shouldn't be too concerned about the means of bringing them about!

"Another issue that preoccupies me greatly is the morality of power. Because of my involvement in the Church and because of my position in the seminary in Nigeria, I feel that I have come face to face with it. My interaction with staff and students drove me to think about it a lot more than I might otherwise have done. In a position of authority, how do I use my power? To me, it's a major issue for everyday life.

"The more visible aspects of Church power as personified by bishops and priests have to be the beecher's brook of the moral life of the Church. Over the years, the Church has been somewhat tied up in the morality of sexual behaviour and it somehow neglected the morality of the use of power. Unfortunately, the history of the Irish Church is full of examples of the misuses of power and a lot of the anger that is directed against the Church in Ireland today is based on memories of clerics in prominent positions using their power in destructive ways. Of course, the misuse of power is the key issue when it comes to clerical sexual abuse. If you examine the New Testament, you will find that the Lord made some very clear and direct statements to his followers about the way they should use authority. He is very insistent on authority being equal to the concept of service and teaches that those who are in power should be the servants of those over whom they have authority. The use of power and authority has to be very central to the credibility of the Church and it is one of the things that I tried to communicate to my students in Nigeria. It's very important because in every society in the world, human beings can lapse easily into domination. It happens in the Church and it happens in civil society.

"During my time on the missions, I have always been keen to keep in contact with Ireland. Now that I am back, I have the opportunity to study many issues more closely. I am very conscious of a need for a purification of the Church and I believe the Gospel and the Christian message needs to be heard in a new way in Ireland. It needs to be communicated in terms that can be understood by twenty-first century people who live in a very secularized environment and in what is now a very complex society.

"There are many good things happening in Ireland and we have many committed people. Our President, Mary McAleese is an example. We are lucky to have such a person in public life because she is somebody who can articulate very well the faith of which she is thoroughly convinced. She is able to find the balance between tradition and modernity and I would also say that she has tremendous powers of persuasion.

"I think bishops and people in leadership in the Church have to be ready to listen a lot more than they did in the past. There is a long journey to be travelled by the Irish Church in this regard. A definite move away from the traditional style of leadership which was authoritarian and sometimes arrogant, has to be made and lay people have to be taken seriously. I would like to see what is happening in parts of America happen in Ireland. There, small groups of lay people come together under the slogan *keep the faith, save the Church*. From what I hear, they are very committed and they are trying to carry on transmitting the faith."

Father Breifne hopes to go abroad on mission again after his current sabbatical comes to an end.

Father Elochukwu Eugene Uzukwu

Spiritan Fathers – Holy Ghost Fathers (CSSp.)
Kimmage Manor, Dublin

Fr. Elochukwu Eugene Uzukwu CSSp.

Father Eugene Uzukwu had spent three years teaching at the Milltown Institute, Dublin and at the Pontifical University at Maynooth when I met him for what we called 'a conversation' at the Holy Ghost College, Kimmage Manor in Dublin. This sprightly and engaging man whose youthful appearance belies his sixty years grew up as a Catholic in Eastern Nigeria and came under the influence of the Irish Holy Ghost Fathers (Spiritans) at an early age.

"I was born in Nnewi in Anambra State and I came into contact with the Fathers away back in 1960. I attended the Spiritan junior seminary at Ihiala which is about twenty-five kilometres from Onitsha and very close to the famous Uli airstrip that was used by the Catholic Church and Caritas for landing relief supplies during the Biafran war. I had just finished studying philosophy in the major seminary when the war broke out.

"It was a terrible time for the Igbo people and we were all feeling sore and disillusioned. The war was disastrous and there was not one family which was not affected by it in some way. I don't know if going to war was the best decision. We found ourselves plunged into it and it was a terrible shock. At the time, most Biafrans wanted to become independent but with hindsight, I am not so sure that it would have been such a good idea. I have since those days been all over Nigeria many times and there is no corner of the country where you will not find big populations of Igbo people. We come from the most populated section of West-Africa so our area cannot accommodate all of us. There's simply not enough space so from the point of view of sheer economics, I think that we wouldn't be able to survive without Nigeria.

"After the war, we started to pick up the pieces. When you are young, you do not focus too much on the trauma and in those days, we did not seek the services of psychotherapists or counsellors! We certainly had group therapy and we understood that there was no alternative to getting up and getting on with life. Some have not recovered psychologically or economically but most did not want to be sacrificed on the altar of war. My group and I were young Spiritan seminarians and when the Irish Spiritans were expelled after the war, many thought that we could not survive. The Nigerian diocesan priests thought it was all over for us. My own memory was that we did not want to join up with the diocese so we became a determined and tightly-knit group and together with the help of a wonderful superior, Philip Obinna Aguh, we somehow survived.

"I was ordained in 1972 and almost immediately I started working in our novitiate house. After three years, I was sent to teach at a diocesan junior seminary. After that, I went to Toronto in Canada for postgraduate studies. When I returned in 1979, I didn't want to stay in Eastern Nigeria because the Church there was not open to the whole idea of indigenization and that is where my interest lay. When I got the chance to teach liturgy and theology to Spiritan seminarians in Congo Brazzaville for three academic years, I was very happy. It was the best thing that ever happened to me as Brazzaville and Kinshasa were in the front line of the theology and philosophy of an African liturgy. The Church in those countries has a long history that goes back to the Portuguese days in the seventeenth and eighteenth centuries.

"In Kinshasa at that time, they had the very powerful Cardinal Joseph Malulu who was totally committed to the indigenization of the Church in Africa. Even before the introduction of the reformed liturgy of the Roman Rite in 1969 (what was commonly referred to as the *new mass*), the Kinshasa Church had already set up their own study group to explore an African liturgy and they started experimenting with a real Congo mass in 1973. By 1981, it was officially approved by the Vatican. The differences between it and the Roman mass are confined to differences in the structure of the liturgy. The Congo mass does not, for example, begin with a note of penitence. It begins instead with an explosive note of joy which you will hear in the opening song, in the drumming and in the dancing. The Gloria is also presented in that way. After the readings and the homily, a time for reflection is introduced and with it comes the note of penitence. During the Eucharist prayer, praise is given to God for the whole ecology, the whole Congo and for all the people of the Congo. Official mention is also made of the ancestors. The picture that emerges from this sort of liturgy is one which recognizes the unity of the *One Church* but which also recognizes that its constituent churches can have their own indigenous liturgy.

"From the time the Church came under the influence of the Graeco-Roman world, her theology, laws, politics and philosophy became married to that world and until recently, virtually excluded all possible variations. It was not until Vatican II that this mono-cultural image of the Church was understood to be harmful to the life and mission of the Church.

"The period after Vatican Council II saw a lot of creativity in Church liturgy in Africa. Pope Paul V1 expressed great delight in this. In 1974, during the Fourth Synod of Bishops on Evangelization (SECAM), the African Bishops gave their full support to a specifically African theology and called for evangelization in co-responsibility. *'They even set aside the prevalent theology of adaptation in favour of a theology of incarnation. The Word must become Flesh in Africa! In other words there must be in Africa, a contextual interpretation of the experience of Jesus.' (Uzukwu, 1996, A Listening Church).* That development proved too much for Rome so in the closing discourse of the synod, Paul V1 warned against the danger of talking about theologies according to continents and cultures. In a subsequent address to SECAM in 1975, he clearly underlined that there was no question of exercising freedom or autonomy in theological research. Despite these pronouncements, the African Bishops continue to believe that the Church in Africa must not be confined to the straightjacket of a uniform Roman style Church. When Pope John Paul II came along, he supported the general idea of inculturation in the churches in Africa but placed strict limitations on adaptations.

"In the 1980's, I was working with a group of researchers in Oka Diocese in Nigeria on this whole issue. When we finished our work in 1986, we presented it to the Bishop who was Nigerian. His response was very negative and he informed us that our ideas could not be applied, that the Church was not ready for them and that he had not asked us to come up with that kind of research. The group was shocked.

"A certain amount of inculturation and indigenization has already taken place in the Nigerian Catholic Church. One example of this is the 'naming ceremony' which happens after the birth of a child. The Yorubas have retained their traditions for this ritual and they have Christianized them by including a reading from the Bible. At 5:00 a.m., the catechist in the absence of the priest names the child. During the ceremony, the child is given some items or instruments that are symbolic of living a life. Life is sweet so he will be given some sweet things. Life is also tough so he will be given some hot pepe to taste. The Yorubas would like to integrate this ceremony with Baptism but personally, I like the separation because I do not think that you could do all of it in one session. Now, the Igbo naming ceremony is not yet Christianized as they do not include a reading from the Bible.

"Aspects of the traditional Nigerian marriage ceremony are also included in the liturgy in some places and all over, definite changes in the way the liturgy is celebrated exist. Not all the changes are approved by the Church so that remains a problem. In November 2003, we had our first ever *National Pastoral Congress of the Catholic Church in Nigeria*. Part of the reflection that went along with it was the examination of where we were as a Church. I did a presentation on Christianity and culture and I found from my preparatory research that we have really done very little from the point of view of inculturation or indigenization. That being said, the reports that came in from the dioceses during the Congress were insisting that we should have a Church that is local and indigenous – one that is related to the structures of the organization of our societies and one that incorporates to some extent, the traditional rituals associated with marriage, naming ceremonies and so on.

"Now, we do not want to turn the mass or other aspects of the liturgy upside down. It really is a question of adapting but we may wish to radically adapt from place to place. What has caught up with us now and it is becoming a problem for the Catholic Church, is the burgeoning charismatic movement and the whole wave of healing ministries and other rituals that are happening in the indigenous Evangelical and Pentecostal Churches. They are attracting a very big percentage of the youth. Some of the rituals carried out play on the superstitions of the people and many are not unconnected to financial gain. These churches are thriving in the context of the massive poverty and massive threat to human life which exist in Nigeria. If somebody tells a poor and desperate person that he has access to the Spirit, that desperate person will want to cling on. This sort of thing has recently crept into the action of some Catholic priests and this is tragic. I was in a consultation in 1991 for the Bishops of Nigeria and many priests who are involved in these kinds of ministries were present. What I heard was quite stunning and some of the priests involved were my own past-pupils. Some were trying to make every mass a healing mass which meant that you could never tell when a mass would begin or end because it all depended on the healing momentum. You cannot make every mass a healing mass but you can announce that on a special day, there will be a special mass for the sick that will include some rituals such as the water rite.

"In the face of all of this, the major challenge which the Catholic Church must grasp with all its strength and ability is the challenge to stem the major corruption that exists in the country. It must also play its part in forcefully attacking the social and political problems at their very roots. There is the official Church position on corruption and this month after the meeting of the Bishops in Makurdi, they came out with a statement condemning corruption, the Government and the manner in which elections are carried out. The Church has been issuing these kinds of statements since the notorious days of the military rule of Sani Abacha. Things were so bad at that time that the Bishops decided to stop preaching in all the churches in every diocese on a Sunday and to read instead a statement from the Conference of Bishops. It would be good for them to go back to that system now because it would show that the Church leadership does not play party politics and it would underline the way the Church feels about the state of the country. Things have not been going well since the return of Democracy in 1999 and as the Bishops assessed at their conference, it has been deceit after deceit. Poverty has increased and even the important *freedom of speech* is not holding because there is so much violence that people are afraid of speaking out.

"Only this morning, I was pondering over all that has happened in Nigeria over the past decades. The image of military dictator Ibrahim Babangida came into my mind. He came to power in 1985. There was a coup which failed to oust him in 1987 and it was followed by terrible bloodshed. I kept wondering how this man can still feel that he can present himself to the Nigerian people as a credible leader. We are now hearing that he has Presidential ambitions for the future.

"The whole area of leadership in our country has been unfortunate but I am still hoping that something will give way. The enormous poverty could bring about a groundswell of revolt that could force the leadership into bringing about change. Will that change come? I don't know! We do know that a great number of people are benefiting from the way things are and we also know that there is massive corruption from top to bottom.

"I feel that I must soon return to Nigeria. My country is beckoning me. My body and my mind are also reminding me that it is time. Next year I will be sixty! Time is passing! When I return, I would not wish to go into parish work as all my life I have been an academic travelling all over Nigeria and beyond giving lectures and courses. I certainly would like to be involved in some parish work but that would have to be in a supporting role. Before I left Nigeria, I was teaching at the Spiritan International School of Theology (SIST) in Enugu and the Institute Catholique in Paris. SIST was established in 1987 to meet the needs of our senior Spiritan seminarians who needed to study the international dimensions of theology in preparation for their future lives as missionaries outside their own country. The other project which I was involved with before I left was the development of a centre for mission research, documentation and animation. This has more or less come to a standstill. If the proprietors agree, I would like to involve myself with that centre again."

The Missionary Sisters
of the Holy Rosary
(MSHR)

An Introduction

The Congregation of the Missionary Sisters of the Holy Rosary was founded in 1924 by Bishop Joseph Shanahan, CSSp. During his early mission years in Nigeria, he became acutely aware that the missionary movement to bring Christianity and education to the people was not reaching women. He approached a number of women's religious congregations in Ireland to see if they would become involved with this work of mission. Because he found that they were reluctant to do so, he concluded that the best thing to do was to form a new missionary congregation.

As a consequence, by 1924, a group of women who had volunteered to join the new congregation first came together under the supervision of the Dominican Sisters in Cabra, Dublin but shortly afterwards moved to Killeshandra, Co. Cavan. Their formation remained under the direction of the Dominican Sisters of Cabra for some years.

In 1928, the first members of the Holy Rosary congregation arrived in Onitsha, Nigeria. They began their mission by setting up a small school for girls and quickly gained insight into what was needed for a productive and fulfilled missionary life. Those who had not been qualified for a profession before entering the congregation were sent to centres in Ireland, Scotland and England for professional training as teachers, medical doctors, nurses and midwives. Their aim was to become specialists in every branch of knowledge that would help them understand all aspects of their missionary calling.

By the time the congregation was celebrating its silver jubilee, seventy sisters were working in various parts of Nigeria.

Today, the congregation works in seventeen countries and its approximate 400 members is made up of sisters from eleven nationalities. For many years, the sisters were mainly involved in educational and medical work but today they help in every area of need. This includes caring for orphans, working among HIV/AIDS victims and caring for refugees in war-torn areas around the world.

Sister Edith Dynan

Missionary Sisters of the Holy Rosary
Enugu

Sr. Edith Dynan, MSHR

At 87 years of age, Sister Edith was the oldest Irish missionary living in Nigeria when she spoke to me in Enugu about her life in Africa. She first described her hazardous maiden voyage to Nigeria.

"It was 1944 and it was an eventful journey to say the least. I left Dublin for Liverpool during the first week of Lent with three other sisters. We had been waiting for months to hear of our travel arrangements. It was during the war so any advance information was difficult to get. In Liverpool, we embarked on a ship called *The Isipingo* which was headed for Lagos and which was one of a convoy of seventy-two ships. We arrived on Holy Saturday. Our journey turned out to be hazardous and the captain had to detour on a number of occasions to avoid enemy vessels. Somewhere south of Spain, we slept over one or more German submarines. The sound of their engines had been picked up. Later our information was that a submarine was hit, that some crew members were killed and that a number of hostages were taken to Gibraltar. We had another scare between Freetown and Lagos when a ship's alarm advised all passengers to stand by the lifeboats. We were apparently in danger of being torpedoed but somehow escaped."

Almost sixty years on, a healthy and very articulate Sister Edith – or Sister Adaeze as she is called in Nigeria – is sitting with me in the parlour of the Holy Rosary Novitiate in Enugu talking about these momentous events. I'm intrigued by the pleasant sounding *Adaeze* – the Igbo name with which she is being addressed. She tells me why she was given it. "I was once very ill in Emekuku in Owerri Province (now in Imo State) and I was taken by ambulance to hospital in Enugu. The Christians began to pray for me and masses were offered. The pagans were also praying to the god of the village called Ezelukwu who apparently communicated with them and told them that I would not die – that I was their Ada (daughter). From then on, they started calling me Sister Adaezelukwu. Over time, it was shortened to Adaeze – which means *princess* I believe."

She was in secondary school in England when the idea of becoming a missionary sister first came to her. "I made enquiries at my convent school and was given some names. One of these was the Missionary Sisters of the Holy Rosary in Killeshandra, Co. Cavan. I think that it was the name Killeshandra that attracted me because straight away I wrote and arranged a visit. The congregation which was founded by the remarkable Holy Ghost missionary, Bishop Joseph Shanahan was just ten years old and I, at the time of my visit was just seventeen and a half. After my interview, Reverend Mother asked when I might consider joining and spoke of 'a nice group' that was coming to join in September, just a few months away! Though I had not intended to make such a quick decision, I found myself telling her that I would come in September. When I came, I knew during the first week that I had made the right decision. On my very first night in the convent, I had a wonderful sleep and when I awoke in the morning, all the tears and loneliness of the previous days had disappeared. Our group built to eleven over the first year and seven of us went through to final profession.

"After qualifying as a teacher in Edinburgh, I decided to volunteer to go to Nigeria. When I arrived with the two other sisters in Lagos on that Easter Saturday night in 1944, we stayed for a few days with the OLA Sisters in Broad Street. While there, two Holy Rosary Sisters arrived from Onitsha by an Ojukwu transport lorry. These sisters who were long overdue home-leave were on their way to our sisters in South Africa having been unable to get passage to Ireland. It was agreed that my two companions would use the Ojukwu lorry back to Onitsha and that I would travel by train with all the 'loads' – 24 pieces in all – crates of all kinds of everything for *the missions*. My journey took two nights and one full day. The train apartment which I was given had three bunks and as the train was crowded, the guard tried to put British soldiers in with me. I refused saying that I had paid for all three bunks. He accused me of being selfish but I did not relent. When night came, I tried to get some rest but the cockroaches took over the floor. I had never seen one before. Later the train ran into a swarm of locusts which managed to enter the carriages. There was great excitement as passengers ran around collecting them for food. I was very fearful and I began to wonder how I would cope with my new life. I never saw a locust after that night! When I arrived in Enugu at 3:00 a.m., I was met by some of our sisters and Father Tom Fox, a Holy Ghost Father.

"My first month in Enugu was very difficult. I found it hard to adapt and kept thinking that I had probably made a big mistake in coming. I lost my appetite and became tired, thin and weary. Then I was moved to our convent in Onitsha where my duties were to give in-service training to the student teachers in Immaculata School, to take charge of the residential pupils and to learn Igbo. I travelled there in a mammy wagon with all the women who were going to the big Onitsha market and had a first class seat beside the driver. I was seated by early morning but we did not depart until after mid-day as the vehicle had to wait until it filled with passengers. On the way to

Onitsha, it broke down and there was a very long delay in the dark. I was pretty scared and of course nobody knew where I was. Our sisters alerted Bishop Heerey of Onitsha so he sent out his driver with instructions to look out for a broken down lorry. Just as he was setting off, he spotted me in the company of some local boys carrying my load on their heads coming through a field.

"I spent a wonderful year in Onitsha. I worked mainly with Sister Mary Liguori Keane who was a great inspiration to me. She had tremendous energy and was a wonderful missionary. She had been just two years ahead of me in the novitiate so we knew each other. At the end of the year, I was transferred to Holy Rosary Convent, Adazi in an area called Agulu where I was put on the staff of Loreto Training College. I was well able for the teaching which I enjoyed but supervising many different programmes and routines in the college took a little getting used to.

"After one year there, I was moved again – this time to Port Harcourt where I was made manager of two primary schools – one in Diobu and one in Ogoni. There were three of us in the convent. One was nursing in the *African Hospital*. In those days, there were special hospitals for Europeans and others for Africans. By 1949, I was due leave in Ireland so I went home and spent some months studying and working in our convent in Killeshandra. By the end of 1950, I was back in Nigeria conducting examinations for students being selected for teacher training.

"In January 1951, I was appointed local superior of Holy Rosary Convent, Emekuku, Owerri. Here our sisters had a large and ever-expanding hospital, an elementary Teachers' Training College and a primary school. We also had St. Mary's Training Centre for young women preparing for marriage and a *Widows' Home* for those widows who were maltreated after the death of their husbands. I was given the choice of being principal of the training college or being manager of the school. I chose the latter as I knew that it would give me more free time to visit homes and take part in the life in the town.

"Relations between the people of Owerri and the mission in general were somewhat strained at that time and I was warned to be prepared for difficulties. I listened to the grievances of the people and unexpectedly found a wonderful opportunity to put ideas before them. As the men were having a new-year meeting at the marketplace, I was passing by and went to speak with them. The headmaster of the boys' school was chairing the meeting. Immediately I was aware of an uneasiness arising from the fact that no woman ever attended this annual meeting of the men. As soon as I spoke, one of the elders shouted in Igbo – 'are you a man or a woman?' 'A woman,' I replied. He told me to stop talking and to go away. A heated discussion then broke out which the chairman dealt with very well. The upshot was that I was to be allowed to speak. I informed them that I had heard some complaints and that I had come to deal with them. I told them of my plans to improve their town and asked them for their help. That day, they promised their help and that promise was kept. The activity which followed over the next few years resulted in their giving land which was ultimately used for the site of a secondary school for girls.

"At the time there was no Catholic secondary school for girls in the whole of Owerri Province. Bishop Joseph Whelan, CSSp., the first Bishop of Owerri, had gone in person to the education authorities to request permission to have one but was told in no uncertain terms that it was government policy to rule out the opening of secondary schools by voluntary agencies. The head of the department – Mr. Quinn-Young, an Englishman, was very strict about this. The Bishop visited our convent after the meeting and was quite downcast. The idea that I might be able to save the situation took strong hold of my mind and I asked the Bishop's approval for whatever efforts I might make.

"I went to the local Chief, Amadi Kelly Obi who suggested a visit to Chief Njemanze of Owerri who was head of the Oratta County Council, which included all the chiefs of Owerri Province. He told me also that I would have to speak to Mr. Quinn-Young. This I did but he was just as adamant as he had been with Bishop Whelan. I then went to Chief Njemanze who told me that he would welcome the idea in so far as it would be progress for girls but that he was concerned that we would try to make Catholics of all of them. I reassured him that the school would be called *Owerri Girls' Secondary School*, that it would be open to non-Catholics, that there would be no pressure on girls to change religion, that the conscience clause would operate but that the school would have Catholic management. He promised to discuss the issue at the next Oratta Council meeting. Several weeks later, while I was on retreat in Onitsha, I got an urgent call to attend this meeting of the Council at Owerri Town Hall. When I arrived, many of the chiefs were wondering about my presence. One pastor stood up and said that he was against whatever I was going to say in advance as he was sure it was going to be for the benefit of Catholics.

"The issue was discussed however, and much noise and shouting took place. Finally, the British District Officer announced that it was obvious that the idea was not popular and he proposed moving on to the next item on the agenda. Chief Njemanze then sprang to his feet shouting *wait! wait!* A long harangue took place in Igbo, the gist of which was that they were falling victim to an age-old British policy of *divide and rule.* Something good was being offered to them, the Chief told them, and they were rejecting it not because of any reality but out of fear of imagined problems. He urged giving the proposal a chance. Further discussions took place and then a majority voted in favour, but insisted on certain guarantees. It was decided that they themselves and not a voluntary agency would request permission for the establishment of the school. *Owerri Girls' Secondary School* exists to this day. It was managed by the Holy Rosary Sisters until the civil war disrupted life in Owerri. It is now run by secular teachers.

"In 1954, I was transferred to America but before departing, I supported the opening of a number of Holy Rosary establishments in Northern Nigeria. A women's training centre which evolved into a girls' secondary school was established in Afikpo. St. Monica's Hospital which is still flourishing was also established there. Our sisters started to work in a joint native authority mission hospital in Oturkpo. In addition, a primary school and training centre were established in Adoka in Idoma country.

"I was sent to America at this time because a few sisters, one of whom was American had been breaking new ground there and had purchased a property in Villanova. Sister Joachim Dwyer and I were sent there to join them in October 1954 with instructions to make the congregation known in the U.S.A. and to raise funds to pay off the debt on the house in Villanova. I had no friends in America and I knew nothing about fund-raising. I took a short course in public-relations in a New York university which was very helpful and which got me on my way. Since those days, our work in the U.S.A. has progressed greatly.

"In 1960, Nigeria gained its independence from Great Britain. To my great surprise, I received an invitation from the Federal Government to be a guest at the celebrations in Lagos. A first class ticket from British Airways was included with the invitation. I went and was present at all the events. I had been booked into the Federal Palace Hotel but I stayed with the OLA Sisters in Broad Street where I had stayed when I first arrived in Nigeria sixteen years earlier. My short and most enjoyable visit heralded my return to Nigeria as in 1961, I returned to go to that part of Northern Nigeria which today is known as the middle-belt region.

"This area was unknown territory to me. There used to be a sign at the boundary with Eastern Nigeria where I had spent all my previous years which said – *You are now entering Northern Nigeria.* As I passed it on my first journey north, I was conscious of the fact that all I knew was to do with the territory south of the sign. The tulip trees were in bloom on the roadside and the forest fireballs were in the grass underneath. They were a joy to behold and I quickly sensed that I was going to grow to like this North Country with its Idoma, Igala, Tiv and Hausa peoples. At this stage we had six convents in the region – Makurdi, Gboko, Afikpo, Oturkpo, Adoka and Idah. It had become a Holy Rosary Region and I was to take over in Gboko from Mother M. Bernard Price as the second Mother Vicar. At the time, the whole region was very underdeveloped and roads and bridges were bad except for the main road going north. In Gboko, the people are Tiv and almost immediately, I felt a special love for them.

"In 1962, girls' education was not encouraged in the North and around this time I got a letter from the Government in Kaduna stating that all girls' primary schools were to be phased out and asking what I had planned to do with the buildings. Phasing out meant – no more expatriates in primary education! After discussion with our Bishop, I proposed using them as girls' secondary schools. To our great surprise, the idea was approved and we opened the school with 18 pupils. There are now 2,000 in that school. Much of this development was happening amid periods of great political unrest among the Tiv people. Riots, clashes, killings and burnings were commonplace. Travelling was risky and frequently eventful. The Kaduna Government eventually had to send the army to the area to deal with the troubles.

"In 1963, a national meeting of sisters from all congregations in Nigeria was convoked through the Catholic Secretariat in Lagos. It was the first of its kind and a suggestion was made that the sisters form a *Conference*. A meeting was called in Holy Rosary Convent Hall in Enugu under the chairmanship of Bishop Joseph Whelan of Owerri. Elections were held after the business of the meeting was concluded and I was elected first national president of the *Conference*. Organizing such a thing nationwide from the small provincial town of Gboko was extremely demanding. It was working quite well until the civil war put an end to all but essential travelling.

"After the war, I was asked by the Apostolic Delegate to revive it and to try to find ways to involve all sisters, not just superiors. By then I was living in Makurdi. The local branches of the *Conference* – the *Area Conferences* as they were called, were the means chosen to accomplish this task. It took time for the idea to take root but today there are *Area Conferences* in almost every diocese in the country. I completed six years as national president and a year later when I had completed ten years as Mother Vicar of our own congregation in the North, I was asked by the new national executive which the *Conference* had established, to become its first executive secretary and to initiate a secretariat. The secretariat was located at different times in Ibadan, Enugu and Ondo. Its ultimate destination will be Abuja. I spent ten years doing that work before handing it over to a Sister from the indigenous Congregation of the Daughters of Mary Mother of Mercy. It now goes to different congregations on a rotational basis every six years.

"In 1985, I was asked to go around Nigeria to visit any place Bishop Shanahan might have been in and to speak to anybody who might have known him. I was given a little Volkswagen and I used to drive off in the mornings with my flask of coffee and sandwiches. I met the most marvellous people and really enjoyed the experience.

When I came to write it up, I called it *Bishop Shanahan as Remembered by the Men and Women of Nigeria*. Before I handed it to our Congregation, I gave it to Father John Jordan, the author of the very fine biography of Bishop Shanahan. When I came to meet him later, he said 'Sister I wish that you hadn't given me this. I know so many of the people in it and it has made me very lonely.' The work was prepared for our archives and was never meant to be published. In the late 1990's however, I was asked to write something that would make Bishop Shanahan known in Ireland so I took it out, expanded it and added more of an Irish interest. I did this during an extended vacation in Ireland in the year 2000. I called it *A Man for Everybody*. It was published by Veritas Publishing and I believe that it is still selling quite well.

"In the 1990's also, I was asked to work to have the *Cause* for the canonization of Bishop Shanahan introduced. Through the wonderful cooperation and hard work of a committee of our Holy Rosary Sisters and in close cooperation with the Archdiocese of Onitsha, the *Cause* was introduced in Holy Trinity Cathedral, Onitsha, by Archbishop Obiefuna in November 1997. I have been vice-postulator of this work ever since but I do hope to pass that role on to another Sister very soon. In 2002, I worked on a committee of sisters which cooperated with the Onitsha Archdiocesan committees, to prepare for the celebration of the centenary of the arrival of Bishop Shanahan in Onitsha. These week-long celebrations took place successfully in Onitsha in December 2003.

"Just a few weeks ago, I made a trip to Cameroon to give a workshop to the Holy Rosary Sisters from Cameroon on the spirit of Bishop Shanahan. The sisters were anxious to find out how they could put this spirit into practice in their daily lives. I was happy to go but I found that it took three weeks to prepare for the workshop. I did my best, prayed about it and worked day and night until I was happy with what I had to offer. The visit also gave me the opportunity to share my experiences on charism and mission with the sisters in Cameroon.

"I cannot say that I knew Bishop Shanahan personally but I met him once in 1934 when I was a novice in Killeshandra. I was given the chance along with another novice one evening after supper to spend time in his company. He just captivated our attention. I had never seen a bishop before except for the one who confirmed me and then I was fearful in case I missed my catechism question! He was retired from Nigeria at the time. He told us lots of stories and talked to us for a very long time. I felt completely at home with him. That was during my first week in Killeshandra."

Sister Nora McNamara

Missionary Sisters of the Holy Rosary
Idah, Kogi State

Dressed in traditional costume after crossing the Niger under a cloudburst!
L to R: Ambassador Joseph Lynch, Bernadette Lawler, Irene Lynch,
Fr. C. Clarke, Sr. Nora McNamara, James Lawler

"My life is as I would have dreamed it to be. There have been terrible ups and downs but if I had it over again, I wouldn't change a thing. To have been able to pioneer something completely new, to have had the opportunity to be involved in development projects which worked hand in hand with the people of Igalaland and to have been able to benefit from the knowledge of so many world class experts for more than thirty years, has been truly fulfilling."

Born into a family of five girls in Lissletown, Co. Kerry, Nora McNamara joined the *Missionary Sisters of the Holy Rosary* in the early 1960's largely because she had a wish since childhood to help the poor in Africa. "I got to know the Holy Rosary Sisters through the mission magazines and I first approached them in 1962. My early years in the convent were quite difficult largely because I felt my free spirit was curbed. I don't mind observing rules but I don't like to be tied down. When I went to University College Cork to study social science, I experienced a liberating force and I began to envisage how my studies would help me with my future work in development in Africa."

We crossed the Niger River at Agenebode, to visit Sr. Nora, co-ordinator since 1971 of the Diocesan Development Services (DDS) in Idah, capital of Igalaland – which now forms part of Kogi State. It was Fr. Christopher who took us to the crowded and colourful river bank to bargain and huckster with the many boatmen lined up for business. Though it was a February morning in the middle of the dry season, stormy rain clouds threatened a safe crossing. Urgent discussions in high decibels and in many languages were taking place – *what if the wind whips up? No, there are no life jackets! By the grace of God, we will cross.* The seasoned boat men were cautious, watchful – and then suddenly, the sky cleared and all were directed to the boats. We were a party of five: my sister Bernadette and her husband James, my husband and I and Fr. Christopher, who took up a standing Christ-like stance beside the boatman – a position which took on a certain symbolism some twenty minutes later when we were half way across the wide expanse of water, rolling black clouds, whipped up by angry winds stirred up the majestic waters and brought from the heavens the mother of all cloud bursts. I speculated on what future lay beneath us in the event of the boat capsizing – images of crocodiles and God knows what else were not comforting. 'I'm an optimist' was Bernadette's retort! Nothing but a forced calm could be read on the faces of James and my husband who were seemingly absorbed in the newness of our surroundings. We know that Fr. Christopher resorted to prayer and the 'calming of the waters' and yes! miraculously, we reached the bank at Idah. If ever there was the image of drowned rats – shivering with the cold!!

Sr. Nora was our ministering angel when we reached the DDS headquarters. In no time at all, she had us all togged out in traditional costumes which were borrowed from her many staff members and was able produce on request, hot whiskeys from a bottle of Irish normally reserved for benefactors and other important persons!

She came to Idah as a newly qualified social scientist in 1970. Her first impressions of the country in which she was to spend the most of the next thirty years of her life were not good. "It was September, just nine months after the end of the Biafran war. The countryside was wet, dirty and altogether miserable. Buildings everywhere were full of bullet holes and Jim Reeves records were playing all over the place. When I arrived in Idah, my heart sank further. There were signs of dire poverty everywhere and all I could sense was apathy and depression. Many things have improved since those days but there is still considerable poverty. Today, we have telecommunications advances but they are not matching existing needs. There are many more good roads but there's still no ferry between Agenebode and Idah.

"Idah is the capital of the ancient Igala Kingdom, which is one of the oldest centralised societies in Nigeria. At one point, the once powerful kingdom extended over a vast territory. The *Attah of Igala* (father) is the traditional head of the Igala people. The exact origins of the people are not known but they share many cultural links with the Yorubas and the Igbos. There are three ethnic groups in the territory – Igala, Bassa Komo and Bassa Nge – and each has its own language. Religion is mixed and the people have a high level of religious tolerance. The majority is thought to be Muslim although no authoritative figures exist. Christians, both Catholics and Protestants are numerous and traditional religion is also widespread. Sometimes many practising Muslims and Christians hold on to some traditional practices. The chief livelihood of the people is agriculture.

"The DDS grew out of Vatican Council II thinking which promoted the extension of Church ministries beyond the traditional ones of education and health. The Council examined the unjust structures that made the fullness of life possible for the privileged few while the majority suffered from hunger and famine. It also took cognizance of the concern of the many socially aware scientists who were studying the problems resulting from the increasing levels of poverty in the ever-expanding populations in the developing countries. As a result of all of this, post-Vatican II years saw the Catholic Church endeavouring to set up specific developmental structures which included involvement in agriculture. From 1969 onwards in Nigeria, development coordinators were being appointed in all dioceses. In 1971, the diocese of Idah set up the DDS and a short time afterwards I was appointed its coordinator. This came during my second year in Igala. Before that I was on my own and I floundered a bit in the early days.

"When I first arrived, I was sent out to a hospital community in Niamba, sixty miles from Idah to learn the Igala language. I did my best but it wasn't my greatest success. While I was there, I didn't have one penny in my pocket. It was a very illiberal climate and Vatican II hadn't impacted sufficiently by then. I travelled the length and breadth of Igalaland on foot or getting lifts from priests, seeing what the people were doing, immersing myself in the life and culture. When I came back to Idah, I did not have any great sense of what my work programme was going to be. I said to my authorities that they should not expect anything from me too quickly as sociologists and social scientists are not meant to rush into projects. I was comfortable with that but many others were not. I was accused of doing nothing or vacillating in my opinions. It was extremely difficult to be so misunderstood. Luckily, a Canadian group which was working in the area took a great interest in the potential of my work. We had many great discussions and there was a very enlightened Monsignor who gave me every support. He got funding for me, got me a car and advised me to take my time – to make haste slowly.

"I was also fortunate at that time to meet with Chief Philip Okwoli who was a tutor at the local College and who I could say became my mentor. He was very pleased that someone had come to do something that was different to the usual missionary work. One of the first things he said to me was 'don't put on all that religious garb – be more casual and the people will speak to you more freely.' He was right and it was very forward thinking for the time. He gave me a great insight into the Igala culture. He was writing a history of Igalaland at the time and he took a great interest in discussing issues with myself and my colleague Sr. Catherine Wallace.

"He introduced me to the traditional institution called the *OJA* or village meeting. It played an integral part in regulating life in the village. Decisions were made regarding the well-being of the community. Responsibilities were taken seriously and tasks were allocated by the *OJA* leaders. It also had a savings contribution scheme which was of great benefit to individual members. A standard contribution was paid each week and one member received the whole sum of all the contributions on a rotating basis. This helped deal with routine and occasional big expenses. Once I became involved with DDS, I felt that the *OJA* which was normally very large could be adapted to facilitate smaller numbers who might wish to form groups for the purposes of raising finance for agriculture. Its elaborate managerial structure also needed to be adapted. In due course and after much work, the adaptation of the *OJA* came about and the farmers called it a *Farmer Council* (FC).

"By this time, I was very much into the farming community and was also in touch with officials in the State Ministry of Agriculture who gave every co-operation. We set up FC's in different locations. It was an idyllic situation in many ways. They had very little but what they had, they shared. Initially they did not elect good leaders as in the Igala culture, seniority is highly respected. That changed with time. The FC's gradually moved into improving crops, using new varieties like maize and legumes, using technical help to deal with weeds and pests and applying artificial fertilizers.

"Once I was appointed the DDS co-ordinator, the diocese brought me around to meet many people who were involved in agricultural development. We had most of our meetings in Ibadan – the base of a community development advisory group who was influenced by the *Liberation Theology* movement that was happening in South America. Within that group were many scientists from the *International Institute of Tropical Agriculture* (IITA) and the University of Ibadan. The IITA was a research institute established to help bring about a *green revolution* in Africa.

"Being in touch with IITA meant that we were in touch with research. They are not a development organization and their research is very much on their own station. On-farm research was not being developed at that time. I found that they were interested in the idea of the Church and missionaries becoming involved in agricultural development. They were able to give us a great deal of advice and a certain quantity of seeds. Initially we were too small for them to visit us in Idah but from about 1976, they came a number of times.

"In 1977, the World Bank came to Nigeria to fund five agricultural projects. The *Ayangba Agricultural Development Project* was located in Ayangba in Igala and it was to concern itself with water projects, infrastructure and agriculture. By this time, DDS was working with 800 FC's and was actively involved in a number of water projects, women's development, adult education and youth programmes. Living conditions were improving and the despondency which prevailed after the war was beginning to retreat. There were a number of areas where DDS and the World Bank coordinated activities. I became their training officer for the Igala project and eventually became head of their extension services. This latter was huge as it involved the whole gamut of agricultural extension which today would be referred to as environment and conservation. I was attached to the bank until 1982 and by that time they had begun to wind down their operations. In many ways, they came to Nigeria at the worst possible time. The oil boom was at its peak and millions of farmers had deserted the land in search of more lucrative positions. Money was plentiful and jobs outside farming were available. Food was imported rather than cultivated. Nigeria began to get dirty in every sense of the word. Corruption crept in and the countryside became littered with plastic bags, sardine cans and so on.

"In the mid 1980's however, oil revenues fell and a *Structural Adjustment Programme (SAP)* which decreased wages, devalued the naira, reduced spending on social programmes and aimed at redistributing income from urban to rural areas was introduced. There were slogans everywhere urging a move back to the land. It was then that people began to benefit from some of the World Bank programmes which had introduced new crop varieties and which had indirectly introduced the whole idea of agri-forestry.

"We set about re-activating the FC's which had declined somewhat during the oil boom. We found that the farmers could not get enough seeds and the IITA were unable to give us sufficient supplies. We decided to set up our own seed multiplication farm. In this we were greatly helped by a Dr. Prendergast who was a researcher with Lever Brothers Nigeria. He gave managerial as well as technical advice and urged putting research aside and concentrating on seed multiplication. He came to the villages with us and taught the people how to maintain tree crops, especially the oil palm which is the main cash crop in Igala. He also introduced the need to care for the bush mangoes which were becoming an endangered species.

"The farm, when we bought it, was a wasteland but we turned it into an oasis with good rotational systems, agri-forestry and green legumes. We improved crop varieties and multiplied seeds, which we were able to sell to the farmers who paid what they were able to afford. Today, our farm has an outreach to an area as big as Cork and Kerry. In addition, we have helped good farmers set up their own seed multiplication farms and helped others set up soya bean farms on farms which had the necessary lighter type soil.

"We are now very concerned with hardwood trees which have become an endangered species. The trees are being felled and are not being replaced. It has been happening for many years. We are coping with this in a small way and with practically no money. Everyone gives lip-service to the environment and conservation but it is extremely difficult to get funding for these relatively invisible areas. Small farmers cannot afford to invest too much in trees as the income generation is not immediate.

"Another area of concern right now is the provision of clean yam planting material. The degeneration of soils caused by clearing for housing and so on has caused a serious deterioration in the quality of yam seeds. Good soil is needed for yams so presently we are in a big project with IITA with regard to good planting material. This however, is only half the battle because it in turn must be put into good soil. We are coping by using everything that will regenerate the soil including the use of green legume cover crops, rotation of crops and agri-forestry.

"The objectives of DDS have changed very little over the last thirty or so years. They exist to encourage the Igala people with their own development. The four major thrusts are farmer self-reliance, agricultural innovation, village development and water development. In all of our programmes, we are working with the disadvantaged and that will always remain a priority.

"With the new levels of poverty Nigeria is currently experiencing, women are particularly at risk and girls are again losing out at school. During the oil boom years, many men married a number of wives. When the boom years ended, a great many of these wives and their children – especially the girls, were abandoned and left to fend for themselves. We are doing a lot to help these women.

"Nigeria is a country with huge potential, yet huge poverty continues to exist. Bad governance and exploitation over many centuries has also a lot to do with it. This cannot be rectified in fifty years. We may very well be expecting too much too soon. Igalaland for example, with its location along the Niger and Benue rivers was one of the places most affected by the slave trade. It accounts for a lot of the fear and lack of trust that people have to this very day. There is inter-tribal distrust and distrust within tribes. During the slave trade era, Igala sold Igala and chiefs co-operated with slave traders. It is a sad admission but it is all documented. Building up trust among people is fundamental to making progress. This is a fragile business and it does not happen overnight.

"All that being said, I have seen significant improvements in my time here. There is a much greater awareness of the importance of education. There is a greater understanding of the land due to the introduction of agricultural science in schools. People are also more aware of their rights and more equipped to fight for them. There is an organic growth going on and it is related to knowledge, self confidence and self respect. The Attah – the traditional ruler, is an enlightened man and the more you keep him informed the more interested he becomes. He has appointed young educated chiefs with whom it is a pleasure to work. They are not there for their own gain."

Having spent more than thirty years in Nigeria, Sister Nora, at the time of my visit was considering the next phase of her life. "I will first take a sabbatical and after that, I may come back in a different capacity. The Irish Government has begun to realize that an abrupt break with the missionaries and their development work in Africa would be detrimental to the continuity of progress. They are introducing the idea of technical advisors who could be missionaries and who could spend short periods in Africa easing in their successors into running projects. I could see myself coming here in that capacity. The *Irish Missionary Union* is currently going through fundamental changes and evolving a new role and new operational criteria. When the new structures are in place, all of us missionaries will be given the opportunity to assess how best we can contribute to mission and development."

Sister Rose Uchem

Missionary Sisters of the Holy Rosary
Spiritan International School of Theology
(SIST)
Attakwu-Enugu

Sr. Rose Uchem - third from the left, second row - at a book launch in Enugu

I met the dynamic and scholarly Sr. Rose when I visited the Holy Rosary Novitiate in Trans-Ekulu, Enugu. Currently lecturing on contextual theologies at the Spiritan International School of Theology (SIST), Attakwu-Enugu, she epitomizes the intellectual strength that exists in many parts of the Nigerian Church. As a young Igbo woman growing up in eastern Nigeria in the 1970's, she came under the influence of many of the Irish missionaries. She spoke to me about that influence and about the Catholic Church in Nigeria.

"The Irish missionaries left a wonderful legacy of education and social concern in Nigeria. Present-day Nigerian bishops, priests and sisters continue to build on that legacy. It is true that the early missionaries who were working within a culture they did not always understand, made a number of mistakes but given their overall accomplishments and given the sacrifices they made on our behalf, there is nothing our people will not forgive them. The Igbo people in particular will never forget the crucial role they played, frequently at great risk to their own lives, in helping them during the Biafran war.

"If you had to use one word to describe the work of the Irish missionaries in Nigeria it would be *dedication*. When I was a novice in Nsukka, I remember one of our pioneering Nigerian Holy Rosary Sisters telling how the Irish sisters used to go to the homes of the people to teach catechism after they had finished their day's work in schools and hospitals. The profound impression that made on me affected the shape of my own style of ministry. I try to keep one foot in the institutional ministry and the other in the non-institutional one of pastoral involvement. While I was teaching in Nsukka and in Sierra Leone during the years following my first profession, I involved myself in quite a lot of pastoral and community work. In the 1980's, when I was a graduate student in Ireland, I engaged in mission education in schools and collaborated with a number of people in the animation of the family mass in Rathmines Parish in Dublin. In the 1990's, when I was candidate formation directress for my congregation in Rigasa-Kaduna, I tried to reach out to people by fostering adult faith groups. During that time also, I was the advising sister to the Catholic Women's Organization of the Archdiocese of Kaduna. During yet another period, while studying in the United States at Fordham University and the Graduate Theological Foundation, Indiana, I became very involved in the work of many parishes. This included preaching at Sunday masses.

"In my present position at SIST, I try to make time to engage in a ministry that creates awareness of the importance of gender equality. I also accept invitations to speak at conferences, seminars and workshops both inside and outside Nigeria on this topic and on many others such as human sexuality and human rights issues.

"I have recently had two books published *Overcoming Women's Subordination (2001)* and *Beyond Veiling (2002)*. I find the positive reaction to them which I frequently receive very encouraging. Bishops, priests, members of religious congregations and men and women from many ethnic groups all over Nigeria and in other parts of Africa are appreciative of the awareness of gender and equality issues that I am helping to create. This good reaction fills me with a sense of relevance for which I thank God. It makes up for the pain and suffering this particular ministry sometimes brings me and it is good to know that my work is helping people find the courage to change age-old patterns which are not life-giving to women in particular, but to others too.

"When I am asked about the state of the Catholic Church in Nigeria, I find myself having difficulty predicting how things will progress in the future. Though the inherent faith of the people is strong, the number of vocations to the priesthood and religious life substantial and the level of laity involvement impressive, many are deserting the Church and moving to the so called *New Generation* or Pentecostal Churches. I do not think our church leaders are paying enough of attention to this. Many are content to put the desertion down to the *Gospel of Prosperity* which many of these churches preach. This is not an adequate response.

"Up to now, our people have largely been unquestioning of the status quo that pertains within the Catholic Church. The increased awareness of issues concerning social justice, human rights and gender equality that is becoming more widespread is beginning to change that. There is now a great need for increased dialogue between church leadership and church membership. There is too much defensiveness on the part of leadership and too much inequality with regard to rank to allow for honest dialogue. I believe that honest dialogue can only take place in the context of equality of all parties. Many of our priests continue to hug ministries as their special property and this tendency has the effect of creating the image of a male church. How this contributes to the exodus to the *New Generation* Churches has not yet been explored. Though these Churches practise their own variety of male supremacy, they are more inclusive of women than the Catholic Church. For one thing, they take seriously the evidence of women's active leadership roles in the early Church. These have been attested to in the New Testament and in the writings attributed to St. Paul, notably his letters to the Romans and Ephesians. Many scholars have pointed to the existence of the tension and discomfort of male Christian leaders with women's leadership from the earliest times. The level of the intensity of the tensions differed from community to community. It can be understood more clearly by closely examining New Testament texts. Furthermore, literary evidence and the studies of tombstone inscriptions discovered by archaeologists, clearly show that women were priests, deacons and bishops in the early Christian communities.

"Regarding the contentious issue of mandatory celibacy and the Catholic Church of the future, I think that we should be reading the handwriting on the wall particularly in the context of the numerous allegations of clerical sexual abuse. If these allegations are true, the Church should be examining how the facts and figures relate to mandatory celibacy. My hope is that honest conclusions will be drawn and that those who are in a position to call for changes, if such changes be deemed necessary, will do so with courage and honesty.

"Inculturation is another subject about which we hear so much in Nigeria and Africa today. Simply put, it is the acknowledgment that the Christian message of salvation of humankind should wear the cultural garb of the people to whom it is preached. The first known act of inculturation in the early church happened at the Council of Jerusalem when it was decided not to impose the Judaic Levitical laws on the gentile converts to Christianity. Unfortunately when the Church came to Africa, many preachers of the Gospel did not allow for a similar process of inculturation. Cognizance of this mistake has since been made and in Africa today, African theologians and missionaries continue to unfold the meaning of inculturation in the African context. There have been many experiments to implement it, especially in church liturgy by introducing African singing, dancing and cultural artefacts. Much more needs to be done and currently some Nigerian theologians are calling attention to the need to inculturate African values within the Church.

"It is often said that Christianity did a disservice to African cultures by disrupting our belief and ruling systems. To this I would say that it was not the Christian message that caused the disruption but the manner with which it was often introduced. We cannot forget that Christian mission and evangelization often went hand and hand with the process of colonization. These mistakes of the past were deeply rooted in ignorance and on the mistaken notion of racial superiority. Unfortunately, traces of such sentiments persist today in all sorts of subtle and indirect ways. This is why it is important to correctly understand the dynamics of past events so that we can chart a better course for the future.

"One aspect of present-day life in Nigeria which must be tackled by everybody including all Churches is the massive corruption that tramples our great country. The belief in the concept of the divine right of kings – the belief that all authority comes from God, has been strangling the imagination of our people for a long time. This has to be replaced by a state of alertness to injustice – similar to the prophetic consciousness which enabled the prophets of ancient Israel to call the kings to order. Church leaders need to denounce all injustice and at the same time announce the good news that God's will is for all people to have the fullness of life, not only in the hereafter but also in the here and now. They need to encourage and facilitate our people to mobilize themselves for non-violent resistance to all oppressive systems wherever they occur and they need to encourage the laity to take informed decisions on their own. The misguided understanding of the role of the Cross in Christian life also needs to be corrected. This understanding is partly responsible for people enduring all kinds of hardships and oppressive situations without protest.

"In our Catholic churches all over Nigeria our prayers for *Nigeria in Distress* and *Against Bribery and Corruption* have to be matched with action and the firm belief that each and every one of us needs to play his or her part in this fight against corruption. I do not think that we can have any hope that the present sad situation in our country will improve if these changes are not made to happen."

Sister Theresa Stapleton

Missionary Sisters of the Holy Rosary
Enugu

Sr. Theresa Stapleton, MSHR

After spending twenty-four years working on social development projects in Zambia, Sr. Theresa was asked by her congregation to transfer to Nigeria and become involved in the formation and studies of young African novices at the Holy Rosary novitiate in Enugu. While the change proved daunting and painful in the early days, she gradually developed a great enthusiasm for her new assignment. She spoke to me in Enugu.

"I first came to Nigeria in mid 1998 on an exploratory visit – a look and see if you like. My congregation knew that it would be a huge change after Zambia so they wanted to be sure that I could manage the transition. When I went to the Nigerian embassy in Dublin to get my visa, the Ambassador who was Igbo said to me: 'Sister, I sense that you are very sorry to be leaving Zambia after twenty-four years. In Zambia, the people are quiet and gracious and they tell you what you want to hear. In Nigeria, we are noisy and aggressive and we will tell you what we think. If you are ready for all of that, I think you will enjoy our country.' And to a large extent, he was right. The Nigerians are very forthright, much more so than the Zambians."

Sister Theresa was an enthusiastic host the day I visited the Holy Rosary Novitiate. This is a large and spacious compound and it is where young African women who wish to join the Holy Rosary congregation spend their formation years. Sister Theresa is a member of the formation team which accompanies the novices on their way to profession.

"I think that I always had a desire to come to Nigeria. The pain and the adjustment of my coming coupled with illness has been nothing compared to the joy and fulfillment I have experienced over the last few years. Being here enables me to be close to the history of the congregation and this is very enriching at this point in my life. Among the people with whom I am living is Sr. Edith Dynan who joined the congregation when it was only ten years old and who met our founder Bishop Joseph Shanahan during her first week in Killeshandra. She was so captivated by him that she has spent a great deal of her time in recent years writing and talking about his work, his life and his spirit.

"I was born in Oola, Co. Limerick – five miles from Tipperary town. It was during my fifth year at the Ursuline Convent in Thurles that I felt a desire to enter a convent. After completing my Leaving Certificate, my health was not good so I stayed at home with my mother for a time. One day as I was doing some domestic chores, the name Killeshandra came into my mind out of nowhere and with it came a tremendous sense of peace. In September 1957, one year after finishing school, I entered the Holy Rosary Novitiate in Killeshandra.

"Before going on mission and after final profession, I did my professional training by going to University College Dublin (UCD) to study for a Bachelor of Social Science. The thinking at the time was that mission needed a diversification of skills. Up to then, all female religious missionaries confined themselves to education and medicine. After UCD, I went to Swansea for post-graduate studies. While there, I asked the Holy Rosary administration if I could relate my thesis to *mission* and I was told that I could take an interest in Kenya. Naturally I thought then that Kenya would be my destination when I was ready to go on mission. Instead, I was sent to Zambia as there was a Jesuit bishop in a diocese in the southern province of Zambia who was looking for a social worker. In those days, there was no consultation about assignments. You were more or less told where you were going and you went.

"The bishop turned out to be a wonderfully free-thinking man so from the very beginning, I enjoyed working for him. Almost immediately, he made me chief promoter of development in the diocese, gave me great scope and had complete trust in my abilities. This as you can imagine was very encouraging to a young missionary. I worked in that diocese for ten years and then in 1980, I went home to Ireland to work in an administrative capacity with the congregation.

"It was a time of transition for the Holy Rosary Sisters – a time when we had to sell our mother-house in Killeshandra. I was appointed coordinator of all the transition activities during this difficult period which brought about many painful changes. All the elderly and sick had to be moved from Killeshandra to Dublin and all others went to our convent in Cavan. I was the person who had to hand over the keys to the Killeshandra Cooperative – the company that bought the whole compound. They were really only interested in buying the land but finally agreed to buy the house with the hope of selling it on to an hotelier. That never happened and to this day the house is very sadly lying idle.

"I went back to Zambia in 1988 on an assignment to open up another diocese in the copper belt of Northern Zambia – an area that was very different to what I was accustomed to in the Southern Province. I was assisted by two companions; one was a teacher and the other a nurse. Our task was to go into pastoral work by looking after parishes – work that was very different to its counterpart in

Ireland or Nigeria due to the great scarcity of priests. We took over a huge parish with about eight out-stations. Here you had people of many nationalities as that was the nature of the copper belt region. The three of us, though greatly challenged, coped very well. Our management and leadership skills, to say the very least, were pushed to their utmost limits.

"At the time HIV/AIDS was becoming a serious issue in Zambia. We were encountering it all the time in the parish and everyday we were meeting with orphans whose parents had died from the disease. We decided to do something for them at parish level. The initiative came from some of the Catholic women in a place called Kitwe where I was living. In 1994 we set up, in a small way, an organization which we called CINDI (Children in Distress). I went on leave in 1995 and when I returned, I agreed to a request to become the full-time coordinator of CINDI. We started working with 80 orphans and when I was leaving in 1998, the number had risen to 8,000. Big as this number was, it was a drop in the ocean compared with the huge numbers that existed in the wider region. We had learned from our research that there were between forty-six and forty-eight thousand orphans between the different cities in the copper belt. Many of them were HIV positive. We found that great numbers of the children we worked with had psychological problems as they had seen their parents die and had then been fostered by aunts and uncles who in turn also died. Another phenomenon that was sad was the many households that were being run by teenage children.

"We set up CINDI groups in many areas in the diocese and allocated people to train local people to run them. Initially all of this was done on a voluntary basis, but after a time we realized that we badly needed funding. *Ireland Aid* became involved at this point and once that happened, the whole project grew enormously and became very demanding. By the time I left in 1998, I had trained somebody to take over my responsibilities. CINDI continues to flourish in Zambia.

"I arrived in Nigeria for my present position in January 1999. Here in this novitiate, because we are training people from different countries in Africa who will then work in different countries in Africa when they are professed, we try to have an international dimension to the staff. Apart from myself, there is Sr. Rosemary who is Igbo and Sr. Mary who is from another ethnic group in Edo State. At the moment, our novices are from Nigeria, Cameroon and Kenya. My own teaching areas have to do with the New Testament, prayer, spirituality and mission studies. I find the work very satisfying but it requires a lot of preparation as the subjects have to be made relevant in a real way to a multicultural group.

"Sr. Rosemary's strengths lie in her leadership skills. She also involves herself in spiritual direction, human development and the understanding of vows. Sr. Mary who studied in Ireland has a degree in theology, liturgy, Old Testament studies and church history. She is also very musical so apart from teaching her special subjects, she does a lot of work with choirs.

"Most of our novices are trained in some profession before they come to us as we don't take them in at a very young age. The members of the group you met this morning are all aged between 27 and 33 years. They have specialized in education, medicine and agriculture. Among the two other groups – the first years and second years, are many who have already specialized in financial management.

"The big motivating factor for those who come to us would be the idea of going on mission. They feel a strong call to go outside their own culture and to be of service. This is of course very much the spirit of our congregation – the spirit of mission – a wish to go out. I have a sister who is a Sister of Mercy in Ireland and she tells me that she would have no wish to go out on mission. A Holy Rosary Sister will say that she cannot but go out. There is also of course the important fact that the young women feel a call from God to dedicate their lives to mission.

"My life in Nigeria is very different to the life I led in Zambia. There I was very well known because of my work in social development and with the AIDS orphans. My contacts were with many people from the President's office down. When I looked at that dimension of my life before coming to Nigeria, I think that I decided that what I needed at that stage of my life was work that was more interior and reflective. I decided that it would probably be good to be a person who was not widely known.

"From the point of view of our congregation having started in Nigeria, I feel that by being here, I am in touch with the whole historical experience. It is also a vital time for our congregation as we are making a determined effort to establish integration between our sisters who are of different nationalities. It's the way forward and I feel that it is important to be part of that development.

"Though there are no Holy Rosary vocations in Ireland right now, I do not see it as a crisis. We are going through a cycle and vocations may come back to us in a different way in a different age."

St. Patrick's Missionary Society
(SPS)

(The Kiltegan Fathers)

An Introduction

St. Patrick's Missionary Society is a society of Catholic missionary priests whose particular aim is to spread the Gospel of Jesus Christ throughout the world. The Society was founded in Ireland in 1932 by Father Patrick J. Whitney who had worked with Bishop Joseph Shanahan, CSSp. in Nigeria in the 1920's.

Currently the society has approximately 400 priests working as missionaries in nine African countries, Brazil, Grenada and the United States.

While the essential work of the Fathers is to preach the Gospel of Jesus Christ to those who do not know him, they are also very concerned with those whose lives are affected by poverty, disease, famine and displacement.

The Society whose headquarters are in Kiltegan, Co. Wicklow is perhaps best known to the Irish people through its magazine *Africa*.

Until 1951, the Fathers worked exclusively in Nigeria.

Father James Sheerin

St. Patrick's Society (SPS)
Abuja

L to R: Rev. Peter Schineller S.J. (in traditional costume);
Fr. James Sheerin, SPS

"My predominant feeling with regard to my life as a missionary is one of deep gratitude. I don't think any other journey through life could have given me the excitement, the richness, the variety or the insight into the lives of so many people. Sometimes I'm asked in Ireland if there were any choices other than the Church in my young days. In fact, I had a number of choices and it was indeed the existence of these that helped me decide to become a missionary priest. For one thing, I got a call, with very high marks, to St. Patrick's Teacher Training College, Drumcondra which was a highly sought-after goal at the time.

Seventy-year-old Father James Sheerin from Horseleap, Co. Offaly had spent more than thirty years in Nigeria when I visited him at *Gaudium et Spes Institute* in Abuja. After completing his secondary education in St. Finian's College, Mullingar, Co. Westmeath, he entered St. Patrick's College, Kiltegan.

"The whole experience of mission – of identifying with other missionaries – of feeling the excitement of working with people in all kinds of mission services – of being engaged in a dialogue with life – of having had the opportunity to engage in a wide range of mission services – has engendered that feeling of gratitude which I referred to earlier.

"I came to Nigeria in 1956. I had come out of a Church that had great energy. I went to a completely different Church, one which was young but very enthusiastic. I came to Ogoja, in eastern Nigeria. The place was just bubbling with development. Schools, teacher training colleges, hospitals and nursing schools were being established all over the place. New parishes were opening up. Agricultural experiments were going on. We were with Bishop Thomas McGettrick from Sligo who was the first Bishop of Ogoja and Abakaliki diocese and who was a very interesting man. First of all, he was powerfully strong. He was also a spiritual man who prayed for an hour every morning and every evening. He was a shy, rough country man who could trek for twenty miles and keep wonderful accounts of same. He was great fun. At supper, he refused to have business discussed. That was time out. When he visited you as a young priest, he did so as an equal.

"The Ogoja mission was set up in the 1930's and the men who came before us were men who had borne the heat of the early days. They trekked and cycled from place to place and there were many tragic losses. The enormous interest, commitment and single-mindedness which they had were very much alive when I came. There was not so much theorizing about where the Church was going; it was all about doing. It might have been better if there had been more of the former. The involvement of the laity was crucial to the Church's development. It was usual for a parish to have thirty, forty or even sixty out-stations. They were visited monthly or quarterly or twice yearly by the priest, so it was the catechist and the Church committees who developed them and kept them going. You could say the missionary was as good as the coordination of his catechists and Church committees.

"The missionary school system in those years was very big. We had thousands of teachers and it was a system run in partnership with the government. Schools were grant-aided and the government paid the teachers' salaries. When the local government got permission to start a school, we frequently offered to run it. We did the same with the teacher training colleges and the hospitals. Relations between us were good. There were many lay missionaries in those days who were serious matter-of-fact people. One of them was Dr. Joe Barnes who had just left before I came but who had in his time, agreed to take on the leprosy project which Bishop McGettrick wanted to establish in Ogoja. It was called the *Ogoja Leprosy Relief Scheme*. The project was eventually handed over to the Medical Missionaries of Mary.

"An Irishman, Gary McKeown, who lives in America, has written that Bishop McGettrick was a countryman who cured a plague. Many people thought the Bishop was too preoccupied with leprosy in the beginning but McGettrick felt that he couldn't go on without addressing the disease that was causing huge distress and that was endemic in the Ogoja and Abakaliki regions. It was the eventual break through in drugs that to a large extent cured leprosy. One of the key discoverers was a Dr. Brown who worked with the Church Mission Society (CMS) at Oji River, Enugu. Barnes would have had great contacts with him and his people.

"During all of this development of parishes, schools and hospitals, more and more people were coming into the Church. Because it symbolized progress and the promotion of human dignity, people identified with it. Nobody would have gained more from the Church than the women as it was a major force in the fight to abolish polygamy which women hated as soon as they got to examine it. While many men continued to have wives and mistresses on the side, the ideal among all Christians irrespective of what was practised was the ideal of the Christian marriage of one man and one woman. Among the women, there was always a marked sense of gratitude to the Church for what it did in this area.

"It was a great time to be alive. There were many conflicts of course. It wasn't a straight picture but it was a great Church to work in – a great Church to be teaching in. I had my teaching years – approximately thirteen – in secondary schools, in training colleges and in seminaries. I enjoyed them. For a while also, I was chaplain to the laity and it was another great experience and one which gave great insight into the quality of Christianity that you can find among lay people in this country. Their capacity for suffering and sacrifice within a frugal society and within their own family commitments was humbling. They were able to give so much and though the Church asked a great deal, they were unflinching in their support. It was a Church alive and I would see the same kind of qualities in the Church here today. Whatever negatives you might attach to it, it's a vibrant Church – one which has great meaning and relevance in people's lives. Their belief is very strong. Almost every African believes in God and the supernatural is always present. They have taken that from their traditional religion. It's one world. There's no compartmentalization between the secular and the spiritual and that would be very important for the continuation of Christianity.

"What are these negatives? Well, some of them are those which have always existed in the Church! We forget that the Church has from the beginning been a Church of sinners. We tend to give the early Church and the Church of the middle-ages which brought about the *Reformation* an easy ride. We forget that the Church is not a perfect institution. Jesus went out of his way to show that it was a Church of sinners. The criticism of the Church today partly derives from the expectation of perfectionism. Here in Africa, an understanding of and a sympathy with the struggles of the people and the pulls of culture are a must, I would say.

"In Nigeria, we have to take care that the Church does not become too institutionalized and that it always asks of itself what it is before asking what it is doing. That was the problem in Europe. The doing was emphasized and when socialism changed the doing by taking over much of the work done by the Church, some confusion with regard to her role developed. That could happen here too.

"A very joyful aspect of the Nigerian Church is its participative nature. If you observe the offertory collection during mass – you will see that it is a prayer – a dance – a song – a celebration. You want to get inside of them for that. It took them a long time to get their own drums and their own rhythms into the Church. They are in there now though more in some places than in others. We have never done that in Ireland. Our rhythms are in the pubs!"

"I was more than thirteen years in Nigeria when I got sick. This caused my return to Ireland which subsequently moved my life onto a different path for the greater part of the 1970's. Somehow or other I got poisoned. I never found out how. Was it deliberate? I don't know. It was an interesting experience to say the very least. I was recovering at home and was about to come back when I was told that the Society needed an editor for *Africa*. I decided to go to Newhouse Communications Centre at the University of Syracuse, New York to train as a journalist. It's where *Newsweek* trains its people. It turned out to be a very good school. I loved it. I found out that I could have been a very happy journalist. I saw the power of journalism. It gave me a great understanding of why the media have grown so big. They are the shapers of public opinion and morals. They are married to industry and the advertising business. Some would say that there are no ethics in the advertising business. It goes as far as it can with sensationalism, sex or whatever.

"There are good things that journalism can do of course. One word is muckraking and the other is investigative journalism and without the latter, so much would have gone undetected in the Church and in society. If control is brought to bear on the media, they thrive on the confrontation. It's not that they have a purpose in society; they are there in a free society as an essential ingredient. They have to have standards and these will come from the standards and values of society. I'd say that politicians and the Church need to look for the prophetic voice and believe that there is tremendous goodwill in every place where human beings operate and that includes the media. Malcolm Muggeridge put Mother Teresa on his television programme *Something Beautiful for God*. Not only was he transformed himself but once he put her there, nobody could take her down – not even the Indian Government.

"I was editor of *Africa* from 1971 to 1978. It was a great experience. I enjoyed it and it had its perks. I got the opportunity to travel to our missions in many parts of the world. That was necessary as I could not have our missionaries in South America, for example, saying that I was seeing our work through Nigerian eyes. I interviewed many great people. Included among them were the bishops – Dr. Birch of Kilkenny, Edward Daly of Derry, Éamon Casey and Cathal Daly. I found Cathal Daly to be very impressive. After retiring, he deputized for Cardinal Hume and the English priests were remarking on the vigour of his mind and intellect. He once gave a marvellous talk on the danger of the coalition between big business and advertising. After that, I felt that he got less publicity. The same happened to Solzhenitsyn after a commencement speech he gave in the United States. He was a hero until he told the West that it was losing its soul. After that, he disappeared from the headlines. It would be the same if a good African like Bishop Desmond Tutu gave a keynote speech in Europe that was critical of some aspect of European society.

"I returned to Nigeria in 1978 and one of the projects I got involved with was *Ambassador Publications* at Iperu in Ogun State. I was asked by Nigeria's first Cardinal, Dominic Ekandem to begin a magazine like *Africa*. I did and it was distributed all over the country. I later combined it with a liturgical calendar. After that, we brought out the *Church Directory/Catholic Diary*. Then we went into books – originals and reprints and at one stage, we had two hundred titles. It lagged a little after I left but it's coming up again at the moment. I notice that they are doing a lot of new stuff and there is a very good fellow who was trained in America in charge. It's still in Epero and its part of the work of the Missionary Society of St. Paul, the first indigenous missionary society in Africa and one which I helped to birth. It's a society of secular priests founded by the Nigerian bishops with the special encouragement of Cardinal Ekandem. It could be described as the Nigerian version of St. Patrick's Society. They have similar constitutions and both have their origins in a diocesan priesthood. The first eleven priests of St. Paul's were ordained in 1986.

"I met my partner and colleague here at *Gaudium et Spes Institute* – Fr. Peter Schineller S.J. at Ambassador Publications. We published his book on *Inculturation* which is a hot topic in the Church in Africa. The Latin liturgy with its very definite format was introduced into the African Church and there was no question in the early days of bringing in drums or any other aspect of African culture. Over time however, drums have been brought in, largely because of the kind of people the Africans are and the kind of rhythms that are part and parcel of their culture. All of that is more acceptable and more desired now and a more serious effort is being made to find out what inculturation really involves. It's one of the things that we haven't in the Western Church and it's one of the reasons that the Church has not kept pace with western culture. Religion hasn't been able to inculturate itself into the rhythms and speeds of our times. Inculturation is not just relevant to Africa. The rest of the world needs it just as much. Basically, inculturation is about the Incarnation coming through at every time among every people. It's about the transmitting of Christ and the Scriptures with immediacy into the lives of the people. This is now an urgent business. How do you make Christ relevant to people's lives today?

"A young girl died of leukemia in Kilbeggan in my brother's parish in Ireland not so long ago. The burial service from beginning to end had a wonderful liturgy and everyone was gripped. Her life was made relevant to the mass – this same mass that so many young people have so little time for. Many years ago, television presenter Bunny Carr asked a visiting Indian bishop what he thought of the young people's attitude to the Church. 'Oh,' the Bishop said, 'I never tell young people to go to church. My job is to invite them to the Eucharist and I wouldn't belittle that invitation by pushing them to accept it.' The Eucharist is at the centre of Christianity and I say to priests and religious that if they do not read something serious about the Eucharist every year, they will diminish that centre.

"My work today at *Gaudium et Spes Institute* gives me tremendous involvement with people. It can be a humbling involvement because we are here to inspire them and initiate them into a higher faith-life. We try to expand their vision by promoting all kinds of programmes for the laity and the religious. We offer seminars and workshops on Scripture, leadership training, marriage, interfaith dialogue and much more. *Gaudium et Spes* (Joy and Hope) – are the first two words of the *Constitution of the Church in the*

World – considered by many to be the finest constitution of Vatican Council II. It stressed that the Church has to be in the world – has to love the world as God's creation and has to relate to the world as it is and not as it should be or as it was fifty years ago.

"It is very exciting for Peter and me to sit down with Archbishop Onaiyekan here in Abuja and discuss the kind of programme he wants and then to go off and craft it. There's a huge partnership in the work we do. Before I came here, I'd have thought that it was an area of work in which I would not have great skill. I have since learned that what it requires most of all is the confidence to put your hand on the people who have the particular skills you are looking for. The Institute, I would say, is trying to provide for the people in this Archdiocese, the underpinning that religion needs because religion must always think and listen at the educational level of the person who practises it. We have many professional people here in Abuja so this kind of centre is vital from an academic, pastoral and spiritual point of view. Fr. Schineller will be leaving shortly but he will be replaced by a young Nigerian priest who is very well qualified academically.

"For the Church in Nigeria, I would see the quality of the priests as an important issue. The Irish Church suffered from complacency. That could also creep in here. Status syndrome has got to be guarded against as it has always killed the priesthood. Father Schineller is always saying that the priest should be a foot-washer as well as a conferrer of sacraments. He should have that foot-washer mentality of serving people – both rich and poor – and reaching out to their needs.

"The Catholic Church always tries to speak out for the poor though some would say that its social doctrine is its best kept secret. The Church lost the poor in Europe during the 1848 Revolution and the French Revolution. Then Pope Leo XIII came in with the first great social encyclical which identified the right of the poor to strike and have trade unions. It took the Church a long time to get that far because it tended, I suppose, to identify with many levels of society. There is a great phrase in Thomas Aquinas called *divine discontent*. It means that the Church and the individual Christian should not go along too easily with secular forces. It doesn't mean that there should be continuous confrontation but it means that we should always be asking questions about the different kinds of models that society creates – models of acquisition and accumulation – success models or models of service.

"I believe that when people get too rich, they can become spiritually disempowered. People are more spiritual when they are close to the struggles of life. We say that power corrupts but so does comfort. There is something to the metaphor of the rich man and the eye of the needle.

"Now, poverty, suffering and struggle can reach the point of being evil. Sometimes Christianity is accused of emphasizing the Cross without the triumph of the Resurrection. We nevertheless have to cope with suffering and St. Paul urged joining our sufferings to those of Christ's and triumphing over them with Christ. That is not to say that suffering in itself is a good thing. There are a whole lot of insights into the processes that purify, discipline and make people grow. There are also many psychological processes that relate to Christianity but never ever is it accepted that suffering in itself is a good thing.

"Here in Nigeria, there is great human suffering. Does my position as an expatriate priest limit my ability to speak out against the causes of that suffering? I would say that it's a question of how to speak out effectively – how to be prophetic. Many people think that what's important is the creation of wisdom. The Church spoke out in South America. Did it achieve so much? Did it create a just society? I believe that the local Churches are speaking out. They may not be as effective as they would like to be. It would be very easy for me to go on about what's not being done here in Nigeria but I am anxious to be fair to the people who host me. The Nigerian Bishops' letters and statements over the years have related hugely to justice and human rights. In the end, it becomes a question of how to put the sentiments in the letters and statements into practice. One of the issues that has been identified since Vatican II is the issue of structural injustice. Before that, it was just personal injustice that was talked about. The question for us here in Africa is – how can we build up democracies that give fairness and that stamp out terrible greed and corruption? I was talking with some Nigerians about all of this just yesterday. We are all searching for answers. I think some Gandhi-like figures will have to be found."

Father Kevin O'Hara

St. Patrick's Society (SPS)
Abakaliki, Ebonyi State

Fr. Kevin O'Hara, SPS

"Just as an ordinary guy growing up, I had a feeling that I would like to get out to Africa and do things but it was in the seminary in Kiltegan in the 1970's that I got really interested in the whole notion of human rights and social justice. I was particularly taken by the *liberation theology* movement that was going on in South America. Needless to say, we had no course on this topic in Kiltegan. What I believe I am practising in Nigeria today is *liberation theology*. It involves liberating people from poverty and promoting social justice and human rights."

When I started working on this book, I was told by many people that I should meet with the indefatigable Fr. Kevin O'Hara – director of *The Human Rights Centre*, in Abakaliki, Ebonyi State and *The Centre for Social and Corporate Responsibility* in Port Harcourt, Rivers State. I was warned that he was not easy to track down but I was lucky. "He's here with me now if you want to make an appointment with him," Fr. Michael Fitzgerald of the Carmelite Fathers in Enugu tells me when I phone to ask him how I should contact Fr. Kevin. We arrange a meeting at the Carmelite mission for the following week. I look forward to meeting a man whose mission is all about social justice and who has had the courage to take on such multinational giants as the Shell Petroleum Corporation.

He sweeps in punctually for our meeting on the appointed afternoon. He is lithe, focused and friendly. Under his arm is a thick report which contains the findings of an investigation carried out by his *Centre* in Port Harcourt into recent oil spills in the Niger Delta region. In his well worn briefcase are copies of the *Human Rights Magazine* which his *Centre* in Ebonyi publishes quarterly: he gives me some of these.

Born in Stranorlar, Co. Donegal in 1955, Fr. Kevin came to Nigeria in 1980, immediately after his ordination. With every passing year since then, he has become more and more dedicated to the cause of human rights and social justice.

"I spent my first thirteen years in Nigeria working in different parishes in the Abakaliki Diocese. In all of them I set up human rights groups. Just as I was getting immersed in the legal aspects of some issues related to the alleged corporate malpractice of certain multinational oil companies, I was asked by my superiors in Ireland to go to London to work on vocations' promotion. It was 1993 and General Abacha had just seized power. The whole area of human rights in Nigeria had become critical. There was great fear in the air and even a blind man could see that the country was reeling towards some kind of national suicide. I was very unhappy about having to leave at that particular time but providentially it turned out to be fortunate, as shortly after my arrival in London, the whole oil crisis involving Shell Petroleum and the people of Ogoni Land in the Niger Delta region blew up. It became a huge issue and London became the meeting centre for human rights and environmental activists from Nigeria. The world was debating the rights and wrongs of the crisis and the role that Shell was playing in it.

"At the time, many of the Churches in the U.K. were investing their money in Shell. As the name of Shell became more and more embroiled in the Nigerian troubles, they began to have huge qualms about this. Just as they were considering moving their money, a group called *Ecumenical Council for Corporate Responsibility* advised continued and increased investment so as to multiply the number of shareholder votes. These votes would enable them to put forward a resolution concerning Shell's work practices in Nigeria at the company's AGM. A resolution demanding that the operating standards of Shell Nigeria be made the same as those operated in the U.K. was duly put forward. It also demanded that human rights abuses such as paying soldiers to go into Ogoni Land to mete out punishment to so-called troublemakers be stopped. The company directors turned down the resolution. Almost immediately, Channel 4 News and the BBC broadcast reports of the rejection and gave huge publicity to the fact that Shell was willing to practise two standards – one for the white man's country and another for black Africa. Things became very difficult for Shell. People worldwide began to boycott their products and its corporate image reached an all-time low. In addition, they were faced with the fact that a substantial number of their shareholders were intent on bringing about change.

"Following all of this, Shell did what no other oil company has ever done; they set up a community development department within the company. They currently spend sixty million dollars a year working with specialists on community projects. As a result, the company is now much more transparent. I, for example, can go into their offices anytime I want to and have access to whatever document I might wish to see.

"Over the last few months, our *Centre* in Port Harcourt has been investigating the causes of two recent oil spills in the Niger Delta. Our report is now prepared. It is very sensitive as it will expose, to say the very least, some serious lapses in Shell company behaviour. After these particular oil spills happened, company officials went to the State Governor to say that they were caused by sabotage. They gave the names of youths whom they said were the ringleaders of the saboteurs. We have since proved that the spills were caused by two slack nuts and bolts which in fact were the cause of two previous spills. The company's internal investigation also identified this problem but they insisted that the nuts and bolts were illegally tampered with. My group happens to have video footage of the company investigation which clearly shows a white man telling the divers to check the particular nuts and bolts which had caused the previous leaks. We also have maintenance reports of what they did to try to correct the problem. All our evidence is now assembled and I have yet to decide how best to use it. We know that there are many groups who are very eager to find out if Shell is still involved in doing unethical things in very unconventional ways.

"Our Human Rights Centre in Abakaliki has no involvement with oil companies. It focuses on access to justice, prisoners' rights, women's rights, children's rights and land disputes. There is a very big problem with the land tenure system in the State and it needs to be addressed. Until we get a mature democratic government which is willing to do so, it will remain a problem. Presently the State Assembly members don't appear to understand the role they have to play. We are trying to work with them but it is very difficult as they have developed a very cozy relationship with the Governor and his executive and they are not interested in a system of checks and balances. Progress has however been made in some areas. We will renew our efforts with vigour after the upcoming elections which may throw up a new group of legislators. We are not expecting a change of Governor as he is far and away too ensconced. I don't expect a very good election as already there have been many allegations of intimidation and fraud.

"There are thirty people working in the centre. It has been developed over a period of twenty years and I have been there from the beginning. Funding initially came from the Catholic bishops in Spain. Then the American bishops through CRS (Catholic Relief Services) came in and helped us increase our capacity. My own congregation has been supportive and has helped in training some of my staff in conflict management at the peace-building centre in Birmingham. Ireland Aid has also assisted us.

"We have made inroads in many areas and our impact is felt. We know this from the way Government reacts and responds to us. They know that we are the only credible group that will challenge them. Recently the House of Assembly passed a bill which would enable them to create a vigilante group. We objected strenuously to the bill on the grounds that such a group could be used by the Governor to manipulate and intimidate. The tragic experience with other vigilante groups in other States has proved this by their completely undermining the rule of law and replacing it with extrajudicial killings and what you could call jungle justice. The Governor actually came up with the idea of a vigilante group when the Federal Government refused to let him have his own State Police. We have recommended that he make the police in his State more professional by training them properly and by giving them adequate equipment. Because of our opposition to the bill, he did not sign it.

"All of this proves that members of the Government are very conscious of our presence and our influence. They know that the people come to us and trust us. This angers the Governor in particular. Sometimes he has difficulty understanding how certain issues we bring to his attention can be regarded as human rights issues. One such issue could be using a man's equipment and time for two years and seriously delaying giving payment.

"Presently, we are extremely busy trying to develop our Port Harcourt centre. There, we have a staff of twelve. We mostly deal with oil-related issues and how they affect community relations. We monitor projects and liaise with the companies regarding human rights issues, spills, compensation and environmental issues. At the moment, we have one lawyer and one environmental geologist working with us. We also have a number of people qualified in community relations and conflict management. Apart from myself, they are all Nigerian and most are from the Niger Delta region.

"We are linked into the CRS office in Washington D.C. The American Catholic bishops are particularly interested in what is happening in Africa with regard to extractive industries because these industries, be they related to oil, gas, gold or diamonds, are often the source of disastrous conflicts. Over the last few years, the bishops have been conducting workshops on this subject in Cameroon. There is a lady, a Professor Carroll, who is a world expert on the way multinational corporations involved in extractive industries relate to governments. She has already led teams of experts to Nigeria, Cameroon, Sierra Leone and Angola to study the issues causing the ongoing conflicts in these countries. She will eventually submit a report and policy document to the Congress in Washington D.C. in the hope that it will enable the powers that be in America and elsewhere to understand how these industries are so often linked to poverty and conflict in Africa.

"Here in Nigeria, I would cautiously admit that some progress with regard to such issues has been made. The *Niger Delta Development Commission* has been set up. It has been charged with handling and channelling 13% of funds deriving from the oil and gas resources of the Niger Delta back into the area. It is a massive task. Professionals have been hired from Germany and other places to help. Ultimately, the Commission will have to oversee and ensure sustainable development projects for this very complex area which is full of waterways and creeks. It will be very important to ensure that those involved understand the true meaning of sustainable development and how it involves working closely with peaceful communities. If there is a big rush to show signs of progress by putting a road here or a hospital there before preparing an enabling environment, results will not be good.

"The future of our own work at our two centres will depend largely on whether we have state and federal governments who respect and understand the rule of law and who understand the meaning of access to justice. *Trócaire Ireland* is coming to our Port Harcourt centre in the near future with the intention of increasing our capacity. They appreciate our objectives and recognize that our work can significantly impact events in the Niger Delta. Hopefully other groups will be inspired by what we are doing and will evolve programmes of their own. Already our centre in Abakaliki has been replicated in five other places. All of them are being run by Nigerian Catholic priests.

"Their task is challenging because in the context of continued and blatant social injustice, it is easy to become discouraged. Many priests feel a powerlessness and many of them resort to channelling all their energies into the heavy workloads of their parishes. I met a priest the other morning who told me that he had four funerals to attend to on that day. I understand this as I was in parish work myself for thirteen years and I found it very difficult to find time for involvement in issues of social justice. It was the reason why I finally went to my Bishop and asked to be released from parish work. I am now doing exactly what I have always dreamed of doing. For me the work is urgent and totally absorbing. It can also be totally draining. It can exhaust you and cause you to lose your balance. When that happens, you know that it is time to take a break.

"Usually I work for a full twelve months and then take a break for about six weeks. At the moment, my Dad is ill in Ireland so I spent time with him at Christmas even though I had my usual summer break. I have fairly good health though like everybody, I get a lot of malaria. The mosquitoes in the Niger Delta are different to those in Abakaliki so I have to accept that despite the medication which I take, there are a variety of parasites getting into my blood and causing fever and headaches. What they are doing to my brain cells, God only knows!

"Hopefully my work in this ministry of social justice and human rights will eventually be widely accepted by the Church as an integral part of spreading the Gospel. For now, this is not fully understood and a very big weakness in formation programmes in our national seminaries is the total lack of courses on the subjects. The hope is that our progress and the initiatives of those who have followed our example will help others in the Church to realize that this is something that all priests should be involved with and committed to."

Father Derry O'Connell

St. Patrick's Society (SPS)
Government Secondary School
Minna, Niger State

Fr. Derry O'Connell, SPS

I met with Father Derry O'Connell in Government Secondary School (GSS), Minna. He has been the school's principal since 1967. Over the years and under his dedicated stewardship, it has grown in size and reputation. It was a lively and busy place on the morning of my visit. Being the final day of term, the mood was upbeat and jolly. That happy sense of relief and achievement that is peculiar to such a day had already permeated the atmosphere. Nevertheless, most classrooms were in full session and teachers and pupils were immersed in a variety of routines and activities.

A porter led me to the principal's office – a pupil friendly place which had many of them roaming in and out relaying messages, asking questions and receiving instructions. The spacious room was overflowing with books, test papers, reports, school trophies and notice boards. The tall and handsome Father Derry was relaxed and friendly but master of all he surveyed. He spoke and listened with a quiet and practised sense of authority. For our interview, we moved to a quieter room a few metres along the corridor. He first told me about his early life in Ireland.

"I went to St. Coleman's College, Fermoy for my secondary education. The school had a long missionary tradition especially with the Columban Fathers. A few of my friends however, went to St. Patrick's, Kiltegan so I suppose that was an encouragement for me to think along the same lines. By joining St. Patrick's Society, you could not be sure of where you would find yourself eventually, as we had missions in many places around the world.

"I was ordained on Easter Sunday 1961. In fact yesterday was the anniversary of my ordination. It's been forty-two years. I came to Nigeria almost immediately and my first two years were spent in Ikot Ekpene, then in the Diocese of Calabar in the south east. I started off as a curate in a very remote place and I enjoyed it very much. I had a very fine parish priest in Fr. James Murphy, a Dublin man who is now retired in the States and who gave me a very good orientation. He was an affable and jolly man, knew what he was about and was well able to communicate with people. I suppose he set the tone for my own life as a missionary.

"A month after I arrived, I was dropped off in villages for maybe three days at a time with a cook and a catechist. It was a bit frightening for the first few weeks. At night, you heard so many strange sounds and you wondered what they were and how ominous they might be! Very soon, I got over all of that and I began to feel comfortable. One fact that bore in on me very quickly was that my training had done little or nothing to prepare me for being a missionary in a remote place. There you were meeting with very simple people and you began with the very basics. It was a learning experience for me just to find out where the people were at, what they needed and what moved them. I was not in virgin territory from the point of view of evangelization. Missionaries had been coming to the area for forty years. There were many cement churches in the villages as people took great pride in having a permanent building for their church. After my initial four months in the area, I was put teaching in a new secondary school – again in a remote area. There were two parishes nearby and at weekends and even sometimes during the week, I helped out with parish work. Furthermore, if the parish priest went home, you could find yourself filling in for five or six months.

"In 1963, I moved to Minna which was at the time the capital of Niger Province in the North but not the far-North. In those days, it was under the Archdiocese of Kaduna. Later, in order to bring the Church closer to the people, a prefecture was created which is the beginning of a diocese. Five Kiltegan priests came to work alongside the SMA Fathers for a number of months. After that, the SMA withdrew and moved to another area further north. Edmund Fitzgibbon from St. Patrick's Society was appointed Monsignor in Minna. He came the same year as I came and remained until 1973 when Minna became a full diocese and got its first Nigerian bishop.

"Minna town is multi-cultural and multi-religious. About 50% of the people are Muslim. When I came here, I did not feel that I was in a place very different to the place I left. The people were just as friendly and welcoming and it did not matter whether they were Muslim, Christian or atheist. My first job was in St. Malachy's Teacher Training College. It's now the Federal University of Technology. There, we were blessed with the wonderful James Campbell, a retired headmaster from Scotland who came to Nigeria as a volunteer for two years. He was an excellent teacher and he taught the rest of us how to teach teachers. We also had an excellent man from Dublin – Fr. Des McKeever, SPS who had been ordained in his late thirties and who had lots of experience as a civil servant and an educator. In addition, there were many excellent Nigerian teachers. They followed a process to the letter. I spent three years at St. Malachy's.

"In summer 1967, I went home on leave and when I returned, Msgr. Fitzgibbon asked me to move to this school as principal. It was then a mission school called Fatima Co-educational Secondary School. It had opened in January 1965 with sixty pupils – thirty boys and thirty girls. Today we have 1,960. It remained co-ed until 1973, the year all secondary schools were taken over by the North-West Government which had its headquarters in Sokoto. Co-ed was not appreciated by the Islamic tradition so girls were phased out and sent to the Maryam Babangida Science College nearby.

"After 1975, primary education in the North suffered greatly from the mass exodus of good teachers who flocked for further training and higher qualifications to the numerous colleges of education, universities and schools of nursing that were opening up. Overnight almost, the primary schools were decimated because once the teachers got on the rungs of the ladder with their higher qualifications, they kept on moving. The primary schools never recovered from that exodus. The good teachers were never replaced and certainly since 1980, the quality of teaching in primary schools has deteriorated. If the children leaving the primary school don't have a good background, they never catch up no matter how much of an effort is put into secondary and third levels later on. Secondary education was also affected in the 1970's as during the oil boom years, teachers found their way out of education and into more lucrative positions.

"I grew to like teaching though my first choice would have been regular parish work. I found that I could communicate easily with the students and I have always had a good relationship with teachers. These are the first two steps towards progress I think. Initially, we selected our own teachers but that changed after 1973. From then on, the teachers you got were sent to you. We started with an excellent core and somehow the new ones followed their example and turned out very well. We do have pupil screening tests here which are not welcomed by our Ministry officials but if we took in everyone who applied, we would have an intake of 2,000 every year. We try to maintain good standards and if you judge by external competitions, we always score very highly. In the competition for the best school in Niger State, we have won the all-over prize for the last two years. You might have seen the big trophy in my office earlier!

"Like the town, the school is multi-cultural and multi-religious. All we have at assembly in the morning is the pledge. Religion is taught separately to the different groups by specialized teachers. We don't experience any problems as there is no discrimination. While you might know the majority of the pupils to see, you wouldn't necessarily know the details of their backgrounds so everyone is treated equally. In any case preferential treatment would not be tolerated in a school like this. Young people are very quick to notice that sort of thing."

Some months prior to my interview with Father Derry, he was awarded the Nigerian national honour of the rank of MFR (Member of the Order of the Federal Republic) by President Olusegun Obasanjo, in appreciation of his work in education. I ask him what the honour means to him.

"It means different things. It is good that the people at the top are taking note of what is going on in schools. The teachers here were very pleased. Parents were delighted and so were the pupils. Even the principals of other schools felt good about it. Then our past pupils, many of whom are in high positions in Nigeria and elsewhere were very proud. We ourselves have always been happy about the school's achievements so any recognition from the outside only encourages us to continue putting in our best efforts.

"The school has the biggest percentage of past pupils at the Federal University of Minna. We also have big numbers at Ahmadu Bello University at Zaria, at Ilorin University (supposedly the premier medical school) and at Sokoto University medical school. Then there are the many polytechnics to which our pupils go. Some students who may not have performed well here on account of being slow learners or whatever occasionally return to tell us that they have received a doctorate or some other good qualification. Today there are many opportunities for third level education in the State. The big problem however is the number of strikes that are taking place in these institutions all over Nigeria. It's a worrying situation for all of us in education.

"The 35th anniversary of the founding of the school was celebrated in the year 2,000. The past pupils rallied around and organized a fund-raising launch. Many of them are not big earners themselves but their positions give them a certain amount of clout. On the day of the launch, we collected twenty-one million naira most of which came from the Niger State Government. You could only describe the reaction to the announcement of the sum as consternation. What we were able to do with that money transformed the school, as on a year to year basis, the school is not well funded. We are supposed to get a certain percentage of the school fees but it doesn't always happen. The parents really have to keep things going. Nigerians are very keen on education so parents are prepared to make big sacrifices to ensure that their children are in good schools. That being said, not all of them consistently give the necessary home supports and some pupils too, can stint on effort."

In addition to his duties as school principal, Fr. Derry also has a parish to take care of.

"I have it by accident really. The parish priest, Fr. Chris McGuinness went home on sabbatical and since SPS has a commitment to the parish, we had to put in somebody. I seemed to be the only person available. I like the role but it is demanding and I am conscious that more could be done if it was my full-time position. It's fortunate that the laity groups are so good. They are highly organized and they know what they are about."

It's a busy life and for relaxation, Father likes to go to the golf course.

"I play every Monday at 4:00 p.m. at the army cantonment. I enjoy it very much. It's the getting away from everything as much as the golf. The walk around eighteen holes is marvellous. There was a time when you could take a walk anywhere around Minna. These days, you have to be more careful."

The town of Minna was established around 1915. It became a melting pot for ethnic groups such as Gwari, Hausa, Fulani, Kamberi and many others. They came into the town to sell their peanuts, yams, pottery, crafts and cloth. Cotton was sent to Lagos along the Lagos Kano railway line for export. Commerce grew up around cattle, indigo, tobacco, kola nuts, weaving, quarrying of marble and the making of bricks. Yoruba and Igbo immigrants from the west and east came looking for work. Driving down the broad avenue that runs through the town and that is dominated by a beautiful golden mosque, I had the impression of being in a cauldron of intense human activity. Despite the heat of an unyielding tropical sun, the incessant onward move of crowds of people of every size, shape and hue was riveting. This was no indolent tropical outpost. Everywhere there was focus, urgency and struggle.

I asked Fr. Derry to tell me about the town.

"Well, education seems to have taken over the place. The school children give it amazing vitality. They throng the streets several times a day. Apart from that, Minna is a place that is very much alive, yet it has a relaxation of a kind. The majority of people are trying to make ends meet for their families. At the present time, there is very little industry around. That's a big disappointment as so many people don't have jobs of any kind."

I enquire if Nigeria's two *Big Men* – former military Heads of State, who live in the town are doing anything to alleviate this situation. The palatial residence of the very wealthy Ibrahim Babangida sprawls itself out in lordly fashion on a hill overlooking Minna while the activities of Abdulsalami Abubakar were rumoured to include the raising of Friesian herds of cattle.

"One of them, Abdulsalami, is building a number of factories around. I suppose they will provide employment for a number of people some day. He also has a big farm out on the Bida road on which he raises Friesian cows. He sells yogurt and fresh milk on the street in the town every day. There were a few small industries in Minna in the past but they failed. The town does not seem to have a big purchasing power and sales distribution to the outside seems to have been poor. There was a big fertilizer factory here but it too closed down. It should have been successful as the area around Minna is a big farming region and the farmers need fertilizer. It's an important yam producing region and there's also guinea corn, maize, ground nuts and some millet. Apart from mangoes, there is very little in the line of fruit though some villages have small orange and guava orchards which were planted due to missionary influence, I think. The mangoes, though not indigenous, grow very well in the area. They were brought here from India."

A notable feature of life in Nigeria is the constantly renewed hope for the massive economic potential of the country. Since gaining its independence from Great Britain in 1960, the country has seen numerous military coups, a bloody and brutal civil war, economic upheavals and much destructive ethnic and religious strife. It is listed among the topmost corrupt countries in the world by the Berlin-based anti-corruption group *Transparency International*. Its vast material resources of oil, gas and agriculture seem to have done little to alleviate the poverty and the daily struggle of the majority. Yet the hope for a turn around, a new beginning, a miracle – is kept alive in the foremost part of the nation's psyche. Since his coming to Nigeria in 1961, Fr. Derry has been a bystander and a witness to nearly all of the country's travails. I ask where his hopes for the country he has grown to love, rest.

"The young people I know are highly principled. The university students are the same. The ordinary people you meet on a daily basis are the best. You wonder how the people at the top are not aware of all of this. You wonder where and how all the corruption builds up. It seems that some people who get into power see it as an opportunity for personal gain. It all amazes me but I believe that eventually it will get through to those in power that the majority of the people want their country to be run properly – with transparency and accountability and all that.

"Since the return of democratic government in 1999, there has certainly been a change for the good in the level of freedom which people experience but there is a great feeling of disappointment about the lack of progress in most other areas. The people expected *democracy* to be the panacea that would solve all problems. They expected everyone to have enough to live on but despite the recent increase in salaries, the buying power of the naira is very low and people are fighting for survival month after month.

"Strong leadership is a must in Nigeria because people understand that and they also understand that when you have authority, you have to use it. I don't think this exists right now. It's plain to see that some people in government behave as if they are their own masters. Unless the authority is there to exercise control, we will just stumble on as we are.

"This country is full of life and energy. The place is throbbing with it. The enthusiasm and talent of the people force you to respond. I love all of that and of course these traits should normally and naturally feed into a march towards progress."

Fr. Derry's contract as school principal was due to expire within a few months. He was being asked by past pupils and others to consider another year. He was in the process of making a decision about the request.

"I still have the enthusiasm and I enjoy the work but perhaps I have done enough! If I retire from the school, I would like to take a break away from the country for at least six months. I have only had one such break since 1961. I have an annual vacation of course which I always spend in Ireland. I often help out with parish work when I am there. I seem to relate well to the people. Bishop McGee of Cloyne told me once that he would welcome me into his diocese should I ever decide to leave Africa. He may have forgotten that!"

I ask if he is disappointed with certain aspects of the Irish Church.

"Well it was always very remote from the people in the past so changes were inevitable. Even yet, I find that the laity is not involved enough. They cannot claim ownership of their Church. From the beginning here in Nigeria, the priests depended on the laity – the catechists, the village teachers and many others to take care of things. This meant that the people, of necessity, were active and involved. In my first year here I used to visit a nearby primary school a few evenings a week and it was a hive of activity. Children were being prepared for Baptism, Holy Communion and Confirmation and most of the work was being done by children not much older than the ones being prepared. They had their different roles. One might tell you that he was a fisher – a boy who goes out to bring in small children for the class. Another might say, 'I'm the teacher.' There was huge involvement.

"I am not pessimistic however about the Irish Church. One problem might be the age of the clergy. In Ireland, it seems to me that young people want to be motivated and enthused by people nearer their own age. The respect for seniority and old age is not nearly as marked as it is here in Nigeria. Since vocations are very thin on the ground right now, we may, for a time, have to depend on priests from the outside. Eventually I think that there will be a totally new attitude that will spring from the involvement of the laity."

Father Noel McGeeney

St. Patrick's Society (SPS)
Kabba, Kogi State

Fr. Noel McGeeney, SPS

Kabba in present-day Kogi State in middle-belt Nigeria is an old colonial town about sixty kilometres from both the State capital of Lokoja and the confluence of the Benue and Niger rivers. During the heyday of the Royal Niger Company, which was the precursor to the British occupation of the territory that became Nigeria, the area around Kabba came under intense British influence. The Company established its headquarters in Lokoja in 1886 and from there operated along the Niger and Benue, sometimes becoming embroiled in serious conflicts while intercepting slave raids or attempting to protect trade routes. It made many treaties with the powerful Caliph of Sokoto and the Emirs of Gwandu and Nupe, which it then used to assert rights of Protectorate over the Caliphate. All the Caliph of Sokoto thought he was conceding to the British traders, however, was a monopoly of European trade with his Caliphate in return for a payment. The Company also used the treaties to keep out their French rivals. In this objective, they were well supported by the British Government. In 1897, the Royal Niger Company's British-backed constabulary sent a force of 500 men to subdue the Emir of Nupe on the grounds that he was allowing persistent raids into Company territory. A new Emir was installed and he was forced to concede the southern half of his emirate which became the province of Kabba. On January 1st, 1890, the British hoisted their flag over Lokoja and from then on, real attempts were made to establish British control over the territories north of the Niger and Benue which were assigned to her by the Berlin Conference of 1885. Today, Kabba has little political importance but its location in the centre of Nigeria, its closeness to the mighty Niger and the state capital means that it remains a significant trading location.

The French SMA priests brought the Catholic Church to the Kabba region. Two of them opened a mission in Lokoja in1884 but both were dead by 1886. They were succeeded by more French SMA. Before these arrivals however, Lokoja had been introduced to Christianity by the famous Bishop Samuel Crowther of the CMS (Church Mission Society) who must have been among the first ecumenists as he gave much cooperation to the Catholics when they arrived. In 1955, the Lokoja Mission was erected as the Prefecture of Kabba and entrusted to the Canadian province of the Holy Ghost Fathers. It was elevated to the status of a diocese in 1964 but the seat of the diocese moved to Lokoja in 1991 when Lokoja became the capital of the newly formed Kogi State. Today, two young Irish priests from St. Patrick's Society, Kiltegan, Fr. Noel McGeeney and Fr. Leo Traynor, occupy the former Kabba compound of the Canadian Fathers. They pursue their ministry which includes an adult formation programme called *SHARING EDUCATION &*

LEARNING FOR LIFE (SELL) with remarkable conviction and enthusiasm. I spoke to Fr. Noel following a much enjoyed breakfast which he and Fr. Leo deftly prepared for my husband and me during a surprise early-morning visit to their compound. He spoke first about the years leading up to his Kabba assignment.

"I'm from Longford town and I went to St. Mel's College there. During my inter-cert year, I decided to be a missionary priest. The decision had something to do with my family background. I had two uncles in the priesthood and an aunt in the convent. One uncle spent a while in Nigeria as principal of schools in Calabar and Abakaliki. He was attached to St. Patrick's Society but not a member. I never wanted to be a priest in the Irish Church. I had a sense that it would be too constricting for me, and furthermore, I did not like the relationship between priest and people that I observed growing up in the 1970's. In those years, moulds were breaking in every facet of life but the Church was resistant and anxious to hold on to all the old power structures. I found myself being very critical of all of that.

"Going on the missions as a priest was for me all about helping and very little about converting people. I felt that there would be job satisfaction, variety and challenge in the life of a missionary priest. Apart from that there was the sense that you would be very much needed on the missions. At that time in Ireland, the place seemed awash with priests and I had often wondered if indeed we had need of all of them.

"My friends were always curious as to how I was able to make my life choice at such a young age. You see, I am totally convinced of the Resurrection and that is the core of Christianity. The Resurrection was the first Christian experience of the Apostles. When all of that grabbed me, the rest fell into place. From a faith dimension, I have never wavered.

"I also believe that Salvation has happened. The world is already saved. It has been saved by Christ for all peoples and races and for all time. That is indisputable as far as I am concerned. The intervention that God made in our world was unique. He became fully human and He was already fully divine. Mankind was utterly transformed by that intervention. It formed the completion of what God had started at the beginning of time.

"Salvation has happened but there will be Judgement. The hopes of the masses of poor people of this world – the oppressed, the downtrodden – rest in the Judgement. If they can get justice in this life, all the better but if they cannot, there will be the final Judgement and justice will be done. It will be God's justice so we don't know how it is going to be. Justice is a very interesting word. Its roots mean righteousness, wholeness and holiness.

"I came to Nigeria in 1984, three months after ordination. I was with another newly ordained priest called Peter Branigan. After we arrived in Lagos, we flew to Port Harcourt where we were met by Kiltegan priests. We were given six months orientation – time to get familiar with the language and absorbed in the culture. Peter and I lived with an older priest, Fr. John Lawler during that time and it was good. We got an understanding of the workings of different parishes and met a large number of Nigerians and colleague priests and reverend sisters. At the end of that time, I was sent to Umuaturu in Rivers State and Peter was sent to Port Harcourt. I was given a brand-new Volkswagen-beetle which was stolen six months later at Onitsha when I was visiting the Cathedral for the centenary celebrations of the founding of the Catholic Church there. I never had a good car again until I got the one I am driving now.

"In Umuaturu (which I think means goat), I was with Fr. Roger Cunnane. Within our parish, we had five zones which included thirty-five out-stations. We worked it on a week in week out basis – a week at the centre carrying out duties and the next week at the out-stations. The latter meant packing up the car on a Tuesday with my mass box, my chop (food) box and my personal bag. When I got a solar light, I had a light box. A young lad called Reggie came with me to help with cooking and other odd jobs. In fact, he stayed with me for six years altogether. On Tuesday afternoons, I usually met the catechumens – children or adults who were studying for Baptism or other Sacraments. The catechists were the ones who prepared them for examination. I would then meet with people preparing for marriage and after that would deal with any other issue needing attention. This parish was excellent as it had priests' rest houses in every village. These were just small rooms into which you moved for an overnight stay. The next morning, you would say mass and as the people all went to the farm in the mornings, you would spend the rest of the morning reading or visiting the old people in the village. That evening, you went to another village to follow the same routine. After six months, everybody knew you and you were made to feel very welcome. I never found anything but friendship and generosity. I was a very happy priest during my stay there.

"After two and a half years, I was moved to Omoko, another town in Rivers State because the priest there went home. It is an oil town and there is a gas injection plant nearby. The town had twenty-four hours light and it was free! This is an abiding memory! I also had air conditioning so my living conditions had reached an all time high! I had nine out-stations which were rather close to one another so I was able to come home to base after every visit. I lived on my own for two years and I would say that the experience almost broke me. I had no emotional support; I was lonely and a sadness came into my life. There were colleague priests around me and we routinely met on Mondays for golf or cards and what I would call superficial communication. We changed all that in later years when the Society opted for a ministry to priests programme in Port Harcourt. It meant meeting every couple of months outside our mission for faith-sharing sessions and serious discussion on prepared topics. These meetings also provided opportunities to socialize and I found that communication was real and sincere. That lasted for three years and it was good. It's no longer happening, due I suppose to people moving and circumstances changing. Out of the nine of us who participated in that ministry, eight of us were very faithful to it and made constructive contributions. We found that it was very helpful to our lives.

"After Omoko, I was sent into St. John's Parish, Port Harcourt – a very good parish. Port Harcourt is the capital of Rivers State and is the centre of the oil industry in Nigeria. It's called *The Garden City* as it has more parks and trees than any other city in Nigeria. It is the second most important port in the country although it did not exist until after 1913. It was built by the British colonial administration for exporting coal from Enugu, and lucrative oil palm products that came from the farming efforts of the densely populated villages in the Bonny River region.

"The peoples of this part of the West African Coast are linguistically and culturally related to the Igbo. However, the demands of coastal life and their contact with coastal trade over centuries have produced ethnic differences that were strong enough to resist the Biafra secession movement when it was pushed by Igbo leadership during the Biafran war. The ethnic groups of Ijaw, Ibibio, Anang and Efik live partly from agriculture and partly from fishing and shrimping in the coastal waters.

"My time in St. John's Parish was good. We were located close to the Shell Oil life camp and were able to use their sporting facilities. There were loads of expatriates to have as friends. A number of them were Irish. One woman was from County Longford and I became friendly with the whole family. My work as a priest was also satisfactory though I didn't have a very comfortable relationship with our Irish Bishop, Edmund Fitzgibbon. He was the reason for my leaving Port Harcourt for Bomadi in Delta State after only one and a half years. In Bomadi, Fr. Tommy Greenan was in charge and we worked very well together as a team and one very good thing we did was establish a *Leadership Training Programme* for all the leaders in the jurisdiction.

"After Bomadi, I moved on to Patani which is not very far from Bomadi. I spent three very happy years there with Fr. Noel O'Brien. It was a tiny parish and we shared a small house. All our work was done by boat – moving up and down the rivers and creeks. Your boat was your car. If you went to an out-station, you stayed for a few days. The freedom was amazing and there was not a monotonous moment. You were hands on with every group and society. No barriers were created and I created none. During my time there, I was coming close to being ten years ordained so I was due a sabbatical. I chose to do development studies for a year in Kimmage Manor, Dublin. After the year which I enjoyed immensely, there was the question of whether or not I would return to Nigeria. Our Superior General, Kieran Bermingham in Kiltegan discussed with me the needs and opportunities in our other missions around the world. I decided to go to the Caribbean – to Grenada in fact.

"Now this is a stunningly beautiful island which rises from sea level to 3,000 feet in a matter of miles. The territory which is largely English speaking now is twenty-five miles by nineteen. It has a small rainforest. A tropical scent of spices and fruit permeates the air. It's a predominantly Catholic island as it was ruled by the French before it was handed over to the British. The French made Catholics of the people and all the slaves in the sugar plantations were automatically baptized. I was there from 1996 to 2000.

"When I left Grenada, I spent six months in a temporary post in Slough in London doing regular parish work. I would have been happy to stay on but there was no permanent slot for me. When I returned to Ireland in 2001, I started looking for a team or at least one other person who might be interested in the idea of collaborative ministry. It was something I was exploring at the time. Essentially it means running a parish collaboratively with men and women, clerics and laity. I believe that it is the approach of the future. I'm trying to craft this method and I'm trying to create a model of Church which could be the way forward.

"Fortunately I met Fr. Leo Traynor around that time. He had the same ideas as I have and he was about my age. I am now forty-three. We came together and wrote a project proposal called *Working with Laity Groups in Nigeria.* It was accepted by our superiors in Kiltegan. A certain amount of stalling then took place with the regional superiors in Nigeria on the grounds that it was difficult to find a point of entry for us. One was eventually found in the Diocese of Lokoja. The late bishop, Most Rev. Dr. Joseph Ajomo was very interested in our ideas and agreed to give us full support. He gave us this pastoral centre here in Kabba which was formerly the seat of the Canadian Holy Ghost Fathers.

"Our work gives witness to team and collaborative ministry. We are currently looking for another person to join us – preferably a woman and if possible an African. Capacity building is an important element of our training programs – the belief that each person has capacities, means and skills to solve their own problems. The style of our work is important and it is based on a concept developed by Fr. Tony Hayden, one of our own Kiltegan priests. It's called *SHARING EDUCATION & LEARNING FOR LIFE (SELL).* We are involved with HIV/AIDS prevention awareness, conflict resolution, gender equality, interfaith dialogue and spiritual direction. We have already given a number of courses. We had thirty-four young Catholic Youth Corps people in for a weekend recently being introduced to leadership training skills in a workshop called the *FIVE CORE KEYS OF LEADERSHIP TRAINING.* Another workshop we did was devoted to human and spiritual growth for young people and some of our own clerical students came from our formation house in Ijebu Ode in Ogun State for that. In a few months time, we will do a training programme for Catholic youths in Federal College, Okene here in Kogi State. I am going over there next week to make initial contact and to make advance explorations. We are also going to St. Matthew's Parish in Amukoko, Lagos to do a programme with the leaders there. Not long ago, we did a workshop on inter-cultural living for our own Irish staff and students at our formation house. We craft our courses with the specific needs of our target groups in mind. Our target groups are usually young adults. This is not easy work. A lot is expected from people who set themselves up as givers of leadership training courses.

"Fundamental to our workshops is the concept of Christian transformation – the need to evolve that inner transformation that is necessary to deal with one's own particular dysfunction – the need to tackle choices that have been made but which have proved bad for the individual and for others. The aim is to try to find that inner balance of body, mind and spirit that is necessary to live in the world in harmony.

"I spoke yesterday at mass about living life in a new way. Baptism alone does not make us truly Christian. I believe most of us have to challenge all our prejudices and all that is dysfunctional in us and make a transformation. The moment of that transformation, I believe, is a gift. People ask how it is possible to arrive at that moment. I say it's by having the desire to espouse the values in the Beatitudes found in the Gospel of Matthew, Chapter V. Each person has to ask how it is going to happen for him or her. It may mean a lot of personal questioning and work and it may mean counselling and spiritual direction.

"I don't believe that Christianity is complex. *Love your neighbour as yourself;* the starting point here would be the self. If for example, you are promiscuous and sleeping around, you do not love yourself and you certainly cannot love the people you are with. In a case like that, there is something in you that you are not dealing with, and it's that something that you have to confront and challenge if you want to achieve that sense of balance and harmony which I mentioned earlier. That's the gift that transformation brings about.

All great religions speak of harmony. In the case of a Christian, it has everything to do with living your life as a fully committed Christian according to the Gospels. On my ordination card, I put a quote from scripture (Colossians, Chapter 1, Verse 27) – '*The mystery is Christ within you, your hope of glory.*' These are powerful words."

Father Jim Noonan

St. Patrick's Society (SPS)
Beji, Niger State

Fr. Jim Noonan, SPS

It is a busy early morning in Minna as Sr. Mary Geraghty from the Mercy Convent and I drive out to visit Fr. Jim Noonan in his very rural parish of Beji. We drive for approximately an hour along an arid country road which weaves its way through a sparsely-populated and semi-desert countryside. The morning is beautiful – clear, sunny, fresh. Father is waiting for us when we arrive. He is sitting, chief-like, in an outdoor circular hut – a stilt-supported, thatched-roof structure which gives protection from the sun but allows a clear view of all the comings and goings in the open and spacious parish compound.

He is a genial and welcoming host. I am enchanted by the setting. "This is a nice place to meet people," he says of his outdoor *pulpit* which was constructed for him by local people. Around us there is considerable activity. The day had started at the crack of dawn – many hours earlier, for the men and women who had gone to farm. A number of older villagers now move easily towards their lighter chores calling out greetings to Father as they pass. Market women with laden baskets on their heads and babies tucked snugly inside securely tied wrappers, stride towards their destination with a more determined gait. Conversation between them is hurried and urgent. One takes leave of her companions as she wants to greet us and show off the beautiful child she is carrying. She beams with joy when we chat and ask if we can take a photograph of herself and her baby. "She is thrilled now that we have acknowledged her in this way," Fr. Jim remarks as she hurries off to catch up with the other women. Closer to the church itself, some very specific tasks are underway. One man is diligently completing the painting of the outer walls of the priest's house. Another is dismantling the engine of an old car. Children too young for school leap in and out of childish games and pranks amidst shrieks of joy and excitement. The whole scene is your imaginary mission station come to life.

Father Jim has prepared breakfast for us. He places a large thermos of hot tea on the table. A carefully-packed cold-box containing bread, hard-boiled eggs, milk and sugar is placed beside it. "We might as well enjoy the outdoors," he says, "since the morning is so cool. There must be rain somewhere close by. Most mornings, I admit, are manageable but later, it can get very hot. The last few months now have been very trying. As you get older, you don't have the same energy. It's only natural.

"I came to this part of Nigeria in 1962. *This part* means distances of hundreds of miles. In size, it's just a little smaller than Ireland. There were three of us – Charlie Napier, Jerry Kiely and myself. The territory was once part of the Archdiocese of Kaduna and it was run by the SMA Fathers. We took it over from them when they moved further north to Kontagora and other places. Here, we are in the Muslim north and in 1962, it was very different from our other missions. The principal tribes of Hausa and Fulani were Muslim but there were smaller groups such as the Gwari who were animists or what we call traditional believers. It was with these smaller tribes that we missionaries hoped to have some success. In a solidly Muslim area like this, you have to be very careful and discreet. When we came, there were a number of other resident missions. The Irish Sisters of St. Louis ran a primary school and a clinic in Minna. They eventually handed over their medical work to the Medical Missionaries of Mary. The OLA Sisters were also here. From the beginning, the human development services of health and education which were offered by the Christians to the people attracted a percentage of the Muslim population. Then in the 1960's, when the pre-civil war pogroms against the Igbo settlers drove them out, greater numbers of locals gradually became attracted to Christianity and many converted to Catholicism.

"I only came to Beji a year ago. I'm not fully settled in yet. Before I came here, I spent ten years in Paiko which is out on the road to Minna, not very far from here. Before that, I was across the Kaduna River out in the middle of the bush. Paiko was a difficult spot. It was very hard to make progress. It's a completely Islamic area. Even the Gwari people there are 98% Muslim. I was dealing largely with Christians who had moved in from other areas. Here in Beji, the people will tell you that denomination is decided – that you are either a committed Muslim or a committed Christian. I'm inclined to think that this is not completely true. I feel that there are many nominal Muslims and Christians around. I'm told that maybe more would be Christian if we weren't opposed to polygamy. There are fifteen out-stations attached to Beji. Beji itself and Maikunkele are the two places that get the most attention. I suppose one reason for that is that there are more people going to the sacraments. The people in the other stations are not at that stage yet. On a Sunday in Beji, you would have about one hundred and thirty attending mass. Most of them are locals and you would be very aware of that. It's not like the big parishes in Lagos and Abuja where you have mighty congregations of thousands made up of people from all over Nigeria and beyond. Here, I work with the Gwari people only. They have their Gwari dialect but they also speak Hausa.

"One thing I try to do here is to get people to do things for themselves. I am totally against handouts. I think that they are very destructive except maybe in an urban situation where you have to build a church or other facilities quickly for artificial communities who have come from other places and who have been Christian for years. In Beji, the Church and the priest's house were given to the people in the past. They were built with overseas money which was sourced by the priests who came before me. I'm trying to change that approach. The house was in bad shape when I came so it is now being reconstructed using money raised by the parish council. We are not talking about big money – about 300,000 naira – less than two and half thousand dollars. The local people are doing all the work. One man fixed up a small generator and an old kerosene fridge for me a few weeks ago. I'm doing things in stages. You didn't see any saucers in that cold box earlier! I haven't got around to those yet!

"I live here for most of the week. One or two nights are spent in Minna as I have to take care of diocesan funds for the Bishop. If you were here yesterday when I came back, you would have seen a whole crowd of young boys and girls waiting for me. When they saw the car coming, they ran out to meet me and then followed me in. They had new ones in tow and some of them were Muslim. A Nigerian priest would find it very hard to bridge the gap between Muslim and Christian. He would come under suspicion. I get a wonderful thrill out of bringing down the barriers and making new friends.

"It's a great experience when you break down that initial fear – the fear of the white man – the fear that I might be evil! There are many different elements in it. I spend a lot of time talking to people. Gradually, you gain their trust. The evangelization idea is always with you but it is much wider than that. You feel pretty close to them when they speak to one another knowing that you are in on the conversation. Sometimes they might even forget that you are there.

"Today now, around one or two o'clock, I will go to a village about twenty miles from here. What will I do there? I'll be teaching the basics of Christianity. I will bring pictures of the Passion and with the help of the catechist who will translate, I'll talk about them. I will probably stick them up on a tree. When I started going to that village, very few would come near me. Now they crowd around. It's all about building trust and relationships. Again I spend a lot of time talking to them. They don't really talk too seriously among themselves. I think that the communication is all a great big jumble – a banter, and I would say that it's the survival of the fittest. I like to joke a lot with them but sometimes you can go a bit too far as they don't always understand our sense of humour. There are Nigerian Sisters living not so far from here and on St. Patrick's Day of last year, they had the Bishop out to visit. Since I wasn't invited, I started joking with them about it when I met them sometime afterwards but I think that the joke went too far. This year, they invited me but I was not free to go. When I went out there yesterday evening, there was something in the atmosphere and it wasn't love! I have to assume that I pushed my joke too far. Sometimes it's different. There's an old lady here who lost her husband recently. She's originally from the Midwest so she travelled there when she had finished her mourning and when it was time to discard her mourning clothes. When she returned, she came to greet me but I joked that I couldn't greet her because she had gone away without saying good bye. We had great fun. She had no problem seeing the joke.

"Since I came to Nigeria in 1962, I have only spent one year out of the country – apart from holidays of course. We had a man here called Fitzgibbon; he is now a Bishop Emeritus. He sent me to Paris to study sociology. I only spent a year there. It was all too much as I had little or no French. It can be really humiliating when you are struggling with a language. I came back here after the year. I learned something from the experience I suppose. For one thing, I got an insight into another side of West Africa by getting to know a number of West-African professionals and students who were working and studying in France.

"I am from Longhill, Co. Limerick. Michael, one of my brothers is well known in politics. Another is with Allied Irish Bank. My father was a teacher. We grew up on the Shannon Estuary looking down on the water. Out here, I miss that water very much. My father died a long time ago but my mother sadly died recently. Looking back on my life as an African missionary, I have to say that it has been great. I have never lost the enthusiasm. The people are wonderful. That man that passed by there just now is a local farmer and he is hard-working, generous and tough. You should meet his little daughter though; she has an altogether higher level of toughness!

"When I arrived in Nigeria, I came up here through Lagos and Ibadan. The huge crowds were overwhelming. I felt that I would never get to know the people as they all seemed the same. Now more than forty years on, I have come to the stage of recognizing a child's voice from its mother's.

"How long will I stay here? I don't know! Health is the big thing out here. At the moment it is quite good."

Fr. Jim's parishioner and her baby

Father Dermot Connolly

St. Patrick's Society (SPS)
Abuja

Fr. Dermot Connolly

Nenagh born Fr. Dermot Connolly was one of the first Irish
missionary priests that I met in Lagos after I arrived in 1998. I
remember him bringing my husband and me around the newly
decorated parish house in the densely populated Mende Road,
Maryland in the western outskirts of Lagos. Everything was in apple
pie order. The Irish women from Guinness Nigeria, he told us, had
made all the curtains. There were bedrooms galore – ones for
visitors, ones for priests passing through and one for us also, he told
me, if ever we wanted to spend the night absorbing the flavour of

'our life out here.' I never did stay over but remember passing some great hours there on Christmas night 1999 when all expatriates were advised by bosses and governments to avoid flying to other destinations in aeroplanes in case of falling foul of the much heralded fears of computer failures at the turn of the new millennium. There were many of us that night being hosted generously by Fr. Dermot and his ebullient co-host Fr. Paudie Maloughney. There was food, drink, music, *siamsa* and great, great fun.

When all embassies departed for Nigeria's new capital, Abuja in summer 2001, we left Fr. Dermot and our many other missionary friends behind. Because I was unable to find a suitable occasion to interview him before compiling this book, I asked him for a contribution. I invite you, dear reader, to enjoy that contribution just as much as I have done.

"OUT FOREIGN"

"Ah, Father, it's easy known you're out foreign!" Sometimes a compliment, the remark could just as well have been occasioned by my showing up sunburnt at a grey time of the year in Ireland, or by displaying my gross ignorance of common affairs at home. Whatever the case, "out foreign" is where I wanted to be – though not always quite this far out. In my early thoughts of a vocation to the priesthood, a diocese in England would have suited me fine, but letters from a classmate in secondary school, who had already gone to Kiltegan, settled the question – St. Patrick's Missionary Society and, as it turned out, Africa. I was ordained on Easter Sunday 1964.

I have to say that I made the choice for priesthood before I knew better; it is the way with most of the great choices we make in life. Then when I did know better, when the years had passed, and things had changed and I had changed, I renewed the choice. It's either that or change it. I find I need to continually renew the choice – it is a sign of life. It is a fact of life, as life changes.

Of course, it is *being missionary* that is the vocation; "out foreign" might be no more than personal preference, no different from *A Year in Provence*. I know it is not an adequate theological definition, but *being missionary means*, in practice, being sent somewhere; as one man put it, being "pusharoundable". For me it meant studies in Rome after ordination; then teaching in the seminary in Kiltegan, Co. Wicklow for a total of ten years. Most of the rest of my priesthood has been in Nigeria: teaching in a secondary school in the Northern diocese of Minna; running a large city parish in Lagos; serving in the Society's administration for twelve years, again in Lagos; and now back to a semi-rural parish just outside Nigeria's capital, Abuja. And it may well be that when I have become *unmissioned and unmuscled, being missionary* will mean settling into another appointment, or retirement, here or at home in Ireland or wherever, or as they say here, "Who knows tomorrow?"

I mentioned that I spent time in Lagos: it was 11 years – running a large city parish. In fact, it was running to catch up! It wasn't just that it was a very extensive, densely populated slum area, but that in Nigeria there is a highly organised system of parish councils, church committees, communities, societies. People are intensely involved, and being a priest means learning to work with dedicated voluntary leaders who know the local scene much better than the foreign missionary could ever manage. They often refer to the priest as the *Father in Charge* – and that's a misnomer, if there ever was one! The image I tended to have was of a packed minibus careering at great speed down a bad road – the parish priest was not the driver, but much more the conductor, clinging to the side of the vehicle, collecting the money and encouraging new passengers to get on board. How or when or whether the bus would reach its destination was, most of the time, beyond my ken or control. Still, I felt it was in good hands, and in a general way, we got there.

If I were to use any one word to describe my sense of the Church in Nigeria, it would be *OWNERSHIP*. The Church is still in its early stages here, despite its several centuries of history. True, there are 55 bishops, nine of them archbishops, and one a cardinal. Concrete is being poured for new buildings everywhere – churches, offices, pastoral centres, nursery schools, clinics. And yet, these are still sowing times, planting times, and beginning times. You will still find small groups of 15 to 20 people in a village holding a weekly service on their own, without benefit of priest or minister – individuals and families with no Christian heritage or history – setting out on a life's journey as new followers of Christ;

communities gathering for mass in a grass-roofed shed – Bethlehem rather than basilica. We are a minority – and young enough and new enough, for men and women still to say, "I carried cement blocks for that church in those days! The most proud title is *foundation member* – as in sport, you can always establish a new record, but you can never beat being the *first* to run a four-minute mile. That has its own, unforgettable cachet. The people own the Church; they built it – it belongs to them and they are proud of it. And they are so extraordinarily generous in their giving: money, time, kind, sons and daughters. And some have given their lives.

Nothing is perfect. We live in denial here in Nigeria about our failures and defects just as people do everywhere in the world. Nigeria scores top of the tables in religious fervour and commitment, but its worldwide reputation for corruption, poor governance, and criminal activity is dire. And, as we have learned in Ireland, there can be an ugly underside to the success and growth of a Church. Sometimes I fear that what the missionaries brought is no more than a slip grafted on to an older and more hazardous stock. It shows in times of crises, when people go back to their roots: these are often buried in the old native traditions rather than in the more-recently arrived teachings of Islam or Christianity. And, of course, what we missionaries brought came wrapped in our own traditions and troubles and temperaments – not always for the better!

And here is where you realize that *mission* goes way beyond buildings or parish organisations or structures. It has to do with trying to get the measure of God; "the breadth and the length, the height and the depth; so that, knowing the love of Christ, which is beyond knowledge, you may be filled with the utter fullness of God" (Ephesians 3:18-19). These are deep waters – this knowing beyond knowledge, but they are not uncharted. At basis, it seems to me, *being missionary* means proclaiming Jesus Christ as the one in whom the utter fullness of God can be found. If we are not doing that, in our words and actions, in our living and liturgy, we are no more than another NGO, doing our best to do good.

So, I have lived here in Nigeria for the past 25 years (a short time in most missionary experience: out foreign, watching my home country progressing in leaps and bounds of one or two years at a time as I come and go on leave. Nieces and nephews growing in non-stop motion inches. Awkward at an ATM, which an old man here described after a visit to Britain as "the hole in the wall that spit money" – exactly my own impression! Always saying goodbye. Cramming family and friendship into days, and a year's shopping into a single visit to Clery's or Dunnes Stores. After a while you realize how much has gone on without you, how much you have missed, how often you find yourself grieving or rejoicing long after the event – out of step, out of synch. And how much your vision of *home* has changed over the years, and how good it is to return there, and that the pearl beyond price is being welcomed.

And what has "out foreign" given me? (apart from a genuine entitlement to have an 'overseas account', if I had the money!) New horizons, other visions, strange and charming fellowships. Unexpected friendship – because in my foolishness I thought I was the bringer of gifts, the herald of Good News, only to find it was there before me in the faith and courage of the people. I have been given faith myself, and the love of very good friends. And hope: I have seen endurance in the face of continuous poverty and disappointment; of injustice and deprivation; how so many people survive and manage to be joyful. I watched people on Sunday morning coming from the most squalid living conditions, but looking resplendent – the women walked and dressed like queens: love and squalor, and a great dignity. New languages, though to my shame and lasting regret, I never learned even one properly. I cannot begin to imagine how much I have lost by that failure. Most Nigerians speak at least three languages – not to mention the language of music and dancing and drumming, and that can be a difficult place to be. I think I know more now than when I first came to Nigeria; whether I know better is another question. But I do not regret the choice that brought me here.

Father Eugene Bree

St. Patrick's Society (SPS)
Amukoko, Lagos

Fr. Eugene Bree, SPS

"I came here to Amukoko in 2000. It was a big change as I had spent thirty-eight years in rural areas in the States of Delta and Rivers. Strange as it might seem, the state of my health led me to this very poor and densely populated area of Lagos. In 1999, while I was in Burutu, in the riverine area of Delta State, I got sick and started to get pains in all my joints. At the same time, I was having a disagreement with Bishop Egerega of Bomadi. He wanted to move me to a station which would require a lot of driving to out-stations and since I had given up driving some time earlier on account of peripheral vision problems, the proposed move was not going to suit me. The Bishop was not sympathetic and he didn't seem to want to pay for a driver. The whole situation forced me to decide that it was time to make a change. I returned to Ireland to deal with my health and to think about what I might do next.

"A doctor in Dun Laoghaire told me that my pains were malaria related. I was given some medication and introduced to a series of physical exercises. I went to Kiltegan and spent four months taking lots of walks and relaxing generally. My health improved so with the blessing of our superior general, I came to Lagos as I became aware of the work that was going on in St. Matthew's Parish here in Amukoko relating to *Small Christian Communities*. This was something I was interested in as in 1999, I had spent time in South Africa doing a *Lumko* training course which was designed to promote pastoral work in *Small Christian Communities* which would be participative and reminiscent of the small groups which gathered together in the early days of the Church, to share what they had and to celebrate the Eucharist.

"Big congregations are good for the devotional aspect of the Church but in small groups, you operate at grass roots level and people aim to live Christianity as opposed to being passive. Here in Amukoko, different groups from the parish meet every Wednesday night in their own areas and in the most suitable venues they can find. They sit in a circle. Nobody preaches. Passages are read from the Bible or from the Gospel of the following Sunday. Words or phrases are picked out for reflection or discussion. Then the events of the week as related to their own lives are shared and enquiries are made about the needs of individuals within the group. These could concern illness, or lack of water, light or employment.

"A certain amount of leadership training goes into the formation of these groups and a whole variety of workshops take place on issues and procedures. The whole idea started in South America even before the days of *Liberation Theology*. Small communities bonded to take part in trade unions and military dictatorships were sometimes overthrown as a result. The Catholic Church was not against this in the beginning but as time went on, it grew wary. I suppose there was a fear that the spiritual aspirations of eternal life and salvation would be lost. Priests who really supported the movement did not climb high in the Church!"

Father Eugene from Cumeen near Strandhill in Co. Sligo spoke to me at the parish house in Amukoko. Our conversation ranged from the carefree days of his youth in the beautiful Yeats country to his life and times in Nigeria since 1963.

"I was born in 1933. Bree is not a common name in Ireland. I think that it has Norman origins. Growing up, I don't think that I was very aware of the sheer beauty of my surroundings but my contemporaries and I had a great time picking blackberries, gathering firewood, climbing up to Queen Maeve's cairn on Knocknarea, throwing stones and scaling walls. We were just three miles from Strandhill beach and we got to it by crossing fields. I grew up on a small farm with a sister and two brothers. We walked two miles up Knocknarea to our primary school. When it came to secondary education, I was sent to Summerhill College in Sligo – first as a day-boy and later as a boarder as my mother felt I would have more time to study. On a farm, you were always being called to do lots of chores so the books often lay idle and homework got neglected. While boarding, I came home for a visit every Sunday. I borrowed a bike from one of the town boys.

"It was during my final years at school that I began to think about the missions. Many priests came to the school doing promotion work, especially the Columban Fathers. Some of our teachers had also spent time as volunteer mission priests in Nigeria. One of these was Father Kevin Dodd – a very nice guy and a guy with whom you could have a good chat. When I told him that I was thinking of joining the Oblate Fathers to go on the missions, he turned me in the direction of St. Patrick's Society who he said were full-time missionaries.

"I arrived in Nigeria in 1963 on the MV Tarkwa ship from Liverpool. There were four of us and also on board were some Holy Rosary Sisters and a fair number of Nigerians. During the journey, we played deck kites and a lot of scrabble! We docked in Freetown, Sierra Leone for half a day. A few of us went up the town and drank iced tea at the Kingsway Stores. We then proceeded to Port Harcourt where we were met by the late Fr. Matt McGrath and a big lorry to carry the one hundred and fifty tea chests we had with us. In those days, the missionaries themselves were used as carriers of all sorts of equipment and provisions for the mission posts.

"My first assignment was as a teacher of Latin, English and geography at *Queen of Apostles Seminary* in Abakaliki, then in the Diocese of Bishop James Moynagh, SPS in Calabar. During the period of two years which I spent there, I got a fair amount of experience in parish work helping out the parish priest, Fr. Pa Walsh in the out-stations. He was later to die in Grenada in 1973 when he fell from a church tower which was being repaired. I then moved to *Central Annang Secondary School* as principal. I hadn't a clue as to how I should go about the job but somehow managed, using common sense. It was a new school and I had to deal with a lot of building. I coped by learning on the job and calling on the experience of other priests. After two years there, I came home for a period of six months. When I returned in 1965, I was assigned to Urua Inyang, another parish in the diocese of Calabar. My work there was divided between teaching and parish work. Quite a bit of evangelization had taken place in the area so it was quite settled. There were villages which were Catholic, Anglican or Methodist. The Catholic Church was very hard-line at the time so if you were in a village which had no catholic church, you were advised to read your Bible at home rather than go to a church of another Christian denomination. Ecumenism was very far down the line. It only existed for an exceptional type of person who might have had vision.

"The civil war broke out while I was in Urua. It was preceded by the military coup of 1966 and the subsequent very brutal and bloody assassinations of the instigators. Great tension developed between Colonel Ojukwu, Governor of the Eastern Region of Nigeria and the Federal Government. When he declared the State of Biafra with himself as President, tension really mounted. Around the same time, an election in the Western Region which had gone badly wrong due to rigging caused further tension. We, in Urua depended on the BBC for any kind of news of this threatening situation and of the talks and discussions which were taking place in Ghana and Addis Ababa. The talks came to nothing and war finally broke out in 1967. Nigeria closed its ports and we began to have the feeling of being hemmed in. Stories of trouble from other parts began to reach us. Bishop Moynagh and some Irish priests were having a hard time in Calabar city as they were being accused of being mercenaries. Food commodities were beginning to get very scarce as nothing could get through the ports. There was a dire shortage of salt. Then, part of a new road between Owerri and Onitsha was turned into an airstrip by the Biafrans so that relief planes carrying salt, stockfish and powdered milk could land. The relief effort was organized by the Catholic Church, Caritas, the Holy Ghost Fathers and others.

"When Port Harcourt, Biafra's main port was taken by the Federal Government forces in April 1968, masses of refugees were on the move. We ourselves had about 3,000 in our secondary school dorms. There were places which were far worse off and which had bigger numbers. People were beginning to die of starvation. We managed to keep the death rate at our place to a minimum as we were able to get provisions from the relief effort. We frequently went to the airstrip with a big tipper and filled up. You had to be careful to protect your load from the looters in the many hungry villages you had to pass on your return journey. Times were quite desperate and everywhere there were starving people on the verge of death.

"By the time the Nigerian troops arrived at our compound, the Biafrans had retreated and our refugees, having somehow got news of the approaching soldiers took flight into the bush the night before. Our compound including the priest's house was taken over and we were ordered to evacuate. I moved to Abakaliki and travelled back and forth to my parish. The officers occupying my home felt a bit guilty and every now and then they invited me to eat with them jokingly saying that they would have to take care of the reverend father. When the war finally ended in January 1970, we were able to return to the house and reopen the school. There was a huge job of refurbishment to be done as the soldiers had stripped down anything they could burn for fuel to cook with. All the walls were black and every window was smashed. It took two years to rehabilitate the place.

"When that was all done, I was moved to the Diocese of Port Harcourt where there was an acute shortage of priests. The Holy Ghost Fathers who had been there in big numbers prior to the war were forced to leave in its aftermath as they were perceived to have identified with the Biafrans. I was sent along with another priest to

St. Peter's Parish, Ahoada, thirty miles outside Port Harcourt. You got there by driving on a disastrous road for four hours. We were also caring for nearby Imiringi, a place that had hardly any roads. We got around by boats, few of which had outboard engines. You depended a lot on the big market boats which chugged along to the different markets in the villages along the creeks and coastline. It was a very beautiful place and since I was never a city man, I took to all this rural and seaside life very easily.

"We went to Port Harcourt regularly to recreate – to play golf, bridge and to eat at the Presidential Hotel which had very reasonable prices in those days. There were quite a number of parish houses to visit and we did enjoy a pleasant camaraderie. We managed to keep fairly healthy but we had more illness than we needed to have. Looking after ourselves was not a priority. When I was in Imiringi, I did have a mosquito net but it was full of holes which were patched up with sticking tape. We had very little funding. In those days, you were sent out and expected to manage on your wits. It was only in the 1980's that your regional superior felt it his job to ask if you had enough money for essentials. We didn't even know how to get the best out of the food available as we had very little knowledge of nutrition.

"In 1982, I moved into Ogoni Land to a place called Bodo. I was asked to go there for a period of six months to act as mentor to two young Kiltegan priests. Shortly after my arrival, the parish priest got sick and had to go home so I ended up taking his place for quite a long stint. By 1985, I was back in Imiringi – by then in Bayelsa State. There, the State government decided to put in a gas turbine to deal with two big gas flares which were burning away. Rolls Royce was contracted to do the work. They set up their headquarters just a hundred metres from my house. I got to know the workers who were mostly English but one, Fred Doyle, had Longford origins. He painted my house and wired it up for twenty-four hour a day electricity – an almost unheard of utility even today in Nigeria! My successor, Paul Hardy is there now with the same facilities, plus the convenience of a speed boat and something I could never manage to control myself – a Honda 50 motor bike. He's just two years younger than me but he is tough, skinny and seems to be made of wire and rubber.

"From Imiringi, I moved to Burutu, a coastal town on the coast in Delta State. It's about forty-five minutes by speed-boat from the big oil capital of Warri and very near Ogulagha, the biggest oil terminal in West Africa. Down there, it was all creeks and rivers and boats. I liked the boat as a mode of transport because it meant that you didn't have to worry about flooded roads during the wet season. Keeping it maintained though was a problem and a costly one. We tended to carry heavier loads than the engine was designed to take so that didn't help matters. You couldn't avoid it really as you were always being asked to bring people to maternity clinics and to help out in all sorts of emergencies.

"Burutu in the flood season was almost floating in fresh water. In the dry season, you were surrounded by salt water and you could buy saltwater fish at your doorstep in the early morning or late in the evening. The people constantly complained about the scarcity of the fish. Oil exploration and spillages were blamed. For this, your sympathies were very much with them because for generations, they have depended on fish. My own opinion is that government should open up the area by building two big roads like the Americans did in the Everglades in Florida. People could then travel in and out. As it is, you cannot get teachers or doctors to go down there. They won't build the roads because of the costs involved. They would not be building on dry land so a series of pylons across creeks would be necessary. Many kinds of different organizations go into the area to give help but much of what is done is not maintained and all sorts of wasteful activities take place. If the roads were there to facilitate a free flow of people, goods and services, the place could be developed more easily. Up to now, if you are there and if you get sick, there is no medical treatment – no hospital. Your best bet would be to contact the much sought after Daughters of Charity who are engaged in medical work in the area.

"Amukoko where I am now is a far cry from those rural regions. Here we are in an extremely overcrowded and unhealthy environment. There is no running water and no real sewage. Some local entrepreneurs have sunk bore holes at the side of the streets and make a business out of selling water. There is no provision for getting rid of the waste so it is piled up along the streets or dumped into the canal. *Canal* is a misleading word because it is really one of the many inland waterways which you have in Lagos. These get clogged up every year during the rainy season and cause serious flooding. I was visiting one poor woman recently – about ten days after the rains. She was trying to get back into her one-room home. The smell of dampness was awful. The waters had risen up as far as the mattress of her bed. You couldn't clean out the place because of all the trumpery she had. There was just enough space to sit down and to make way to a bed. She is not well enough to come to church so we visit her. The people in Amukoko suffer terribly from flooding and many other deprivations so people living here get out if they can find any means of doing so.

"A few weeks ago, a building collapsed and about sixteen people died. The Governor arrived and said he would have the landlord arrested. He also identified other unsafe buildings and ordered that they be evacuated and knocked down. He never mentioned help – where the people might move to – nothing!

"My own health is holding up but I still get pains from time to time and it's important to do the prescribed exercises. Right now I'm looking forward to my holiday in Ireland. I'll spend a month in Kiltegan meeting people and walking the Wicklow hills. Then I will do four mini workshops related to my work here."

Fr. P.J. Sexton, former parish priest of St. Matthew's parish, Amukoko enjoys Galilee Day with parishioners (photo: Eugene Bree)

Father Billy Greene

St. Patrick's Society (SPS)
Minna, Niger State

Fr. Billy Greene, SPS

"The concept of evil spirits and their part in suffering is very strong around here. The explanation as to why a person is sick might be found in the thinking that somebody is wishing you ill. Alongside all of that, you have a people who are truly generous and who have a great wish to come to God. They are very open about their difficulties when they come to you. A woman might bring a friend to help her discuss a problem. The men come on their own and they open up much more than the average Irishman. A major problem for the men can concern *the wife. She won't obey me Father* would be a common complaint. Of course, there are different types of women. Some like to challenge and oppose the man; others are placid, passive and gentle. Men are slowly but reluctantly becoming aware of the concept that a woman is his equal. I always mention this fact at weddings but many don't want to believe it. Even the educated man can find the concept hard to accept."

Sixty-year-old Father Billy Greene is talking to me in the sitting room of the parochial house in St. Joseph's Parish on the outskirts of Minna. He is the parish priest. He is also Vicar General at the Diocesan Secretariat. This position he doesn't want to talk about. "It just happens that I am able to give some help to the Bishop. I don't want to make a big thing out of it. I'm behind the scenes when it comes to all of that. I'll be happy to hand the duties over to a local man when one becomes available." Father Billy has been in the Minna area for twenty years. Prior to that, he was further north in Zuru in the Sokoto area. He first came to Nigeria in 1969.

"I was born in Kingswell (Tobar an Rí) in County Tipperary. King Brian Boru is supposed to have washed his wounds in a well in a place nearby. I have one brother and one sister. My mother was killed in a car crash when I was a seminarian. My father coped quite well. He was a man who had an old-style faith. We had a small farm and if the hay was down and the weather bad, he'd say, 'we will get a fine day yet, please God.' That was his attitude. I had the idea of becoming a priest when I was growing up but coming to a decision about it when the time came was not easy. I had a girl friend and I liked the home life. My uncle was a champion waltzer and I was able to dance and waltz from a young age. In those days, that meant being able to get around to dances to enjoy yourself! We used to get the mission magazines in school and the images of Calabar and palm trees created some kind of idyllic desire. Of course, at the time, I believed in the doctrine that proclaimed that there was no salvation if you were outside the Church, so there was the noble idea of evangelization and bringing people to God. It was never an easy doctrine to accept. I remember a Protestant girl from home doing her exams in front of me. She was the loveliest of girls and I could not imagine her not getting into heaven. In 1949, that teaching was actually condemned as false doctrine by Rome but somehow the news didn't filter into all parts of the Irish Church. I was brought up with that belief but when I came out here, I never for a moment thought in that way. I believe that any person who has love, truth, justice and forgiveness in his life is going to heaven. I have no problem with all of that but it's a problem sometimes trying to explain the demands the Catholic Church makes on people. A Catholic man can ask you why the man with five wives can get into the same heaven that he is hoping to get into. My explanation is that people have to live according to their lights. The explanation is simpler if the Catholic has gone through the different stages of commitment as a catechumen. He or she will then have understood what they have to commit to if they want to be baptized. If they feel they cannot commit, they know that nobody is going to force it down their throats.

"All of us missionaries here are trying to plant the local Church among the people. We are helping it to grow and develop so that it will survive when we leave. We are trying to let Gospel values seep through the people's own culture. We must not forget that the ground we walk on was holy ground long before we ever came and the people have worshiped here for thousands of years. What we are doing is offering them the chance to know, love and serve Jesus Christ. We do not baptize them if they do not have the knowledge of Jesus Christ and if they are not prepared to live in a Christian way. Sometimes you get people who become Christian wanting to cling to some aspects of the traditional religion. I remember baptizing a guy one day and he brought in a cowrie to protect him from *the evil one*. He felt that he needed to keep a foot in both camps!

"I have my priorities when it comes to planting the local Church. I think it is important for the people to have their church – their house of prayer. Praying is part of their pagan culture. Gods were prayed to when the rains didn't come or when the crops failed. When a child was ill, sacrifice was made to the crocodile god. I believe that it is important for the priest to help the people to pray – to be with them when they do so in their own way – to be patient and to help them to bind their prayer around the Eucharist which is at the heart of it all. I think that it is also good if the priest can give a well-prepared homily every day during mass. This is a privileged moment. It can be demanding for the priest of course. I myself am not able to travel very much on account of back problems so I put my energy into creating a homily a day which would relate to people's lives. I have found that the people like this very much.

"They also like the *Stations of the Cross* in a big way. They are able to identify with the sufferings of Christ. Most of their own suffering comes from poverty. I saw figures recently which said that 60% of Nigerians were now living below the poverty level as compared to 40% twenty years ago. Huge cultural upheavals can be brought about by a bad economic situation in survival-level families. If the father has no work, the mother may have to be out of the home for long hours trying to bring in some income. This situation can cause family life to go quickly downhill as all the mother is fit to do when she finally gets home is put some kind of food on the table.

"When I was in Zuru during my early years in Nigeria, the people there were very poor but also very gentle. The diet was mainly guinea corn. If the crops failed, there was great hardship. In that area, if a husband wasn't able to pay the bride price, he had to work for his father-in-law for seven years. Despite the seemingly harsh side of this tradition, it provided the positive of binding two people together in a marriage. Seven years is a long time to work for something, so jettisoning it after all of that was not likely to become an easy option.

"This country has an enormous population so there's a great struggle to get out from under the poverty and to progress or make it in some way. How you make it does not always seem important, unfortunately. You cannot blame a poor man for wanting to get out of poverty because everything he does will be tied up in that poverty. If he has no income, he will not be able to have a nice wife, a nice home, a nice family and he will not be able to send his child to a good school. There is also the shame of being poor and the poor man really suffers when sickness comes. If he has any savings, they will vanish. If he has not, he will be lost.

"Many people here in Minna who have jobs with the Government don't always get their wages on time. They can be railway people, teachers, policemen or civil servants and they can quickly fall into poverty when the money is not paid. We have a little welfare society here in the Church and we have a very good St. Vincent de Paul Society. I have noticed that it is always the poor who run these societies. My security guard out there at the gate wouldn't earn very much money, yet he is actively involved in the welfare society. The people here can enrich your faith. My own faith has been greatly enriched and my whole notion of God is completely different to the one I brought out with me. For me now, it's God the merciful – God the compassionate. There was fear in my father's God. We have moved away from all of that.

"Sometimes the poor in this country perceive the Church to be connected to people with money and the Sunday masses are often seen as masses for people who have a goat or a cow to present at the *offertory*. The people will tell you that it is part of their culture to share their riches with the Church and they can be tremendously generous in this respect. They want to give God His share. That attitude was never in Ireland to any great extent.

"The negative side of this is that the poor man feels bad if he has only two eggs to offer. A priest I know had nobody to bring up the gifts at a Sunday mass recently. He asked a certain member of the parish if he would bring them up. His answer was 'Father, I am a poor man. How can I bring up the gifts?' We stopped having bazaars and harvests in Our Lady's Parish in another part of Minna when I was there because I felt that they were a display of wealth which made the poor man feel out of it. In Church laity groups, the poor man tends to have no position unless you make a point of bringing him up-front the whole time. It's what we do and I do it in this parish but sometimes I feel like the lone soldier. If we lose the poor, we lose the Church.

"Laity groups in the Nigerian Church are wonderful and in many ways the Church could not survive without them. They play a tremendous role but they can sometimes be aggressive and forceful. The priest is the leader of course but it is not unusual for laity groups to try to lead the whole way and never give the priest a chance. We had a very young curate here for a while and after six months he was made parish priest in another parish. He was younger than all the parish laity leaders and they were always telling him what he could and could not do. It became very difficult for him. At parish meetings, you might have your position on an issue but you might be told that another position is preferable. A vote might then be taken that could out-vote you. In our situation here, we have a veto but mostly we do not have many problems and I have to say that the laity in general makes good decisions, especially if you are there with them at all the meetings.

"One thing that the Catholic Church is not strong enough on here in Nigeria is the *sacrament of the sick*. It used to be called *extreme unction*. I feel a little sad about that as it is a great sacrament and we have kind of let it go. You don't get too many sick calls unless you encourage them. Perhaps people feel that they will have to make an offering or give you something. Many have nothing to give. Whenever I go on a sick call, I never accept anything. I might take a coke or a sprite. In the old days, the priest was always given a chicken or something. In Ireland, the priest and the doctor are still called but out here, it doesn't happen very much.

"Looking back on my life – how do I feel? I wouldn't like to have had it any other way. Mission life though is always a struggle. It's not a life of driving around in a *504*. You have to struggle the way anyone else has to struggle. I plan to continue doing what I am doing as long as my health holds up. I have major problems with my back and to date I have had about nine operations. Lots of medical mistakes were made and a right mess was the result of them all. One of the many things that I really love about Nigeria is the interest people have in God, in the Church and in prayer. It all comes from their traditional religion. As I said earlier, the ground on which we are walking was holy ground long before we came."

The Benedictines

Order of St. Benedict (OSB)

An Introduction

St. Benedict lived at the end of the fifth century when the idea of a religious order had not yet been conceived. Although he organised a number of 'houses of God' where people could live the Gospel life according to a monastic wisdom, already popular in the East, he was not conscious of having founded an order.

This same informality continues to this day in Benedictine monasteries worldwide. The Benedictines are not an order in the sense of a strongly centralised organisation.

There are approximately 8,000 Benedictine monks and 16,000 nuns or sisters spread widely in Benedictine monasteries on all continents. They are mostly grouped in loose congregations or federations – 21 for men and 61 for women. Each of the groups has its own history and traditions.

Benedictines are not essentially identified with any specific apostolate, unless it be the over-riding principle that Benedict took from Scripture and enshrined in his Rule, "that in all things God may be glorified" (1 Pe 4:11).

If men and women today are still turning to communities where peace, work and prayer are the familiar watchwords, it is surely not in search of sophisticated ideas or esoteric wisdom. They are attracted by the simple art of spiritual living.

The Benedictine Monks

Ewu-Ishan, Benin State

The Benedictine community at Ewu-Ishan
Fr. Andrew Nugent, sixth from left, second row

When in the early 1970's, Bishop Godfrey Okoye, CSSp. of Enugu heard that the Benedictine monks at Glenstal Abbey were interested in making a foundation in Africa, he travelled to Ireland to persuade them to do so in his diocese. By Christmas 1974, Frs. Columba Breen and Ambrose Tinsley of Glenstal and Fr. Columba Cary-Elwes of Ampleforth Abbey in England had established themselves in Eke in the Enugu Diocese in a large colonial style house built by Bishop Broderick, SMA in 1940 as a rest home for missionaries. There were difficulties however. The land assigned to the monastery – though extensive, was sandy and largely infertile and would not be able to support a sizeable community. By November 1977, the community had decided to investigate the possibility of moving elsewhere. Several invitations from bishops and traditional rulers all over the country were received and many sites were visited. Eventually with the invaluable help of Fr. Dick Wall, SMA who knew the territory west of the Niger very well, a suitable place was found at Ewu-Ishan, 100km. north of Benin City in the diocese of the same name.

I paid a memorable visit to this oasis of peace during my stay in Nigeria. The monastery is situated in Ishan territory, part of a buffer zone of small tribes between the great ethnic groups of Igbo to the east, Yoruba to the west and Hausa to the north. Here Christianity, Islam and traditional African religion are almost equally balanced. There is cultural richness and this is reflected in the Benedictine community itself whose members represent a great many different ethnic groups.

Monastic life began at St. Benedict's Priory in Ewu with the singing of the *Salve Regina* at midnight on the feast of St. Benedict, July 11, 1979. The community then consisted of Fr. Prior Columba Breen, Frs. Ambrose Tinsley and David Conlon, Brother Colman Hingerty, Fr. Andrew Nugent and two Nigerian novices. One of these novices was Vincent Mordi, a young Igbo chemistry graduate who, having survived the horrors of the Biafran War, decided to give his life to God. Ordained to the priesthood in 1985, Fr. Vincent has been Prior of St. Benedict's since Easter 1996.

Before the arrival of the community at Ewu, Fr. David had spent months, with the help of local labour putting up essential buildings and providing rudimentary services. Much development has since taken place and in addition to many fine buildings – some of which were designed in African idiom by celebrated Nigerian architect, Demas Nwoko, there are many workshops, a large poultry unit, a palm oil factory and an excellent herbal medicine clinic and factory which is run by Fr. Anselm Adodo. Recently a state-of-the-art pharmacy has been added to the clinic. Several of the monks and up to twenty local people work at the clinic where they attend to the scores of patients who come daily, and produce medicines, herbal teas, soap and ointments which are marketed in several major cities throughout Nigeria.

The community provides its own requirements in fruit, vegetables, poultry, brown bread and eggs and these products are also marketed to outsiders who particularly appreciate the brown bread made to the recipe of the Medical Missionaries of Mary. Candles, honey and art works are also made at the monastery and sold.

From the beginning pastoral work has been an important part of the community's activity. As well as helping in neighbouring parishes and serving as chaplains in the nearby Auchi polytech, the monastery serves four major sectors in its local parish. Six members of the community have now been ordained to the priesthood and many others have completed third level studies in various places.

The traditional monastic apostolate of hospitality has also been of major importance from the very outset, and the completion of its new guest house will now accommodate the great numbers of people who come to the monastery from every walk of life in search of inspiration, peace and hope. The Glenstal monks who laid the foundations of this admirable work which continues to grow and develop are now either gone to their reward or have returned to Ireland.

The day my husband and I visited Ewe, we were warmly welcomed by the quiet spoken and dignified Prior Vincent. We were fortunate also to meet Abbot Augustine O'Sullivan who on his retirement as Abbot of Glenstal served as superior in Ewu from 1981 to 1996. He then remained on in the community and was in the words of Fr. Andrew Nugent: "a living sign of God's gentleness and love until his death in December 1999." He is buried in Ewu. So too is Fr. Kevin Healy who died four months earlier at the height of his powers. Again in the words of Fr. Andrew: "He served from 1992 to 1999 as bursar, chanter, and prime inspiration of the rich liturgical life of Ewu." Indeed, it was Fr. Kevin who personally made the wonderful pot of Irish tea which we were so badly in need of on our arrival at Ewu after our long journey from Lagos. Their two graves rest under the palm trees at Ewu and are venerated as holy ground and a sacred guarantee that the monks have come to stay.

If the Glenstal community's commitment to the African project was initially tenuous, the two communities have grown together over the years. Since mid-2000, there has been no permanent Glenstal presence in Ewu. This is simply because Glenstal's task is largely done. Its contribution now is to stand back and let the Ewu community take responsibility for itself. It is, however, the hope that the two communities, now so inextricably linked in apostolate, personal friendships and shared history will continue to love and support each other for all time.

Father Andrew Nugent, now prior at Glenstal Abbey spent more than ten years in the Nigerian monastery – in the role of novice master and prefect of studies for young Nigerian monks. He also engaged in pastoral and development work. A former lawyer, he became a Benedictine monk in 1961 and has worked mostly in Glenstal Abbey School as teacher, housemaster and headmaster. His many published writings have appeared in specialist reviews in Ireland, England and the United States. In summer 2005, he published his first book of fiction and is currently finishing a second. Having read his sensitive and beautiful feature on African spirituality and the spirituality of the African child in particular, I asked permission to include it in this book: it was graciously granted.

The Little Black Girl (or) Boy in search of God

(Text from 'Slow Release Miracle' published by Paulist Press, 2006. Text first published in 'Spirituality', Dominican Publications September/October 1997)

African children have beautiful teeth. Everybody knows that. Teeth dazzling, in perfect alignment; and they are strong. Your host's son may set *your* teeth on edge by opening beer bottles with *his*. These children smile a lot. It seems reasonable to suppose some correlation between smiles, nice teeth and psychological and even spiritual well being.

Spiritual? Yes I think so. We accept the psychosomatic, the interaction of mind and body. Why not the pneumasomatic* as well, the epiphany of the spirit in the forms and language of the body? Was it not Jung who said that by age forty, every man has the face he deserves?

So why do African children have beautiful teeth? There are no doubt genetic reasons but diet too is a principal factor. No sugar, no additives, no hormones or cowboy chemicals, no junk food to poison the system and rot the teeth. Besides, these children rarely eat between meals and, though adequately nourished, do not often eat to their hunger. Fasting, in the sense of eating no more than one needs, is the everyday experience of almost any African child. This, as ascetics of all traditions have forever known, is good for the body, good for the mind and the spirit and good too, for the teeth.

We should remember too that the great majority of African teenagers do not smoke, drink alcohol or take drugs. Quite simply, they are unpolluted. The comprehensive freedom from toxicity, with the self-discipline and temperance it implies, goes deeper than the purely physical. The smiling face and flashing teeth attest to an inner freedom and a self-respect that many youngsters in the Western world have lost or never had.

It's not just teeth of course; it is a whole way of inhabiting the body, a poetry of poise of movement, a rhythm of dancers, drummers, and effortless carriers of everything on the head. A veteran Olympic medallist raised protest for suggesting that young blacks are more gifted naturally for athletics than others. Some said that this is racism, and racism going in an unfamiliar direction too. Well, just watch African children at play, skimming the earth, shimmering through the air, like silver porpoises in and over the water. No equipment, no coach, no commercialism, no fulsome praise for the clever little darlings. It is all pure fun and second nature. That too gives glory to God, and is very good for the soul.

Liturgy is by its very nature pneumasomatic. The spirit dances, sings, welcomes, processes, proclaims, offers, receives, rejoices and mourns. That is the theory. In Africa, it is the reality, as it can be only where people rejoice with Christ to say, 'You gave me a body….Here I am!' (Heb 10:5). It is sad to be in churches where there are too few bodies, with nobody appearing to be very happy inside the ones there are.

Dress, too, for the liturgy of life. In conditions where water is scarce, where climate, housing and insects go hard on fabrics, how do people manage to be always immaculate? Their clothes are home-made or the work of village tailors. A kaleidoscope of colour, which never seems to clash, worn with hieratic elegance. Besides, these are

217

real clothes which express the personalities of their wearers, not the anonymous gear which seems to have invaded the rest of the planet.

I know an out-station of a small country parish in Nigeria where the people are determined to provide six sets of Mass servers' outfits, each with five cassocks, and one in each of the liturgical colours. A total of thirty garments. It is crazy of course and the people can ill-afford it. But that is what Judas said about the lady in the gospel with the jar of ointment. In Africa, clothes are sacramental, and there are priorities.

Strong bonds of family affection and the still close ties of village society make for children who are open and self-confident. At the same time, there is a strong sense of hierarchy. Children, teenagers even adults show marked respect for parents, elders and traditional rulers. The respect manifests itself in speech but also in an expressive and captivating body language. Girls curtsy gracefully; boys make solemn bows of head and shoulders. In some tribes, these reverences come nearer to genuflexion and prostration. One is never casual. In giving or receiving even a nondescript gift like a biro, a young person will hold out both hands in an almost liturgical gesture. To accept a gift, a boy may drop down on one knee, like a knight to his dubbing. Even more alarming is the unsolicited valeting service. At any point in conversation, an ebony hand may dart out to pick insects, vegetation or debris off one's face, hair or clothes. No commentary or explanations. These civilities are all rendered spontaneously, without the smallest trace of servility or awkwardness. 'Manners maketh the man,' and 'Grace builds on nature' – two clichés, of course. They both happen to be true.

In African society, overt flirtation between boys and girls is strictly taboo. It is perfectly normal however, to see teenage boys or young men holding hands. Any suggestion that this could have sexual overtones would be received with open-mouthed astonishment. Young Africans are generally disgusted by the sexual crassness of much Western cinema and publishing.

There is a common myth in the West that blacks are highly sexed. They are hardly deficient in that regard, but the catastrophic incidence of Aids and venereal diseases in some areas can be attributed to many factors besides depravity and promiscuity.

Whatever their sexual exploits, African boys and girls are mostly notably different from many Western contemporaries in their unshaken belief in the family, their hope to marry some day and their ardent desire to be blessed with children. These values do seem threatened in the Northern hemisphere where young people grow more and more preoccupied with their individual fulfilment, not to say gratification, so that whole nations are rapidly becoming vast fortified colonies of the elderly. Perhaps the most fundamental question about any culture or any spirituality is, what do people hope for?

Another important difference is that when young African feels guilty, they are disposed to believe that they have done something wrong. It would not be correct to attribute this attitude to a puritanical Christianity which one might say, has contaminated the joyful springs of native African spontaneity, especially in the area of sexuality. The myth of the 'noble savage' and of the good times he had dies hard. Traditional society as also the influential Islamic culture, are in fact rigorous in most areas of morality and indeed disapprove of churches which they perceive as dispensing facile forgiveness for serious infringements.

Transcending all purely moral questions is the massive reality of African spirituality. Christian, Moslem, traditional believers, all live in the presence of a 'cloud of witnesses,' ancestors, good and evil spirits, God himself. There is fear and superstition certainly, but also a deep core of trust and hope. In the context of religious conversion or to follow a vocation, young people will accept great hardship and will not be deterred by intimidating and even violent opposition. They believe, they care and they go for it.

In too many African countries, corruption and malpractice of every kind have reached such proportions that it is no longer a question of cheating the system; cheating is the system. Children will have learnt that bitter lesson long before leaving school. It is hateful to see them sucked inexorably into this soul-destroying miasma. And yet, Africa is not just a bubbling cauldron of bribery and corruption, nor yet neither one vast refugee camp, nor a continent inhabited by skeletons and begging bowls. Africa is rich in things that matter. Not least of these is a vibrant and youthful spirituality.

The Medical Missionaries of Mary
(MMM)

An Introduction

The congregation of the Medical Missionaries of Mary is composed of over 400 women from 17 nationalities who are committed to providing medical services and a service of healing to people in areas of great need in many countries around the world.

It was founded in Ireland by Mother Mary Martin, a Dubliner, more than seventy years ago. The first formal steps towards its establishment took place in March 1934 when Marie Martin and her companions arrived at the Benedictine Monastery, Glenstal, Co. Limerick. In return for the group's assistance with the domestic arrangements of the monastery and boys' boarding school, the monastery provided the spiritual formation for the future missionary congregation.

The MMM have been in Nigeria for more than 66 years. Today they are involved in health care at 12 different locations in 6 States and in the capital city, Abuja.

They have a multicultural novitiate in Ibadan in Oyo State and nowadays many professed Nigerian MMM sisters work in Nigeria, in other African countries and in many other parts of the world.

Sister (Doctor) Leonie McSweeney

Medical Missionaries of Mary (MMM)
Ibadan

Sr. (Doctor) Leonie McSweeney, MMM,
at the Irish Embassy Residence in Abuja

"When I joined the MMM, I told our foundress, Mother Mary Martin, that I'd be interested in becoming a nurse. When she asked if I would like to be a doctor, I opened my mouth in amazement but received her suggestion with joy. I didn't know that she had been checking my school reports at the Holy Faith Convent in Haddington Road, Dublin. After my pre med. examination, I went to the congregation and told them that they were wasting their money, that I found medicine too difficult. I was encouraged to persist and at the age of twenty-six, I graduated with an M.B. Shortly afterwards I was sent to Nigeria."

Seventy-one-year-old Dr. Leonie McSweeney had spent forty-four years in Nigeria when she spoke to me during one of her many visits to Abuja. She was born in Dublin in 1932 and grew up on the South Circular Road. Her devotion to her medical work in Nigeria, a country she now refers to as *our country*, has been selfless and prodigious. For nearly thirty years, she has been in the forefront of promoting natural family planning. Her organization *Pro-Family Life Association of Nigeria (PLAN)* which is based in Ibadan has, in recent years incorporated a HIV/AIDS prevention programme which she calls *The True Love Wins Campaign.*

Her first post in Nigeria was in Urua Akpan in the south east where the MMM had a hospital. She recalls her early days as a young doctor as being very nervous. "The doctor I started working with became ill a few weeks after my arrival so I was left alone to cope. I remember how I trembled during the night when I heard the nurses' footsteps coming to get me. Very soon, another MMM doctor came to replace the sick one. She was a fantastic teacher who gave me confidence and got me on my feet. Unfortunately, she also became ill and suffered from a lot of malaria so it was not long before I was more or less on my own again. There were no consultants so you had to accept the fact that you were probably the best within hundreds of miles. You had to take your courage in your hands and get on with the job. I remember doing VVF surgery (Visceral Vagina Fistula) with a book on the operating table to guide me. We had only done the smallest bit of surgery during our training so I had to rely on it, the book and whatever the senior doctor had taught me. My training in obstetrics also came from doing the work in the field. When I came home in the late 1960's to do my MRCOG (Master of Obstetrics and Gynaecology), I was not given enough time to finish the course as I was invited back to Nigeria by the Federal Government to help with the war effort on the Federal side. Previously I had been working within Biafra. This time, I found myself working alongside a wonderful Nigerian doctor called Major Albert Ekup. His first child is now an MMM doctor in our hospital in Abakaliki in Ebonyi State.

"When the war ended in 1970, I was transferred to our hospital in Eleta in Ibadan. The staff situation in the hospital at the time became critical and after nine months, I found myself as doctor in charge with yet again an excellent Nigerian doctor at my side. By the end of 1970, a raging cholera epidemic which originated in East Africa, swept through Ibadan. Our hospital became the main cholera hospital and we were obliged to close to all other services. Over a three-week period, we had more than four thousand patients. The whole experience turned out to be the most wonderful example of co-operation between nurses, priests, reverend sisters, Protestant leaders and seminarians from the local major Catholic seminary in Ibadan. I remember Sr. Dymphna Drury of the Sisters of St. Louis in Ibadan being one of the first to offer help from the outside. Initially the Nigerian nurses left the hospital refusing to work as they were afraid of bringing cholera home to their families. Eventually they returned bringing with them many lay helpers.

"We developed a strict routine and people worked in shifts. We had maypoles for hanging drips. A huge effort had to be made to get people better quickly in order to free the beds for the new patients arriving. As soon as they began to pass urine and stopped vomiting, they were on to stage two which had them sitting around taking marmite from a sister who went around with a big bucket of it. They were also given lots of oranges. On the following morning, I came to give instructions about the third stage of recovery which would take place in their own homes. Like the pied piper, they followed me out to the gate where we said our goodbyes. Many did not want to leave but anyone who got a relapse was told to return. Very few did. We estimated that the death rate after the whole epidemic had passed was less than 1 per cent. The people in the market in Ibadan claimed that the Catholic Church and Eleta Hospital saved Ibadan.

"Not long after all of this was over, I had a very bad car accident. I had been very tired and I had driven out to a quiet place in the country in search of a little peace. I cannot remember what happened but somebody found my car and reported that the doctor from Eleta was in it and appeared to be unconscious. I remained unconscious for three weeks and then I woke up speaking gibberish. One marvellous neurosurgeon came to visit me every day from the University College Teaching Hospital in Ibadan. He later died himself of a brain tumour. The accident affected my memory and I am still a little scattered about events immediately before and after it. Otherwise, I am quite good.

"One of the areas I have always been concerned about is how to help my people with family planning. In 1973, when I was working in a small one-doctor hospital in Ondo, I came across the Billings Method (BM) of family planning when I read a book written by Australians, Dr. John Billings and his wife Dr. Lynn Billings. In fact, 2003 was the fiftieth anniversary of the start of the research into the BM and there was a big conference in Australia, which I attended, to celebrate the event.

"It all started when a friend of Dr. Billings came to him requesting a method of family planning that worked. The friend had been put in charge of marriage counselling by the Archbishop of Melbourne. Dr. Billings who was a very busy neurosurgeon said that he would devote three months to the quest. He went to the university libraries and searched all the literature for the previous hundred years for references to signs of fertility in women. He came up with the information that there was such a thing as the mucus sign. A woman can use that sign to achieve and avoid pregnancy because it identifies the time of ovulation. Once that time can be identified and its significance understood, a woman will know how to control her fertility. Dr. Billings proved his theory by working with a number of women and scientists in Melbourne.

"It is a natural family planning method. It is not the safe period method or the rhythm method. It does not make use of a thermometer or a calendar. Neither does it involve the use of a pill, coil, condom or withdrawal. A recent WHO report stated that the BM is unsuitable for only one woman in every three hundred and it also noted that 95% of women can recognize the mucus sign after one cycle. There is no method of family planning with 100% success. With BM, if adequate instruction is received and rules properly followed, the success rate is between 98.5% and 99% – about the same success rate as the pill when *it* is used properly.

"I began to teach this method in a few towns around Ondo after practising it on my own body for about a year. The Bishop of Ondo, Bishop Field, SMA, heard about what I was doing and asked if I would speak to the Bishops' Conference. I spoke to them for about an hour on the subject. With great foresight, these Bishops of Nigeria asked me to try to get myself relieved from my hospital duties so that I could go all over the country to teach BM.

"I started to travel around to the different dioceses within the States. Only once (and our country is not so good for time keeping and our roads are often dangerous) did I fail to turn up on time and when I did arrive, the people were still there. From the beginning I made a strict rule that I would never teach classes of men only or women only. I deliberately used English as everybody I taught was a potential teacher and I wanted them to do a big exam at the end of the course. One fifth of the numbers who persevered got their exams and they went on to teach in the villages in the vernacular. We called ourselves *The Pro-Family Life Association of Nigeria (PLAN)*. I went to every State in the country and I appointed leaders and instructors. Today there are some brilliant people whom I trained in those early years who continue to be instructors. Before a man could become one, he had to teach his wife the method. Since my classes were arranged by the dioceses, most of the participants initially were Catholic. Gradually as the word got around about the content, I found that there were many people from other religions attending. I never experienced any squeamishness or embarrassment simply because the use of correct language and terminology dispels all of that.

"The whole exercise did wonders for marital relations because BM will not work if there is not a good marital relationship. Initially I used to leave the class I gave on sexual harmony between husband and wife until the end of the course because I suppose I didn't want to be getting into the whole subject of sexual orgasm until I knew my students. Then one evening after a class in Awka near Onitsha, when I asked for comments, many people requested that I give that class early in the course so that they could start putting it into practice. Another evening, a man stood up and said, 'Dr. McSweeney, I wish I knew all this thirty years ago.' There was always affirmation and good feedback. I remember two ladies in Calabar coming to me to tell me that they had experienced orgasm for the first time in their lives after following my guidelines. Another man who recognized me from the television series which I did came to me to tell me that I was transforming the lives of millions of men and women all over Nigeria. Only the other evening, in the John Paul II Centre here in Abuja, a woman in the restaurant who wanted to know if I was who she thought I was, told me that she hoped I realized how much I meant to the men and women in Nigeria.

"I have had so many joyous experiences in all parts of the country. Once I was on my way to Port Harcourt and my driver and I pulled into the side of the road in a nice rural area to have our coffee and sandwiches. A car suddenly stopped and the driver jumped out, came over to me and lifted me up in the air and said, 'thank you Dr. for my lovely baby boy.' He had learned from my television series how to achieve sex pre-selection. It's a special application of the BM and it is 96% successful for a boy and 90% for a girl. Initially Dr. Billings didn't encourage using it for a number of reasons but at a certain point, he announced publicly that he thought the time had come to use the knowledge God had given us especially as too many girl children were being killed in certain societies.

"In 1996, I began to introduce a HIV/AIDS prevention programme which I called *The True Love Wins Campaign.* It's a campaign to control the sexual spread of AIDS by group behaviour change programmes. The objective is to give people scientific, medical and social information combined with a deep spiritual input which will enable them to commit to pledging themselves to total abstinence from sex before marriage and absolute faithfulness within marriage. We have found that love is a far bigger inspiration than fear when it comes to achieving these goals.

"Many international experts now believe that the most effective way to control the spread of the disease is by group behaviour change. Uganda, which at one time had the highest occurrence of HIV/AIDS in the world, is the great proof of this belief. In 1999, the BBC reported that following a significant group behaviour change which was backed by the Government and which involved abstinence and fidelity, new infections in Uganda had dropped by 75%. Furthermore in 1991, people from many nations who met in Dakar, Senegal to explore the issues of behaviour change as a preventive strategy against the epidemic came out with a statement of belief which said behaviour change is the most powerful strategy in overcoming HIV/AIDS. The statement also expressed the strong conviction that individuals and whole communities had the inherent capacity to change attitudes and behaviour but that the power to fulfil that capacity is often denied by defeatism preached by others.

"Since 1996, we have been working with our campaign and we have a plan of action which has different stages. We use poster kits, companion books, videos and pledge forms. We are trying hard to change attitudes by dispelling myths. For those suffering, we console them with the words of Pope John Paul II which stated that people suffering are sharing in the redemptive work of Christ. Their lives are not useless as they are helping every human being. St. Paul also referred to 'completing the redemptive work of Christ.' In 2002, a Capuchin theologian delivered a remarkable and inspiring paper in Rome on the infinite value of suffering for all mankind.

"Fr. Michael Golden who worked in Nigeria until he got polio and became paralyzed now ministers to alcohol and drug addicts in Ireland. His understanding of suffering is that God is giving us an opportunity to share in his love through our suffering. He believes that suffering and love go hand in hand and that sharing another person's suffering is the essence of love.

"In many countries, there are myths which militate against fidelity in marriage. In parts of Nigeria, there is a widespread belief that sexual intercourse should not happen during breast-feeding. It is believed that semen can enter the breast milk and poison the baby. Another myth concerns sexual relations after menopause. Here it is believed that the absence of menstrual fluid to dispel the semen causes the growth of fibroids in the womb. In addition, there is the belief that sexual intercourse after the menopause is ungodly as the Bible states that reproduction is the only reason for sexual relations.

"Every mass I speak at now, I aim to dispel these beliefs. Traditionally during these periods in a marital relationship in parts of Nigeria, it was more or less accepted that the husband could have sexual relations with other women. This of course created the habit of infidelity and promiscuity which later was difficult to drop. Many fine men have come to me to say that they try to be good but that it is very hard to sustain abstinence during the pregnancy period and the long breast-feeding period which follows.

"I have found that the people are very open to accepting the knowledge that helps dispel old beliefs and myths. I once spoke to a group of wonderful chiefs who invited me, a white woman, to talk to them about the strongly held belief which exists in parts of the country concerning twins. It is believed that one is possessed by an evil spirit and since it is not possible to identify the possessed one, both have to be killed. Fortunately this belief is dying out.

"I feel a great gratitude to the people of Nigeria for the happiness I have enjoyed in their country. From my earliest days in medicine and surgery right up to the present time, I have felt their encouragement. They are a wonderfully tolerant people and their tolerance of white people and the mistakes we make is remarkable. I want to continue to work here for as long as my health permits. I have let it be known that I should be sent home if the time comes when I need care. I do not want to be a burden. Before that, I hope to have prepared somebody to step into my shoes."

The Late Sr. Regina Diamond

to whom this book is dedicated

The author and the late Sr. Regina Diamond in Ekpoma, Edo State

Capturing the Colour of Nigeria

A young woman from Benin delivering a speech at her school
on the occasion of the 8th Commemorative Birthday Observance
of Dr. Martin Luther King Junior

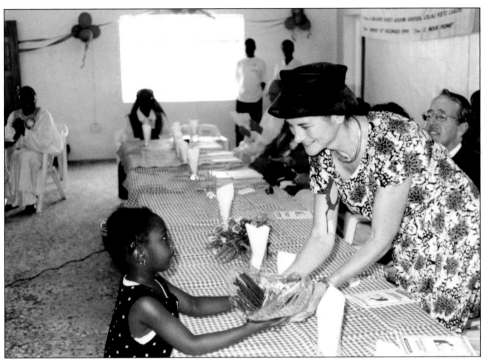

The author receiving flowers at the official opening of Ketu Cinic, Lagos
which was funded by Irish Aid

The author officially opening Mount Carmel School, Ekpoma, Edo State.
To the left is Archbishop Ekpu of Benin

L to R: The Onogi or King of Ekpoma; Irene Lynch; Bernadette Lawler;
Joseph Lynch, Irish Ambassador; Fr. Christopher Clarke; Fr. Chrisogenous Okorie.

Ambassador Joseph Lynch and Mrs Irene Lynch being received
by the Emir of Kano, Alhaji Bayero

A Carmelite Sister in Enugu dressed in her traditional Indian costume

*The author with Monsignor Pedro Martins, born 1910
- the first indigenous Catholic priest from Lagos*

*The late Father Slattery - an extraordinary missionary - who was conferred with the title of
Officer of the Order of the Niger by President Olusegun Obasanjo of Nigeria
- seen here with Fr. Fachtna O'Driscoll, Irish Provincial Superior of SMA (photo: sma)*

*L to R: Brian Kerr (manager); Fr. Frank Diamond, SMA; Robbie Keane;
Barry Quinn (captain) and Noel O'Reilly (assistant manager) after the
Ireland v Saudi Arabia game during the 10th FIFA World Youth
Championship in Ibadan, Western Nigeria, April 1999 (photo: sma)*

Fr. John O'Hea, SMA, at the Ireland v Saudi Arabia match in Ibadan (photo: sma)

At the bi-annual residence staff party at the Embassy of Ireland, Abuja: Nicaise Zoumatoum (cook) extreme left; Godwin Akpamekpa (steward and compound supervisor) extreme right; Luke Bala, head security guard making a speech of appreciation

L to R: Laoise Kelly; Sharon Shannon; Steve Cooney; Maighread Ní Dhomhnaill and Mícheál Ó Dómnaill performing at MUSON, Lagos at a concert sponsored and organized by the Embassy of Ireland, Nigeria in 2002

Fr. John Trout, St Patrick's Society and Ambassador Joseph Lynch
at the official opening of Ketu Clinic, Lagos

L. to R.: Fr. Christian Mai of the Diocese of Maiduguri; Fr. André Oliveira de Sanpaio,
Embassy of the Holy See, Abuja; Joseph Lynch, the Ambassador of Ireland; Irene Lynch;
Most Rev. Dr. John O. Onaiyekan, Archbishop of Abuja;
Fr. Raymond Hickey, OSA, Embassy of the Holy See, Abuja
following the inauguration of the first Nigerian Bishop to the Diocese of Maiduguri

239

Enugu children performing traditional dances

Cultural dancers from Nazareth School in Festac Town Lagos,
run by the Religious Sisters of Charity (photo from Sisters of Charity)

Archbishop of Abuja, Most Rev. Dr. O. Onaiyekan celebrating St. Patrick's Day
at the Irish Embassy Residence in Abuja with Ambassador Joseph Lynch and Mrs. Irene Lynch.
The Archbishop was educated by Irish missionaries.

Missionaries, the author and others enjoying St. Patrick's Day, 2000
at the Irish Embassy Residence, Lagos.
Third from left is Sr. Maureen Dowley of the Congregation of Jesus and Mary Akoka, Lagos.

Missionaries enoying Christmas dinner at the Irish Embassy Residence in Lagos,
December 2000. L to R: Fr. Christopher Clarke, Fr. John Trout, Fr. Noel O'Leary

Missionaries enoying Christmas dinner
at the Irish Embassy Residence in Lagos in December 2000.
Fr. Máirtín Conroy in red shirt with Sr. Maureen Dowley on his left.
Fr. Dan Murphy is in the background with check shirt.

Sr. Cecelia Azuh MMM, co-ordinator of the HIV/AIDS prevention programme for the Archdiocese of Abuja

Children from Onitsha, Anambra State

Some children at school at Holy Family parish, Abuja with teacher and author

Children playing in the grounds of Holy Trinity Cathedral in Onitsha

Traditional dancer, Kogi State

245

The Irish Ambassador, Joseph Lynch and Mrs. Irene Lynch being welcomed to St. Louis Secondary School, Kano by the then principal, Sr. Mary Connellan and students

A market scene in the outskirts of Abuja

Presenting a bouquet of flowers to the author after the opening of Mount Carmel Social Centre, Ekpoma, Edo State which received funding from Irish Aid

Children from Holy Family Parish School, Qwarimpa, Abuja

Father Con Cronin, Kiltegan Fathers (second from left), helping to load a pick-up truck in preparation for a trip to the local market in Kontagora, Niger State (photo from Africa magazine)

A school girl from Holy Family Parish School, Qwarimpa, Abuja

Sister Sally Davis

Medical Missionary of Mary (MMM)
Amukoko, Lagos

Sr. Sally Davis, MMM

Amukoko lies buried deep in one of the poorest and most densely populated areas of Lagos. There you will find the primary health care clinic which is run by the calm and conscientious Sr. Sally Davis and her team. The clinic is located within the compound of St. Matthew's Catholic parish church which is something of an oasis in an area hugely overcrowded and rife with disease, stemming from that overcrowding. In Amukoko and in the adjoining neighbourhood of Ajeromi, the population of children is estimated to be 1.7 million while the number of adults is believed to be close to five million. A very great mix of people comes to the area from all over Nigeria. They come looking for employment – something which is very difficult to find. They don't have any accommodation when they arrive so they share the already inadequate and sparse living quarters of a relative or an acquaintance from their native village. The clamour on the streets of Amukoko is terrific. Vast numbers of people move with intensity to their myriad destinations. Young men on okadas (motorbikes) shriek past at ungodly speeds and swerve by pot holes the size of craters. Market women with stalls bulging with grains, fruit, vegetables and just about every imaginable commodity, engage in a noisy and boisterous trade. Their sleeping babies rest cozily, tied onto their backs inside gaily coloured cotton wrappers. Raucous music pours out of every corner and motor cars in every conceivable stage of decrepitude inch their way forward on the narrow streets they share with the constantly moving throngs of men, women and children.

Sister Sally first came to Nigeria as a lay missionary in 1966. She spent two years nursing at the MMM hospital in Urua Akpan near Calabar in the south of the country. "It was quite the trend at the time," she says. "There were lots of Irish graduates here who were teaching, nursing and working as doctors. When I qualified as a nurse in Dublin, I spent a few very enjoyable years working in the city and then I got a bit restless and felt I needed to put a little more into life. When I returned from my first assignment in Nigeria, I joined the MMM and I was back in Nigeria towards the end of 1969. The civil war was in its final stages when I arrived at my assigned post in the Abakaliki Diocese in Ebonyi State. Apart from a few short periods, I remained in that region for the next thirty years.

"I was based at our hospital in Mile Four but we had a network of clinics all over the diocese. We were mainly into mother and child care. Our mobile clinics and our community outreach programmes provided curative and preventive care and we attached great importance to the whole area of community health education. Community participation was also a very important element in the programmes. We would, for example, set up a village health committee with the chief and his councillors and give advice on how they should proceed. Women were not allowed on these committees in the beginning, but later as they became more empowered, they were. Eventually the village communities selected their own candidates from the village and had them trained as health workers in schools of health technology. They then set up their own basic health care centres in the villages. All this worked quite well. There was Government involvement in it from about 1987. The late Professor Olikoye Ransome-Kuti was Minister for Health at the time and he was very interested in community health. From that time on, we were able to get free vaccines. Primary health care centres were being established all over the country and wide-ranging immunization programmes against measles, diphtheria, polio, tetanus and tuberculosis were being carried out. As there was quite a bit of neonatal tetanus around, vaccines for pregnant mothers were also available.

"I loved the life from the beginning. I was blessed with good health and that meant that I had lots of energy to enjoy what I was doing. In those days, there were big numbers of Irish sisters in the area so in the evenings we came together to talk and to pray. All of that was a great help.

"Unfortunately the progress of these years did not continue. Right now, vaccines are very scarce so there is a breakdown in the immunization programmes. This is a great pity as it took years to build it up and to educate the mothers. Nobody knows for sure why there are no vaccines. We are now told that they will be available from June of this year. I am always telling the local government people here in Amukoko just how devastating the situation is.

"When I left the Diocese of Abakaliki, I came here to St. Matthew's Parish. It's a very poor area and it has hardly any utilities. The population is huge and the health problems are enormous. People only live here if they cannot afford to live in a better place. Sometimes when I go out to see a patient, I'm frequently told that he or she 'has packed out'. This could mean that they were unable to pay the rent or that they had found a better place. Most people call one room home and as many as five or six can end up sharing that room. Somehow the people seem to be able to accommodate themselves to the congestion, the noise and the pollution. They are wonderful at coping with whatever circumstances they find themselves in. Despite all this hardship, when you go out into the streets, you are not met with an atmosphere of misery. The whole scene is quite upbeat and there is a garrulous sense of camaraderie which is quite warmhearted.

"The staff in our clinic is made up of staff nurses, health workers, community health workers, cleaners and drivers. We don't have visiting doctors. We could have if we wanted to but our policy here is purely to deal with primary health care and community outreach work. We also involve ourselves in a number of health education programmes. When necessary, we refer patients to a number of different hospitals. Very sick children will be referred to Massey Street Children's Hospital which is run by the State. It's a very old hospital but it has moved with the times and it has a twenty-four-hour service. Adults with TB are referred to the IDH (The Infectious Diseases Hospital) which is the TB centre for the State of Lagos. There is also a fairly good general hospital nearby and they have four doctors on duty every day. They have an ambulance and if they cannot cope, they will send people to Lagos General. In addition to all of these, there are a number of small private hospitals around which often accept referrals from us.

"Our own clinic is open five days a week and among the services we provide are antenatal and postnatal care. On any given day, we might see one hundred babies. We do immunization every day just to keep the numbers under control. We have a nutrition department which treats low weight babies. TB patients are treated once a week and our numbers are about one hundred. In the general outpatients' department, we can deal with three hundred patients needing treatment every day. We manage this with four full time staff and a number of assistants.

"I mainly concern myself with the TB and AIDS patients. Both are on the increase. The message of the seriousness of AIDS is only very slowly getting through. There is a great deal of denial and the whole subject is very much underground. If people come for pre-test counselling, they will then often disappear because they become too scared. Their attitude is one of doom and they figure if they have it, well then they have it; they don't want to be told they have it. It's understandable. They see people dying with it every day. We are presently working hard to get the people who are HIV positive on the anti-retroviral medication. It offers hope that the virus can be suppressed for a number of years at least. It's possible to get the treatment at the Nigerian Research Institute in Yaba or at LUTH (Lagos University Teaching Hospital). Of course it is very costly. We have sent some infected pregnant mothers to LUTH before delivery as they need to be treated during labour and after the birth if the babies are to be born free from the infection. For that treatment, we are trying to screen as many antenatal women as possible but they are not always willing to come forward. We like to have their permission and offer pre and post-test counselling. Other clinics just have a policy of testing with or without permission. It's very traumatic and calamitous for the expectant mother when their tests prove positive. They react very badly and often disappear for many weeks. Some eventually come back and are prepared to talk.

"You have met Sr. Levinia this morning! She is one of the senior nurses here and is on mission to us from her native Tanzania. She is very experienced and has a wonderful rapport with the people. Apart from her very busy schedule which includes work in the ante-natal clinic and the outpatients department, she takes time to talk with and counsel patients who become traumatized when they learn that they have the HIV/AIDS virus. Her attitude is always positive and she projects a radiance that shows the joy and satisfaction she achieves from her work.

"We are presently in the middle of a fairly extensive building programme here at our clinic. It's largely to provide for our TB patients and we also need a daycare centre. We have had to find funding for all of it. Funding is always difficult but we get donations from a number of sources within Nigeria. Some would come on an annual basis and others would be on an irregular basis from individuals and groups who appreciate what we are doing.

"It is a very busy and absorbing life. We have good systems in place and I believe that we cope quite well. Weekends are for relaxing. We might go shopping or go to the beach. There are two other MMM houses in Lagos so we visit back and forth. We also get a number of visitors coming through. When they are passing through Lagos, they sometimes like to spend a day or two. I take an annual holiday of two months in Ireland. I first go to our mother house in Drogheda for a rest. Then I visit my family in the West. After that I usually do a retreat in Dublin.

"My future! Well I'm here until the Lord calls me! Of course it all depends on my health. There is no retirement age for an MMM. It depends on the individual. Some like to retire early, go to Ireland and become involved in work there. Others prefer to stay on the missions for as long as their health permits."

Sister Sally was born into a farming family of six, three miles outside Roscommon town. After completing her secondary education at the Mercy Convent, Roscommon, she trained to be a nurse at Baggot Street Hospital, Dublin.

Sr. Levina Samky

Sister Chris Gill

Medical Missionaries of Mary (MMM)
Fuka, Niger State

Sr. Christine Gill at the well-baby clinic, Fuka.
(photo: MMM)

We are at a gathering to mark the opening of the MMM clinic in Fuka, an arid, rural location less than one hour's drive from Minna, the capital of Niger State. The spirited and dynamic Sr. Christine Gill is master of ceremonies. She is using a clever mixture of Irish charm and hard sense to beguile the invited *Big Men* from the local authorities to commit to some level of support for the clinic in the years to come. Her audience is not oblivious of her motives and she is frequently cheered on with claps of approval and affirmation. Later, during a carefully prepared lunch planned to cater for European and Nigerian tastes, she presents a lively exposé of the work of the sisters since their arrival in Fuka.

In the afternoon, Sr. Christine took time out to talk to me about her life and work in Nigeria.

"When we came to Fuka in 1996" she tells me, "there was nothing here. Our Nigerian sisters from Gussaro, further north in the State used to come down with their medicine and bush box and the people were always begging them to establish a permanent place. Eventually, Sister Joan Melinn and Sr. Dervla O'Donnell were given a mandate to do a survey of the area and it was found that 30% of children had died of measles the previous year and that many mothers were dying in childbirth for lack of antenatal care. That was only the tip of the iceberg. A submission was made to *Misereor*, the German funding agency, and they gave us the money to get started with the sisters' house. Later *Ireland Aid* came in and funded the clinic which was formally opened today. We have been in operation now for a short while and we plan to go from strength to strength. At the moment, we are adding a small TB clinic as the response to our TB programme has been very good.

"We are also having four bore holes sunk to provide water in nearby villages. Funding for those has come from *International Christian Childcare* in America and from collections in England and Ireland. All the villages have formed committees and are working very hard with an engineer from Minna and contractors from Kwara State to ensure that this project is quickly carried out. I have come to realize that the best thing you can do in Nigeria is provide water because when you go, the hospital might fail but the water will remain. When you have clean water, the waterborne diseases decrease by 50%. Sr. Joan Melinn has proof of this as she works exclusively on our outreach programme which is community based, and includes immunization programmes, health education and HIV/AIDS awareness classes. It is she who oversees the water projects.

"I am mostly in curative medicine and I deal with TB, AIDS, malaria, typhoid and a number of other tropical diseases. There are twelve of us on the staff. Sr. Cordelia is a young Nigerian sister and she can turn her hand to anything. She was trained in our hospital in Afikpo so she has the MMM ethos. We have six trained community health workers, and a community health assistant to work in our pharmacy. Some local people are also trained to carry out administrative duties.

"We deal with many different ethnic groups. The Fulani who are largely nomadic and who drive their cattle from area to area following the pasture, come regularly for treatment. Then there are the Kadura, the Koro, the Hausa and some Deltas who have come to live in the area. Hausa is the predominant language. I am not very good at it so I always have to have an interpreter. Sr. Cordelia is excellent and Sr. Joan is quite good."

Sr. Christine was born between Castlerea and Ballintuber Castle, Co. Roscommon. Before joining the MMM, she had qualified as a nurse in Dublin. Her arrival in Nigeria in 1967 coincided with the outbreak of the Biafran war. She was first posted to the MMM hospital in Afikpo which was within Biafra in the south east of the country. "As soon as the war started," she recalls, "our hospital became very busy with casualties. It was a big teaching hospital with many departments, including a maternity clinic. Nine months later, the federal troops silently crossed the nearby Cross River and came into our compound while we were carrying out surgery in the theater. We were all called out and accused of supporting Colonel Ojukwu and the Biafrans. We were then ordered to assemble in one room. Any of the patients who could move had also to assemble. You can imagine how fearful we were. We tried to convince them that we were there for all casualties and that we were on neither side in the war. They eventually went away but returned a few days later in the midst of heavy shelling. It was quite frightening and one of our nurses was killed. This time we were ordered to evacuate and we were marched down to the river. As the bombs were falling, we were being accused of being collaborators and traitors and threatened with deportation and prison. We knew that these were not idle threats. Some priests, one Nigerian (now Bishop Michael Okoro of Abakaliki) and one Irish, Fr. Rory O'Brien, came to intercede on our behalf. Eventually, they agreed to let the Fathers take us across the river to where the Kiltegan Fathers had a mission. After several months, we were allowed back to Afikpo. It was in a terrible state. It took time, effort and outside help from the *International Red Cross* and other agencies to get it up and running and fit to receive the great number of war casualties that were pouring in.

"My greatest fear during those years was that we might be brought home. We got word saying that anybody who felt they could not cope should come home. We all stayed. Now it was quite terrifying at times and on a few occasions, we were lying on the floor under tables while shrapnel was flying. We were determined however, to help the people in their greatest hour of need. They had more fear than we had. Naturally, we were all thinking of our families at home who were hearing the news because it was a much publicized war and the awful suffering of the Biafrans caught the world's attention. It was a lonely time too as we were not able to get any letters from home and we were cut off from other MMM in other parts of Nigeria. We were able to tune into the BBC from time to time and that is often how we got information about the whereabouts of the federal troops and the general state of things. Those of us who went through those times together developed a great bond which exists to this very day.

"I was in Afikpo in January 1970 on the day the Biafrans surrendered. It was then that we had some of our more harrowing experiences. Fr. Dónal O' Sullivan (Kiltegan Fathers) and I went down to the river in a huge lorry to select the people who we thought would live: the rest we had to leave. It was very difficult and emotionally draining. So many mothers were by the riverside crying and trying to locate any family member that might have survived. Some families were just left with the grandmother. The rest had been killed or had starved in the bush.

"During the war, many children had been evacuated to the islands of Sao Tomé and Fernando Pó off the West African coast. When they were brought back, the MMM were among the groups who went with parents and family members to help identify and allocate the children. Many had to be deemed war orphans so extended family members had to be found to look after them. It was heartbreaking.

"When the war and its aftermath came to an end, I worked in a number of different hospitals in the east and mid-west of the country. I spent five years in Ndubia which is eighteen miles from Abakaliki. There, it was largely midwifery, community health, immunization and all that. We had a number of expatriate doctors helping out. One was Dr. Michael Cleary from Ballyhaunis, Co.

Mayo, who came with his wife Bríd to spend time. Bríd was an administrator.

"In 1980, I was transferred to Mile Four Hospital in Abakaliki as matron. I remained there until 1990 dealing largely with TB, leprosy and maternity. We had funding from the Austrian Government for our TB clinic and *GRLA* (German Relief Leprosy Association) funded the leprosy treatment. The funding enabled us to develop good clinics. When I was there, the number of our TB patients escalated to 250 at one point. Leprosy, during my time decreased from 2,000 to 800. There is now a cure for it so it is not as feared as it used to be. Like TB, it is an airborne disease but it is not very contagious. Handling dressings and that did not present a problem. Very intimate contact is dangerous but we were always very careful about hygiene. In the early days, lepers were ostracized. They were just brought to us and dropped. That is now changing and we have, through the years, been able to resettle some cured lepers with their families. Being able to do this often depended on the economic situation of the families. Many were unable to take on an extra burden. Close to the grounds of our hospital, we have a village for the cured lepers who can cater for themselves. Our sisters visit and the inhabitants have access to the facilities of the hospital services when necessary. Sr. Joanne Kelly who is a nurse and Sr. (Dr.) Deirdre Twomey continue to co-ordinate and manage all of that. In my years at Mile Four, HIV/AIDS was not the big factor that it is today. We had begun to screen for it after the Nigerian Government gave us the go ahead to do so. They were very slow to do that as they were not at all keen to admit that people in Nigeria were affected.

"The economic situation in the country has always impacted greatly on healthcare services and in recent years, we have been affected ourselves very much. In the 1960's and 1970's, we were really able to run our clinics with the revenues generated, but over the last decade at least, the patients simply cannot afford to pay even the very low fees of mission hospitals. From the mid to late 1980's onwards, things deteriorated rapidly and since then, we have had to depend a lot on funding.

"I am now sixty-seven years of age. I have no immediate intention of leaving Nigeria. Everything will depend on my health. At the moment, it is very good thank God and I have a lot of energy.

I love Nigeria and the Nigerians. I know that there are some rascals but essentially they are a really lovely people who are friendly and warm and who have values we have not got. We are workaholics but they bring hospitality, kindness and compassion into all of our lives."

Sr. Cordelia

Sister Joan Cosgrove

Medical Missionaries of Mary (MMM)
New Lugbe, Abuja

*Sr. Joan Cosgrove, MMM, discussing the details of a proposed health post
at a village near Abuja (photo: MMM)*

It was a great pleasure for me to spend a morning with Sr. Joan
Cosgrove at the MMM house and primary healthcare clinic at
New Lugbe in the outskirts of Abuja. When her team moved there
in the late 1990's, it was a desolate and bush area. Since then
extensive housing estates have been built on their doorstep and the
whole neighbourhood has begun to be absorbed in the frenetic
growth that has come to be associated with Nigeria's new federal
capital and its ever expanding suburbs.

Sister Joan was born in Enniscorthy in 1935. Her mother died
in 1940 so she and her two siblings, a brother and a sister were raised
by their grandmother in Roslea, Co. Fermanagh. Later they came

back to Dublin where Joan and her sister attended the Dominican-run secondary school of Sion Hill in Blackrock.

"My sister entered the Dominican congregation immediately after secondary school. I had ideas of doing the same after my Leaving Certificate exam but I felt that I should first spend some time getting a little experience *out in the world*. I now believe that I was trying to fight off what I thought was a vocation. I kept putting it out of my mind. Then one night following a party which I had looked forward to very much, I experienced a sense of disappointment and unease which led to my thinking that there had to be more to life than going to parties, dressing up and so on. I had known about the MMM as I had seen the film *The Visitation* which depicted their work with leprosy patients in Nigeria. Seeing it, motivated me into visiting our foundress, Mother Mary Martin in Drogheda. I was nineteen and a half at the time and I considered myself very old! I found her to be wonderful. She really impressed me. She was welcoming, friendly and not in the least bit pushy. I remember that she spoke with a beautifully educated accent. Two months after that meeting, I joined the congregation.

"As a second year novice, I went to the College of Pharmacy in Shrewsbury Road. As soon as I was qualified as a pharmacist in 1963, I was sent to the MMM hospital in Afikpo in south east Nigeria because the needs there were very great. It was in fact in Afikpo that my final profession took place. I spent ten years in that hospital which had attached to it a nursing school, a training school for young doctors and a laboratory training facility. It had been established in 1947, ten years after the founding of St. Luke's Hospital, Anua, which was our first hospital in Nigeria. Today, these two hospitals are still run by the MMM.

"Working as a pharmacist in Africa in those days was very different to what it would have been in Ireland. We had to make up all treatments from ointments to cough mixtures. We made gallons of the latter. One of my tasks was to teach the nurses and midwives pharmacology and English. All their exams had to be taken in English so while on duty, they were not allowed to speak any other language.

"In 1966, I was transferred to Obudu, a beautiful area in Cross River State. A devastating massacre of Igbos had taken place that year in Nigeria and it precipitated the civil war between the Igbos and the Federal Government. Igbos were fleeing from all parts of the country back to their villages. Thousands trekked through the bush and trainloads of schoolchildren returning to their homes from schools in different parts of Nigeria were being attacked. Many of the children were killed. When the civil war actually broke out in 1967, our area which was within Biafra was heavily shelled so we had to flee with our patients to a school in the middle of the bush. We were there for ten very fearful days. Strangely, I felt very calm and had a sense of peace. On the eleventh day, our regional superior, the bishop of the diocese and Éamon Ó Tuathail from the Irish Embassy in Lagos managed to come to see us. It was decided that we would move to Ikom, about ninety miles away, where we had a house. Obudu at this stage was almost deserted. We drove through the town on our way to Ikom and the people who had remained had their palm branches out to welcome the soldiers from the federal side. This was done for their own protection. When our party arrived in Ikom, it was decided that some of us would move on to Afikpo. I was among a group who did.

"One day in April 1968, bombing by the federal soldiers started in Afikpo. It was totally unexpected and all the people were in the market. They started fleeing and we received huge numbers of casualties at our hospital. During this period of bombing, we ourselves were very scared and feared for our safety and that of our patients. Just when we thought the soldiers had passed on, they returned and came into our compound. We were all brought down to the banks of Cross River as prisoners. There were about fifty of us which included staff and any of the patients who could walk. There we had a tense time for many hours in the middle of all the shelling. Finally, we were told to go to Ugep on the other side of the river where there was a mission run by the Kiltegan Fathers. The fathers came to fetch us and they brought us away in relays in a few battered cars and trucks. We remained there for about four months and then we were allowed back to Afikpo to continue our work in co-operation with the International Red Cross teams who had arrived in Nigeria to help with the war effort. We set up a programme of action which was quite effective. I myself had to move to our

263

hospital at Mile Four in Abakaliki to help co-ordinate the assignments of drugs which were coming in from abroad through Enugu airport. They had to be distributed among the different Red Cross teams from Canada, Ireland, Belgium and other places. People from *Save the Children Fund* were also helping as was a special Irish team of volunteers which I presume was sponsored by the Irish Government. That particular team stayed on for some time after the war came to an end in January 1970.

"By then I was able to return to our hospital in Afikpo and join the rest of the team picking up the pieces. Much had to be re-built and we had to re-start our training schools. It was a difficult time. I remained there until 1974 when I went to Abakaliki as MMM regional superior. One of the jobs I had to do was to find a house in Benin City that would be suitable for our regional headquarters. We first rented one close to Benin University and just beside the Jesuits who were also on the look out for more permanent premises. We and they subsequently got land and built new houses close to each other in the same neighbourhood.

"In 1982, I returned to Obudu to spend what I would call the best years of my working life. They came to an end in 1997 when we returned the hospital to the diocese as the Church was well established in the area and there were a sufficient number of medical personnel available to continue our work. I found it very hard to leave because in addition to my pharmacy work, I had become very involved with the local people. I looked after physically handicapped children in the villages and had programmes with the women that taught them to cook and care for their families.

"I returned to Ireland for a year and took courses in Dalgan Park on *Faith and Mission* which I found very relevant to my life. By 1998, I was back in Nigeria looking into the possibility of setting up a primary healthcare centre in the Abuja region. We had been invited into the diocese in the early1990's by Cardinal Ekandem, the first Archbishop of Abuja and in fact the first indigenous Nigerian Catholic priest. By 1999, we had purchased this house and land at New Lugbe but since it was initially uninhabitable, I stayed for a while at our mission at Fuka near Minna in Niger State and commuted. The MMM congregation owns the New Lugbe compound and that is good for the Nigerian sisters who will come after us. When we left other clinics and hospitals such as Obudu and Ogoga, everything went back to the diocese and we had no claim on anything despite having spent decades building them and working in them.

"Here in New Lugbe, I am the administrator of the project as regards reporting, funding and management. Sister Felicitas, a Nigerian MMM is the leader of the medical team which runs the primary health care clinic and which provides outreach programmes in the nearby villages. The team goes out to the villages to survey the needs and to talk to the people. They meet the chiefs and village heads and discuss practicalities. What the people want sometimes can be different from what is needed. They may want a hospital when their real need might be clean water. The team caters for about thirty villages and serves approximately 25,000 people. The whole idea of primary healthcare is that you don't give out too many medicines and that you try to be preventive. When treatment is necessary of course it is given. Immunization of children under five years old for the five killer diseases (measles, polio, diphtheria, tetanus, tuberculosis) is routine. Anything else that presents itself like cholera and typhoid are dealt with as they arise. Malaria is very prevalent and there are many water-born diseases such as dysentery. Typhoid is very rampant right now and it is often misdiagnosed.

Sr. Felicitas Egeolu, MMM on a home based care visit (photo: MMM)

"We have a large HIV/AIDS awareness programme which often takes place in the evenings. Archbishop Onaiyekan of Abuja is very interested in the whole AIDS's issue and Sr. Felicitas is very involved in our programmes here. Sister Cecilia Azuh, another Nigerian MMM oversees the general AIDS's programmes for the Archdiocese. The MMM worldwide are very involved in HIV/AIDS and we have an international programme which is sponsored by *CAFOD* (*Catholic Aid for Overseas*) which is supported by the English and Welsh Bishops.

"Sister Felicitas would not always go to the villages herself as she has to be at the clinic to treat the many people who come for emergency treatment. In addition, she has a great deal of work to do with the new clinic which is being constructed and for which we received some funding from Ireland Aid.

"There are a number of government and local authority-sponsored health centres in the wider Abuja area and we co-operate with them as much as we can, i.e. on national immunization days. We wouldn't have a clinic in an area where any of these centres operate. We don't encroach and we are not into religious propaganda unlike some of the evangelical Churches. Anyway we have to be very careful here in the North which has a strong Muslim ethos. I would say that we live the Christian message through our work. We treat all who come to us irrespective of religion. We are not into any overt evangelism. Our clinic and health work is part of the medical service provided by the Catholic Archdiocese of Abuja. For two days every week I work as pharmacist in the diocesan health co-ordinator's office. I purchase the drugs for all the health posts in the diocese which number about ten, when they are all operating.

"I have found my work as part of a medical team in different locations in Nigeria very satisfying. I became an MMM to be a missionary. I didn't know what I was going to be doing within the congregation when I joined. I was prepared to do anything but I imagined that I would be nursing. Spreading the Gospel has always been to the fore in my mind. This I have done more by example than by anything else – by respecting the dignity of people and by reaching out to those in need.

"Now that I am over seventy, I have begun to consider the future. Sometimes I wonder if it would be better to move on and let the younger people coming up take over and do things their way. I have not come to any decisions about all of that but I have begun to reflect on options.

"The rule of St. Benedict inspires the work of the MMM congregation. The spirit of the rule goes hand in hand with our constitution. It's a spirit of freedom rather than one of dogmatism with regard to prayer and life and it's a very human rule. I love to read it. The words are very beautiful and though they were written many hundreds of years ago, they are pertinent to our lives today."

Sister Maura Ramsbottom

Medical Missionaries of Mary (MMM)
Mafaluku, Lagos

Sr. Maura Ramsbottom (Photo: MMM)

The petite, lively and highly motivated Sister Maura
Ramsbottom welcomes me warmly to the MMM house she
shares with colleagues Sr. Jacinta Roche and Sr. Helen Omeya in
Mafaluku in the outskirts of Lagos. Concerned that I have been
travelling all day, she immediately offers me her room so that I can
shower and have a change of clothing.

Having spent most of her life teaching and lecturing, she is very much at ease talking about herself and her work. She was a primary school teacher in Dublin enjoying a carefree life and much travel before she joined the MMM. "Every summer as soon as the schools closed, a big group of us headed off to the continent for an extended holiday. Highly enjoyable as all of that was, it had a kind of a temporary feel about it for me because from an early age, I remember having a longing for the missionary ideal. I was an only child, and growing up I regarded Jesus as a friend to whom I could talk. When I came to the realization that there were children in the world who did not know Jesus, I felt a sadness and a need to do something to rectify this. My becoming a missionary then had nothing to do with evangelism or saving souls; it was all about enabling other children to have Jesus as a friend.

"I was never interested in joining any congregation other than the MMM. When I was introduced to them, I found that they were welcoming, generous, practical and very human. After I joined, I came to know our foundress, Mother Mary quite well as I had the privilege of working close to her for a time. She died in 1975 aged almost eighty-three years. She was a woman of great humanity and vision.

"My first four years as an MMM were spent in Clonmel where we had a nursing home. I was mostly involved in the formation studies of the young sisters even though I was quite young myself. After that, I was sent to Rome to study and I was quite fortunate to be there during the second Vatican Council when all the new developments and changes in the Church were being debated. When I returned, Mother Mary asked me to go out to all our communities in Africa and introduce our sisters there to these developments. I was unable to go to Nigeria at the time as the Biafran war was raging but I went to Kenya, Uganda, Ethiopia, Tanzania and Malawi and held workshops for our own sisters and for those of other congregations who made requests. My mission was to articulate the new vision of the Church – the Church in the world – the Church open to the world – the Church in dialogue with other religions and ideologies. Mother Mary was very excited by the whole approach of Cardinal Suenens of Belgium, a very important figure during Vatican II, regarding the apostolates of religious orders being an integral part of religious life. Up to then, there tended to be a dichotomy between prayer life and work life and a rather rigid timetable for prayer was always followed. Since Mother Mary herself had always insisted that your work was your first prayer, she was particularly happy with what Cardinal Suenens was articulating.

"After my trip to Africa which lasted about five months, I returned to Drogheda and taught in our formation programme for a short period. Then it was back to Rome for further studies in theology at Regina Mundi and at the Gregorian University. When these were completed, I was sufficiently qualified to go to Nigeria to become co-directress of an institute being set up in Ibadan by the major superiors of many different congregations to provide theological formation, which encompassed the new thinking that emanated from Vatican II, for religious sisters and brothers. The teaching staff was mostly drawn from the major seminary of St. Peter and Paul and the Dominican Institute, both of which were in Ibadan. From time to time we had visiting lecturers. Our students came from many countries in Africa and their many cultural influences provided stimulating and challenging interactive sessions during courses. I found that everyone felt a huge sense of involvement in the new Church developments and in the different apostolates which we were all involved in within our own environment – in parishes, in schools and in hospitals.

"I returned to Drogheda in 1974 to work with the MMM central administration team. Like all religious congregations in the post-Vatican II period, we became engaged in updating our structures and constitutions. It became my job to travel to all MMM houses in Ireland and abroad and engage in dialogue with our sisters about the updating process. I then reported back to the committee charged with actual updating. Fortunately, I love travelling because during that assignment, I covered many thousands of miles. An added bonus to my work was the fact that I got to know great numbers of our sisters all over the world.

"In 1979, I was asked to work with the Irish Missionary Union (IMU) in Dublin and to become for a year, the coordinator of a formation programme which it was setting up for novices from a great number of different religious congregations. Previously, each religious congregation had its own formation programme but with the drop in vocations, it was decided to pool resources. This turned out to be a very productive exercise because having pooled resources, we began to see the value of it for its own sake and the interchange of ideas brought about practical innovation and development.

"By 1980, I was back in Ibadan teaching Scripture and courses on *The Church in the Modern World* at the Dominican Institute. Again we had an inter-congregational programme involving seven congregations of men and women. I liked this work very much. I always tried very hard to relate what I was teaching to everyday living. During this time also, I became involved in the *DELES (Development, Education and Leadership Services)* movement. The inspiration for *DELES*, which is largely concerned with leadership training, came from an ecumenical movement in Kenya. Fr. Dónal Dorr from St. Patrick's Society, Kiltegan was the person who introduced it to Nigeria.

"In 1991, I became MMM Regional Superior in Nigeria and remained in that position until 1994. It was a demanding time which again involved much travel. At the time, Nigeria and Liberia made up one MMM region and there was a horrific war going on in Liberia. It was a very dangerous place and I recall in particular one very frightening experience during which I was held up at gunpoint by a boy soldier who had no sense of what he was doing and who was liable at any second to pull the trigger just for the fun of it. We have since withdrawn from Liberia as the protracted troubles made our situation and work practically impossible. The people of Liberia have been suffering for too long and now it is very sad to see the Ivory Coast which was a peaceful and stable country for many decades, sink into conflict.

"After all my moving around and nonstop work, I was due a sabbatical and I took a mini one in Louvain in Belgium in 1995. I attended the Catholic University there and did advanced studies in Scripture and Church History. I love history and in Louvain, I was well situated to explore the context of many historical events. I travelled around a great deal and I especially liked to visit the many galleries and museums in Brussels and the beautiful Flemish cities of Bruges, Ghent and Antwerp. Another highlight from this time was being able to go into Holland to view the glorious tulip fields.

"When I returned to Dublin, I joined my Nigerian colleague, Sr. Elizabeth Ikechukwu in the work of preparing a group of intra-cultural sisters for final profession. It was an exercise of accompaniment and of being present for them rather than one of teaching. Sr. Elizabeth and I worked very well together and I found that my experience with the inter-congregational groups at the Ibadan institutes greatly enhanced my own capacities. Sr. Elizabeth who is a nurse is currently working in our clinic in Amukoko, Lagos and she is also the vocations' directress for Nigeria.

"I returned to Ibadan in 1996 to work again in formation and *DELES*. I also became involved in facilitation work at conferences and workshops in response to requests from different congregations.

"I came here to Mafaluku in 1998. We are in west Lagos and as you can gather from the noise of the aeroplanes overhead, we are quite close to the airport in Ikeja. Here, as well as having a continued involvement in formation programmes and facilitation work, I manage the running of this house and take care of all the travel arrangements of the sisters who come through Lagos. At times, it can be very busy and exciting and it is especially lovely to see our young African sisters coming and going to different countries in Africa. We have recently started a mission in the nearby Benin Republic and the three young sisters – one Tanzanian and two Nigerians – who have started it from scratch are doing marvellous work in their clinic in Zaffe where they treat almost 7,000 patients annually and provide greatly needed services in their outreach programmes in the many surrounding villages.

"Here in Mafaluku, we have our own primary healthcare clinic which is called *Catherine of Siena Medical Centre*. It is run by Sr. Jacinta Roche and her staff of thirty. She is currently introducing the work there to Sister Helen Omeya who has not yet taken her final vows and who is engaged in the work experience which is part of her formation programme. Sister Jacinta is from Wexford and has been working as a nurse in Nigeria for almost forty years. She set up *Catherine of Siena* with the help of funding from *Misereor* of Germany. It caters for the poorer people of the region who cannot afford to go to private hospitals. Its work is both curative and preventive. Sister Jacinta's nursing skills and capabilities are renowned. From her early days in Ibadan when she helped cope with a virulent outbreak of cholera, through to her different assignments in various MMM hospitals in many parts of Nigeria and right up to the work she is doing here, she has been diligent, dedicated and totally professional. She loves her work and though like myself, she is now more than seventy years of age, she has no wish to retire.

"My own future? I am very happy in Nigeria and I thank God for my good health. I also have no plans to stop working. I want to remain active and engaged in contributing in whatever way I can for as long as I can. My wish for Nigeria is that democracy will take root and that somehow the great numbers of people of integrity, kindness and vision that are in this country will find the strength and courage to influence the future. I am praying that goodness will not be strangled by power, corruption and greed for money."

That evening in Mafaluko, I greatly enjoyed the company of the three sisters over a carefully prepared dinner. To round off a very good visit, Sr. Maura pulls from the dining room sideboard a bottle of *Frangelico* liqueur which had been given to her as a gift and which she graciously claimed to have been keeping for a special occasion. She and her driver then drove me into the Lagos night and to the OLA guest house in Maryland, Ikeja where I was staying.

Sr. Helen Omeya, Sr. Jacinta Roche (right)

Sister Helen Omeya

Medical Missionaries of Mary (MMM)
Mafaluku, Lagos

Sr. Helen Omeya, MMM

I met the soon to be professed Sister Helen Omeya while visiting the MMM compound in Mafaluku, Lagos. She spoke to me about her reasons for joining the congregation.

"Ever since childhood, I believed that I was destined to join a religious order. During my school years, I was an altar girl and I was always involved in religious groups and societies. I was also in close contact with DDL (Daughters of Divine Love), an indigenous religious congregation. At the age of nineteen after my secondary education, my people wanted me to marry but I ran away to my sister's place and refused.

"I first heard about the MMM in the *Ambassador* magazine which is published by the Missionaries of St. Paul in Gwagwalada near Abuja. Then when I was doing my midwifery training at Awgu General Hospital in Enugu State, my sister took me to visit the MMM hospital at Mile Four in Abakaliki in Ebonyi State. I had heard of the work being done there for TB and leprosy patients but hadn't known it was an MMM hospital. That visit and the impression it made on me caused me to ask to be put in touch with Sister Joanne Kelly, the congregation's vocations' directress. Sister Joanne subsequently visited my school to interview me and to give me all the information that I was requesting. She invited me to attend the MMM aspirants' retreat which happened to be commencing the day after I finished my exams. When it was over, I went to visit my parents to tell them of my decision to join the congregation.

"My father was content for me to choose whatever was going to make me happy. It was more difficult for my mother. She wanted me to work for at least a year so that I could help the family financially. We are a Catholic family of eight, five boys and three girls and it was very hard for me not to comply with her request. Eventually, she came around to accepting my decision.

"My first year with the MMM was spent in our hospital Urua Akpan in Akwa Ibom State. Then I spent two years at our formation house in Ibadan. That was followed by some months at our clinic in Fuka near Minna in Niger State. Now I am here in our clinic in Mafaluku working with Sister Jacinta Roche. We are getting on very well and I am learning a lot from her and gaining much experience. When I finish here in a few months, I will go back to the novitiate to take my final vows.

"Ever since Vatican II, the pattern in formation is that during the novitiate years, novices go out to different communities to get involved in an apostolate. Since I am a nurse, my apostolate is to work with the sick in our hospitals, clinics and in our outreach programmes. This pattern is meant to integrate more fully our work life with our prayer life.

"I have never doubted my decision to enter religious life. I love the way of life of my congregation. The work can be stressful at times but it is rewarding and I enjoy the fact that I am getting better at it all the time. I have excellent teachers so I keep on learning and all of it helps me to help my people here in Nigeria. Leaving my family and entering a completely new world which had an international dimension was not easy. I had to let go of certain things. It was quite a challenge, especially given the attitudes of today's society. Not too many people want to devote their lives to the type of work we do. I am happy and I thank God."

Sister Rose Eruvwaegwainre Mogun

Medical Missionaries of Mary (MMM)
Benin City

Sr Rose Mogun, MMM (photo: MMM)

Imeet with Sister Rose Eruvwaegwainre Mogun at the MMM headquarters in Booterstown, Co. Dublin. She is one of the six councillors elected to assist the superior general of MMM worldwide so she is in Dublin to attend meetings. She first talks to me about that part of Nigeria from which she comes.

"I was born in Sapele in oil-rich Delta State in 1957. I come from the Urhobo ethnic group. It is the biggest group in Delta though others might dispute that claim. In my language, the name Eruvwaegwainre means *experience is a good teacher*.

"The landscape of my area is unique. It is covered with rivers and creeks. Many of the rivers form part of the Niger Delta; others flow directly into the sea. People mostly travel and get around by boat and canoe. Between the rivers and creeks are huge mangrove forests. These re-grow themselves because the land is wet and swampy all year around. In British times, the place was very prosperous as there was a very big timber and plywood manufacturing company in Sapele which employed great numbers of people. That all changed with the discovery of oil in the 1970's. Warri and Port Harcourt are now big oil capitals and Sapele is very much a poor relation.

"Fishing is a big occupation in Delta and a great source of food. Both men and women fish. Our farmers produce great quantities of yams, cassava and fruit. The big source of wealth however is now oil. It has proved to be a mixed blessing. Those of us who come from the region cannot say that there is a fair distribution of the wealth that emanates from the people's own land and it is very distressing to see the poor living conditions of the vast majority of the ordinary people. Frequent oil spillages have polluted many of the rivers which have fed our people for generations. Farm land has also been affected. The oil companies attribute such problems to vandalization by youths but this is not always true.

"My grandparents were farming people. My grandfather on my mother's side was a very good farmer who owned a number of rubber and palm plantations. My own parents lived in the town as my mother was a trader and my father worked for a private company. There were ten in my family as my father had two wives even though he and my mother, who is his first wife, were married in the Catholic Church. They had four daughters together but because our tribal culture expects you to have a male child, my father took a second wife who gave him four sons and two more daughters. My mother remained his senior wife and since his second wife is no longer with him, my parents are together.

"I attended Our Lady of Apostles primary school in Sapele, a school which was founded by the Irish OLA Sisters. For my secondary education I went to St. Ita's Grammar School also in Sapele. Following my graduation, I started teaching in a local school even though I had no training. While teaching, I became friendly with my Irish parish priest Fr. Jack Ryan, SMA from Dundalk and his assistant a Nigerian priest. This friendship led me into quite a lot of contact with church voluntary groups and with many congregations of reverend sisters. I began to admire the sisters' sense of sharing and their total dedication to their work. The idea that I myself might like to be in religious life began to take root. I started reading up about the congregations I had come in contact with and just as I was considering writing to the OLA Sisters, I was given information on the MMM by a cousin of my father's who had met a number of them while he was studying at a seminary in Ibadan. He talked to me about their impressive work and their warm hospitality. I was then nineteen and it was 1976. I wrote a letter to their vocations' directress and was invited to visit them in Ibadan. Soon after that very happy visit, I entered the congregation and in 1980 made my first profession in Ibadan. From day one, I felt I fitted in with the MMM ethos and charism and I have always loved the mixture of races that the congregation is made up of. I find it encouraging to see how blacks and whites can live together and work for a common purpose.

"After my first profession, I was assigned to our community in Abakaliki where we have a leprosy settlement, a TB clinic, a HIV/AIDS treatment centre and a maternity hospital. I started working with the malnourished children. Teaching the mothers about nutrition brought about very good results. Within weeks, the babies began to gain weight. Indeed it often happened after just one week of good feeding. Bad diet in a family nearly always sets in where you have poverty and disease. In the Abakaliki area where leprosy, malaria, guinea worm, TB and now AIDS are common, the men who work hard under the heat in the fields are often the first to get sick. The women then have to take over the management of the family with no income, so poverty quickly comes.

"Leprosy, though very prevalent in the Abakaliki region in the past is now greatly on the decrease as there is a cure. The incidence of TB and AIDS however is increasing all the time. The impact of the latter is not yet felt in Nigeria on account of our huge population but those of us who are working in healthcare see it every day and the numbers are very big. It is being transmitted by sexual intercourse and by the use of unclean needles in badly run clinics and health posts.

"When I left Abakaliki, I trained as a nurse in Benin Teaching Hospital. Benin is an ancient city dating back to the 10th century A.D. For many centuries, it was the seat of government of one of the oldest and most powerful African kingdoms. At the height of its power in the 16th century, it extended westwards to include Lagos and Dahomey (the present Benin Republic). The king or traditional ruler was the Oba and life centred around him and his court. As well as being king, he was also the religious leader. Even before colonial times, Benin had good urban structures and was world famous for its bronze art works. During my training at the hospital, I enjoyed being in the city and getting acquainted with its ancient culture and history.

"When my training was completed, I was assigned to Obudu in Cross River State where the MMM then had a general hospital. I worked in the different sections of the hospital and gained a lot of experience. I enjoyed my time in this green and beautiful area which is in the midst of the rolling green hills close to the border of Cameroon. It is there that the Government runs a famous cattle ranch which attracts many visitors and which was built in the 1950's by Scottish ranchers. At a height of about 1900 metres, it has no mosquitoes and has a cool and very pleasant climate. After leaving Obudu, I went to our hospital in Afikpo in the same State to do my midwifery in the nursing school there.

"I made my first visit to Ireland in 1986 and spent five months working in *Our Lady of Lourdes Hospital*, Drogheda. There I was able to qualify for my international registration which entitles me to work in any country. I also used the time to update my nursing skills and to become familiar with all the latest techniques and equipment. Though I arrived in the middle of summer, I felt the cold intensely. No matter how much clothing I wore, I could not get warm. In fact I got pneumonia and was not at all well for a while. When I returned to Nigeria, I took time out preparing to take my final vows.

"This is a very serious and important period for all of us in religious life as it is a time for confronting any self-doubt or unhappiness. To be honest, I have always been happy in my vocation but from time to time you do question yourself about the decisions

282

you have made. I have always accepted that this type of questioning is very much part of the journey towards final profession.

"An assignment of two years at our hospital in Urua Akpan in Akwa Ibom State in the south east followed my final profession. After that, I was asked by our regional superior to work with our formation team. This request took me by surprise as I did not feel that I had the ability to work with the young novices. It was explained to me that I would receive training. I was sent to Kent in England and to Chicago in the United States for extensive studies. In Kent, I focused on human development, counselling and spirituality in a course which was run by the Mill Hill Fathers. In Chicago, I first attended the Institute of Spiritual Leadership and then went to the Jesuit-run Loyola College for theological studies.

"Equipped with knowledge, skills, the humility to be challenged and an awareness of my own personal journey, helped me cope with the responsibility attached to the ministry of formation. Interacting with the human person, trying to be present to God within that person, in her own culture and in her own personality, is quite an onerous duty. The role is one of accompaniment and exploration rather than one of teaching or leading. I spent five years at our novitiate in Ibadan on our formation team.

"A general chapter of our congregation worldwide was held in 1997. This is where the congregation's leaders are nominated and elected. During the chapter, I was nominated to be one of the six counsellors to the congregational leader or superior general who is Sr. Margaret Quinn from Co. Clare. Though I was very surprised by the nomination, I welcomed it because my commitment to the congregation means that I am available for whatever my leaders call me to do. At a general chapter a lot happens. The operations of the whole congregation are studied and discussed. Its mission in the world of today and its response to that mission are carefully examined. Leadership is looked at and new leaders are nominated and elected. When my name kept coming up in the nomination counts, I was encouraged to go forward and was promised that I would be greatly supported. For many years now, the Irish sisters have been empowering us and preparing us for leadership. Our time has now come to put that preparation into practice as there are very few Irish sisters left in Nigeria.

"Since my election as councillor, I have become the co-ordinator for the West African zone. Within MMM worldwide, there is the congregational centre in Ireland and four zones – West Africa, East and Central Africa, Europe and the zone for the Americas. Within my own zone, we have three areas – northern, eastern and western. This last includes our newly established mission in the Benin Republic. I work with the area leaders in the MMM communities in my zone. We constantly evaluate our lives and our apostolate and make changes and adjustments where necessary. I am based in Benin City but I do a lot of travelling within West Africa and between it and Dublin.

"The Nigerian Catholic Church has achieved a lot but there is much to be done. It remains a very patriarchal Church and I would like to see that changing. I would like to see greater participation by women in religious orders and by women in general. I would like to see some oppressive traditions die. Sometimes Church leaders cite the importance of guarding culture and tradition as an excuse for stalling change. I believe that change and innovation should grow out of culture and tradition as they are not static things. I also believe that the Church in Nigeria could do more when it comes to speaking out against corruption and bad leadership. We have a country which is rich in natural resources yet the vast majority of our people are struggling to live.

"Internationally, we are frequently voted as being among the most corrupt nations in the world. In my travels, I have found that the Nigerian passport is like a red flag at any point of entry. The other day, I was happy to read an article in *The Irish Times* which said positive things about Nigeria by referring to our hospitality and our willingness to help other West African countries through peace-keeping forces. We as a people will have to take the redeeming of our country into our own hands. For years, we blamed our colonial masters, but since those days, too many of our own leaders have betrayed us. We may have to get deeper into our own mismanagement before we begin to turn things around. One thing is certain: the vast majority of the Nigerian people want to solve their problems and want to be proud of their country.

"In my own life, I am currently in the middle of my second term as provincial councillor. I will continue to give my best support to our congregational leader and to our communities in West Africa until my term comes to an end. When that happens, I would like to go on mission outside Nigeria as I feel I would learn a lot by contributing for a while in another country."

Congregation of the Mission
(CM)

(Vincentian Fathers)

An Introduction

The Congregation of the Mission was founded by St. Vincent de Paul who was born into a small farming family in Puoy in the south-east of France in 1581. From the beginning, the Congregation of priests dedicated itself to reforming the Church and to evangelizing and caring for the poor.

A significant number of Vincent de Paul's early followers were Irish. Religious persecution had driven many priests to France and more than twenty of them joined the CM. A request was eventually made to Rome for Vincentian missionaries to be sent to Ireland. A party of ten was sent in 1647. They first worked in the Dioceses of Cashel and Limerick.

Their work in Ireland was basically the same as what it was in France. After the First World War, missionaries were sent to China and in 1960, a mission was sent to Nigeria to work alongside the other Irish missionaries there, especially the Kiltegan Fathers and the Medical Missionaries of Mary. That mission grew into the indigenous Nigerian Province of the Congregation within which are many Nigerian Vincentian Fathers.

Father Rod Crowley

Vincentian Fathers (CM)
Christ the King Catholic Church,
Akowonjo, Agege, Lagos

Fr. Rod Crowley

'Reverend Father Rod Crowley is a true Vincentian. He is the luckiest man to have chosen a career he so richly fits into' – words from Sir Pius Ehiagwina, International Vice-President of the Society of St. Vincent de Paul.

It was a career he had not considered "until late in the day" he tells me. "I had graduated from university with a B.A. in economics and a B.Comm. There was a place reserved for me in the accounting firm of Craig Gardener in Dublin. It looked as if I was going to follow my father who had founded Kennedy and Crowley and Co. and my three brothers into the world of accountancy. I went away on holiday and found myself thinking that there must be more to life and living than money and fame. I began to think about other options. I had this vague and niggling desire to do something worthwhile – something that had value. I started thinking about the priesthood and decided to give it a try. I'm not sure if I ever believed that I would persevere. To my surprise, it seems to have worked out."

I met Fr. Rod shortly after my arrival in Lagos. I had the opportunity of being present at a parish anniversary celebration in his church in Akowonjo, Agege in the outskirts of Lagos. It was a joyful occasion and one in which his devotion and his commitment to his huge Nigerian flock was clearly in evidence. This is a parish that has an attendance of approximately two thousand at all four masses on Sunday. Most of his parishioners struggle to make a living.

He first came to Nigeria in 1963. At the time of this interview, he was packing his bags and preparing to retire in Ireland.

The Congregation of the Mission (CM) – commonly known as the Vincentian Fathers was founded by St. Vincent de Paul in France in 1625. It forms a part of what is known today as the Vincentian Family which comprises the Vincentian Fathers, the Daughters of Charity, the St. Vincent de Paul Society, the Ladies of Charity and the Marian Vincentian Youth Movement. The Vincentians came to Ireland in 1647 when a party of ten missionaries was sent there from France. While the words mission and charity personify the charism and the work of all branches of the Vincentian family, the early Vincentian missionaries to Ireland focused on a ministry they were engaged in in France, that of the revitalization of Catholic Church.

Rod Crowley was educated in Castleknock College in Dublin by the Vincentian Fathers. "They were not professional educators as such though most of them were very well qualified. They had a good spirit and were concerned with giving a sound all-round education. When I was thinking of becoming a priest, I didn't immediately think of joining them. Neither did I ever imagine myself going on mission and spending a large part of my life working with the poorest of the poor in Africa. I first considered the diocesan clergy and a number of other congregations such as the Jesuits. In the end, I came back to the Vincentians as I was attracted to their community life and the variety of their work. This includes teaching at different levels, spiritual direction, parish and mission work. They also work with the deaf and with the travelling people.

"I was ordained in 1956 and taught for two years in St. Paul's, Raheny before moving to Castleknock College. I was on the 14th tee on Newlands golf course in Dublin when I was asked by my golfing partner Fr. Frank Mullen, if I would put my name down on a list of priests who might be willing to work on the missions in Nigeria. I agreed as it all sounded vague, abstract and in the remote future. I was in no way gung-ho about going. Some months later, to my great surprise, my name appeared on the board in Castleknock as a person appointed to Nigeria. I was slightly shocked but I do remember feeling some degree of excitement about the possible adventure of it all!

"I came by plane to Lagos and I recall being overwhelmed by the heat. I felt I was being wrapped in a wet blanket. The frenetic activity and the surging crowds disturbed me a fair bit. Somebody drove me to Ikot-Expene, now in Akwa Ibom State. It was our only mission house in Nigeria at the time. Very soon after my arrival, I became parish priest and that threw me in at the deep end and tied me down a fair deal. I did however get away from time to time to give some missions and retreats.

"We had started the parish in Ikot-Expene a number of years earlier so there were a fair number of Catholics there. I found that I liked the people and that I integrated well with them. I had many ways of gaining an understanding of them. Visiting the prison as chaplain was one. That sort of thing when combined with the normal duties of a parish priest brings you right into the people's lives. You become very involved in their joys, their fears and their aspirations. After a few years, I began to feel that somehow we should be more specialized as missionaries if we were going to be able to add that extra dimension to the activities we were involved in. I introduced this idea at a meeting and the man in charge suggested that I go to America and study with the Jesuits at Fordham University who offered courses geared to mission work. I didn't fancy going really but I found that it was inspiring once I got started. Though the courses were good, they were not as geared to what I was looking for as much as I would have liked.

"After two years in the States, I found myself back teaching in Dublin – in St. Patrick's Teacher Training College, Drumcondra and in All Hallows College. It was understood at the time that I wouldn't be able to get back into Nigeria because of the raging Biafran war. I did however manage to make one visit to Biafra in 1969. I came in on a cargo plane which landed on Uli airstrip – a converted piece of road halfway between Onitsha and Owerri and right in the heart of Biafra which was used to land relief planes which were organized by the Catholic Church and Caritas during the war. Landing a plane was always a challenging business and it frequently had to be done after dark and without lights, for fear of attracting enemy fire. My visit was preparatory to my coming back and though the war was still being fiercely waged, we managed to tour around and meet our own priests who were still there. Force of circumstances had pushed them up into Biafra and that is where they stayed for the duration of the war. They became largely associated with the Biafrans as they were cut off from the territory controlled by the Federal Government. Part of the discussion in our congregation at the time was related to whether or not we could move them back into Federal territory. In the end, it was decided that I should go back to Federal territory and that the others had no option but to remain in Biafra. Subsequently when a number of Irish priests – mostly Holy Ghost Fathers – were deported from Nigeria at the end of the war, some of our own were included in that number.

"My attitude to the war at that time was somewhat ambivalent. Many of the people I had worked with in Ikot-Expene were Igbos and therefore Biafrans and I certainly had sympathy for them. Indeed I spent much of my time in Ireland during the war collecting food and relief supplies for them. It's not that I ever became anti-Biafran but I began to feel at a certain stage that if they were to win the war, they might very well try to suppress the surrounding ethnic groups who lived within the territory which became known as Biafra. These smaller groups had become very fearful.

"Almost the day the war finished in January 1970, I was one of two priests who went down to Port Harcourt which had been largely deserted by the Church during the war. We went at the suggestion of the Kiltegan Fathers who had always ministered there. Straight away we got into relief work which ranged from rebuilding hospitals, schools and bridges to digging bore holes, supplying food, water and seeds for planting. We were also dealing with a number of cholera epidemics. The whole thing was amazingly challenging and it touched bells in me that I didn't realize existed. The more powerful feelings of wanting to get things moving again submerged those of pessimism and frustration.

"During this time also, I was asked to get involved in the refurbishment of the Sacred Heart Minor Seminary in Port Harcourt which had been totally destroyed by occupying soldiers. It took five years to complete. All of this work was combined with parish work in three parishes, one of which was on the Niger River up at Bonny which today is the location for huge oil and natural gas export facilities. I had a boat to do my rounds!

"In 1977, I was moved for one year to Emmanuel College in Ugbokolo in Makurdi Diocese in the relative north of Nigeria. It was like moving to a different country and I was just beginning to come to terms with it when I was transferred back to Ikot-Expene to be spiritual director and teacher of English at the Bigard Seminary there. Somehow I felt ill-equipped for this role but to my surprise, it worked out well. Interacting with young people of a different culture is challenging and it places you in a position of great responsibility. I spent seven very happy years at Bigard. They were peppered however with a few bad experiences. One of these happened one Christmas when four of our students were killed at the gates of the seminary by a passing vehicle. I had the sorrowful task of conveying the corpses to the families in various parts of Nigeria.

"My next move was to Orafite in the Onitsha Diocese in the east where I became involved in missions and retreats on a full-time basis. I enjoyed this assignment very much. The parishes I went to, especially the big rural ones, were a revelation as I came into contact with quite a lot of the traditional rituals which had to do with juju and charms. One involved a teacher who invited myself and another priest to bless the stream from which she drew water and in which she claimed were water spirits. We entered the stream after dark when everything was quiet, said prayers and did a blessing. As we were coming away, the local people rushed out in great numbers and wanted to attack us with knives because they believed we were performing rituals and offering sacrifice. Real human life faced us on these kinds of occasions but I regarded what we were doing as removing the fear from the lives of the people. Some aspects of many of the traditional customs and rituals were good but fear was often a dominating feature.

"One evening a man from another location came to our house and invited me to carry his juju to the mission. He was too afraid to touch it himself. It was composed of all sorts of things tied together in knots. He wanted me to burn it but after a day or two when we wouldn't baptize him because he had not taken instruction and had been a committed pagan up to then, he wanted the juju back. He felt he needed it or baptism for protection. I had to leave the area shortly after that but I asked that he be given instruction and baptized at a later date.

"On another occasion we had to go to cut down juju trees which the people were afraid of. The trees appeared perfectly normal to me. There was a shrine in the middle of them which was used to appease the gods. I wasn't in any way frightened while engaged in these tasks. I understood that people needed help to be released from their fear. I felt it was a worthwhile task to offer that help. We were meeting this juju fairly regularly at that time. Its incidence is now decreasing. Water spirits are still very much believed in, especially in rural areas. These beliefs do not die easily and we frequently found that people liked to combine them with Christianity. They feel secure if they keep a foot in both camps!

"Their belief in and respect for the ancestors I liked but again a lot of it had to do with fear and appeasement. If you didn't appease them, they were likely to wreak vengeance. Because of this, it was very important to have proper burials which sometimes had notable excesses which tended to wipe out all the family's savings. The notion of respect for the ancestors in itself is good and it is close to the Christian belief in the communion of saints.

"In 1987, I made a choice to go to the Gregorian University in Rome for a year to read spirituality. It was my first time to spend any length of time in the city. I found the history that can be discovered under every stone to be fascinating. I wasn't too focused on observing church politics though I did go to some functions around the Vatican which were very impressive in the way they were conducted. One group of people with whom I came in contact that year was a lay group called the *San Egidio Community*. They were very enthusiastic and involved in prayer and social work. They brokered a peace in Mozambique at one stage. I believe they have a branch in Ireland.

"I was very pleased to return to Lagos in 1989, to St. Leo's parish in Ikeja. It's a mighty big church and it was started by Fr. Hugh Ford, SMA who is now retired in Ireland. We took over its completion and it's now a thriving parish.

Sir Pat Igwilo, one of the parishioners from St. Leo's and an admirer of Father Crowley describes the church 'as a work of architectural magnificence' but claims that Father will be remembered even more for the wonderful work he did among hundreds of drug addicts, HIV victims, prisoners awaiting trial and helpless people suffering the effects of all kinds of human rights' abuses. 'Fr. Crowley was a man,' he said, 'to whom people gravitated from far and wide. Even other priests came to him for help in solving their problems. When he was transferred from St. Leo's to Christ the King parish in Agege, he set up Ozanam House for the homeless. He initiated skills acquisition programmes for many of his parishioners. He packaged a health insurance scheme and ran a daily clinic where medical services were virtually free for those who could not afford to pay.'

Moving to Christ the King was just another challenge which Fr. Crowley approached with eagerness.

"When I moved there, we set about building it up as it had once been an out-station of the nearby bigger parish of St. Sabina. Today all four Sunday masses have huge congregations. We developed it by putting in various facilities and now it is a full parish with out-stations of its own. The parishioners and many church groups work very hard to keep up high standards. By and large, they are wonderful people and I have been working with them to try to deepen their faith. They sometimes tend to settle a lot for devotions and practices which will obtain this and that for them.

"When I retire, a Nigerian Vincentian priest who will be appointed by the superior general of the order will take my place. We are at the point of performing the essential exercise of mission which is passing our work on to the local Church. They will do things their own way and it will be a little different to our way. We have about forty Nigerian Vincentians. Whoever takes over the parish will be helped along by the very strong laity groups which have quite a lot of drive and power and this is especially true of the women's groups.

"After spending almost forty years in Nigeria, I admit to feeling a little uncertain about the next phase of my life. I know that I have come to the end of a particular road and it would not be right to continue on that same road. I feel that I have done all that I could. At the same time, I have been here for a long time and it may not be that easy to fit into the next situation which will be in Ireland."

Father Crowley celebrated his 70th birthday in Nigeria shortly before he retired.

The Company of the Daughters of Charity of St. Vincent de Paul
(DoC)

An Introduction

The Company of the Daughters of Charity of St. Vincent de Paul is an international organization of women in the Catholic Church which was founded in France in 1633 by St. Vincent de Paul and St. Louise de Marillac. From the beginning, these women dedicated their lives to the service of the poorest of the poor.

The Congregation of the Mission (Vincentian Fathers), which was founded by St. Vincent de Paul in 1625, has always acted as spiritual directors to the Daughters of Charity.

Today, the Daughters of Charity number over 22,000 and work in more than 80 countries in every continent.

Their work responds to all types of poverty which includes child and family services, services for people with intellectual and physical disabilities, services for older people and services for the homeless.

The Daughters of Charity came to Nigeria in 1963. Today, Nigeria has become a fully-fledged Province of the international congregation and the Province with its 120 strong membership continues to serve the poorest of the poor in 17 locations throughout the country.

Sister Elma Hurley

Daughters of Charity (DoC)
Eleme, Port Harcourt

Sr. Elma Hurley with women from the St. Vincent de Paul Society,
Eleme, Port Harcourt

It is Sister Elma who is waiting for me at Port Harcourt airport when I arrive for my visit to the provincial house of the Daughters of Charity (DoC) which is located in Eleme in the outskirts of the city. When I emerge with my luggage, I spot her making a friendly enquiry of one of the porters about my arrival. I call out and there she is – more than seventy years old, sprightly, friendly, welcoming and full of chat. As soon as Benjamin the driver is introduced, we set off on the forty-five minute journey to Eleme. It is late afternoon, traffic is rapidly building up and the streets are packed with people. Crowds pour on and off the public transportation buses. Taxis in various states of dismantlement do a rattling trade. Okadas (motor bikes) flit recklessly in and out of non-existent spaces while their swaying passengers disinterestedly hold on. Roadside fit-up restaurants grill bush meat, chicken, yams. Women with tiny babies on their backs crouch over low kerosene stoves or open wood burning fires cooking aromatic dishes of rice, bean-cakes and much more. Streams of school children in uniforms of purple, green and pink languidly wend their way to their homes. Some stop at small stalls to purchase a snack, a drink or a sachet of ground nuts.

Sister Elma clearly relishes giving me a running commentary on all these activities. I am enchanted by my surroundings. I pour questions at her. The sultry late afternoon heat cocoons us in a place apart.

When we arrive in Eleme, I see that the compound of the Daughters of Charity is an impressive one, set in spacious grounds. Imposing entrance gates open on a long avenue lined on each side with majestic palm trees. They were planted by American Benedictine Fathers who were the first white owners of the compound and who ran a very good school there before the civil war.

In the grounds there are many buildings. First there is the chapel – simple, peaceful and tastefully furnished. There is the office block, the conference hall, the staff house, the priest's house, the guest house and the accommodation block where the sisters sleep. It was Sister Elma who was in charge during much of the building programme.

"In 1975, when I came to Nigeria, I was forty-four years old. I had always let it be known that if I were ever needed in a mission post that I would be willing to go. Nevertheless, when I was asked to go to Nigeria, I got a bit of a shock. The congregation was planning to open a new house and school in Uyo in Bendel State (now Akwa Ibom State). My first few years there were spent teaching *home economics*. Then I became our local sister-in-charge.

"In 1986, I came here to Eleme again as sister-in-charge or sister servant as we say in our congregation. Our founder St. Vincent de Paul did not believe in the concept of superiority. For him, the person in charge is the person who serves the others. In fact the Holy Father's official name is *The Servant of the Servants of God*. My work in Eleme over the years involved the development of what we see here today. My team and I learned as we went along and got advice from many quarters. Today, Sister Christina Quinn is sister servant but I continue to have a number of responsibilities. I am the provincial bursar and that means that I supervise and manage the finances of all our houses. Sr. Christina who was born near Castlerea, Co. Roscommon came to Eleme in 1995 after spending almost eighteen years teaching at second level in Uyo in Akwa Ibom State. In addition to her duties here, she serves on the provincial council. She is a highly competent person who has the talent and personal qualities for her demanding role.

"I am also very active in the St. Vincent de Paul Society. We meet here in the house every Sunday. Presently, we are building a transit camp at Eleme Junction for people without means who find themselves stranded in Port Harcourt. This happens quite often especially with prisoners who have just been released and have trouble finding accommodation before returning to their own area. Eleme Junction is a very suitable location for the camp as from there you can head in many directions."

I found Eleme to be a very busy place. Staff from DoC houses from all over Nigeria and Ghana had assembled for management training. There were lectures, workshops, presentations. I met a great many young Nigerian and Ghanaian participants – the young women who will carry the work of the Irish DoC into the 21st century and beyond.

I visited *The Child* – the school for the mentally disabled which is run by the sisters in the Catholic cathedral compound in the centre of the city. We arrived just as the children were about to be released for the day. During the few minutes we had to chat, they poured out their stories with huge excitement to Sister Elma who was well known to most of them. These tapered off as soon as the arrival of the buses to take them home was announced. Despite their disabilities, all we could see through the windows as they waved good-bye were joyful and exuberant faces.

On the way back to Eleme, we take a tour of the city centre. Port Harcourt which was once known as *The Garden City* has lost most of its flowers and much of its former charm. Today its fame comes from being the oil capital of Nigeria. Wealth has made it one of the country's most expensive cities. The once elegant, former colonial mansions have given way to sprawling complexes of office blocks which house government and business employees. It's a low-slung city with few tall buildings. The once lovely downtown area is now largely an extended market. "There are many huge markets in the city," Sister tells me. "Trading is intense and displays of every conceivable commodity draw huge crowds on a daily basis." We pass an impressive church named *Mater Miserecordia*. It was built by the Irish Holy Ghost Fathers more than fifty years ago and is the most beautiful in the city

An obtrusive and extravagant building comes into view. It was built for General Sani Abacha, the former military Head of State and given to him as a gift by the Rivers State Government. We pass *The Presidential Hotel*, once the best in Port Harcourt but now losing out to a big downtown Chinese-owned hotel. The names of long established P.H. companies loom large as we drive around – *UTC, Peugeot, Nissan, CFAO, Union Bank, John Holt, Mandilas, Federal Express, Frenchies* (a well liked Lebanese-owned restaurant and bakery) and the expensive supermarket *Park and Shop*. This supermarket which has branches in other Nigerian cites is owned by an Indian company and is largely patronized by wealthy Nigerians and expatriates employed in multinationals.

We pass local and state government offices. The latter comprise of nine carefully maintained buildings set in well appointed gardens. The upcoming elections are heralded on numerous posters which claim that *Odili* (the incumbent Governor) *is the Man*. "He's been very good," Sister Elma says, "but of course he has his detractors as well as his followers. He is expected to be re-elected." Other electioneering posters loom large – *The Future of Nigeria Depends on You; Dignity of Labour; Save the Woman – Save the Nation*. "There are many powerful women around and they are trying their best to move things forward," Sister Elma informs me.

We return to Eleme for lunch after which I visit *Rosalie Home* for destitute women. It's run by the sisters totally on donations. Many of the women are mentally ill. Some have been driven from their homes – their families believing that their *madness* is associated with evil spirits. All members of staff are Nigerian. Sister Catherine who is in charge of the home is assisted by Sister Esther who did her psychiatry training in St. Vincent's Hospital, Fairview, Dublin. Sister Lucy, fresh out of the novitiate hopes also to go to Ireland for professional training. Toyin, a very enthusiastic psychology student is doing an internship.

Alongside *Rosalie Home* is a vocational school for local people and for any resident of the *Home* who is fit to attend. The students learn sewing, cooking and English. An impressive display of women's dresses, wrappers and blouses provides evidence of considerable talent and industry. Cake baking is a specialty and some very fine examples of wedding cakes and party cakes are on display.

Sister Christina Quinn at a Rehabilitation Centre for destitute women at the Sisters' compound, Adiaha Obong, Uyo, Akwa Ibom State

Sister Elma was, at the time of my visit, contemplating returning to Ireland, not to retire, she emphasized but to become involved in some new project. "When I joined our congregation, it was more or less understood that you would spend your life working in the Irish province. Once the foundation in Nigeria was established, it became an extension of the Irish province so those of us who came always intended returning home eventually. Nigeria has now become a province in its own right and within a few years, it will be totally run by Nigerians. Our objective was to establish the mission and then leave it to the local church to take over. Our Nigerian sisters will do things a little differently to the way we did them but I am confident that they will be successful. What is most important is that we all retain our spirit and our charism – which is working with the poorest of the poor and working at grass roots level."

Sister Francesca Edet

Daughters of Charity (DoC)
Eleme, Port Harcourt

Sr. Francesca Edet

"I come from the coastal city of Calabar in the south east of Nigeria. The landscape is very green as it gets twice as much rainfall as Lagos for example. The city which is small by Nigerian standards is situated high on a hill commanding a wonderful view of the Calabar River. It is a safe and pleasant place to walk through and visitors are happy to go there. The people are hospitable and friendly. It is there that you will most often hear the phrase 'you are welcome.' The local women love to dress up with wonderful styles. They also love good cooking and delight in presenting great dishes. Sometimes it is said that they use their cooking skills to attract good husbands! They have mastered the art of cooking many delicacies and within any one week, the woman from Calabar will prepare a variety of different soups for the family. Our soups are not like yours. They consist of aromatic sauces which have lots of meat or fish in them. The soup is the main part of the meal.

"Calabari women are also said to be very creative. They show lots of initiative, confidence and independence. All of these characteristics have evolved to a large degree from the fact that Calabar is a coastal city and has for many centuries been exposed to outside influences. We have always been required to understand, absorb and learn from these influences. The Niger Delta and the port of Calabar which were once notorious for the export of slaves subsequently became well known for the export of palm oil. Still later, when Nigeria discovered crude oil, Calabar remained an important port."

I met the handsome and poised Sister Francesca at the regional headquarters of the Daughters of Charity in Eleme in the outskirts of Port Harcourt. She is the first Nigerian to have been elected regional provincial of her congregation. At the time of our meeting, she had completed half of her six-year term of office. "I was absolutely amazed," she told me, "when my name kept coming up in the elections. I was in Ireland taking a two-year leadership training course when I was given the news and told that I would have one week to consider whether are not I would be willing to assume the responsibility of accepting the position. I was unsure of what I should do but after speaking with experienced reverend sisters in Ireland and having received all sorts of messages of support from Nigeria, I felt sufficiently encouraged to accept. Like all my fellow Nigerian reverend sisters, I have always understood that the day would come when we would have to take over from the Irish missionary sisters but of course, I never expected it to affect myself in such a direct way.

"Following my decision, I quickly returned to Nigeria to meet our Superior General who travelled from Paris for my installation ceremony. She came with my work mandate which had every detail in written form. It also mandated every sister to offer their co-operation and obedience to me. After the ceremony, a big celebration took place which was attended by many of our sisters from all over Nigeria and indeed from Ireland.

"I am based here in Eleme and on my provincial council, I have six councillors. They are very experienced advisors and they represent our different apostolates in the fields of education, health, pastoral and social work. In addition, Sister Geraldine Henry who is based in Abuja but who has lots of administrative and management skills comes here on a regular basis to assist me. At the moment, we are working on a plan which will depict a vision for our congregation for the next three years.

"My work involves a lot of travel to visit our communities in different parts of Nigeria, Ghana and Cameroon. This gives our sisters in these locations the opportunity to speak to me in groups or as individuals. Local superiors or sister servants as they are called in our congregation are also given the opportunity to have consultations with me."

Sister Francesca was born in 1954 into a large polygamous family. Her father had many wives even though he considered himself a Catholic. Her mother who was the third of his five wives gave him six of his twelve children. "She was the wife for whom he paid *the bride price*. Being part of a polygamous family was not easy for my mother who was an assertive woman and who found herself frequently at odds with traditional customs and demanding marital in-laws. Preferring to be independent during one period of illness, she moved out of my father's house and into Port Harcourt with her children. She spent all her energy educating us up to class three in secondary school. It was then that my father stepped in and took over our education in preparation for the GCE.

"We were all very fond of our Dad and during the years we spent with our mother, we were never detached from him. He in turn was very fond of us and he never failed to give my mother the financial help he could afford. He is dead now and Mum is seventy-four. She is very well, very happy and working hard.

"When I was a seminary sister (a novice), my father took a wife whom he wedded in the Church. It was a big blow for me as I had always wished that my mother and he would be the ones to wed in Church. I used to listen with great sorrow to my fellow seminarians talking about their parents who had had Church weddings and who had families who were living tightly-knit lives. When the Irish reverend sisters came to visit my family, they had to visit my parents separately. This was hard for me to bear although polygamy was understood by everybody to be part of the African culture.

"The latter part of my own secondary education took place at a mission school run by the indigenous congregation of *The Handmaids of the Holy Child*. At the time, I had no idea that I might like to become a reverend sister. I had never been a member of the aspirants' groups in school which were made up of young girls interested in religious life. I remember having a great interest in helping the elderly and I was a member of *The Young Christian Association*. I took delight in doing helpful chores like fetching firewood or water for the sick and elderly but I was not doing them for any religious reason.

"It was after I finished school and during a period when I was teaching as an auxiliary in a small village school that I got this clear and strange feeling that I wanted to become a *Daughter of Charity*. At that point, I had no memory of ever having heard of them. The name mysteriously came into my mind. Some time afterwards, while I was visiting my former school, the sisters there managed to put me in touch with the *Daughters*. When I told my mother of my plans and thinking, she did not approve and did not wish to have her first daughter leave her in that way. My Dad on the other hand had no problem giving his approval as he had two reverend sisters in his own family. My mother eventually came around and after that, I never looked back.

"I became eagerly involved in the work of the *Daughters of Charity*. After some time, I was put forward to train as a teacher of deaf children – firstly in our centre at Ikot Ekpene in Akwa Ibom State and then in Jos in Plateau State. I found the training to be daunting but with generous help from my colleagues, I managed to master the techniques. I later did further training in the field in Dublin. In Ikot Ekpene, many of our sisters were involved with all kinds of disabilities ranging from those emanating from polio to disabilities resulting from the tragedies of our civil war. They had earlier taken over that particular apostolate at the request of the Bishop of the diocese."

Sister Francesca admits to feeling disheartened that her country which has so much natural wealth still suffers from enormous poverty. "It's quite overwhelming to have to suffer the consequences of huge corruption and the serious mismanagement of our resources. We are conscious that as reverend sisters, we carry part of the load for the Government. The financial aid we get in return is very little compared to what we should get. For our funding, we depend mostly on aid agencies and on donations from both within and without the country. In the institutions which we run independently of the Government, we don't give ourselves salaries no matter how highly trained we are. The small number of us who work in government-run schools and clinics are remunerated with a meagre salary. The financial struggle is an ongoing challenge. We live quite frugal lives ourselves – sometimes not being able to spend money on the fresh fruit that is abundant in many parts of Nigeria.

"Despite these difficulties, we see a bright future for our congregation. The young women who join us will already have reached exacting personal and academic standards before they apply to us. We are quite strict in this regard. All have to have secondary school GCE certificates and their motives for joining are very carefully examined. The seminarians are subsequently given ongoing assessment during their formation period. Presently, our Nigerian reverend sisters and aspirants are highly committed. If, by God's grace, we continue to get good candidates and we continue to give them an excellent training, I think that we can have confidence in the future.

"Our Irish reverend sisters have always been a wonderful example of what true commitment is all about and of what living simple lives in accordance with the charism of our founder St. Vincent de Paul means. St. Vincent continually stressed to his Sisters that they should have faith in the providence of God. This is what we strive to do. People see and appreciate our work and for those reasons, are frequently willing to offer their sincere support."

Sister Annette O'Shea

Daughters of Charity (DoC)
Eleme, Port Harcourt

Sr. Annette O'Shea at the opening of Bue Leka clinic in Ogoni Land

I am travelling with Sister Annette O'Shea to the clinic she is
building in Eeke in the heart of Ogoni Land in Rivers State in
south eastern Nigeria. It is gloriously warm and sunny at 8:00 a.m.
as we depart from the Daughter's of Charity (DoC) provincial house
in Eleme. The clinic which is nearing the end of construction is the
focal point of our outing but during the morning, we will also stop
to observe a mobile clinic which moves daily with Sister Annette's

medical team among the tiny villages of Ogoni Land and which today is operating out of the grounds of a Methodist Church in one such village. Here her team will treat up to a hundred people who will come from the surrounding areas with their pain and their suffering. Monthly, the number of patients treated averages about one thousand.

"You are actually in Ogoni Land when you are in Eleme," Sister Annette tells me "though it is not called that. During the crisis years of the mid 1990's when Ken Saro Wiwa and the activist group Mosop were fighting Shell and the Government of Nigeria for the rights of the Ogoni people to their land and to a share in the profits of its rich yield of oil, many Ogonis came to Eleme and formed little settlements. Some of our own staff are originally from the many small villages we will pass through today. Nobody in Ogoni speaks the same language. The four areas which you have within the region all have differences in language. Whether or not you understand them depends on how well you mixed with the different groups growing up. One of our sisters who is from the area of Khana understands all four as she went to school in Bori, the capital of Ogoni, where all four were spoken. Another sister who was brought up in the Gokhana region speaks only Gokhana.

"The area, as you can see, is quite poor and undeveloped though I have seen improvements in the four years that I have been here. There are some better roads and electrification has increased especially for people in places that are fortunate to have a good local political councillor. It is said that Shell Nigeria is behind some of the improvements and you will see that they have posters claiming sponsorship for a number of development projects.

"Since the crisis of the 1990's, the people have refused to let Shell back into their region which of course is bad for employment but they are prepared to put up with that. Shell is only waiting to get in again and it is said that they have changed for the better, many of their work practices. Nevertheless, they will not be let in and many people around here will tell you that their crops have begun to improve now that there are no oil spillages. Of course many things are said, but with what veracity one is never sure.

"The DoC have been working in Ogoni Land since the 1970's. It all started when Sister Nora Lally, a nurse, found herself visiting the sick in the various villages there during her irregular visits to Port Harcourt from our house in Akwa Ibom State further west. When she subsequently moved to Eleme on a permanent basis, she started visiting four villages on a regular basis. Initially, she and her team were paid by the Government to do immunization programmes and the like but then came the late 1970's and the Government's take-over of hospitals and clinics. From that time on, indigenes were employed to do the work which the sisters had been doing.

"In 1993 however, at the height of the Ogoni crisis when demands of compensation for damage to land of more than $300,000,000 were being made by Ken Saro Wiwa and Mosop for the Ogonis, we were asked by *Trocaire Ireland* to be the coordinators of food distribution for the people who were starving in the villages involved in the conflict. This food was actually being paid for anonymously by Shell Nigeria but distributed and channelled through European Union and Trocaire agencies. It was an enormous operation. We were distributing among other things huge sacks of rice. All around there was huge starvation as people had stopped working or were unable to work. Many were also being killed. Sr. Elizabeth Fallon who is now in Ireland was in charge in Eleme at the time."

While Sister Annette is relating all this information, she is keeping a close eye on the road and staying in touch with the driver who is not her normal driver and who is not totally familiar with the route. "Benjamin," she calls out from time to time, "be careful, take it easy, there is a lot of traffic." At one point Benjamin comes to a complete stop. We are surrounded by big heavy trucks and the noise is deafening. The dust is rising and affecting everybody. "The trucks are all on their way to the refinery," Annette says. "Yesterday, there was no electricity so they probably didn't manage to get filled. There could also be trouble up there between the people of Eleme and the village of Okrika. It's often about who gets employed and who doesn't. Both groups claim that the refinery is on their land. This morning, the pile up is huge so there must be a dispute. We are very close to the refinery now. It's run by the Nigerian National Petroleum Corporation."

The delay is not for too long so Benjamin drives on over potholed and bumpy roads for another few kilometres until he is flagged down by the police. Annette passes him twenty naira so that he can give it to them. "They are searching for stolen cars," she says. "If you pay them a few naira, they won't bother searching the car! If you don't, they will become demanding and give you a lot of hassle. It is said that they are often sent out by one of their superiors. They will divide the collected funds between them this evening. It's an easy way of making some extra money!"

The further into the villages we drive the poorer and the narrower the roads become. At times we seem to be bringing the car over narrow virgin tracks. The countryside is green and very beautiful. Only the occasional cement construction spoils the natural beauty of the traditional village dwellings which are made of mud and straw. Subsistence farming is all around. We pass a very old lady who is bent over her shovel digging her patch of cassava. "The women," says Annette, "all have their rented patches. The farming is very hard but they are devoted to it. Even if they are dying with fever, they will go to the farm. Some will go as far as leaving a sick child at home rather than miss the morning's work. It's their bread and butter – their life. The daily diet is cassava and yam. If you are well off, you will have rice and beans. The cassava is to them what the potato was to us in the past. They eat it with soup. Out here, they are able to have some fresh fish and dried fish is eaten quite a lot. Meat is rare and it's for the well off. They are great farmers around here though and each side of this road, you can find villages that go in and in and in. All have mud houses. You might find a few made from blocks.

"From close to here, you can get across by boat to a place called Andoni and that's another eye-opener. There are loads of people living over there – all in tiny mud dwellings. They were the people who came in and caused a lot of trouble during the Ogoni crisis and the Ogonis allege that the Government paid them to do so. They maimed, killed, slashed and burned. It's extraordinary but they have been sort of forgiven. Some villages however, will not now allow their women to marry Andoni men. They will accept these people superficially but there rests a deep-seated distrust and when it comes to jobs or marriages, it's an absolute no-go situation. They will also say harsh things about the Andonai such as claiming that they do not bury their dead or that they hang bodies from the trees. I don't know if this is true or not.

"We are now approaching Bori, the capital. It's the only real town around. The rest are all villages and markets. The local government is here. There are a few good schools and a polytechnic. The market is huge and it spreads over a vast area and trading of every imaginable variety is carried on. Bori is in the Khana region and the Yeghe people who are in the adjacent Gokhana region feel that they should have got the capital and the market for their area. For this reason, you can have all sorts of trouble with irate youths from Yeghe. They are the ones who burned all the houses we are just passing now.

"Over there where I am pointing, you will notice a general hospital. I wouldn't like to go into it. One of our sister's brothers had a road accident and he was brought there. Because nobody could produce the money – though they would have been able to bring it later as the man had a good business – they wouldn't admit him. He subsequently died.

"Around here also, you will notice men going around tapping trees to extract the palm wine. There are different kinds of palm trees but the palm wine ones are mostly what you get in this area. The wine is available in the bars including the one on the site of our clinic. The builder went around one day and offered us all a drink! Palm oil on the other hand comes out of the giant nuts that grow on the palm oil trees. They are plentiful in other areas along the coast. There are also coconut palms that produce coconuts.

"If you went straight on from where we are now, you would come to Bane, the village where Ken Saro Wiwa was born. His grandfather used to be in charge of the big market area in Bori. He was a very strong business man and he educated all of his children abroad. He now regrets that they are all living outside Nigeria but he's proud of their success in the different professions. Just now, we are on the road to Kaa and it is the last village before you meet the river water that is close to the sea. When you go over to the coastal town of Bonny which is not far from here, you have sea water. Bonny, for centuries has attracted European traders and today it is a port from which liquefied natural gas and petroleum products are exported. Among the ethnic groups that are to be found along the coastal regions are the Ibibio, Ijaw, Anang and Efik. They are linguistically and culturally related to the Igbo. Nevertheless, they feared domination by the Igbo when the concept of Biafra – an Igbo nation – was fought for during the civil war. For this reason, most did not support the Igbo aspirations."

We arrive in Eeke shortly after 9:00 a.m. The signs say *Welcome to Eeke*. It's a village but the people, Annette says, argue constantly about whether or not it should be called a town. She instructs Benjamin to drive right into the clinic site. "We will first take a look at the sisters' house. The funding for that came from *Missio* in Germany and *The Seton Institute* in the United States. *Ireland Aid* is funding the clinic. No agency will give you the full amount so you always have to make up the short fall from some source or other. We hope to be able to open the clinic in a few months.

"The invitation to establish the clinic came from the local chief. Immediately after the crisis years, a group of about forty farmers came together and offered small plots of land for the establishment of a clinic. The chief then wrote to the DoC and offered the land. He was told by our provincial that the proposal would be considered. Then during the *Jubilee Year* of 2000, the Pope gave out donations for development projects. We were all asked by the Bishop of Port Harcourt to come up with ideas. The DoC proposed acquiring a mobile clinic for the Ogoni villages. Funding was granted so we have been operating it successfully for a few years. Working in the villages in that way pushed us towards committing ourselves to building the clinic in Eeke. When it is up and running, I hope that many of the patients whom we are now treating in the little villages all around will come there. Then I will look at the map and see what other villages we might serve with our mobile facilities.

"The mobile clinic has been providing a greatly needed service. We negotiate in advance with the villages and then go and set up in a location in a different village every day. We deal with many conditions – pains, aches, ulcers, fevers, inflammations, immunization, ante and post natal care. We do not deliver babies, though it is something we hope to do in Eeke. I lead the team. I'm a qualified nurse. I also have a Nigerian nurse/midwife as well as some local people who do a lot of work like giving out drugs and keeping records. My regular driver, an Ogoni man is very good at helping with all sorts of tasks. This year I took on a community extension worker whom I hope to send into the villages to do health education.

"The people pay what they can and we charge very little for drugs. We don't generate enough money to pay the staff and that is done with the help of a sum of money which I get every year from the International Women's Club in Port Harcourt. I also get other donations from time to time.

"The work is always increasing. HIV/AIDS is now a very frequent occurrence. You cannot afford to think of it in the way you would at home. You find for example, a patient in your clinic who is very sick. The sickness can take many forms. It might be an ulcer that is oozing. You put her on antibiotics because she looks terrible. You feed her because she is thin and fragile. In six months, you realize that this lady has HIV/AIDS and that her immune system is nonexistent. You could then get her tested which would cost an amount she cannot afford. If the test is positive, what can I do or what can she do? You are largely dealing with an illiterate population who will find it very hard to grasp the significance of the disease or who will refuse to believe in its existence. A couple once came into my Nigerian colleague. She felt that HIV/AIDS was their problem. The man was a pastor so sister explained that she would like them to take a test. He sent his wife along to take one but refused to do so himself. Most people will not want to be tested. We often get tuberculosis and AIDS together. We treat the TB as we get the drugs from *GRLA* (German Leprosy and TB Program). Then there are a few clinics in the region which will accept people I sometimes send."

Before leaving the Eeke site, we walk around to look at all the buildings. There is great excitement and the site manager who is a small, plump man jumps up and down with glee even if Annette is finding fault with one thing or another. The sisters' home is finished and the clinic itself with its different departments is taking shape. The workers are proud of their achievements and the villagers are eagerly awaiting the opening. Annette's regular driver's wife has set up a canteen on the site which sells snacks and soft drinks to the workers and to passers by. She's a jolly, mother figure whose congeniality spreads warmth in all directions.

We leave Eeke and drive to the location of the mobile clinic. Annette chats on. "The pressures here," she says, "are very different to those you have at home. At home, you might have everything you need to carry out your job but the staff stresses and the demands of superiors can be very wearing. Here it's a question of having enough money to pay your staff and buy the drugs. It's nevertheless very satisfying work and the people are grateful and appreciative. I also have great scope. I'm building this clinic now and before I came here, I didn't know one end of a brick from another. Now I hear myself saying to the contractor – 'look, I want this window so high and these doors so wide and so on.' I have to keep a close eye on prices because I know that I can be fooled and that may not be deliberate or with a bad conscience. The dealers will start with a huge price and expect you to know that you have to start with your own. Then it's a question of where you go from there. You are in the end never quite sure of the advantage that might be taken and that can be frustrating. I try to inform myself as much as possible about the prices of raw materials and current labour costs and so on. When big money is involved, I consult with others who have been involved with building projects."

We spot the mobile clinic in a shaded area alongside the beautiful old stone built Methodist church. Were it not for the hot sun filtering through the tropical foliage, the shrieks of the beautiful black children on break from their cool classrooms within the church and the circle of sick and pained people who sit patiently around the mobile clinic, one might have imagined oneself in an Irish churchyard. Most of the sick look wretched. The ministering angels from Annette's team are on hand. They are caring and interested. I ask how old some of the really wizened looking patients are and am astonished to be told that most were not more than fifty. Life with its strains and suffering had ground them down. Aside from the joyful children, the atmosphere is subdued and respectful. It's also full of hope – hope in what sister and her team might be able to do to relieve, to rescue. Annette knows most of the patients. They are happy to see her. She walks among them, greets them, has a kind word. Many of the regulars have already been treated and have gone home. Before the clinic closes its doors later in the day, the remaining forty or more patients will have been seen to.

Annette O'Shea was born in Limerick City. In 1963, she joined the DoC in Blackrock, Dublin. She was by then a trained psychiatric nurse. After a short period in the novitiate, the congregation sent her to the DoC run *North Infirmary Hospital* in Cork to do her general nurse's training. After that, she was appointed to *St. Vincent's Psychiatric Hospital* in Fairview, Dublin. For six years she took charge of the acute admission ward there and then returned to general nursing in Cork until such time as the hospital was closed down. She then transferred to *Our Lady's Hospital* for sick children in Crumlin, Dublin and worked in the operating theater there for six years. It was after that period that she volunteered to come to Nigeria.

"I will not stay here indefinitely. I will stay until my project is up and running, but you know, one thing leads to another and one never knows what the future has in store."

Reverend Sister Geraldine Henry

Daughters of Charity (DoC)
Abuja

Sr. Geraldine Henry

I grew up in the west of Ireland observing *the nuns from Knock*, with their enormous white butterfly headdresses shopping in my uncle's grocery. These were efficient ladies who went purposefully about their business. Though I often stood in the shop as they meticulously went through their written lists, I never dared utter a word, because my child's mind had categorized them as women whose busy lives of prayer and good deeds left little time for the normal exchanges of everyday shoppers! The *nuns from Knock* were also known as the French Sisters of Charity.

Many decades later, I am sitting with Sister Geraldine Henry in the dining room in the beautiful compound of the Daughters of Charity in Abuja, asking if there is any connection between her community and *the nuns from Knock*. "We are the same community," she tells me, "but we stopped wearing the huge bonnets in 1964. We are not nuns because nuns are cloistered and our founder St. Vincent de Paul was very insistent from the beginning, that we were to be a group of women who would have total freedom to be out in the world working amongst the poorest of the poor.

"He founded our congregation in France in 1633 with the help of Louise de Marillac. We are known within the Church as 'The Company of the Daughters of Charity of St. Vincent de Paul, Servants of the Poor'. In less than thirty years, we will be four hundred years old. The Company was established in response to the huge needs of the countless poor people in France. We were the first female religious order to be active out in the community. In Paris, the early volunteers to offer their services were ladies of high rank and while they were sincere in their offer, it was found that they were often obliged to put family and social obligations before service to the poor.

"St. Vincent quickly realized that what he needed were women from the country towns and villages who would love the poor, be totally available and be willing to undertake the lowliest of tasks in the poorest of areas, especially in the cities. He collaborated with Louise de Marillac. The first woman to answer their call was Marguerite Naseau, a young and self-taught shepherdess from Suresnes. She was soon followed by others and together under the direction of Louise de Marillac, they formed the Company of the Daughters of Charity."

Sister Geraldine was born and raised in West Belfast and was sister servant (superior) of the Abuja house of the Daughters of Charity at the time of our interview. She came to the city in 1998 to establish the congregation and to accept the invitation of Archbishop Onaiyekan of Abuja to be his diocesan health co-ordinator. She engaged in the latter assignment for five years and then handed it over to Sr. Cecilia Azuh of the Medical Missionaries of Mary.

Being naturally outgoing and possessed of a will of iron when it comes to accomplishing the most daunting of tasks, Sr. Geraldine was the ideal person to tackle two formidable assignments in the newly-built political capital of Nigeria with its ever-expanding poor suburban villages and shanty towns. "When I came, we didn't have any structure and I had absolutely no funding. Apart from a newly established mission hospital in Gwagwalada in the outskirts of the city, there was little else. The Archbishop was not very forthcoming with funds in the early days so I started to approach funding agencies such as Ireland Aid, Misereor from Germany, CRS (Catholic Relief Services) from the U.S. and CAFOD from Britain. Ireland Aid was the first to come to my rescue. They funded my car and the setting up of my office. I then carried out a study of the needs of the diocese. These needs turned out to be totally related to primary healthcare. I sat down and crafted a number of projects. Some were accepted by funding agencies so I was able to go into partnership with them. By this time, the Archbishop had begun to understand more clearly my financial needs and was willing to fund certain developments. Over time, a number of other religious congregations came into the Abuja diocese so we were able to divide up the area into different zones with different groups taking responsibility for a variety of services.

"We – that is the diocesan services team under my leadership opened a number of health posts and clinics. These were small places which basically dealt with primary healthcare and maternity services. We also established small hospitals in Gwari and Gaski in the city. In Gwagwalada, the diocesan services for the disabled collaborated with the Christoffel Blinden Mission and built a unit for orthopaedic and ophthalmic surgery. We ourselves, The Daughters of Charity built a clinic in Kubwa in the outskirts of the city and the MMM built their clinic in New Lugbe, also in the outskirts.

"I spent a lot of time in the early days raising funds, but my team and I were also very active developing health-policies for the diocese, setting up structures such as management boards, management committees and committees charged with introducing correct employment terms and conditions. We started a HIV/AIDS programme which the Archbishop is very interested in. It is now very developed. A HIV/AIDS co-ordinator is being funded by CRS and there's a big support network in operation. One of the men in the support group died yesterday. His wife is demented because her father-in-law doesn't want to have anything to do with the body. It's there in the morgue and nobody is claiming or paying. You have these sad situations cropping up all the time.

"Despite the many AIDS awareness programmes that are going on, there is still terrible stigma and great denial. The Daughters of Charity have a small hospital for TB and leprosy down in Ondo State in the South. A large portion of the TB patients have AIDS and it's just taboo. Our sisters were telling me that there have been incidences of families poisoning relatives who are known to be infected. Contaminated food is brought into the hospital and given to the infected patient. It's very easy to do this and get away with it as there will never be a postmortem. If a person dies, he dies and that's it. AIDS, all over Nigeria is being spread through contaminated blood, unclean needles and sexual activity. It is putting great pressure on the already stretched health services.

"When I resigned from the diocesan position, I was assigned to be the Daughters of Charity projects' coordinator for the Province of Nigeria and Ghana. This involves a lot of travel. I am also the community leader for the DoC project here in Kubwa which consists of a primary healthcare clinic with an outreach programme to the villages, a women's development centre and a centre for the education of children with special needs. Each of these facilities has its own executive manager."

Growing up in West Belfast, Sister Geraldine says that she couldn't have escaped contact with the DoC who first came to the city in 1900 to open a school for the girls who worked in the linen mills. "At the time, the city was rampant with disease and poverty. Young girls aged between nine and eleven had to work in the most terrible of conditions often having to wade in water up to their knees. All my aunts worked in the mills and they got TB and anything else that was going. When the sisters came with their school, they made some arrangements with the British authorities for the children to work part-time so that they could spend the rest of the day at school. This was the school I attended myself and I also went to the DoC secondary school which was opened in 1958 in response to a dire need for affordable secondary education for the poor. Currently there are two thousand pupils in that school and through the years, they have had excellent results with some pupils getting places in Oxford and Cambridge. The principal is still a DoC but these days, we have only two sisters in education in the whole of Belfast. The school remains because there is still a great need to help poor students.

"Our company was found to serve the poor and St. Vincent always said that the day we stop serving the poor is the day we will cease to exist. Every decision we make takes this into account. Before we involve ourselves in any project, we will always ask the questions: *can anybody else do this? is anybody else doing it? will it serve the poorest of the poor – the most neglected – the most abandoned?*

"Here in Nigeria, our work is with the handicapped, the very poor who are sick, the mentally ill and the people whom nobody else cares about. When we were invited into the country by the Bishop of Calabar in 1963, we came to Uyo in his diocese. The sisters started off educating the poor at secondary level but when the Government took over the mission secondary schools in the late 1970's, we moved out. Our house in Uyo which was our first in the country is now a home for the destitute. We have a sister there who also works in prisons and with women's training and development.

"The Company of the DoC is different from other religious orders in the sense that we renew our vows every year and only make them for one year at a time. I think that makes us more committed because every year, you have to make a decision. If anyone decides to leave, they just don't renew the vows."

Sister Geraldine is a highly qualified professional. She first trained in mental handicap nursing at the DoC run centre in Lisnagry in Limerick and then went on to train in paediatrics in the DoC-run children's hospital in Crumlin, Dublin. Later, she went to Edinburgh to take a master's degree in healthcare management. In addition to all that, she is a qualified and experienced nurse tutor.

"I always knew that I would be willing to serve on the missions if I were asked to do so. That opportunity came at Christmas 1995. The Provincial sent for me and told me that she needed two sisters to join a three-person *GOAL* team in war-torn Sierra Leone within a matter of days. The third person was a man called Norman, who was very experienced in the logistics of dealing with crisis work in war zones. In Sierra Leone at the time, there was a huge displacement of people taking place and practically the whole population of the country was crowding into Freetown, the capital. Our team was to take charge of a refugee camp which was so appalling that no NGO was willing to take it on. It was an old, disused, windowless warehouse and it housed 20,000 refugees. Among them were men, women and children from ten different ethnic groups. Most of the children were distraught and wandered around looking for parents who could not be found. Our job was to start a feeding programme and to deal with the most basic of healthcare.

"There were just the three of us. One of our first tasks was to build a little hut to deliver babies as prior to that, they were being delivered on dirty floors. Mornings were horrendous as you had to face the corpses of those who died during the night. At other times, there was sheer terror in the camp when rumours of approaching rebels reached the refugees. I saw riots in that place over the tiniest thing like a bar of soap or an item of clothing. Somebody once gave me clothes to distribute but I had to abandon the exercise as the rush and scramble became too dangerous.

"A purpose-built camp was eventually built. Moving the people turned out to be a huge operation. In the end, the new building could not house everybody and there were many who did not get places. That caused further consternation as there was no question of people staying in the old camp because as soon as it was emptied, it became infested with rats. I remember one old man coming to me and saying that we must be experiencing the nearest thing to hell. The stench and the heat were almost unbearable. That was 1996. I came home when our work in that camp was finished and handed over to another agency.

"I resumed my job in Ireland but I could not settle. What upset me most of all was listening to people complaining about tiny unimportant things. When our Provincial asked me if I would return to Sierra Leone when things settled a little there, I gladly volunteered. I never did get back as the war continued for years. I went instead to Romania to help out with the HIV/AIDS orphans. In 1998, I came to Nigeria and I have been here ever since."

Sister Brenda Hunter

Daughters of Charity (DoC)
Kubwa, Abuja

Sr. Brenda Hunter with children from
'Hope Centre for Children with Special Needs'

"I had just finished my Montessori teaching training when I was asked to get involved in special education. I refused saying that I couldn't do that type of work. To be honest I found the whole idea upsetting. Fortunately, the woman who had asked me had more wisdom than I and she persuaded me to try it out at our centre for disabilities in Lisnagra, Limerick. I found it extremely difficult for the first few months. I'd set up everything the way my Montessori training had taught me only to find the children pulling it all down. One day, I seriously questioned myself as to what I might be doing wrong. It dawned on me that I was trying to change the children to my own way of thinking. From that day on, I decided to let them lead me, to go with their flow, even though that was also difficult. I soon realized however that it was working, so with that new beginning and the support of the staff, I started to enjoy the work in a real way and was in fact heartbroken when I had to change some years later. I am now back in the field here in Nigeria and I have to say that I am enjoying the most fulfilling time of my life."

Set in the wide open spaces of Kubwa in the outskirts of Abuja is *Hope Centre for Children with Special Needs*. This is where Sister Brenda Hunter and her team lovingly and constructively cater for approximately forty-five children with a variety of special needs. The school opened its doors in 2000.

Sister Brenda's coming to Nigeria came as a complete surprise to her. "I was in hospital recovering from surgery when Sister Geraldine Henry whom I had never met before then came in to sit by my bedside. She proceeded to tell me how much I would love Nigeria and how much I would love to work with the beautiful children with special needs there. I was only coming out of an anaesthetic and I kept saying that I was sure that I would. The following week, my Provincial came to tell me that Geraldine Henry had told her that I was anxious to go to Nigeria. I decided to give it a try and came directly to Abuja some short time afterwards.

"By the time I arrived in 1999, Sister Geraldine had already started a clinic in Kubwa. She had also purchased the land on which this school is standing. My early days here found me struggling with the climate and I also found the complete lack of any social outlet very difficult. I have always enjoyed going downtown for a coffee or going to a film or to the theatre. Suddenly all of that had come to a sudden end and I found myself having to depend totally on my own inner resources. On the other hand, I found the people here happy, joyful, bright, full of vitality and very, very welcoming. In every home that I visited and it remains the same to this day, I found that a little food and maybe a drink of maltina was put in front of me.

"My own background lies on the two sides of the divide in Belfast. My father's family are Presbyterian and very pro-British, Ulster and all that. My mother's side was Catholic and very Republican. My father was the first of his family for eighteen generations to marry a Catholic. I am the eldest Hunter grandchild so it was very difficult for his family to accept my Catholicism. At the time, the Catholic Church demanded that all children of a mixed marriage be brought up Catholic. During my childhood week-ends, I was always moving between the Protestant Shankill and the Catholic Falls Road. My two sets of grandparents taught me different songs. I went from singing *I'm a little Catholic girl, I love my home and place . . .* to *. . . Do you think that I'd let a dirty Fenian cat destroy the orange of the lily . . .* without having much of a clue about what it all meant.

"Growing up, we lived in a place called Ballymurphy and then suddenly, we had to move on account of *the troubles* in the 1960's and the burning of many Catholic homes. After that, *the peace line* went up and we were totally cut off from my Shankill relatives. I remember the suddenness of it all. It meant that I did not see my Presbyterian grandparents for five years.

"Being the eldest, I think that I have always felt caught between two families and to this day, if I feel that I am in the middle of a dispute or if I am in the position of having to take sides, I begin to feel very uncomfortable. It's only in the last five years or so that the two sides of the family have been able to come together. They now even go on holiday together in Donegal."

It was the troubled times in Belfast that brought Brenda Hunter into contact with the Daughters of Charity. "I had grown up in Ballymurphy, a place that was badly affected by sectarianism. The area was in decline and there was severe depression. Mother Teresa and her sisters came in to help and though I was very young at the time, I could see that they were unable to raise the spirits of any neighbourhood or relate to the people. When they left, the Daughters of Charity came and I remember taking great notice of them. One of them set up a flower and plant stall and I used to hear her saying to the men – 'look, I'll give you this rose bush. Why don't you plant it and see how it grows.' Then I began to notice the men out cutting the grass, painting doors and railings and suddenly the area began to look attractive. I said to myself that these women must have very special qualities to be able to get through to the notoriously tough-minded Ballymurphy people, to be able to visit them in their homes and to be able to set up relationships.

"Since then, I have learned that it was their charism, their wish to show respect for the dignity of people, their wish to give what we call today a quality service to the poor and rejected in society. Their work was social work – women's development – men's development. They were the first who saw the great need for the latter. They brought the men together and encouraged them to talk about their problems – something that was traditionally difficult for them to do. The sisters had a holistic approach towards raising the spirits of the people and the contribution they made was good. I was young and idealistic at the time but I knew that I wanted to be part of making that same kind of contribution. Ultimately, all of that led me to joining the congregation when I came of age!

"Here in this totally child-centred school in Nigeria, we aim to give a service of excellence. That includes a pleasing, physical environment. We want to develop a sense of the aesthetic in the children and we want them to learn how to appreciate beauty and fine things. Many of them live in mud huts with open sewage at their doors. They have no running water, no toilet facilities and no electricity. I honestly don't know how the mothers manage as before they do anything, they have to go to the nearest bore hole to fetch water and carry enough back to cook, wash clothes and bathe the family. Doing all this and caring for a child with a disability is very taxing. They only cope because they have to.

"Every parent wants a perfect child so having a child with a disability is a burden and growing to love that child is a process. Here in Nigeria, the parents have also to deal with all the mythology that is attached to children with disabilities. Who is the sinner? Is it me or is it the father? Who put this curse on us? Is this child a snake who is going to put a curse on the rest of the family? This thinking is all very much part of the culture and it influences greatly the acceptance level of parents. Acceptance does not always come and even today, some disabled children are killed or left to die in the bush.

"I've seen mothers make enormous sacrifices and I've seen the great love mothers give to a child who suffers, for example, from cerebral palsy or *Down syndrome*. I've seen these children strapped to the backs of the mothers as they walk to the farm. It's only in recent months that I am beginning to see the fathers' side of things because more fathers are now coming into this room we are sitting in and becoming more open. They feel very inadequate because they don't know what to do and they are not always allowed to express their emotions. It's my hope that this place will be a haven for parents, a place where they can express their thoughts, feelings and anxieties and know that they will not be judged.

"I have witnessed many emotional outpourings and it's something that I find quite difficult and emotionally draining. If you have a father breaking into tears because he feels that his autistic child is rejecting him, it is very sad. Last week, I had a mother who wanted to know if her child was a devil. There is so much they have to break through before they even begin to accept that having a disabled child is not their fault. You have to deal with their anxieties from an educational and medical point of view but sometimes I think that what people need mostly is a listening ear and a little compassion. If there is a complex explanation involved, Sister Geraldine Henry who is the sister servant (superior) of our community here, has a great background in the area of special needs and she is always around to assist. When I am in Ireland, I frequently bring back a number of little books which give simple and concise explanations to parents.

"We have children with a variety of disabilities. Some are blind, some are deaf, some are autistic and some suffer from cerebral palsy or *Down syndrome*. We have children with *Williams' syndrome* (hyperactivity) and some who are micraphalic which means that the brain does not develop all its parts. They have all to be dealt with in a different way. In a sense, each child sets his own curriculum because the child tends to lead you in certain directions. We try to do an individual programme for each one and our approach is holistic. It takes a while to observe the child, determine its potential and see where its gifts may lie. Following the observation period, all of the staff come together to design a programme.

"The children all have gifts and they are gifts we need in life – like the gifts of kindness and generosity. I often watch a three-year-old helping to feed a child who cannot lift its own hand. I have seen four-year-olds put aside their own needs and become conscious of the need of the child beside them. We have a little girl called Sandra and she often forgets which room she is supposed to be in. Other children will run to take her by the hand. Once at a staff meeting, we came up with a list of their gifts and they are compassion, acceptance, forgiveness, and empathy – the higher gifts if you like. These qualities pour naturally out of them so I think that if I were to spiritualize all of this, I would say that children with special needs are God's gift to society. These children are not competitive and they have a deep sense of friendship. We have a sport's day here every year and they are told that the first one over the line will get the prize. They all set out together but children with *Down syndrome* might stop half way and wait for their friends to catch up. With these children, everyone is their friend.

"Every morning when they come off the bus, I get a huge hug from each one. The same happens in the afternoon when we wave them good-bye. This school is their place – a place where they are given the dignity they rightly deserve. They know and sense this because children with disabilities are ultra-sensitive.

"These higher gifts which the children possess help the parents to love them. Let's not forget however that there is always a cross to bear for the parents and they do need a lot of support. We have a support team which goes out on visitation to the families and the importance of this family contact is one of the reasons why we opted for non-residential care in the school. We believe that the child has a right to a family and a right to live in a community.

"For our forty-five children, we have five on the teaching staff. They are all professionals who are highly qualified and suited to the work. They are on trial for a year after they come to us as we need to establish if they will fit in with our ethos and work programmes. As well as teachers, we have teacher assistants, drivers, cooks and domestic staff. Our running costs come from charitable donations. We get no government funding because as far as I know, there is no government policy on special education in Nigeria. *Misereor* of Germany has funded us as has *Ireland Aid*. We are constantly fundraising but I have to admit that we are never without and that is an extraordinary thing. Every month, I have enough to pay the staff, feed the children and run the buses. The children bring forth people's natural generosity and sense of goodness."

Sister Brenda's purpose-built school has a variety of rooms specially designed to cater for the special needs of the children. The relaxation room is apparently particularly good for children who are autistic and hyperactive. The aromatherapy room is where children are massaged and where a lot of rocking exercises are done to help calm them down. In another room, light-therapy combined with soft music is used, also to engender calm. "Sometimes I find that an autistic child who has been playing with the lights – switching the different colours off and on, will then come and lie down beside me to have a little rest or sleep. We have a language and speech therapy room and the children go there for twenty minutes every day. This is in addition to the speech therapy they have in their classrooms. The art room is where the children draw, paint and play with sand and water. There is an integrating thread connecting and relating all the activities."

Sister Brenda thinks it is important that the DoC have a presence in Nigeria.

"Our presence is important as I think that the poor in this country are a forgotten population. I think that we can be a voice for the voiceless – a voice that says that these people have a right to services – to water, to education, to healthcare, to safe birth and to development. There is huge wealth in Nigeria and I find it sickening when I walk up to Biaji which is five minutes from here and see whole families living in a room smaller than this small room we are sitting in with no running water, no light, no sewage facilities. I see the local government school in a rundown state and I ask myself – does anybody care about these people? I have to tell you that I honestly think that nobody does.

"Before I came to Nigeria, I was very much of the opinion that all third-world debt should be cancelled – written off. Now I am not so sure because who will make sure that the money saved will ever reach the people I am talking about?"

The Augustinian Fathers

Order of St. Augustine (OSA)

An Introduction

Tradition has it that monks and hermits dispersed by the Vandal invasion of North Africa in the fifth century fled to Europe and established monasteries, particularly in northern and central Italy. In 1244, Pope Innocent 1V formed the Order of Hermits of St. Augustine by uniting many groups of monks and hermits and ordering them to follow the Rule of St Augustine. In 1256, Pope Alexander 1V joined other groups to the existing Order of St. Augustine. The Order spread rapidly throughout Europe and took an active part in ecclesiastical and university life. The Augustinians first came to Ireland in 1280 when they established a foundation in Dublin.

Today, there are 3,000 Augustinian Friars in 45 countries. In addition to parochial and missionary apostolates, members of the Augustinian Order teach in schools, colleges and universities around the world. Many also work closely with the poor and the sick.

Numerous groups of religious women are affiliated with the Augustinians.

In 1936, the Irish Augustinians applied to Rome for a mission territory in Africa. This was given in 1938 when they were offered a territory which then comprised the Province of Adamawa in Northern Nigeria and the adjoining Northern Cameroons.

Father Raymond Hickey

Order of St. Augustine (OSA)
Abuja

*L to R: Sr. Dymphna Drury, Embassy of the Holy See, Abuja;
the late Fr. John Ofei (Catholic Secretariat of Nigeria, Abuja);
Fr. Raymond Hickey*

Dubliner Fr. Raymond Hickey spoke to me at the Apostolic Nunciature in Abuja about the history of the Augustinian Fathers' mission to Northern Nigeria and about the part he himself played in that mission.

"The first Augustinian Fathers arrived in Yola in Adamawa Province in north eastern Nigeria in 1940. They sheltered in the only Catholic church which existed in the province. This was a grass-matting structure which was erected ten years earlier by a handful of Catholics who came mainly from the south and who settled in Jimeta, the commercial district of Yola. The fathers' assigned mission station was ninety miles further south at a small village called Sugu. To get there, they had to make a track through the bush. As the second world war had started, they were destined to suffer from severe shortages of building materials and foodstuffs. They had learned Hausa in preparation for their coming but on arrival, found that the language was unknown in Adamawa. They immediately set about learning Fulani. Their nearest Irish fellow missionaries were the SMA Fathers in Jos in Plateau State which was hundreds of miles to the south. You reached it by a road that became impassable during the rainy season.

"The station at Sugu was slowly built and after some months, the fathers were given permission to have a residence in Yola. In 1951, the Apostolic Nuncio asked the Augustinians to take over the evangelization of Borno Province in the extreme north-east of Nigeria. A mission was set up in Maiduguri, the capital of the Province in 1953. The Prefecture of Maiduguri was established in due course and it became a diocese in 1966 with the late Bishop Cotter, OSA as its first bishop."

"I arrived in Maiduguri in October 1960, the month Nigeria gained its independence from Britain. The mission was still in the very early stages of development. The complete newness of everything was a bit of a shock but not a negative shock. Three of us landed in Kano and waited two days for a connecting flight to Yola. From there we travelled by public transport to Maiduguri. It was still at the first stage of having a Christian presence. Fr. A. J. Hanly, who was the first priest to arrive there in 1953 had built a church, a small mission house and a school to serve the local Catholic population which was regarded as part of the non-Muslim stranger community. In many ways, our priests found that it was easier to establish the Church in Maiduguri than in Yola as the Kanuri indigenous people, though Muslim for many centuries, have the tradition of tolerance and hospitality towards strangers.

"There were restrictions placed on missionaries during the colonial era and these largely continued after Independence. They had to sign that they would not go near any Muslim household, that they would uphold the correct order of things and that there would be no open-air preaching. Their work, they were told, was to be restricted to the Christians who had migrated from the South. All this was based on treaties worked out between Lord Lugard – the so-called architect of modern Nigeria and the Emirs of the North. It had the objective of safeguarding the Islamic culture and religion. In the beginning, we were also prohibited from making contact with pagan groups but that restriction slipped over time.

"I was very conscious of the history of the Augustinians in Maiduguri so I was very delighted with my appointment there as junior priest to Waterford man, Fr. Michael O'Floinn, who was born in the gaeltacht of Ring. He was a wonderful missionary who gave good example and I learned a great deal from him. My new life on the missions was a complete change from the world of study, books and exams. For the first three and a half years, I was in Maiduguri town working largely with the Igbo Catholic community who had migrated there. I was also teaching in a primary school where the students were almost as old as myself. It was a very good experience in an environment that was completely new and exotic in many ways.

"From the air, Maiduguri appears like an evergreen oasis in a dusty bowl. It is evergreen thanks to the neem trees which were brought there from India by a British colonial officer while he was the Resident of Borno. They give shade and relief to half a million people. They do not however give protection against the invasive dust that comes with the cool harmattan wind that blows from the Sahara Desert between December and March and which gives respiratory problems even to those who know no other home. The city started off as a trading post on the *pilgrim road* east to Chad, the Sudan and Mecca. Nowadays, few pilgrims go overland to Mecca.

"From my very first days in Maiduguri, I started learning Hausa but it was not until I commenced my second mission tour in 1964 that I came to grips with it. I was sent out to a station in the bush to work with semi-pagan and partly Islamic peoples who were really open to the good news of the Gospel. I was first in Gwoza in the mountains you pass if you are travelling south to Shuwa from Maiduguri. After that, I was in Potiscum where again you had pagan people who being pagan were historically very much underdogs and therefore fair game for slave hunters and all the rest of it in pre-colonial times. They were accustomed to fleeing to any place they could find protection – to the mountain tops, to swamps, to forests.

They had always lived on the fringes. I loved working in these places and Fr. O'Floinn had whetted my appetite for what we call *bush mission* which meant being out among the people of rural areas, living with them, preaching to them and starting up mission stations. Potiscum is on the road between Cameroon and Maiduguri. There, I was able to open up villages and establish a number of small mission stations. It was hard work as the prevailing wind was Islam. In 1970, I was asked to open up Buma, down in the deep south of Borno State, south of Biu. There were no Christians there and you could get very discouraged if you were expecting quick results. I spent my time going out among the people in the villages, explaining who I was and why I was there.

"In 1973, I was asked by our Provincial to take a doctorate in theology at the Gregorian University in Rome. I was somewhat dismayed as I did not want to re-enter the world of academics believing as I did that all that was very auxiliary to the main mission work of being out amongst the people. I managed to postpone my move to Rome until 1975. My time there turned out to be a very valuable experience. I was very familiar with the place as I had studied there before being ordained. I have tremendous admiration and respect for all the Jesuit professors at *The Greg* as it is fondly called. They come from all over the world and live there in their small rooms which combine as offices. They dedicate their lives to education and learning. They are wonderful educators and great thinkers and leaving religion aside, many would rank amongst the world's greatest scholars. I recall Bernard Lonergan in particular. He was a great philosopher and psychologist who would be in the top bracket of twentieth century thinkers in his field. Latin was the lingua franca at the university during my first period there. After Vatican II, Italian was introduced.

"Since I didn't want to go into academia, I was allowed to return to Nigeria after my studies. I went back into *bush mission* for a period and then changed to a training centre for catechists in Kaya which was very close to Shuwa and about two hours south of Maiduguri. I spent two years there and it was during that period that my voice broke and I began to have recurrent laryngitis. It grew progressively worse during every dry season and would not respond to antibiotics. It was particularly bad in 1979 when my dear sister

Gladys came to visit for Christmas. I returned to Dublin with her in January and spent six months under strict medical instructions to completely rest my voice. A certain relief was brought about but there remains a permanent weakness. I have a facility for a certain amount of speech. After that, pain sets in.

"In 1983, in great sadness, I had to leave active mission work in parishes. Bishop Cotter, my bishop was very understanding. He took me over to St. Patrick's, his compound in Maiduguri and appointed me Chancellor and Secretary at the Bishop's office. My life changed drastically that year and I have been at a desk ever since. Bishop Cotter died unexpectedly in 1988 and Senan O'Donnell was appointed administrator and later Bishop. I was recalled to Jos to become secretary of the Augustinian Order in Nigeria but not before spending a year researching the history of Yola Diocese.

"In 1992, I went home to help with my mother's final days as she was suffering from Alzheimer's disease. This was a sad but very rewarding experience. She died in November 1993 and I returned to Nigeria the following January, this time to Benin City for a short period. In April of the same year, I was asked to serve at the Apostolic Nunciature in Lagos as my predecessor there died unexpectedly.

"The nature of my work at the Nunciature is confidential and behind the scenes. The work provides a link between the Pope and the Nigerian Church. The outlets and potential for doing good are substantial. The Church being a human institution as well as a divine one will inevitably be involved in rows and misunderstandings and appeals for the resolution of these are often made to Rome. The records of the work in the Nunciature are kept in archives for thirty to forty years. There is no instant information available. I could tell you in a general way what is involved in a given case but I could never go into the specifics. We moved from Lagos to Abuja in 2001. I was delighted to be back in an area that is closer to the North. I never enjoyed living in Lagos very much. My work here in Abuja is a continuation of what I was doing there. I find that there is a certain challenge in paperwork and someone has to do it.

"At weekends I help out in St. John's Parish, Mararaba outside Abuja. Fr. Richie Hughes, OSA from Julianstown, Co. Meath is the parish priest there. This I enjoy very much as it gets me out into the countryside and the small amount of work I do resembles somewhat my own earlier days in parishes. Mararaba is one of the *dormitory towns* of Abuja. Ninety percent of the people who live in these towns do so because they cannot afford to live in Abuja. In a sense they are the real Abuja, the African Abuja, the Soweto of Abuja: a hotchpotch of unplanned housing and makeshift roads, a seething cauldron of humanity where people commute to work, live off one another, buy and sell from small roadside tables and where sanitation is primitive and privacy unknown.

"From time to time, I like to visit Maiduguri to meet old friends and colleagues. Fr. Charles O'Reilly who works at the Cathedral has been in Nigeria for a very long time. So has Sr. Rita Currivan, OSA who runs a maternity and child care unit in Shuwa, south of Maiduguri. It was partially funded by *Ireland Aid* and was formally opened by the Bishop of Maiduguri in 2004. Sr. Rita also spends much of her time in the service of the novitiate and the community. "

I first met Fr. Raymond in Lagos in 1998. Later when all diplomatic missions moved to the new capital of Abuja, I came to know him well. He is a quiet spoken man whose gentlemanly qualities, impeccable manners and willingness to help endear him to people. He generously gives of his profound knowledge of Nigeria. He enjoys a regular game of tennis and those who know him, quickly sense his pride in his native Dublin and his love of the Irish language.

"I was born in Dublin in 1936. My father was a Limerick man who came to Dublin in 1922 from the Christian Brothers School in Sexton Street to become a civil servant. At the time, there were lots of vacancies as the English civil servants were leaving. He was first with the Department of Industry and Commerce but later moved to the Board of Works. My mother was born in Wales but grew up in Dublin after her father, a medical doctor died at the age of thirty-seven.

"I went to primary school in Scoil Treasa in Mount Merrion just down the road from where we lived. I later attended Willow Park and Blackrock College. After two years in the latter, I was sent boarding to Good Counsel College, New Ross, Co. Wexford. It was an Augustinian school and I had an uncle in the Augustinians.

"I think that I always wanted to be a priest. I don't remember a time when I didn't have that wish. I was probably influenced by a combination of factors – the home, the school, the people I met and the times in which I grew up. I was always interested in politics, society and the wider world and when I was growing up, it was a time of great certainties. You had Stalin and atheistic communism on the one side and Christ and the Gospel on the other.

"I was attracted to the idea of going on the missions and spreading the Gospel would have been very much part of that. After my Leaving Certificate, I went straight to the Augustinian novitiate in Orlagh, Rathfarnham, Dublin. From there I attended the Augustinian Internal School of Philosophy in Raheny. The study of philosophy was for me a real eye-opener as it introduced me to the wider world with all its different philosophies – starting off with the Greek thinkers and finishing with the major philosophers of the day. All of it made me think in a new way and it introduced me to logic. In school, I was not one to reason things out so I struggled. When I finished philosophy, I went to the Gregorian University in Rome to study theology for four years. This was also a very broadening experience and living in Rome was very educational. It was a new world, a new culture. I loved it."

Being in his late sixties, Fr. Raymond frequently thinks of a future in Ireland. "I've no wish to carry on out here until I die. I would like to be semi-retired in one of our smaller communities in Ireland. These are located in Drogheda, Dungarvan, Fethard in Co. Tipperary and New Ross in Co. Wexford."

Sr. Rita Currivan with OSA postulants, in Maiduguri

The Franciscan Missionaries of the Divine Motherhood
(FMDM)

An Introduction

The Franciscan Missionaries of the Divine Motherhood had its origins in a group of women who worked among the poor in the woollen mills in Lancashire in the north of England over a hundred years ago. Initially the FMDM were known as the Order of Franciscan Sisters (OFS). *Divine Motherhood* was eventually added to their name as they were the first group of women in England to practise midwifery. Over the years, the congregation grew and houses were opened in many countries including Ireland, China, Australia, New Zealand, America and the Philippines. The Augustinian Fathers invited the Order to Nigeria in 1950.

Sister Celsus Nealon

Franciscan Sisters of the Divine Motherhood (FMDM)
Assisi Convent, Rantia, Jos

Sr. Celsus Nealon, second from left, and Sr. Katie Naylor, second from right with Nigerian aspirants, Jos

Apart from meeting a number of the FMDM Sisters as they passed through Abuja on business or for our annual Christmas dinner for the Irish missionaries, I had the privilege of visiting two of their mission stations during my time in Nigeria. The memory of the indefatigable and capable Sister Finbar treating the two Irish missionary Fathers who had been struck down with malaria and typhoid as well as keeping a close and caring eye on the many other patients in the FMDM-run clinic in Yakoko in Taraba State, will always stay with me. There also I met Sister Helena McEvily who spent her days treating the hundreds of patients who availed of the clinic's outreach programme in many different rural out-stations. So respected is the work of the sisters that patients come from hundreds of miles in the surrounding areas to avail of their services.

In Assisi Convent, Rantia in Jos, I was once guest of Sister Celsus and her colleagues for a weekend. After what turned out to be a very busy and social few days, Sister Celsus and I took ourselves aside to talk about her story as an FMDM in Nigeria. She first took me back to her early days in Ballina, County Mayo.

"I was born on December 31, 1942 – the first of thirteen children – eight boys and five girls. I was christened Alice Mary Nealon. Both my parents came from farming stock in the Ballina region. I attended the Mercy Convent in Ballina for a few years but in the late fifties, my father, my eldest brother and I moved to England and that is where I finished my education. While there, I was introduced to the FMDM and from the moment I met them, I knew that I wanted to join their congregation and give my life to God by becoming a missionary.

"I returned to Ireland in 1960 and after much discussion with my parents and family, I renewed my contact with the sisters. On March 26, 1961, my parents, grand-aunt and cousin drove me to Portiuncula, Ballinasloe, Co. Galway to take the first steps of my postulancy with the congregation. Tears still come to my eyes when I remember the pain of parting with my family wondering indeed if I would ever see them again. That was part of the sacrifice in those days – putting your hand to the plough and never looking back!

"On September 26, 1961, I made my temporary vows of chastity, poverty and obedience. My feelings of joy were intense and though my vows were only temporary, I knew that I was dedicating my life to God for life.

"Very soon afterwards, I was appointed to the FMDM community in Yola in north-eastern Nigeria. Two of us – both inexperienced travellers, flew on a BOAC flight to Kano. Because of stormy conditions, the plane had to divert to Lagos. The next day, we returned to Kano and landed on what seemed like a strip of land in the middle of nowhere. From there we made our way to Yola.

From Yola I was sent on a short assignment to Sugu, which was to the south-east of Yola and where our sisters operated a mission engaged in the ministries of health work and adult education. When I returned to Yola, I prepared to take my final vows but also became involved in parish work, house visitation and hospital visitation. It was during that time that the Biafran war broke out and though we were far from the very dangerous war zones, we were able to hear from our hiding place the screams of terror as the Igbos were being hacked to death. It is a time of my life that I shall never forget. Though things calmed down rather quickly in the North, the atmosphere remained redolent of the blood that was shed.

"It was during the war that we transferred from Yola to Yakoko. The German funding agency *Misereor* funded the building of a registered clinic and maternity unit. At the time the area was very remote and underdeveloped and there were little or no medical facilities. The late Sister Bernard Rudden, Sister Teresa O'Sullivan, Sister Kitty Cashman and I pioneered the Yakoko mission. The indigenous people at the time were known as the *Mumuya* but they later changed their name to *Yorro*. They are a very large tribe who were famed in the past for their warrior skills. Their main source of income comes primarily from farming yams, guinea corn, sweet potatoes and maize corn. The guinea corn is used for producing a local beer called *brukutu* which is sold in all the market places. Every Sunday there is a really big market where foodstuffs are sold from early morning. By evening, every man, woman and child moves to the other side of the road where an extensive beer market is set up. The high spirits, good humour and fun that emanates from this gathering accelerates by the hour and lasts well into the night.

"When we first opened our clinic, we were inundated with patients who came from as far away as Jalingo, Yola and many other places. Our work was varied. We held general clinics, leprosy clinics, primary healthcare clinics and a maternity clinic. We operated in more than six stations and we tried to visit each of them once every two weeks. Before we could afford to employ qualified staff, the sisters were on twenty-four-hour call. Our greatest joy was being able to see people getting cured and returning joyfully to their homes. To this day Yokoko continues to give a wonderful service and for that its reputation has spread.

"I found my life in Yakoko very absorbing and exciting. I became very involved in the work of the parish. I walked to all the surrounding villages with a catechist – instructing adults and young people in the faith. I carried out Sunday services in villages when there was no priest available. I had a small classroom built and equipped so that I could get involved in the education of the local women in home economics, literacy and crafts.

"It was while I was there that I made my final vows in the local church. Though the occasion did not have the style and romance of my first profession, the grandeur of the organ was replaced by exuberant drumming and shakers rang out with gusto to the acclaim and excitement of a huge gathering of Yorro people. They had never before witnessed such a ceremony. At the time, there were no Nigerian priests in that part of the North but present for my big day were twenty Irish Augustinian Fathers and eight FMDM Sisters.

"By 1974, I was ten years in Nigeria and the time had come for me to go to England to commence my nurse's training. This I did at *St. Thomas' Hospital* in London. Three years later, I was back in Yakoko in my new role as a qualified nurse. Straight away I got involved in the different types of nursing from general outpatient to primary healthcare to the treatment of the endemic diseases such as leprosy, typhoid and malaria. Every week, I travelled to our out-stations. My life was extremely busy.

"During that time, quite a few young, local women began to be drawn to our way of life and I became interested and involved in their spiritual growth. By 1987, we had eight such young people who wished to experience our life by passing some months in our convent. Because of this development, it was decided to establish a new house in Yola and to set up an aspirancy programme. Sister Kathleen Lynch and I were put in charge of this project. Prior to coming to Nigeria, Sister Kathleen had spent twenty years teaching in New Zealand. Coming to Africa was a complete new experience for her. The two of us forged ahead and opened in Yola – this time right in the centre of the town.

"Once we were settled into our new ministry, our congregation asked us to look for an outreach apostolate which would be specifically geared to the poor. As a result of this request *St. Mary's*

Clinic was founded in a place called Yadim which is one hour's drive north east of Yola. Without fail, I visited Yadim every week, initially for one day and eventually for two. I held my clinics under trees, in the marketplace and in classrooms when the rains were heavy. Eventually the bishop paid for a couple of rooms so that I could have a permanent site. The little place was plastered and roofed and I thought it was the most wonderful clinic in Nigeria!

"One of the highlights of this time was caring for a little boy called Beni. His mother had died giving him birth and the father wanted him buried with his wife. On hearing this, the grandmother stole the baby and ran to me. He was the most beautiful baby and though he had been starved of food for more than five days, he was chubby and healthy. I was lucky to find a childless woman in the village who was delighted to help me care for little Beni – who now by the way, is almost fourteen years old.

"In 1992, I left Nigeria for what I thought would be a year long sabbatical. My intention was to return to Yadim as soon as was possible. My sabbatical lasted three years and instead of returning to Yadim, I was asked to go to Jos to accommodate our Nigerian sisters who were training for the different apostolates on their way to profession. Humanly speaking, I was bitterly disappointed not to be going back to my beloved Yadim. I felt a great need at this time to pray and indeed to question God. The answer came – loud and clear – *what I need from you is obedience and humility*. I was being reminded that I have a vow of obedience! I went to Jos, was appointed vocations' director and settled into my new ministry. Some of the Nigerian sisters began their nursing training at *Vom Nursing School*. Those who were wishing to train as teachers attended *The Federal College of Education* at Pankshin. We actually found it very difficult to find a suitable community house and we changed three times before we found the one we are now living in. It required an enormous amount of refurbishment and for years our chapel which is underground and which was a former *pub* frequently became flooded. In the rainy season, we often found ourselves ankle deep in water. We were enormously grateful to *P.W.* – the Irish construction company that sorted out the problem for us in the end.

"Presently our ministries in Jos are varied. Sr. Katie Naylor who was nursing at the OLA Catholic hospital for five years became the health co-ordinator for the Archdiocese of Jos. Sr. Josephine Langan works as secretary and spiritual director at the major seminary in Jos. Sr. Fidelia Wamgomsu, one of our newly professed Nigerian sisters is teaching at St. Murumba's Secondary School, Jos. In addition to my role as vocations promoter, I was appointed leader of the community.

"In July 2003, I became seriously ill with a heart condition and very soon afterwards, I was admitted to St. George's Hospital, London for angioplasty. I spent twelve months recuperating and was able to return to Jos feeling very well and able to resume my work in April 2004. Sadly, Sr. Katie Naylor has since then had a very bad car accident and had to be flown to England when her condition deteriorated rapidly. We thank God that she is now on her way to recovery.

"I have been in Jos for more than six years. I am thankful to be healthy enough to continue God's work. You asked me why I became a religious sister! The only reason I decided to consecrate my entire life to God was to find a way to God through serving Christ in my neighbour. In one of the Gospels, Jesus told us that loving our neighbour is the only way to prove our love of God. I won't deny that it has not always been easy!"

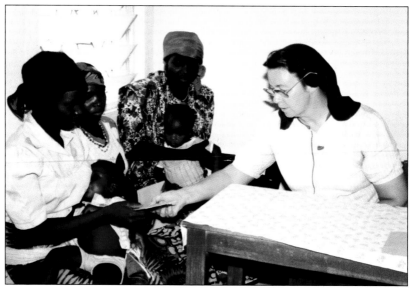

Sr. Celsus at St. Mary's Clinic, Yadim

Sisters of St. Louis
(SSL)

An Introduction

The Institute of the Sisters of St. Louis was founded in Juilly in France in 1842 by a French priest, l'Abbé Louis Bautain. He was born during the French Revolution and grew up during the troubled years that followed. From an early age, he developed a great wish to re-introduce the truths and practice of the Christian faith to the people of France.

While the sisters from the newly established Institute engaged in a wide range of activities, priority was given to the education of girls, something practically non-existent in France at the time.

In 1859, the first Irish foundation of the Institute was set up in Monaghan in the Diocese of Clogher. Though it broke its formal links with France in 1861 for almost 90 years, the Irish foundation thrived and spread to many parts of Ireland and abroad in the succeeding years.

After World War II, Pope Pius XII appealed to religious orders to include missionary work as part of their apostolates in order to assist the congregations which were specifically established for missionary work.

In 1947, the first St. Louis missionaries arrived in Ghana and a year later, the first group arrived in Kano in Northern Nigeria.

In the years that followed, the sisters set about introducing Christianity by teaching and by example and involved themselves with great devotion and energy in the fields of education, health and all categories of social work such as prison and home visitation.

In 1963, they opened a novitiate for the formation of young African women who wished to become members of the St. Louis Congregation. This venture has been very successful and today a great number of Nigerian Sisters of St. Louis are taking over and perpetuating the work started by their Irish colleagues.

Sister Máire Blair

Sisters of St. Louis (SSL)
Abuja

Sr. Máire Blair, second from right with from the left,
Sr. (Dr.) Deirdre Twomey, MMM Hospital Abakaliki;
Dr. Virginia Anohu, Abuja; Sr. Sylvia, Little Sisters of the Poor, Enugu;
Sr. Joanne Kelly, MMM Hospital Abakaliki

"The Institute of St. Louis was founded in France in 1842 by l'Abbé Louis Butain, a French priest who wished to provide education for women. Sisters from the Institute first came to Ireland in 1859. Since then they have devoted their lives to providing a quality education for girls. In 1947 they added a missionary apostolate to their work. I was in my final year in secondary school at the St. Louis Convent in Rathmines, Dublin when the first sisters departed for

Africa. As seniors of the school, we were allowed to be present at the send off. I found it very moving.

"My interest in mission however, was awakened long before that as Miss Gavin Duffy, the principal of my primary school in Scoil Bhríde in Earlsfort Tce., Dublin was very interested in the work of the Irish missionaries in Africa and elsewhere. Our school made regular collections for them and I remember once being shown a film called *Damian the Leper*. It concerned a priest who had devoted his life to caring for the lepers in Africa. After seeing it, I think that my interest in joining a religious congregation that worked in Africa took root."

Seventy-four-year-old Sister Máire Blair from Dublin spoke to me in her office at the Apostolic Nunciature in Abuja. She first came to Nigeria in 1955, five years after entering the Sisters of St. Louis (SSL) in Monaghan. Her final profession took place in Ondo in south west Nigeria in 1956.

"I was born in Dublin as were both my parents. My father was a civil servant who was very interested in the Irish language so I was sent to the renowned all Irish Scoil Bhríde for my primary education. Miss Gavin Duffy who was a sister of *Young Irelander* Charles Gavin Duffy was an educator to her finger tips. She herself had been partly educated in France. She included in the school curriculum the study of French and Shakespeare. We all loved her and as school girls, we speculated a lot about her personal circumstances. We believed that she was involved with the troubled times of her brother and we imagined that she probably had a fiancé who was killed in the fight for Irish freedom. She was a wonderful disciplinarian and she maintained open lines of communication with our parents.

"In 1955, when I was told that I was to be sent to Nigeria, I was really pleased. Two of us set out on a cargo ship which sailed from Liverpool carrying forty passengers. Sister Geraldine my companion, was a trained nurse who had always longed to go to Africa. It took fourteen days to reach Lagos. On the ship, we met with other missionaries – *the Missionary Sisters of the Holy Rosary, the Medical Missionaries of Mary and the Holy Ghost Fathers*. I remember teaching a priest called Fr. John Byrne how to type. I didn't meet him again until the 1980's when I was a seminary secretary in Jos.

"When we disembarked in Lagos, Sister Geraldine and I were met by two of our own sisters. We had fourteen pieces of luggage with us – tea chests filled to the brim with all sorts of necessities for the missions. We proceeded to Broad Street in the centre of Lagos where *The Sisters of Our Lady of Apostles* (OLA) – missionaries in Nigeria since the 1860's had a house and a school. In those days, it was just a small wooden structure. Today it is an impressive modern compound. Straight away, Sr. Geraldine was brought off to *The Nursing Council* to register. I remember being left on my own for hours, being too nervous to set a foot outside the door and not being able to find a single thing to read.

"After a few days, we set out for Ondo Diocese some hours to the east of Lagos where the SSL had three houses in the Yoruba towns of Owo, Ondo and Ado. It was all a bit mesmerizing. All the people looked alike. I wondered how I would ever get to know them. The roads were quite frightening. We were constantly passing huge lorries loaded down with huge trees tied together with a bit of a chain. Sister Geraldine got off at Oyo and was taken to her post at Ado. I continued to Ondo where I was to remain for the next nine years. On arrival, I don't know whether I was delighted or disappointed to see our grand house with its beautiful long avenue. Bishop Field, the SMA Bishop who had invited us to the diocese was very particular about the sisters having a comfortable house. The SSL had just started a secondary school in the town. Secondary education for girls was in its infancy at the time though free primary education had been introduced as early as 1954. That meant that primary school teachers were paid by the government and grants of £100 per classroom were available for the building of schools. In those days, you could build a school for £600. Most of the Catholic mission schools were built by the missionary priests themselves who kept tight controls on costs.

"My years in Ondo were spent teaching and providing secretarial services at our secondary school. I also spent time working as a supervisor at two primary schools. When in 1965 I was moved to the town of Oye-Ekiti, now in Ekiti State, I started teaching secretarial and commercial subjects on a more full time basis in the SSL vocational school. By then, I was a much more confident teacher. Our school in Oye-Ekiti was non-denominational but the ethos was Catholic. The pupils were residential and we never had more than one hundred. Many were drop-outs from more academic schools and generally they settled in well and benefited greatly from the programmes we offered. These included biology and health science as many of the girls would later train as nurses. As staff, we knew each pupil very well and were able to give a lot of individual help and guidance. Education was extremely important to the Nigerian parents though they didn't always see the value of vocational subjects.

"In addition to my school duties, I got involved in many church and pastoral activities such as the visitation of the sick in homes and hospitals. I also visited the prisons. We were surrounded by eight small villages and the people in their one-roomed circular huts regarded our visits as a blessing. They were beautiful people who were welcoming and generous. They would bring out their last portion of food and put it before you. You felt bad accepting it but you knew that by refusing to do so, you would be offending them.

"My years in Oye-Ekiti were very happy ones. I left in 1972 to spend a year in Antigonish in Canada to do a social leadership course which was being offered by the Jesuit university there. I joined sixteen people from many parts of the world. It was a Father Cody – a priest associated with that course, who coined the phrase – *Give a man a fish and feed him for a day, teach him to fish and feed him for life.*

"I returned to Nigeria in 1973, this time to the much bigger Yoruba town of Ado-Ekiti. Today it is the capital of Ekiti State. There I was appointed administrator of the SSL run Maria Assumpta Hospital. It was a booming place. Sisters of St. Louis worked as doctors and nurses and we also had a big lay staff. It had started out as a small clinic and grew to be a flourishing hospital and training school. I enjoyed my work very much and it gave me many opportunities to have meaningful contact with the people. Our congregation was greatly respected in the area as we had been there for quite a long time.

"It was during my time at the hospital that the State Government took control of all hospitals. That development has not been successful. Free medical services were introduced and the government while agreeing to pay the salaries of the staff gave no other funding. Things went downhill rather quickly. Stocks and stores became depleted and equipment deteriorated. Bishop Faun of Ekiti wanted to privatize our hospital but I knew that if that happened, we would have to charge high patient fees and would then end up treating only the rich and well off. I made my reservations on the matter known to the Bishop but he stuck to his own ideas and grew more and more anxious to appoint a new administrator who would be of his way of thinking. He was nevertheless keen to retain my services because of all the experience I had. In the end, my own congregation decided to transfer me. The hospital today is being run by the Diocese.

"In 1984, I was assigned to St. Augustine's Major Seminary in Jos as secretary. This seminary which is now run by the Archdiocese of Jos was then administered by the Augustinian Fathers and it had clerical students from many parts of Nigeria. Two sisters of St. Louis were teaching there when I first arrived.

"I grew to love my new post which lasted until 1992. Initially it was difficult as I found the abrupt change from the Yoruba territories of the south west to the middle-belt region to be quite an upheaval. It was as if I had moved to a completely new country, as the people, the culture and the languages spoken were all different. I had grown to love the Yoruba people who are outgoing and friendly. I had developed a high degree of rapport with them and also with all the other Irish missionaries who were quite numerous in the south-west. Many were SMA Fathers and we worked closely with them.

"The ethnic groups which inhabit the Jos region are initially reserved. They take time to look you over, as it were, before they begin to trust and accept you. Once that happens however, they offer a high level of support and friendship. The Birom are the indigenes but there are also populations of Hausa, Fulani, Kanuri and Tiv.

"I ultimately became the only woman working in the seminary as the two other St. Louis Sisters were posted elsewhere. I made a point of communicating as much as possible with the seminarians as I felt that they were completely isolated from the natural female influences they would have had in their own families. They grew accustomed to approaching me for a chat and I enjoyed very much asking them about their families, their studies, their joys and their difficulties.

"In 1992, when a request came for me to go to Lagos to take up secretarial duties at the Apostolic Nunciature, I was dismayed. I was sixty-two years old at the time and had no wish to make any more changes. I put forward considerable resistance but in the end, I knew that I could not avoid going. My departure from Jos created a big problem for the seminary as the then rector was about to be made bishop and it meant that the incoming rector would be left without secretarial support.

"My arrival in Lagos in August 1992 coincided with that of the new Apostolic Nuncio, Archbishop Carlo Mario Vigano. The Nuncio represents the Holy Father in Nigeria so many aspects of the work of the Catholic Church in Nigeria are closely associated with the work at the Nunciature. Six new dioceses were created in the country during my time in Lagos. That meant a huge amount of work as there are very strict criteria involved.

"I settled in fairly quickly in Lagos and grew accustomed to the work. I lived with two of our sisters in Ebute Meta one of whom was Sr. Dymphna Drury who was already working at the Apostolic Nunciature and the other, Sr. Hannah Boylan, who was involved in a very big *Samaritan* project. Ebute Meta is not so far from the centre of Lagos and it was at one time a very pleasant area. That changed with the huge population explosion which started during the oil boom of the 1970's. The area is now very congested and huge numbers of people find it hard to eke out a living

"One thing that distinguishes the Catholic Church in Nigeria from that of the Church in Ireland is the serious involvement of the youth and the laity. It has been like that from the beginning. A seventy-four-year-old Irish missionary priest, Fr. Jim Sheerin, SPS, gives courses in Abuja on pastoral and collaborative ministry and the young people attending are very involved and interested. Collaborative ministry involves the lay community. The priest is the leader but he is always in consultation with a participating laity. Fr. Tom Walsh, SMA, also in Abuja, is a typical example of a priest involved in this type of ministry. He discusses every step of Church and parish development with the people and he enlists their help which is always given as the people feel ownership of their Church.

"Another aspect of the Nigerian Church that is being explored is the leadership of women. Last week, I attended a lecture given by a woman who had traced women's leadership to the Old and New Testaments. Highlighting this history is very important here in Africa where traditionally women have taken second place to men. A very good discussion followed the lecture.

"One very good way of coming face to face with the heart of Nigerian society is by visiting the prisons. I did so in Jos and I did it again in Lagos. The prisoners very gradually gain enough confidence to speak to you about their plight. Many are left in prison awaiting trial for years. In Lagos there were two prisons. I used to visit the maximum security one which was called Kiri Kiri. Between eighty and ninety percent of the prisoners were always awaiting trial and most of them protested their innocence. Few could ever hope to engage a lawyer. They spent their days in cramped conditions with few facilities and poor nourishment. Some had families who weren't even aware that they were in prison or who didn't want to acknowledge that they were there. Prison numbers increased greatly in the 1990's during the regime of Sani Abacha. Executions were also more frequent. I was present during one and it was quite terrible. Twelve prisoners were lined up in the prison grounds and tied to stakes. They were then shot, to the cheers of an audience who had gathered to witness the event. In the past, executions took place down on Bar Beach in Lagos and they attracted huge numbers of spectators.

"One day, I visited Kiri Kiri with a wealthy Lagos lady who had organized three giant pots of food out in the open prison grounds. As feeding was about to commence, a huge number of wretched skeleton-like men of all ages rushed out. I was absolutely shocked. While they were eating, they were being handled roughly by six stalwart well-fed prison guards. In my horror, I approached the guards and begged them to show some compassion.

"My post in Lagos came to an end when the Apostolic Nunciature had to move with all other embassies to the new Nigerian political capital of Abuja. My work here is more or less the same as what I did in Lagos. Here in Abuja however, the SSL do not have a house so for the moment, I live in the accommodation section of the Nunciature as does Sister Dymphna Drury who is also here.

She, who is some years older than I am, will be returning to Ireland in the near future. Before coming to the Nunciature in Lagos, she was the principal of the SSL School at Mokola, Ibadan for more than twenty years. She loved teaching and missed it greatly when she retired in 1983. It will be a huge wrench for me when she returns to Ireland.

"As for myself, I have to accept that I too am approaching the end of my time in Nigeria. I intend to stay as long as I am able to do my day's work and as long as I am in good health. If I had a choice, I would like to live out my days in this country. This would be unfair of course to the young Nigerian sisters who would have to take care of me if I became incapacitated. Leaving Nigeria will be difficult as I have been here for all of my adult life. I came before Independence when people were idealistic and lived simple lives. Over the years, materialism has crept in and unfortunately, the leadership of the country has not always been good. Nowadays the level of corruption is very high. It has become part and parcel of everyday living. It will take leadership of extraordinary calibre to turn the country around. The people of Nigeria are intelligent and gifted in so many ways and their country has enormous natural resources. It should be a very great country. The hope lies in the fact that there are huge numbers of people who continue to have faith and hope and who never stop praying for leaders who will lead them out of this troubled time.

"In 1963, the SSL started a Nigerian formation house in Akure in Ondo State and today we have about eighty Nigerian Sisters of St. Louis. They are all very good and they are capable of carrying our work into the future."

Sister Maura Flynn

Sisters of St. Louis (SSL)
Kano

L to R: Sr. Maura Flynn; Irene Lynch; Sr. Kehinde Ojo; Joseph Lynch, Irish Ambassador; Sr. Christiana Ogundele; Sr. Brigitte Burke in Kano

The first Irish Sisters of St. Louis arrived in Kano in 1948. They were invited there by Bishop John McCarthy, SMA. Their mission was to educate girls in his diocese.

Kano is the oldest city in West Africa, dating back more than a thousand years. For centuries it was one of the most active commercial centres within the broader region of Nigeria and its surrounding countries. Vast numbers of traders moved northwards across the Sahara desert and southwards to Zaria and beyond. Today Kano is still an important city but the old Hausa city with its extensive market and century old indigo dye pits contrasts greatly with the modern industrial section.

When the sisters arrived, they were conscious of moving into a largely Muslim territory whose people regarded the education of girls, especially secondary education, with a certain amount of suspicion. They knew that it would take much courage and diplomacy to establish their schools. They started taking morning classes at one of the primary schools in the city and at the request of the British District Officer, agreed to give afternoon classes to expatriate pupils.

By 1949 however, plans for a new secondary school to be run by the sisters were unfolding and by January 1951, St. Louis Girls' Secondary School opened its doors to twenty-two residential pupils at Bompai, not far from the centre of Kano. From the beginning, it accepted pupils from all denominations but in the early days, the vast majority was Christian. This changed in the late 1970's when the Government of Kano stipulated that 80% of the school's intake had to be Kano indigenes who were predominantly Muslim. By this time the school had grown in size and reputation. The new government stipulations created a challenge for the sisters as it meant going beyond their objective of teaching pupils mainly from their own faith. They rose to the challenge however and entered wholeheartedly into the education of both Muslim and Christian, in keeping with the spirit of the founders of their congregation whose motto was *Sint Unum* (may they be one). It meant many changes, not least of which was the provision in their compound of a mosque and the employment of two Imams to come daily to conduct the five recommended prayer sessions. This practice has continued.

It was to this much respected establishment that I went to meet Sister Maura Flynn. She herself was the school's principal from 1989 to 1993. At the time of our meeting, she was preparing, at the age of seventy-three, to say a final farewell to Kano and the country to which she first came in 1959 at the age of thirty. Farewell parties were being given by friends, staff and past pupils. She was putting on a brave and cheerful face but admitted to feeling a wrench. "The country is part of me now. I have imbibed it and it is really my home. I almost feel that I am turning my back on it but I know that one has to make a decision at some point to return to the country of one's birth. It will not be easy.

"When I came here in 1959, I was appointed headmistress of St. Louis Primary Residential School in Zonkwa in the Archdiocese of Kaduna which is further south than Kano but very much in Northern Nigeria. Before long, my brief was changed by the Archbishop who gave our congregation a big piece of land and told us to establish a teachers' training college in Zonkwa. I worked on the assignment with Sister Mary Ibar who was longer in Nigeria than I was. As you can imagine, we had no experience of setting up training colleges. We sought advice and help from the OLA Sisters who had a training college in Akwanga in middle-belt Plateau State. We went to visit them on a particular Monday and during the course of four days, we learned everything that was to be learned about setting up a Teacher's Training College! I remember Sr. Finian who by the way, is still alive in their mother house in Cork, emphasizing how important it was for me to understand how the pit toilets worked. She then brought me to the kitchen to meet the butcher who explained how the meat was cut, stored and cooked. That day the cooks were in the kitchen grinding on two stones the various ingredients that went into one of the regional aromatic stews. Out in the compound, the sisters' two carpenters worked to make and repair every stick of furniture in the college.

"During the days of our visit, the student teachers happened to be on teaching practice in the local primary schools so we were able to meet with them, observe their preparations and sit at the back of classes while they gave their lessons. The whole experience was the most rapid and most inclusive training I have ever had. We returned to Zonkwa and proceeded with our own college which was ultimately opened in 1961 with Sister Mary Ibar as principal. When she departed for postgraduate studies in 1963, I took over as principal. Some hectic years followed and then came 1972 and the move by the Nigerian Federal Government to take over all the training colleges. I remember a team of six arriving at the college from the ministry. They were very keen to find out how I ran the college so economically. I was invited to remain on as principal and they suggested that I apply to be interviewed by the Public Service Commission for the position. I complied with this and was thereafter appointed formally as principal and paid a government salary. In 1977 however, when I felt that my vice-principal who was

Nigerian, had her eye on my job, I sensed that it was probably the right time for me to resign and to head for pastures new. I have had that same intuition a few times during my career and it has always proved to be correct to pay attention to it.

"Following my resignation, I went on a year's study leave and then returned to Nigeria to give adult literacy classes in Kano. These classes were being conducted as part of the *Option for the Poor* programme that was being put forward by the Catholic Church. This work, which I did for six years was very rewarding and fulfilling as I was helping great numbers of poor illiterate women. It was with joy that I faced forty women in St. Elizabeth's Hall in our compound on the first night of classes. Many were women I had known in Zonkwa who had come to Kano to accompany their husbands who had found work in factories. There they were, singing their hearts out in Hausa as I entered. I asked if they would like to learn English. Their excitement was electric. 'We want to be able to read in church and we want to be able to help our children with their school work' they told me.

"I put beautiful charts all over the place and used drawings and Hausa words alongside the English ones. Some came to the hall in the early mornings to spend time learning the charts. I am a Carysfort-trained primary school teacher so all this was second nature to me and I loved it. I taught groups at three other venues, two of which were at army posts. Today if I were asked to identify the most meaningful part of my work in Nigeria, I would choose the work of those six years, as I felt it made a real contribution to the poor.

"At the end of that period, I was asked to engage in fund-raising for our congregation in Ireland. This request dismayed me in a big way. I was sure that I would hate it. In the end, I decided to take it on. Sister Patricia Moloney, a former principal at the secondary school in Kano pointed out some perks of the job – great freedom, my own car and a chance to visit regularly my mother who was living in Clare and approaching ninety years of age. 'Every time I visit your mother,' she told me, 'she wonders what is wrong with her Maura who cannot get a job at home!'

"Over the next six years, I visited and stayed with my mother as often as I wished until she died at the age of ninety-six. I travelled around the country in my own car and successfully raised the impressive sum of £200,000 outside expenses. The fund-raising itself was not easy. The SSL, not having been founded specifically for the missions, was not allowed by the Irish Missionary Union to raise funds through the normal diocesan channels of appeal or through mission magazines. Just as I was feeling fairly down about the whole business, I ran into a cousin who suggested that I do *cash and car drives*, something she and her group were doing for the Augustinian Fathers in Limerick. After that, I never looked back.

"Back in Kano, the sad and unexpected death of Sister Eileen Burns, principal of the secondary school occurred. I was asked if I would think about taking the post. Though I was then 62 years old, I jumped at the idea as I had had enough of fund-raising and I was also missing Nigeria a lot. When I arrived some months later, I remember the little messenger Daniel who only died last year, taking me around and introducing me to just about everything. He was absolutely fabulous. I picked up on things quite quickly and even though I had no clue about science labs and the like, I had a team of teachers who were top-class. I stayed for three years and then I handed over to Sister Patricia Ebegbulem who became our first Nigerian principal.

"I myself proceeded to Gonzaga University in Washington State in the United States and joined a master's degree programme with no compulsion to sit exams. I attended lectures on spiritual studies, liturgy and catechetics. Then we had lovely extras like yoga, dream analysis and calligraphy. I found it all very broadening and renewing and I made a great many new friends. It would be my dream to revisit the friends of those days but that will hardly happen now.

"Once the course was finished, I was back in Nigeria – this time to replace as principal of our primary school, the young Nigerian sister who wished to study abroad. I was to remain in that position for six years. It was a busy time as the school which had 1,300 pupils was developing all the time.

"Just as I was taking a breath after that position, Bishop Sheehan of Kano persuaded me to teach English at the new Diocesan Seminary in Kano. I agreed to do so for two years. After that, I spent time coaching our own Nigerian sisters who were preparing to enter university.

"This country has witnessed my many entrances and exits. The exit I am about to make will most probably be my last. I am going home on 27 February. I will be given six months of freedom at our mission house in Dublin and then I will be assigned to one of our communities. I have plans to do a course on retirement during the summer at Balinter, County Louth. After that, I intend to relax and visit a number of places around the country. I am hoping that nobody will put too much pressure on me for a while. Ultimately, I would like to spend about four days a week engaged in computer studies, adult literacy and visitation of the elderly. There are a great many lonely, elderly people and I think that I have many stories I could tell them.

"I am optimistic about the next phase of my life. I believe in the power of positive thinking and I always strive to avoid negativity. I think that I have benefited from living among the Nigerians. They are open, upbeat, hospitable, gracious and fun-loving. I feel a certain amount of contented fulfillment and am thankful that I have been able to serve in a variety of worthwhile positions during my working life. I shall be seventy-five on my next birthday and I cannot believe how quickly the time has passed. When I came to Nigeria, we had approximately one hundred Irish Sisters of St. Louis and maybe ten Nigerian sisters. Now it's the opposite. That's how quickly change comes about. The Nigerian sisters will carry on our work."

In 1998, Sister Maura was awarded the Papal Benemerenti Medal 'for her fruitful and meritorious service to the Church in Nigeria.' In her acceptance speech, she said that she was accepting it on behalf of all the Sisters of St. Louis and their lay collaborators who were involved in the ministries of education, health, social and pastoral work in Nigeria over fifty years and that it was an honour to have her name included with those of the pioneering sisters who also received this medal."

Sister Brigitte Burke, one of Sister Maura's colleagues in Kano was more recently honoured by the President of Nigeria, Olusegun Obasanjo with the award of *Members of the Order of the Niger (MON)* – 'in recognition of her meritorious and remarkable contribution to the growth and development of education in the nation.' Sister Brigitte first came to Nigeria in 1970.

The Congregation of the Religious Sisters of Charity

An Introduction

The Congregation of the Religious Sisters of Charity is a religious congregation of women dedicated to working with the poor. It was founded by Mary Aikenhead in Ireland in 1815. She saw social, economic, educational and spiritual deprivation all around her and her desire was to 'give to the poor for love what the rich got for money'. Today the sisters continue to do this work on four continents by working in schools and hospitals but especially with people who are ill, poor, homeless, depressed, suicidal or addicted to alcohol or drugs. They also work with refugees, asylum seekers, prisoners and those suffering from disabilities or affected by HIV/AIDS.

The Congregation established a foundation in Nigeria in 1961 and today they are involved in healthcare, education, pastoral and social work in six locations in Southern Nigeria.

Sister Ann Lally

Religious Sisters of Charity
Port Harcourt

Sr. Ann Lally with her pupils at 'Sancta Maria School' Port Harcourt

I travelled to Port Harcourt to meet Sr. Ann and her colleagues Srs. Rosaleen, Pauline and Sylvia. The sisters came to Port Harcourt in the early 1990's when the Bishop there invited them to take over the running of a primary school, a home for physically handicapped children and a hospital. Because of insufficient personnel, they declined the management of the hospital but undertook the two other projects. At the time of my visit, the spirited and highly motivated Sister Ann who had earlier in the year celebrated her 70th birthday was administrator of *Sancta Maria School*. In a lively after-supper conversation, she talked about her work there and also recalled her earlier years in Nigeria.

"I have spent almost twenty years in Nigeria. People often ask if I love it here. Love is not the word. I have found it very fulfilling and I wouldn't be without the experience. You become very involved with people here and you feel that you can help a great deal. I had been teaching in England for twenty years when I was asked to come here in 1977. It was a whole new beginning at a time when I thought that I had arrived at a settled period in my middle life. Since then, I have had many new beginnings.

"I have in fact retired several times. I was running a school in Festac in the outskirts of Lagos in the early 1990's when I got sick and had to return home. As soon as I recovered, I was asked to stay on in Ireland and head up our primary school in Crumlin, Dublin. At age sixty-four, I was thinking of retiring but the following year an emergency developed in Festac, Nigeria in the school in which I had worked for nine years. I thought that it was cruel to ask me to return and though Mother General gave me a choice, I felt that I could not honestly turn down her request. I decided to go for a year. I stayed three.

"That school had been set up in 1983 as a private school belonging to the Archdiocese of Lagos. Two months after it was opened, I became principal and administrator and it became a very academic and first rate place which won many national awards. In 2001 after forty-five years of teaching, and after completing my second assignment in Festac, I finally retired or so I thought. After being given a wonderful send off, I returned to Ireland with the intention of studying theology at Milltown Park Institute in Dublin. I was not long there when I received another call from our Mother General asking if I would go to Port Harcourt and help run *Sancta Maria School.*

"The school was originally set up by a former reverend sister from an indigenous order for handicapped children. She was running it in conjunction with a home for the handicapped. It was when it all became too difficult for her to sustain that the Bishop of Port Harcourt sought the help of our sisters. On arrival, Sister Sylvia Uwwalaka, our Nigerian colleague who was just out of the novitiate took charge of the school and developed it by bringing in non-handicapped children. She, after some time, had to leave for studies and in her absence the school ran into new difficulties. It was then that I got the request to help out.

"I arrived in late 2001 and when I first went down to view the whole set up, I have to tell you that I got quite depressed. I wondered how at my age I could start all over again to tackle problems which would have proved daunting to a much younger person. At this point it was the awareness of my past experience that came to my rescue. I knew that I had been a successful administrator and a good teacher so I dug deep I suppose and came up with the courage to tackle the new assignment. I called a meeting of the staff and we discussed every aspect of the life of the school. Somehow or other, I became very enthusiastic and motivated as I spoke with them. I first told them that their salaries would be gradually and quickly increased from the 11,000 naira a month they were getting to 18,000 a month. Now government-run schools get a lot more than that and in Festac, we were able to come close to the government salary. *Sancta Maria* is funded from school fees and since most of the parents are very poor, we cannot afford to have very high fees. Already they are paying 5,500 naira a term and that is a huge amount for them. Most live in one room and some never know when they will be turned out by an unscrupulous landlord. Education is very important to them and they will starve rather than be short of the school fees. There are some children whom we take in for nothing. Sister Sylvia has now returned to the school, and she and I make decisions on all these kinds of issues.

"I was given one million naira by our congregation in Ireland to develop the school. We have two hundred children attending now and that number includes the handicapped children. I hope to have three hundred by next September. One of the ways that I managed to increase the number was by starting up a nursery school for children between two and a half and three years. This was set up in the old home for the handicapped which was replaced by a new one and which was next door to the school. I knocked down walls and pushed in windows and in the space of a few months, we were ready to open. I get hypertension when I think of all we went through. We opened on January 13, 2002 and we were still painting the night before.

"The whole ethos of the school needed to be changed. The teachers needed in-service and development and the buildings needed substantial improvements. We have made tremendous progress in just a few months. The morale is high and the parents are happy. When I call a parent-teacher meeting, I make sure that at least one parent of every child attends. I get great co-operation on this. All in all things are going very well and we plan to continue to grow and raise standards. The children are very happy and enthusiastic and at my age, it is a privilege to be involved in such a venture and to be able to share in youthful joy and enthusiasm. The early days were undoubtedly exhausting and initially I had planned to stay only for a year. Now my plan is more fluid. I pray about it so whatever the Lord wants me to do, I will do."

When Sister Ann first came to Nigeria in 1977, it was to Pacelli, the school for the blind run by the Sisters of Charity in Surelere, Lagos. She remembers that it was the year that Nigeria hosted the second *World Black and African Festival of Arts and Culture* in Lagos. "There was a great buzz about the city. The country was in the first flush of oil revenues and lots of roads, bridges and flyovers were being built. Things seemed quite organized and in those days corruption was not as rampant as it later became.

"Our school in Surelere was a fantastic school. I was first charged with looking after the blind pupils who were to be integrated into the federal public schools all over Lagos. I co-ordinated their transfers and made sure that they all had the requisite number of brail text books. The prisoners in the high security prison of Kiri Kiri in Lagos did the brailing of the books. Our sisters taught them how to do it just as they did with the prisoners in Dublin prisons. You have a little machine with six keys and the brail is a permutation and combination of these keys.

"While in Surelere, I took time out in Birmingham to do post-graduate studies in education for the visually handicapped. Among the things I did when I returned was to get in touch with a very good ophthalmologist who was able to perform surgery which yielded great results for some of the young people. The cases that were too serious for the Nigerian medical facilities were brought to London. To cover the costs of that venture, we had to mount a big fund-raising campaign as we were bringing the children to a top Harley

Street clinic. Nigerian Airways helped us greatly by giving us first-class return tickets to London. I travelled with the children and for six weeks, we stayed in one of our convents in London so as to be near the clinic for all the necessary post-surgical aftercare treatment. The whole project was a huge success and it got huge publicity at the time with photographs of the children and me appearing in many newspapers around the world!

"During my time in Lagos, I also got involved in prison visitation. One day as I was leaving, the prisoners who were doing the brailing for me, a group from the condemned cells who were walking towards the medical section approached me and asked if I would come and visit them. It was necessary to get permission from the prison authorities for that type of visitation and nobody thought that I would be given it. I asked for permission to talk with them, pray with them and bring them small useful items like soap and it was granted. There were about twenty cells with fifteen prisoners to each one. A great number of them had been picked up off the streets and never given a trial. Many had been there for years awaiting trial. Their clothes were just rotting off them. During my visits, I started bringing clothes collected by the families in our schools. This always caused wild excitement. The cells were mosquito infested and crowded and the prisoners didn't even have the space to lie down. The doors were covered in metal but had little peep holes at the top. I used to climb up so that they could see me as I spoke. I found them to be ordinary, everyday guys and when I looked around at their young faces, I could only think of my own brothers. As I got to know them, they began to relate their stories to me. I got on to their level and I learned that prisoners can be very prayerful and can be brought to a spiritual level very easily. I never had any fear or trouble as I believe that they trusted and respected me. In the beginning, I was brought to them under armed escort. That eventually became unnecessary. When I left Lagos, that work was continued by our sisters and today it is one of their main ministries."

Sister Ann was born in Dublin and attended the Irish Sisters of Charity Schools in Kings Inn Street. After completing secondary school she worked for a period in the Dept. of Finance. "The idea of entering the convent kept gnawing at me. It was as though a magnet was drawing me in that direction. In the end, I felt that I couldn't do a better thing with my life and I liked very much the idea of having a closer relationship with the Lord. I entered in 1954 and cut off all my long red hair which my mathematics' teacher and others could not bear to think of me doing! I have never regretted my decision."

Sister Pauline Butler

Religious Sisters of Charity
Port Harcourt

Sr. Pauline Butler

"I come from Freshford, Co. Kilkenny. I broke off a six-year relationship with a man friend when I decided to enter the convent at the age of twenty-six. It was a difficult decision of course but I believed that I really had to give the religious life a try as I was conscious of something drawing me in that direction for a long time. I have never regretted my decision and I feel that I have led a fulfilled life. I came to Nigeria in 1979 and I believe that it is important for me to be here.

"I went to school to the Presentation Sisters but when it came to joining a congregation, I knew that while I wanted to give my life to the Lord, I didn't want to teach. I searched around in various magazines and found that the Religious Sisters of Charity were involved in nursing, childcare and pastoral work. I felt that I would fit with them. Shortly after joining, I was sent to train as a nurse in St. Vincent's Hospital in Dublin which was run by our congregation. It was while I was waiting for the results of my exams that I got a letter from my superior asking me if I would like to go to Nigeria. That was twenty four years ago. I came to Uromi in the mid-west and started working in our hospital there. It was a general hospital with a midwifery training school. We moved out of it in 1991 because we were being pushed into a profit-making situation which meant treating the rich at the expense of the poor. Since our charism is to care for the poor, we found we couldn't continue. After that I went to Delta where we had another mission hospital and I was there in charge of it and its out-stations when this project which I am now in came up. The Bishop of Port Harcourt invited us here to take over the running of a school, a home for the handicapped and a hospital. We agreed to take on the school and the home but declined the hospital as we didn't have sufficient personnel. At that point I went home for eighteen months to train at the orthopaedic hospital in Cappagh, Dublin. During the training, I was conscious that I was looking forward very much to returning to Nigeria. I have now spent ten years in Port Harcourt.

"In our compound here, Sister Rosaleen Desmond is the superior and she is responsible for all buildings, staffing, delegation of work and the buying of all equipment and food. I take care of financial matters and in the home for the handicapped children, I basically oversee all the care programmes. We have children who are polio victims and we have quite a number who suffer from cerebral palsy. Ultimately we would like to devote ourselves fully to polio victims until such time as polio is eradicated. The caring that is needed for both groups is very different. After surgery, the polio children can more or less care for themselves. They can go to school and get around as long as you make sure that they are wearing their callipers. Their reactions are normal and you can observe them growing in intelligence and so on. A child suffering from cerebral palsy can be eighteen and act like an eight-year-old. Mostly they suffer from congenital problems which might have been caused at birth by prolonged labour or by jaundice which was not treated properly. Sometimes an affected child can be sitting up or walking before anything wrong is detected. The problem can be initially slow to develop but then it can progress rapidly to the point where you find serious non-coordination of muscles or speech defects. Mentally, some are better than others. One of the boys you met this evening is a very fine boy and he can speak and do things but he is very spastic. You can relax him with physiotherapy but within minutes he can become very tight again. It takes these kinds of children a long time to perform an action as the message from the brain takes time. Most have speech defects but some are more severe than others. The cases we have here are not actually as bad as some I have seen in our facility in Baldoyle, Dublin. It may be that the worst cases in Nigeria do not survive.

"The new and modern facilities which we have here in Port Harcourt are very suitable for the work we do and they give the children a real sense of home. We have four separate houses and the children are grouped as families with eight to ten to a house which is managed by two members of staff. Boys and girls share houses but there is space and privacy. The children feel that they go from their own home to school every morning and when school is over, they are allowed to have visitors and behave in a way similar to children who go home to family homes. If there are any serious clashes of personality, we have the option of moving children around. This does not happen very often. On the whole, they have all responded marvellously to their conditions which are so much better than those they had in the old buildings.

"It was our congregation in Dublin that provided the money for the new buildings. Our contractor who was well known to our sisters in Lagos came down here and lived with his team outside the gates for a year and a half. He had his site manager and we had ours and any problem that emerged was sorted out very efficiently. Our regional superior here in Nigeria had a huge say in all the development decisions but first, we here, submitted our plans and ideas.

"My days are full. There is never a dull moment. The children keep you young and alert. In the morning I am with them for an hour and a half before they go to school. During the school hours, we treat children who come in from the outside and care for the post-surgical children. In the afternoon, when the polio children come in from school, I find that there are always a fair number of problems to deal with.

"Despite their disabilities, the children are very active and they love to dance and perform to music. You saw that today during the cultural display they put on for you. It is no problem for some of them not to be able to use their legs if they can use their hands, and some dance very well with their hands. This evening, there were three cerebral palsy children dancing with their hands and they were enjoying all the movements they were making in a big way.

"I am sixty-three now. I'd like to go home before I'm too old as I would like to be able to fit into Irish society. A lot of things have changed since I left in 1979. We are free to go home whenever we choose but you need to have someone to replace you and here, we need very specialized staff. We are always planning for the future with regard to this. If I went home, I would like to do something with a caring dimension and I would also like to continue with my hobby of gardening! This is something that I have enjoyed doing here in my spare time.

"I have found that I fitted easily into the life in Nigeria. I like the sun and I have no problem being out in it. Sometimes the struggle and poverty which you see around you can get to you and you wonder if there will ever be an end to it. There's rich and poor in Nigeria but the vast majority is very poor. The poor seem to have an ability to rise above their suffering and they have a huge capacity for life. They live for the moment and even if they are weighed down with problems, they can be optimistic and upbeat. People are suffering much more now than when I came in 1979. Food and transport were then affordable and the constant struggle was not as evident. Now you can go to the market and find the trader telling you with delight that you have *opened his market* because you are the first to make a purchase. When I was in Uromi, a person in need could nearly always depend on help from somebody within the extended family. That is no longer the case because the members of the extended family are likely to be just as badly off. If sickness hits a family, there is usually no money for hospitals or any kind of medical attention. If a family member gets into trouble with the police, there is no money for a lawyer or for bail. Life is hard at every level. Rents are high and unscrupulous landlords can increase rents or evacuate tenants whenever they feel like it. Many of our own staff are constantly requesting advances from their upcoming salaries for all sorts of emergencies. I do the salaries and I find it extremely difficult because with all the advances, you end up giving them hardly anything."

Some resident children at the Sisters' Home for the disabled, Port Harcourt

Sister Ugomma Sylvia Uwalaka

Religious Sisters of Charity
Port Harcourt

Sister Ugomma Sylvia Uwalaka with her pupils

Sr. Ugomma (beautiful eagle) Sylvia was deeply engrossed in the lesson she was giving her fifth form pupils when I was introduced to her at Sancta Maria School. You are immediately aware that this handsome young woman is no run of the mill average teacher. She simply loves being in the classroom and this is sensed and rewarded by her charges. Sister Sylvia joined the Sisters of Charity in the early 1990's.

"When I was in school," she tells me when we chat later that day, "I never really thought that I would enter religious life. I did want to be a good Christian and all things spiritual drew my attention. I was a member of the choir and anything to do with the Bible was of great interest to me. I went into a college of education with two friends who were interested in becoming reverend sisters. They were always checking out congregations and talking non-stop about their plans. At that stage, I had a young man in my life and I had plans to marry him. Very unexpectedly, I began to think of the possibility of becoming a reverend sister. I wished the idea away and told God that He was too late, that I had other plans! The desire kept growing so when I graduated from the college of education, I went on youth service and for a year, I stayed very much apart from everybody as I wanted to think clearly and see if I could come to a decision about my future. By the end of the year, I was convinced that I would not be able to combine the desire I had for God, prayer and spiritual things with the commitments of marriage. I met my young man and told him that I could not marry him. He was devastated and to this day, even though he is married, he continues to visit my family. My sisters tease me saying that no matter how many veils I put on, his heart will always be married to me! I felt very sorry for him at the time but I also felt that if God wanted me to devote my life to Him, I would not be able to make him happy in marriage. It was all very clear in my mind.

"I had been introduced to the Sisters of Charity during my college of education years so I contacted them and was invited to spend a week in one of their convents. After the week, I somehow felt that their life was for me. I felt that my spiritual life and my desire to serve would find expression in their congregation. I was very impressed with their commitment to the people they were serving and I loved their community spirit. They were happy and joyful amongst themselves and they made me feel very welcome.

"My parents were not opposed to religious life but they were worried about my going outside my own country. I had an aunt in the indigenous congregation of the DDL (Daughters of Divine Love) and their work in health, education and social work is very respected. My aunt was in fact their superior general at the time. I didn't feel drawn to them as I wanted to be anonymous and had no wish to have people saying 'she is the niece of the superior general, make sure that she is treated with respect'.

"My father resisted my going away before studying for my degree at university. I had to seriously negotiate with him as I was intent on joining as soon as I had made up my mind. It had been his ambition to send all of us to university as his own father had struggled long and hard to give him his own university education. My father is from Owerri in Imo State and that is where I grew up. He became a principal of a secondary school and my mother was a primary school teacher. They were both educated by Irish missionaries – my father by the Holy Ghost Fathers in Enugu and my mother by the Holy Rosary Sisters in Emekuku which is close to Owerri. I am the fourth of their nine children. One of my brothers is studying for the priesthood.

"As soon as I joined the Irish sisters, I was sent to Ireland for my formation. Everything was strange and new and even though it was summer when I arrived, I felt extremely cold. We were three Nigerians and we gained a great deal of experience in different apostolates during our formation years. While in Dublin I worked a lot with the travelling children and I helped prepare them for school every morning. After my profession, I went to Cork to work in our facility for women who were not able to cope with living on their own. I got to know them all very well.

"In 1990 I came back to Nigeria and taught in Lagos in our primary school for two years. Then I was sent to Port Harcourt to help out with the school here. After four years, I went to Zambia to do a course in spirituality and it was after I returned from Zambia that I was given the opportunity to go to university to do a degree. My father was very happy. Following my graduation, I returned here to teach primary five. I am very happy being a classroom teacher and if I were to remain being one forever I think that I would be fulfilled. To be working with children, to be shaping their lives, to be helping them with their academic work and to be assisting them in their growth is what fulfillment is to me. I am very content in my work right now. I do not know where I will be sent next or what the future holds.

"There are very few Irish sisters left now in Nigeria. My own wish would be that we would always have some of them with us. I recognize the realities however and I am confident that whatever happens, we Nigerian sisters will carry on and pass what we have learned from the Irish sisters to the ones coming after us. I couldn't see us settling for anything less."

Carmelite Fathers
(OCD)

Discalced Carmelite Friars

An Introduction

The Discalced Carmelite Friars are priests and brothers who follow a way of consecrated life inspired by the Rule of St. Albert as it was interpreted by St. Teresa of Avila and St. John of the Cross. The distinctive feature of this way of life is their focus on personal prayer and meditation. They feel called to witness to the importance of prayer in the life of Christians.

The Friars have their origins in a group of pious pilgrims who, after the victory of the crusaders in Palestine and the recapture of the Holy Places, settled on the slopes of Mount Carmel to live life as hermits in imitation of the prophet Elijah. The main elements of Elijah's life – total dedication to God, solitude, penance, prayer and contemplation – became the way of life of the first Carmelites.

In 1988, the Discalced Carmelites from the Anglo Irish Province were invited to bring their apostolate of prayer and spirituality to Nigeria by creating a foundation in Enugu. Today, Nigeria has 21 Carmelite priests, fifteen of whom are Nigerian and there are also over 45 Nigerian Carmelites in formation.

Impressions of Nigeria

by
Father Nicholas Madden (OCD)
Carmelite Fathers, Donnybrook, Dublin

The Carmelite Community in Nsukka, Enugu State
Fr. Nicholas Madden - second from the left, front row

I was fortunate to meet with Fr. Nicholas Madden during a number of his visits to Nigeria. His keen interest in every aspect of life in his host country led me to invite him to write about his impressions of Nigeria. He graciously accepted my invitation.

"I have been to Nigeria three times; these visits did not go beyond three months. The first was in 1998 to attend the ordination to the priesthood of four Nigerian Carmelites, a joyful event that presaged numerous vocations in a burgeoning Church. I went back twice after that in 2000 and 2001 to provide brief courses for novices and students at Nsukka and to give a few short retreats to Carmelite nuns in a missionary seminary in Ibadan and in the Dominican Faculty of Theology there. I also got a taste of parochial ministry in Ekpoma where we have a parish. Fr. Tim Buckley, a seasoned Spiritan missionary, asked me why I was 'out here' and having mused for a moment on my reply said: 'I see, you are a class of a commercial traveller.' I have no argument with that as it underlines my lack of qualification to speak. However, the invitation to do so derails the admonition to be 'forever silent'.

"Those who have given their lives to work in mission fields admit the difficulty, if not the impossibility of getting inside the minds and culture of another people. It is not that there is no communication but it is an encounter between people conditioned by generations of a different way of feeling and of thinking. It might be said to be another way of being human. I have seen this illustrated by a missionary writing about the use of language. Language is a means of communication but it has another use in Nigeria: it is the way that a trusting relationship is established. Until this has been achieved the 'facts' can be multifaceted and the slide-rule between 'yes' and 'no' can have a very nuanced calibration. The communication requires patient exegesis from both parties. Add to that the levels of usage that your interlocutor has in mind as he runs multi-storey linguistic rings around you and then you might well say: 'what have you?' To offset this I have tried to listen to writers like Chinua Achebe with his *Things Fall Apart*, Wole Soyinka, dramatist and author of the haunting memoir, *The Man Died* and poets like Clark and Okigbo.

"Nigeria as an entity was largely the product of colonisation. At a time when European powers were looking beyond their frontiers for expansion, exploitation and the opportunity to share their civilisation, Africa was obviously ripe for the harvest. Gandhi spoke for whole generations when asked what he thought of Western civilisation: 'I think it would be a good idea'. Parallel to that is

Chesterton's riposte when told that Christianity had failed: 'It has never been tried'. Analysing those insights would require considerable knowledge and finesse. History cannot be turned back and it would be a caricature to see its unfolding in a simplistic outline of black and white. There were advantages and disadvantages; there was good fruit and rotten fruit. The country began to take shape at the same time as other colonised regions. It was the creature of adventurers, heroes and villains, educators, missionaries, philanthropists and blackguards.

"As Achebe has demonstrated, *things fell apart.* Foreign ways and organisation were imposed on peoples with different cultures. Traditional wisdom and style of life were not integrated into the emerging nation. Nigeria has not had the benefit of a Mandela.

"While keeping the many distinctions that characterise the peoples of Nigeria in mind and despite the opaqueness that challenges perception, it is obvious that they are intelligent, industrious, warm-hearted and above all resilient, with reserves of stoicism that enable them to survive crushing setbacks. Today Achebe consoles himself with the knowledge that his passport, which used to describe him as 'British Protected Person', now identifies him as 'Citizen of Nigeria'. A dawn has broken and there is much work to do in the heat of the day.

"Two examples may illustrate some of the problems that confront Nigerians. When I visited a university campus, I could not avoid seeing a huge unfinished building, roofless and with gaping windows. The intention was that it should serve as the library. The 'big man' who was sponsoring it had lost power and the money assigned to complete it had disappeared – I was told. Too much depended on the protagonist; another 'big man' would prefer to undertake a new project than complete the unfinished work of his predecessor; huge sums of money vanish into thin air which is a magnified instance of widespread venality. The younger people make no secret of their concern about the prevalence of corruption. Any observer will note the fascination which money has in every quarter of the population. This is linked into a deep urge to better the family fortune and family can be extended family.

"Driving along any road you come across sprawling schools. There are hundreds of children coming and going but it is impossible to overlook the crumbling state of the buildings. Often the missionaries left them in excellent condition; those who took over do not seem to have either the will or the means to maintain them. Public services are often unreliable. The electricity scheme, NEPA, is an obvious example, a byword for failure and disruption. Proper sanitation and a reliable flow of pure water would improve basic welfare immeasurably. While the people are meticulous about personal hygiene, the colossal garbage of a city like Onitsha exemplifies the widespread need of a ruthless Germanic clean up. The capital, Abuja, shows what can be achieved, but it shows other things too.

"Sister mosquito ensures that malaria is rife. If the State were to extirpate malaria the country could develop its tourist potential. This would also require the elimination of brigandage, a constant threat to travellers even on those splendid new roads. Incidentally, it did not stop Fr. Máirtín Conroy from travelling far and wide, often on 'secondary' roads, to visit the homes of prospective candidates. But Fr. Jude, who was shot and died, was not so fortunate. The Aids epidemic is a more recent and challenging scourge.

"Nigeria stimulates all the senses. It is possible to look at the sun with the naked eye through the early morning fog. Theophilus invited me to look at the sunspots, giving me kinship with Galileo even without the use of his telescope. It was a delight to walk up and down under a starlit sky in Nsukka and discuss the day's or year's or aeon's events. Being about 7° north of the equator, I knew that a brother in Dublin was seeing the moon from a slightly different angle. Walking reminds me that Nigerians do not 'go for a walk'. A woman in Ekpoma, true to custom, asked me where I was going. When I told her that I was merely out for exercise, she was perplexed but eventually gave me the benefit of the doubt and concluded with considerable charm that I was 'strolling'.

"The landscape is seldom dramatic in the sense that there are no lofty mountains, picturesque valleys or stretches of inland water. There is of course the Niger and its majestic rolling waters, rising in distant Guinea and wending its way through Mali to turn south and traverse Nigeria before entering the Atlantic through the Delta. Seeing it is to have images of generations of people, washing, fishing, canoeing, trading, warring, celebrating. It is unlikely that parties ever set out just to look at it. The Romantic imagination does not seem to have emerged in Nigeria in that way. When the white man came, he realized the significance of the river for conquest, trade, education and evangelisation.

"Probably, the most typical thing to strike the eye in tropical Nigeria is the palm tree, especially the coconut palm and the oil palm. The former provides latex and the white flesh is eaten alone or with other food; the latter is used to procure oil as well as kernel oil and can be tapped for wine, which in turn may be distilled as gin. Palm trees have many uses, medicinal, cultural and practical like building and finally they are used as firewood when they die.

"The most significant cultural symbol in Nigeria is the cola nut. It is offered as a sign of hospitality and has more than one cultic use.

"To drive north-east from Enugu to Zing in Taraba State is to note a change of scenery, a rapid change if Frank is at the wheel. The palm-trees gradually give way to grass and eventually you find yourself in an austere landscape with a ring of low bare mountains, where there is some agriculture, tillage and stock. Compounds become more numerous, a sign that polygamy is common in these belts. The rising ground gains higher altitudes around Jos. Here the European can breathe more freely and find a more familiar habitation. Regularly, small groups of Fulani herdsmen drive their long-horned cattle by the roadside, their drovers' sticks held in the crook of their elbows behind their backs, their broad brimmed hats keeping their faces in shadow, their assets carried in a satchel swinging at their sides. They are said to have an uncanny telepathic rapport with their animals. Here and there a group of convex tents just breaks the skyline. These house their women, renowned for their beauty but prematurely aged, and their children. The encampments move in rhythm with the herds.

"It is said that there is little or no wild life in Nigeria. One reason given is that there was such scarcity during and after the Biafran war that anything that moved ended up in the pot. Of birds, the one to stand out in the memory is the vulture. He is not a very engaging creature on the ground, with hunched posture, scrawny neck, beady eye and lancet beak but he is majestic in flight. The local varieties in Nsukka seem to keep an eye on the butcher. They came in numbers with him when he set out for the monastery where he slaughtered animals for a feast. They had to be content with what they could nimbly snatch from the discarded entrails. Carrion is their speciality and sometimes this is human, whether the result of an accident or criminal activity or summary police justice. The taboo attached to corpses works in their favour.

"It is fair to say that the house or home is not necessarily the primary focus of life in Nigeria. The places where people meet that play the most important function in their social life. The house provides shelter in which to eat and sleep and preserve personal belongings. It is true that if a man makes good he will go back to his village and build an imposing house. You may be told with a flashing smile that of course he is 'a 419'. The market place, the church, the school, the play-ground are the centres of gravity. They are full of life and colour. The milling crowds of traders in Onitsha must be seen to be believed but markets in full swing or empty market places punctuate any journey. They are not confined to towns; they just seem to spring up by the roadside. They are places for trade but also for conversation, information, humour and social exchange. Men and women take part without any seeming reservations of rights. Bargaining is built into the system. There is a wide selection of goods for sale, the stalls forming a pattern of supply for diverse demands. The traders do not doubt the quality of what is for sale, their animated gestures and expressions a stimulating contrast to the po-faced demeanour of your Western salesperson. Nor do you or your vendor take the marked price literally. It is understood that a bargain is the occasion for an *entente cordiale* contrived by an interplay of wit and ingenuity. It is reminiscent of those rituals that had to be observed at Irish fairs not so long ago. Children are everywhere, weaving in and out between the stalls, playful, charming and still trusting. Even a spin on an okada, the local motor-cycle taxi, through the rutted and slippery gangways between the stalls invites the offer of fruit, bread, soft drinks or the inspection of the victims of ratsbane being swung tantalisingly from a stick for the benefit of the *anocha* – the white man – riding pillion.

"Every gathering of people is a concentration of colour. Reds, blues, yellows, violet, green, orange, tertiaries, hues, shades and tints shift and change in a living kaleidoscope. The traditional use of indigo for dying brings ingenious forms into sight on hangings and tablecloths. Younger artists delight in the whole spectrum and use it to produce stylised images of their surroundings or release the teeming contents of their imaginations. Both men and women dress colourfully. But it is the women especially who display such variety and vitality in their choice of cotton, skirt, wrap and matching headgear. The designs are generally abstract but occasionally they unselfconsciously wear a representation or motto or logo. Ornaments, especially gold, find a favourable setting against the dark pigment of the Nigerian. Many of the younger people prefer western styles. This is probably symptomatic of something more generic. It is hardly an exaggeration to suggest that the United States of America is the Nigerian's *Shangri-La.*

"All the people bear themselves with dignity, but it is the women who move with such grace, not least when they have a child pitched on their haunches.

"It is a joy to watch them dance or even sway up the church at the offertory, the inner impulse emerging as harmonious movement. It has been noted that Nigerians do not suffer from a sense of dualism, that the opposites in their makeup are not in strife. The tiny tots celebrating their patron at an out-station school gave a stunning display of traditional dance in the presence of the elders, adults and the visitor. They have the sense of flow from being carried on their mothers' hips. To awake to consciousness was to awake to rhythm.

"Then there is the din. The Ishan humorist, Peter Enahoro, has said that God created the world but that Nigerians created noise. I was only in Nsukka for one night when I was startled by a series of explosions very early in the morning. I discovered later that it was part of the funeral ritual down in the valley. It seems that the spirit's transitus is facilitated by a final blast of sound from this side of the chasm. The bombardier has been known to join the spirit unceremoniously through carelessness in the execution of his duty. The same procedure is used to signal the importance of an occasion. We were told to brace ourselves for a thunderclap after the ordination of our confrères. I wonder if it is a relic of the foreigner who marked solemn occasions with a twenty-one gun salute.

"Wherever there is a group of people there is a rise in decibels, whether it is a cluster of women in conversation, the exchanges of traders in the market, the instructions or jibes of men in the workplace, the children at play in school yards, the guests at weddings, the mourners at funerals – often accompanied by a band, or inevitably the crowds in the football stadia where the range of emotion is dramatic, plunging from wild exultation to sullen depression. The roar of traffic on the highways and the staccato of the okadas in the towns begin before dawn and do not end with nightfall. That innate rhythm comes out in sound too. Popular music throbs with a deep sense of the ebb and flow of vital energy.

"The singing, not least in church, is strikingly robust and harmonious. The religious sense is alive, and rolling through the harmonies is a powerful feeling of 'how great Thou art'. Inculturation provides the challenge of creating a genuine religious music. I heard choirs at Fr. Crisogono's first mass, and in the cathedral in Enugu for the profession of native Carmelite missionary sisters which proved that the classical repertoire is within their range. The liturgical task would seem to be the creation of a distinctive musical dialect that would be the fruit of profound religious experience and would marry technical competence to a genuine Nigerian idiom. The Benedictines at Ewu achieve a restrained contemplative spirit in their chant to the accompaniment of Senegalese harps.

"The other senses are said to be too bound up with nutrition and basic functions to provide a range of vivid impressions comparable to what comes to us through eye and ear. However, to recall Nigeria is to remember the climate and especially the heat. When a confrère saw me close a window, he reminded me that 'there are no draughts in Nigeria.' It was pleasant to drive with all the windows wide open, in a stream of warm air, with no fear of a crick in your neck or a sore eye.

"One of the pleasures of the early morning was to walk straight into the shower to be refreshed by a douche of cold water. That was the norm if the supply had not been cut off. In that eventuality you had recourse to anticipation and the bucket. The bucket reminds me of a visit to the gaol in Enugu with my confrère, Michael Fitzgerald, the founder of CAPIO, an organization for the benefit of prisoners.

While he was in conversation with a man condemned to death, another old man, obviously a bit disturbed, kept pestering him about getting him a new bucket. I do not know if he got it. I do know that the condemned man was taken back to his village and executed in public. The prison conditions were appalling. CAPIO, as well as helping the inmates spiritually and legally also had the sewerage improved and the water supply enhanced.

"It was moving to celebrate mass for the Nsukka prisoners, to hear them sing lustily, not least the Credo in Latin and to try to speak to their condition. The occasion I remember most distinctly was the feast of the Resurrection. To contemplate their entombment in spite of brilliant sunshine and the jacaranda blossoms in the prison yard was not easy. Some visitors, their 'holy women', had come with gifts which were distributed after mass. Soap was the most prized item. On one occasion the prison authorities arranged that Fr. Jim Noonan would bring a prisoner, who had broken down mentally and was violent but sedated, to Enugu as he was driving there anyway. Jim and I sat in front while a warden, the sick man and a prisoner on parole sat behind. As we went along I heard some clinking of metal and suggested to Jim that he was having engine trouble. I was told not to worry, that the handcuffs had been removed and were rattling on the floor. We pulled up near the gaol. I can still see the prisoner, wrapped in his impenetrable story, being led across the street to the huge gates.

"My sense of smell and taste is impaired through age so my memories of those sensations are few and faint. Taste is said to be largely a matter of smell so that we can lump them together. My hosts thoughtfully provided me with familiar food. It is not easy at first to accommodate much of the local staple diet as the smells of dishes such as gari doused in a variety of pungent sauces are new to the western nose. Goat and chicken are kin to their northern cousins. I never want to suppress the memory of the delight I got from seeing playful little pigs snuffling around village huts. The honey was very dark but pleasant. I managed one glass of palm wine, slowly. You are advised to choose carefully your supplier. A large shandy after sundown did wonders for dehydration. Fruit was always available, varying with the season. It is hard to recall a European tyro up to his ears in a mango without the impulse to produce a cartoon.

The pineapples at Ekpoma must be the best in the world. I have to take it on faith that body odours differ with colour. Perfumes and unguents are popular in Nigeria and I was assured, with mischievous humour, that the untreated skin of a European is quite unpleasant to the African nose!

"The montage which follows is necessarily quite subjective, but I hope that the tiny vignettes will convey something of Nigeria. The silent old bishop of Nsukka comes to mind, standing perfectly still in the sacristy before a long, colourful and very audible ceremony. I was told that before he retired, when on visitation, he sat bold upright in the back seat of his car looking neither to the left nor to the right. Bishop Shanahan's work was in prayerful hands. When I was a child in Tipperary, I saw Bishop Shanahan who came to give confirmation in place of the local ordinary. This was a matter of interest to anyone in Nigeria to whom I mentioned it as his memory is revered. He now lies in Onitsha Cathedral far from his native Glankeen.

"There is an upsurge of native religious congregations in the Nigerian Catholic Church. This is a sign of hope but in the interests of healthy growth, they may require the metaphorical pruning knife. I had a slight contact with one of these congregations. The foundress, a professional woman who radiated zeal and purpose, might have been cast in another role in a matriarchal society.

"Sitting beside a priest at a ceremony, I asked him during an interval, where he had studied. He had taken a doctorate in history at the Gregorian University in Rome. I then asked him if he had taught. He replied offhandedly: 'No, but it was useful culturally.' Nigerians take learning in their stride. There is much vitality in the Nigerian Church. The people themselves realise that it takes time for the baptismal water to percolate down to the remoter genes. Like the rest of us, they have to rely on energies beyond human resource to attain to the full stature envisaged.

"We had an audience with the *Onogi*, the King in Ekpoma. He exuded authority but without arrogance. Shortly before, he had been ambushed by thugs who tried to force him into the boot of his car. He resisted – showing another kind of authority and was shot in the leg. It was he who conferred an honorary title on Fr. Christopher Clarke for his religious and social contributions to the district.

"A final memory may convey something else about Nigeria. Fr Emmanuel drove me to his village nestling under the giant irokos, to see his father and mother. His father had been a teacher and both he and his mother had travelled to the United States. I noticed the reverence and respect with which they treated their priest son. An uncle came in. He too had fought in 'the war'. As I drank a soft drink with my back to an open window I felt little hands making sure that it was hair in spite of being straight and white. They were reprimanded and scattered giggling with mischievous pleasure. It was good to be trusted.

"These haphazard remarks should convey some of the splendid qualities I noticed in my superficial contact with the people. There is an incalculable treasure of ability spread throughout the country. I met lawyers, doctors, nurses, teachers, builders, sculptors and painters, business men and labourers and many in other walks of life. These men and women deserve a stable and productive community.

"If a profound respect and affection for Nigerians cannot be read between these lines, then it is a failure in communication."

Father Michael Fitzgerald

Carmelite Fathers (OCD)
Carmelite Monastery, Enugu

Fr. Michael Fitzgerald, OCD

Talking with Father Michael is like being sucked into a racing, high tide of enthusiasm, learning and anecdote. At the end of a three-hour-talk, you want to go on absorbing his engaging recollections and insights from his former mission post in the Philippines, and his current one in Nigeria.

We meet in the beautiful house of the Carmelite Sisters who are the close neighbours and sisters in religion of Fr. Michael. The location is the tranquil and green Government Residential Area of the well laid out Igbo city of Enugu which is set in the midst of rolling green hills. It's the State capital and its people are renowned for their warmth and friendliness. Tree lined streets provide beauty and shade. It was here that the Carmelites founded their first house in Nigeria. They were invited to do so in the mid 1980's by the Bishop of Enugu, Michael Eneje. Father Michael was among the first priests to arrive.

He first spoke about his early days in Ireland.

"I joined the Carmelite order and had lots of doubts about my decision at different times during the early years but I was always fortunate to meet somebody who was able to address them and help me over the hurdles. From a very early age, I felt a strong and deep instinct for the missions. It had its source in the type of community I came from and also in the influence exerted by Philip Jones, one of my primary school teachers. He treated the school-boys regularly to heroic and spellbinding stories. Many were related to mission, many were not.

"I was born in Broadford, County Limerick in 1941. I had a number of relatives who were in the Carmelite Order. In 1950 when I was a youngster, a cousin went to the Philippines on mission. There were family stories but mostly I was influenced by Philip Jones. He was a slightly withdrawn man, who was a great reader and religious in a non-apparent way. He had a great interest in church liturgy and in the Bible. When he was principal of our school, I and a number of the boys went in a half-hour early in the mornings to take his optional Bible class. There we were also introduced to the lives of the great missionaries such as Bishop Joseph Shanahan and Bishop Charles Heerey of Nigeria and Bishop Tom Quinlan of Korea. The Korean War was on at the time and there were five boys from our village in Korea fighting with the American forces. The famous Korean *Death March* was a tremendously real thing to me as a boy. I had all sorts of fantastic images of it in my head. A large group of prisoners were marched by the communist forces over a long distance from one camp to another. Huge numbers died on the way. The people who were involved in that march became super-heroes to me. Bishop Tom Quinlan was one of them.

"Philip Jones also talked a lot about Bishop John Howe of Burma. Years later, when I was in the Philippines, this same man walked into my sitting room in Manila. He had been expelled from Burma and the Archbishop of Manila had taken him on as an auxiliary. He represented an extraordinary verification of my childhood feelings and images. In my child's mind, this man had iconic status.

"I believe that I have that nomadic gene which has enabled me to live the life of a missionary. Understood in that is knowing that you stay in a place for only as long as you are needed. That being said, I know that my soul was a theatre of conflicting emotions when I had to leave the Philippines after fifteen years. My human instincts were telling me to stay because I loved the place and the people so much. At the same time, I felt that as a missionary, I had played my role and that the time had come for me to move on.

"I arrived in the Philippines in 1973 and during my time there in Ilo Ilo on the island of Panai, in Bokola on Negros Island and in Manila, I became involved and absorbed in a variety of ministries and activities. I taught in a seminary, was a parish priest and was the Carmelite superior for a time in Manila. Predominant among my memories however are those connected with my inevitable involvement with the whole issue of social justice which arose out of the many unjust aspects of Philippine life, not least of which were the sugar and land issues. This was during the Marcos regime. The whole justice issue exploded and some of the local priests were saying that we should be preaching Mao Tse Tung and distributing guns instead of sermons. This was all very much inspired by the *Liberation Theology* movement in South America. I myself became somewhat confused for a while as I found myself in a totally new reality. My instincts told me that what was happening around me was right but for a while, my mind could not catch up. I was not sure who I was or where I was headed but I did know one thing and that was that I wanted to be associated with the oppressed.

"Eventually, I became very involved with the people who were committed to this fight for social justice. Some were deeply Christian in their convictions, others were deeply humanistic. I felt both sides shared a common denominator. I kept thinking of the statement that was issued from the Synod of Bishops which was called by Paul V1 to examine social justice in the world – *that action for justice is an integral part of preaching the Gospel.* Gradually I began to feel an extraordinary deep impulse within me which indicated that I wanted to commit myself fully to the justice issues and that I wanted to take action. Furthermore, I knew then that if ever in the future I found myself teaching student priests, I would make the justice issue the principal thrust of my work.

"The opportunity to take action came rather quickly. On a particular Shrove Tuesday, I was having lunch with American Trappist monks who had a monastery on an island adjacent to Ilo Ilo where I was living at the time. During lunch, a man came to the house to ask if he could borrow a tape-recorder. I had been telling the people never to speak to the military without recording what was said. I asked what the problem was and was told that he and some others were being evicted from their homes by a woman I happened to know very well and who had indeed come to me days earlier to say how delighted she was that the church had woken up to social and justice issues. I went straight to her house. All she would say was that the evictions were legal and that they had been authorized by the courts. I told her that what was just in the courts was not necessarily morally just. She got very angry, asked me to leave and suggested that I go to clarify issues at the court. 'It's exactly what I intend to do,' I told her.

"We had an old jeep at my house at the time. I filled it up with people and went to visit the judge who had issued the eviction orders. He asked that we present ourselves in court two days later. In preparation for this, we found a so-called honest lawyer but as we were entering the court on the appointed day, we met him coming down the steps saying that the judge had told him that he was not needed. It was obvious that he had been bought off. The proceedings took place without a lawyer on our side. I was accused of being in defiance of court and it was one of the times that I was threatened with deportation.

"That particular case dragged on and there were many other cases which meant that we were regularly in and out of courts. The rights of tribal Filipino people to the land they were sitting on were the central issue at stake. There were in fact presidential decrees in existence which declared that these lands could not be touched.

Nevertheless problems and disputes arose and many involved multi-national conglomerates trying to get their hands, by hook or by crook, on the people's land for their own business purposes. In all the cases I was involved in, I had a policy of never speaking for the people but encouraging them to do so themselves.

"After fifteen years in the Philippines, I was told by our Superior General, Philip Sainz de Baranda that he would like to send me to Nigeria. I arrived here in November 1988. Father Charlie Newell and Fr. Tom Curran were already here in Enugu. The change for me was enormous – not only culturally but also in terms of the local Church and the work that lay ahead of me. When the Bishop invited the Carmelites into his diocese, it was to provide that extra dimension to a Church which was already established. He wanted us to share the Carmelite spirituality with his people. That exercise of sharing is very much part of what we do and it's something I believe in very much. We put our heads together and decided that the best way to do this was to establish a Carmelite foundation and to start looking for young men who might have a vocation for our way of life. The Superior General, who came to visit us for a week, wholeheartedly supported our thinking and also gave approval to the buying of a piece of land suitable for building a formation house. It was located high on a hill overlooking the university town of Nsukka not far from here. Funds for this expensive acquisition came by way of an Asian connection.

"After the Communist take-over in China, many of our Carmelite monasteries in that end of the world became very uneasy. The one in Macau uprooted itself and moved to Canada. The money from the sale of what turned out to be an extraordinarily valuable property in Macau was enough to establish in Canada and provide substantial funding for the Nsukka venture. Nsukka is now our main formation house. It is called *Tabor Carmelite Community*.

"The stages of formation are as follows: there's first of all a year which we call *postulancy* and it can be done in any of our houses. *Novitiate* which is a very strict year comes after that. That is done in Nsukka. It's a structured and supervised time and a period during which the novice can be severely tested from the point of view of vocation. Those who continue after that year go to Ibadan to study philosophy at the Dominican Institute for three years. A commitment to a year at a time is undertaken at this point. After Ibadan, they go to Tangaza College in Nairobi, Kenya to study theology. This is a great college run by a consortium of religious orders. For a number of years, Father Paddy Harrington, SMA (now Bishop) was rector there and he was outstanding. Aylward Shorter, another great scholar and English missionary was also rector for a period. He is a very learned man who has devoted most of his life to the study of how the Christian message can be in-culturated into African culture and how Christianity can in turn learn so much from Africa.

"Because there were all sorts of complex difficulties attached to the early days of the Nigerian foundation, we decided to provide the best possible educational opportunities for our students. This, we believed would help forestall problems which are particular to Africa such as the tremendous ethnicity which causes great rivalries between groups. The realities attached to religious life such as community life and the taking of the vows of chastity, poverty and obedience also prove very challenging for Africans.

"When tasks were allocated in the beginning, I was appointed vocations' director. All applications were vetted initially by me and at a later point, by all of us in committee. We selected a first group of eight out of hundreds. Nobody from that group survived. Two subsequent groups were more successful and from them came our first Nigerian Carmelite priests – Father Chrisogenous, Father Remegius and Father Sylvester. We built on that small number and took in five or six students annually after that. Out of those numbers, an average of two or three reached ordination.

"Because of my own experience in the Philippines, it was not long before I believed that our presence in Enugu with its emphasis on spirituality would be more authentic if there was a justice dimension. I wasn't sure how to introduce this but felt that the plight of prisoners offered an opening. We started paying visits to the prison here in the city. Our Nigerian students were initially not at all keen on this as they felt that the prisoners should take their punishment for whatever it was they were in prison for. We began to examine this attitude with them and tried to encourage a more humane and Christian approach. We also tried to make them understand that prayer and contemplation alone can take you into a stratosphere of unreality unless your feet are well grounded in day to day reality. Our foundress, St. Teresa of Avila was always realistic and very practical.

"Out of our tentative early steps in prison visitation has grown CAPIO (Carmelite Prisoners' Interest Organization). We have made significant progress when it comes to improving the conditions in the prisons and we also focus on helping to bring the cases of prisoners who have been awaiting trial for years before the courts. As a result of our work in this field, quite a number of prisoners have had their cases heard and some have been found innocent and freed. This work is ongoing and our Nigerian priests and students are now fully involved. In addition, the priests have reached the stage where they are directly handling formation work. The progress we have made during the course of about twenty years gives me great hope for the future of our order in Nigeria.

"As Carmelites, we have always to be conscious of our commitment to a life of prayer and contemplation. We are a contemplative order with an active dimension. This last can often cause tensions if it interferes with, or submerges the true nature of our calling. When I was in the Philippines and involved in all the social justice activities, I started to examine how this was working in my life as a Carmelite. Every evening for a period, I sat down and thought through my situation. I came to the conclusion that the issue of justice was for me, at that time, the ideal way to be both contemplative and active.

"The fruit of contemplation is something that has to be shared and this is very basic to the Carmelite understanding of itself. How to share it is not in the last analysis up to the individual to decide. The Carmelite priest or brother has to look at the local Church and its needs and ask how he can contribute in the light of what his Carmelite charism has given him. This means that we go into a diocese with an open mind and are willing, within reason, to do whatever it is we are required to do. If for example, we are asked to run a parish, we will do just that. When Bishop Eneje invited us here, he did not want us to run parishes. He did not even want us to attend parish meetings. His successor Bishop Gbuji came and changed all that. What all of this means is that we have to be flexible enough to accept changes within the local Church."

After fifteen years in Nigeria, Father Michael has a philosophic approach to the considerable injustices that are ongoing in his host country.

"It is very difficult to observe all that is happening in the line of injustice but as a guest in the country, you have to be very careful about what you say and how you say it. My Christian faith makes me believe very, very strongly that there are seasons in our lives, that we are going through a winter season here in Nigeria but that there will be a spring. This is the basic Christian message of hope and the most conclusive and definitive fact that I know of in literature is – *they placed His body in the tomb and rolled a great big stone over the mouth of the tomb and went away.* Our faith starts there – with the resurrection. There are situations in which we need to exercise patience. St. Teresa said that patience was a most important virtue. I believe that she was right. I could do something rash here tomorrow morning and destroy the whole Carmelite mission. St. John of the Cross, the other great Carmelite said that there were two ways to tackle a serious problem. One was to face it head on and have it crush you; the second was to skirt around it and find more effective means of approaching it. This is the way I try to deal with the justice issues that are all around me here."

Given his earlier stated understanding of how long a missionary should stay at a mission post, I ask Father Michael how long he intends to stay in Nigeria.

"I will stay as long as I believe the signs and the circumstances of the time indicate that I should. That may not be for much longer. You can reach a point in a task where your presence could present more of an obstacle than a help to the young people you are preparing to take over. As long as you are there, they may be inhibited in exercising leadership qualities. This may be especially true in a Nigerian culture where the understanding of age is one of respect and deference. If I were to leave Nigeria in the next few years for an assignment in Ireland, I would be very happy to come back for a few months from time to time to do a particular job in connection with formation, for example. I would be happy to remain in contact but would not in any way want to be a fly in the ointment."

While Father Michael has an open mind about the timing of his possible return to Ireland, he is sure, he says, that it is something he would cherish.

"I get an enormous thrill when I go back to Ireland even if it's just for a week. There are so many people and so many things that I love to see. I think really that the very stones in Ireland can cry out to me. I haven't fully worked out what I would do in the event of my returning there on a permanent basis. Some that I know – priests and religious, tell me that there might be an interesting and fruitful area of involvement for me in working with priests to help them have a deeper spirituality. Priests are so much in the limelight now and some have let the side down. Many are wonderful men doing very good work but great numbers are suffering. I would hope to introduce to those in need a kind of spirituality that would enable them to cope effectively with their lives and with the celibate aspect of it. Now I don't know whether or not celibacy is going to remain as part of the Catholic priesthood. If it were my decision to make, I would keep it as an option and not a requirement. I think that at a particular period in Church history, it was desirable but that period has now passed. We now need the freedom to be able to choose and that requires a fairly deep spirituality. I have thought about the issues involved in all of this and I believe that there are great needs to be addressed.

"Another ministry that I would enjoy would be to work with lay people to help them develop a deeper sense of the reality of God and the saving grace of Christ. I would like to help them understand what that means in their daily lives because I believe that the essence of spirituality can be found in that understanding.

"In Ireland today, despite diversions by many from the more traditional religious practices, there is a more thinking and reflective attitude towards religion. I welcome that. It's an old principle of human nature that every action provides a reaction. There was so much rigour in the past that there was bound to be an equally rigorous reaction. I think that eventually the pendulum will swing back to a more balanced place."

Father Christopher Clarke

Carmelite Fathers (OCD)
Nsukka, Enugu State

L to R: Fr. Mícheál MacLaifeartaigh, Aliyu Haruna, Irish Embassy Abuja;
Fr. Christopher Clarke at Nsukka

When I first arrived in the strange world of Nigeria, it was a bonus to know that one of the missionary fathers was my cousin. Father Christopher's smiling and welcoming presence in *Mary the Queen Parish* in Ekpoma in Edo State meant that one of the first trips we made upcountry was to visit him. In his capacity as parish priest there over a period of six years, he has been responsible for an impressive amount of social development which includes two schools and a community social centre. His great capacity for this type of work as part of his religious vocation is accompanied by a sharp business sense and an ability to keep a sustained focus on a project until it reaches completion. His keen insight into the behaviour and outlook of different Nigerian ethnic groups combined with a telling sense of humour which illuminates the foibles of those it encompasses, are traits that are particularly suited to his multi-task role in Nigeria.

He first came to Nigeria in 1995 following assignments in Carmelite communities in Ireland and London. Shortly after his arrival, he went to Ekpoma as part of a team to run Mary the Queen Parish. His order was invited to do so by the Archbishop Patrick Ekpu of Benin.

During a conversation I had with Father Christopher in Nsukka shortly before I left Nigeria, he explained why the Carmelites came to Nigeria and spoke of many other aspects of his life there.

"They came to establish a Carmelite presence. The early missionaries had done the primary work of evangelization and as religious life began to be a feature of the life of the Nigerian Church, there developed a desire to establish some of the old religious orders and so many Nigerian bishops invited these orders in. It was the Bishop Eneje of Enugu who invited us by writing to our Superior General in Rome. Fathers Charles Newell and Tom Curran, both from Headford, County Galway were the first to come. They were followed by Fr. Michael Fitzgerald and Fr. Frank Considine both of whom had spent a long time in the Philippines.

"In those early days, the primary work was to establish the order so they started with the formation of young Nigerian candidates and set up a monastery in Enugu. It was the main feature of our work and life in Nigeria for a number of years. Then as the young Nigerian Carmelite priests came on stream, we had to anticipate their need for work and that is when the idea of running a parish came up. When the invitation to do just that in Ekpoma came, we were very pleased to accept it. The parish was already set up so we were not in any way involved in primary evangelization.

"Now, running a parish in Nigeria entails an enormous amount of work. Congregations of thousands and the upkeep of many out-stations create a huge workload. As Carmelites whose main apostolate is a life of prayer, we have to take care that the demands of a very busy parish do not force us to lose sight of that apostolate. We have to endeavour to maintain a balance between prayer and community life.

"The school and the social centre which we have built in Ekpoma was in response to the needs of the parish. When we arrived in the mid 1990's during the military regime of General Sani Abacha the financial situation of the country was dire and the psychological fear among the people palpable. Also a great lack of freedom of speech created extremely oppressive conditions. It did not take us long to observe the acute needs of the parishioners. The teachers of state schools and other public servants were not being paid regularly at the time so every morning, we noticed that there were great numbers of children hanging around the church compound. Following enquiries, we learned that the teachers were not turning up in school, because not being paid, they were forced to go to the farm, trade at the market or engage in some activity that might earn them money to care for their families. Because of this situation, we decided to build a school.

"With financial help from the Irish Carmelites, we were able to build a beautiful school which can cater for seven hundred and fifty pupils and which is now up and running. It is being managed by Sister Zelia of the Sisters of Jesus and Mary who came to Ekpoma from her community in Lagos with her companion Sister Regina Diamond for that purpose. Unfortunately and tragically Sister Regina developed an illness in late 2002 which brought about her untimely death and much grief to her community, her family and to all of us who knew and worked with her. Despite this early set back, the school is thriving and the parents of the parish have been hugely supportive. Its success encouraged us to plan for a secondary school. The building of that is now well advanced and we look forward to opening it in the near future.

"Ekpoma is a university town with thousands of students. Many of them have neither space, light or any other facility in their homes to allow them to study. It was after noticing this need that we decided to build a social centre which would include a place of study for the students, a creche for the children of working mothers or mothers attending the university and a basic health post which would offer advice, health education and deal with basic health problems. This last is being run very well with the help of the Catholic nurses group of the parish. I was in the social centre the other day and I was surprised to see a great number of students there even though the university is closed because of strike action. There were also about fifty secondary students totally engrossed in their studies. For the building of the social centre, we were grateful to receive funding from Ireland Aid.

"One of the things that never ceases to amaze you in Nigeria is the great love the people have for education. They see it as a way forward which of course it is. The parents will do anything to find the school fees. Mothers will work long hours in the market if they know they can earn more for that purpose. What the future holds however, even for the educated ones is questionable, because the whole economic system is not promising. You already have vast numbers of graduates with no work, and no doubt that is contributing to the lawlessness of the country.

"Nigerians are clever, very enthusiastic and upbeat. How they manage to be that way given the circumstances of their country is a great tribute to them. They have a great desire to better themselves. They are convinced of course that everything is greener on the other side so they will do anything to get to Europe or America. Some are prepared to lose their lives in the effort. Since *Democracy* was restored in 1999, few things have improved. My impression was that in the beginning things improved quite a bit but recently a marked deterioration in every facet of life has set in. However, the greater freedom of speech has thankfully endured.

"Nigerians are also very optimistic by nature and they seem to have a natural faith. There is very little atheism in their culture and their belief is spontaneous. The present Holy Father when he was cardinal remarked that he believed that Catholicism in particular appeals to the African because *The Communion of Saints* corresponds with their own belief in the *Ancestors,* and the Catholic world of sacramentals connects with former African pagan rituals. The priest in Nigeria has won half the battle with his people because before he even gets started, he can assume that they are on his side and that they believe in God. It is so difficult for the priest at home right now. He has to deal with much skepticism, his authority is suspect and he is faced with the weakened faith of the people. Nevertheless, if the priest believes in God, he cannot but remain optimistic and we must not forget that the Church has been through far more difficult times in the past.

"As Carmelites, we focus on the spiritual. Every religious order has its own charism. Prayer is ours. As one of the Popes said: *Carmel without prayer is nothing.* It's our tradition. Right from the beginning, the early hermits, many of whom were crusaders who had thought at first, that killing Muslims was the way forward became disillusioned with what was being done in the name of God and decided that a life spent in prayer on the slopes of Mount Carmel would better serve the Church. St. John of the Cross would later state that more can be achieved by prayer than by any other activity. As a Carmelite, you are very conscious of being part of that great tradition. Lots of religious orders were founded by bishops for apostolates such as nursing or education. Over time, in many places in the world, these apostolates were taken over by lay people. That situation left the orders founded for them in a sort of limbo. In the end what gives meaning to our lives and our work is our relationship with Christ.

"I have now moved to Nsukka though I commute regularly to Ekpoma to oversee the building of the secondary school. Our monastery in Nsukka is a beautiful Italianate palazzo-style building over looking the small but pulsating Igbo university town. Beyond the bougainvillea-draped walls, a vista of brown, drumlin-like hills punctuate a seemingly endless expanse of green landscape. It is quite beautiful to my eyes but my colleague Fr. Mícheál Mac Laifeartaigh who was brought up with the glories of Lough Swilly on his doorstep is not so sure. Naturally he misses the sea!

"Our monastery in Nsukka is primarily a novitiate or house of formation. The life there is experiential and the day to day routine is much more regular than life in a typical parish. We receive young men from English speaking African countries and introduce them to the tradition and life of the Carmelite Order. At the moment, we have students from Malawi and Kenya as well as Nigerians.

"In the monastery also, we have approximately twenty five rooms which form a retreat house for priests and reverend sisters. We aim to provide a place of respite for them – a place where they will not have people making demands on them and where they have an opportunity to pray in a peaceful environment.

"Presently the Carmelite community in Nsukka is totally Nigerian apart from Fr. Mícheál and myself. Fr. Mícheál came here about eighteen months ago to work with the young African seminarians. He is hugely enjoying his interaction with them though he is the first to admit that interpreting young minds of a different culture is not always easy. Language can be a problem because even though they speak English their vocabulary can be limited and you are never sure how they imbibe what is given to them in terms of Carmelite culture which is coming to them via Europe.

"Fr. Innocent Chrisogenous Okorie who was among our first Nigerian Carmelite priests is currently the house superior. He also plays an important role in the formation of the young postulants. To them he is a powerful figurehead who, being in his early thirties is not a great deal older than many of them. They feel that they can identify with him and they also know that they can share their doubts and difficulties with him without inhibition. In performing his duties and in his everyday life, Fr. Chrisogenous is a man who has compassion, understanding and superb leadership qualities. He is also a man who has a passionate interest in Nigeria and a powerful wish to be in solidarity with his people – something he believes present-day political leaders are not."

On the eve of my talk with Fr. Christopher, he, Fr. Mícheál and I took a tour of the exciting and densely populated nearby city of Onitsha which is situated in the heartland of Igboland. As we crossed the bridge which is the main east-west artery across the banks of the mighty Niger, we were immediately sucked into the noisy whirlwind of activity that is the hallmark of this hugely commercial and colourful city whose gigantic market is the most vibrant in West Africa. Everywhere we went, we were met with a barrage of the most bizarre, the most colourful and the most inventive of human activity. Not least was the skill with which two laughing young men on battered bicycles managed to steer their way through a packed street balancing four enormous mattresses on their heads.

Chatting with Fr. Mícheál as we pushed our way through the thronged walkways, he remarked that it is this boisterous and full of life aspect of life in Nigeria that is so seductive. "The sunshine of course is wonderful and because of it, the people are extrovert and full of vitality. In the monastery, I think that it is the youthfulness of the community that is so attractive to me. In our Carmelite houses at home, everyone is a little old and tired and maybe lacking in inspiration. There is no young blood pushing things forward, so a certain amount of introversion is inevitable. Here, things are just beginning. There is newness, hope and promise. The young people are brimming with life and everywhere you go is full of intense activity."

As Father Christopher is my cousin, I can conclude by referring to an aspect of the lives of all the missionaries which is rarely mentioned, least of all by them: that is how much they are exposed to danger. What has happened to Fr. Christopher could happen to any of them, and in many cases has. While walking the streets of Ekpoma one afternoon, he was mercilessly though accidentally torpedoed by a recklessly careering motor cycle (okada) which appeared suddenly and without warning. Fortunately the wounds he sustained were not serious and his recovery was quick. At a later time, after he had moved to live in Nsukka, the Carmelite Monastery there came under armed attack from a gang of local thieves who among other things ransacked Fr. Mícheál Mac Laifeartaigh's room and put a gun to his head. Later in the year, there was another attempt by robbers to enter the monastery which brought the following reaction from Fr. Christopher. "I found that we think of strange things when we find ourselves in tense situations. I remember that night thinking that I must get dressed and ready for these visitors, after which I took my rosary and sat at the end of the bed and waited without praying. It was not long before I heard a quiet knock on my door – it was my companion Fr. Mícheál. He slept on the floor of my room that night. The message here might be that no one is meant to die alone! Fortunately, our intruders did not get beyond the outer gates of the compound that night."

More recently, while driving from Lagos to Ekpoma on Nigeria's notoriously dangerous roads, he was involved in a very bad accident from which he was fortunate to escape. Indeed it was on this very same road some three or so years ago that the very young Carmelite, Fr. Jude came to a sad and tragic end. Having been waylaid by armed robbers, he was shot in the leg and left to bleed to death on the roadside.

These are but a few of the many stories that came to my attention during my stay in Nigeria. Some such stories have a comical side as occasionally, less vindictive thieves and gangs who sometimes plunder the homes of the missionaries have been known to ask for the priest's blessing or the sisters' prayers as they depart with their spoils – explaining that times are hard and that they are forced into their unsavoury activities in order to feed their families. This indeed is often the case and in Nigeria, it is well known that much of the everyday crime is caused by dire and oppressive poverty.

Fr. I. Chrisogenous Okorie

Father Michael Spain

Carmelite Fathers (OCD)
Mary the Queen Parish, Ekpoma, Edo State

Fr. Michael Spain with the author at the Carmelite House in Ekpoma

Father Michael Spain, a Tipperary man now in his late forties recalls a big hearted Carmelite coming to his school looking for vocations. Thirteen years later, he was ordained. "My mother cried when I lifted the chalice. Her tears contained the pain of her brother Paddy's death before his ordination." After spending twelve years in Carmelite monasteries in England, Fr. Michael came to Ekpoma to help run the Carmelite Fathers' first Nigerian parish. He is currently the parish priest there. During my many visits to Ekpoma, I was always welcomed warmly by him. Abiding memories are of Fr.

Michael outside the parish church in flowing white Carmelite robes engaging patiently and caringly with the many who came to have a private word or discuss a personal problem once the major crowds from the mass had departed; or of him arriving at the Teaching Hospital in Irrua to give the last rights to the late Sister Regina Diamond; or of him arriving back at the mission on a Sunday, after saying four masses at the out-stations announcing his hearty appetite for Madame B's substantial and well prepared lunch. He recently sent me a copy of this following letter which I think describes beautifully and evocatively his early days in Africa. He might agree with me if I say that while many things have changed since he wrote it 10 years ago, much has remained the same.

Dear:

I am in our first Nigerian parish with two companions – Fr. Charles and slightly senior Fr. Christopher. No account would be accurate without my telling of our first Sunday here. It was the first Sunday in Advent and also the one for harvest thanksgiving. We were not prepared!

The church from the outside resembles a very large ware house with a rusty galvanised roof. 2,000 people can find seats but they spent little time in them that Sunday. What we experienced was a four-hour music-powered feast of giving to the Church. Participants were dancing – dignified youths to wriggling mobile old lassies. They boogied the length of the church with gifts held high like a goalkeeper after he snatches the football off an opponent's head. 36 parish groups made the joyous carnival shuffle from door to altar rails. 50 university students roared out a different song for each group as rice and chickens and cocks and pineapples and yams and things like embroidery got presented. A reluctant goat got a mild kick from a server as he tried to dig his hooves in while being led up the aisle. We laughed and sprayed buckets of Holy Water, and noticed many ducking out of their group to be part of a following troupe of donors. The priests were in group 36. We were summoned to the back and made to hooley all the way up. Charles clicked his fingers and pedalled his arms for about ten seconds before breaking into a blessing like the one that comes from the Pope-mobile. The beaming faces shone welcome and I knew what St. Patrick saw in his famous dream.

That joy-filled morning was followed by an afternoon auction of inflated prices. Chiefs and dignitaries dispensed charity competitively. Some of the bidders were comical. Occasionally a man dashed into the selling arena and ran away, in jest, with a bucket or a chicken for which he had already paid treble the market price. Lascobo, a youngish business man and one of the entertainers dashed pompously into full view and did a public head-scratching exercise – pondering on whether to compete or not. Invariably he attracted a flamboyant opponent to contest the price.

I feel a surge of happiness and privilege to be here. Firstly, it's the genuine thing and what one imagines a mission to be – poor people – devout and God-fearing – loving to be blessed – regularly praying for God's protection – and repeatedly thanking God. Mass intentions are read out in full – to be delivered from drunkenness; for a relation to have a change of heart; for a successful business trip; in thanksgiving for surviving a fatal accident; for the coco crop to deliver fruit. The only people who have secrets are thieves. Sometimes a parishioner will come with a marital problem like divorce. No one is expected to leave the room. The problem is announced; everyone joins in with questions and suggestions. One old woman I took Communion to was unable to speak English. She gushed her confession to the catechist in the local Ishan language. He transferred the sins to me with a big smile and I trusted him to pass on the relevant penance.

Our house, church, parish centre and staff quarters are known as a compound which measures 150 sq. metres. The S.M.A. Fathers built it back in the fifties and left us with a legacy of 7,000 parishioners, fifteen out-stations, a dozen catechists, two seminarians and 7 goats. The house is made of brick and has a dark galvanised roof. Precautions include having a lock on the fridge. One plump 14 yr. old innocent has twigged that 6 a.m. mass-time is a good time to go for bread and marmalade to the priests' kitchen. The day I write coincides with him locking himself into the toilet when one of the altar server spies caught him.

The out-stations can only be served once in 3 weeks. The eventual aim is weekly mass for everybody. A new parish has been started from 5 stations which were previously the responsibility of us here. All our stations are off the beaten track but accessible by un-tarred roads. The furthest is 20 kilometres away. Like most of the others, it is a 4 walled mud-brick building with a roof, an entrance with no door and windows with no glass. Some have stilt-like bamboo structures covered with dry branches for open-air masses when the indoors gets too steamy.

Without exception, the people are warm. The men greet with a bow while shaking your hand with their two. Women curtsy with the right knee. Children topple over one another to give the sign of peace though the odd one still squeals in dread of the big white man. Fr. Chris has a party piece for which scores of the curious ones gather. He suddenly enlarges his eyes, waves his huge arms high and the ghost impression triggers panic. They are back within seconds for a repeat of the make-believe terror.

Christmas was a big surprise. There were no buntings, trees or lights and there were no shop windows. There was a bigger fowl, grain, goat and vegetable market. On Christmas Eve, Emmanuel, one of our ODC students tied 3 lines of string across the sitting room on which he hung all our cards. They brought pleasure to us and such fascination to visitors that many asked to take one home. Sending a Christmas card to us then is like sending it to hundreds. We had a mighty Christmas with lunch 15 miles away with the Benedictine monks. They first came to Ewu about 20 years ago from Glenstal Abbey. Now they number 4 Irish and many young Nigerian monks. In case you're curious, there was rice, beef and plum pudding for lunch! No obvious depression was caused by a nearly totally abstemious Christmas.

In case I've painted an idyllic innocent picture, the tenuous nature of life was imprinted the week before Christmas. Clement, a young and gentle father of 3 was dealt one murderous blow while earning an honest living on his motor-bike. An 18 year-old parishioner died of TB; a civil rights campaigner – Ken Saro-Wiwa and the other Ogoni leaders were sent to the gallows; a plane crash killed the eldest son of General Abacha who ordered the executions. I've been to the police station to mediate a dispute – to prison to smell filth and bring consolation – to hospital to anoint – to dark little homes to say hello and bless the occupants. I'm also in charge of the parish purse so many is the good story I hear! May your light shine in 1996……

Fr. Michael Spain

P.S.

As I write to send you this Irene, I am nearing 10 years in Ekpoma. If I didn't love the people, I would wish to go home. Since coming here, mother has passed on – so have my two aunts. Tragically my sister Mary's husband was killed last year by a bull. I could spend a lot of time with their 8 children but the parishioners here say 'Fadda' in such an appealing way. Life is very full!

Carmelite Nuns
(OCD)

An Introduction

The tradition of women dedicating their lives to God's service by a particular commitment dates from the beginning of Christianity. During the thirteenth and fourteenth centuries, a number of pious women placed themselves under the direction of the Carmelite Friars (priests and brothers) and began to follow the Carmelite Rule which they adapted to their life's situation. Frequently they were women who lived in absolute solitude and continual prayer. Others formed loosely knit associations and lived in community without taking vows. In 1452, the then General of the Carmelites obtained the approval of Pope Nicholas V to organize these groups into a second order, thus giving them canonical status. Blessed Frances d'Ambroise, the Duchess of Brittany, was among the first to join one of the convents she herself endowed. This was the modest beginning of the almost 13,000 who make up the 895 communities of Carmelite nuns worldwide today.

Our Lady of Mount Carmel Monastery

Zing, Taraba State

Sr. Regina, left and Sister Mary Bridget

Our visit to Zing was a memorable one. We set out from Enugu at a very early hour and drove for more than seven hours through fascinating changes of scenery until we reached the austere but beautiful landscape surrounding the Carmelite Convent in Zing, Taraba State. There we were welcomed with great joy and excitement by Sister Mary Bridget and her team. The sisters, being contemplative normally spend most of their days in silence. However, since the visiting party included my husband who, as the Ambassador of Ireland was the representative of the Irish President, all rules regarding silence and contemplation could be suspended for the duration of our visit! As a result, the conversation was non-stop!

We were housed in the beautiful guest house adjacent to the convent grounds and for two days, apart from enjoying the generous hospitality of the sisters, we had the opportunity of exploring this little known area of Nigeria. We also visited the Irish Mercy Sisters in Yola and the Irish Franciscan Sisters of the Divine Motherhood in nearby Yakoko.

In 1981, Bishop Patrick Sheehan, OSA, Bishop of Yola, invited the Carmelite nuns in New Ross, County Wexford to establish a monastery in his diocese. In response to this invitation, three sisters

Back row left to right: Srs. Angela and Veronica
Front row left to right: Srs. Annunciata, Regina, Catherine,
Ruey, Breda, Maura and Sr. Mary Bridget

went to Yola in 1993 to explore the possibilities of setting up a Carmel there. After a three-week visit they returned convinced that the time had come for such a foundation.

The sisters sent letters to Carmels in Ireland and Britain asking for volunteers and they got a generous response. After spending a number of months with the Mercy Sisters in Yola, they moved to their new monastery in Zing in 1995. The Diocese of Yola had by then been divided: Zing was in the new Diocese of Jalingo and the sisters were given a warm welcome by the Bishop of Jalingo, Dr. Ignatius Aya Kaigawa.

There was immediate interest by Nigerian young women in the Carmelite way of life and by February 2003, the first entrant made her final profession. There are now seven Nigerians in the community.

The community makes a frugal living from making altar breads and vestments. They also receive support from the local people but the widespread poverty that exists in the area limits what they can expect in this regard. The nuns have now begun to develop a small farm to supplement their income and to attempt to make the monastery financially viable.

Sister Mary McGlynn

Carmelite Nuns (OCD)
Tranquilla, Knock, Co. Mayo

*The Carmelite Community at Owerri with Sr. Mary McGlynn
standing on extreme left - second row*

Seventy-eight-year-old Sr. Mary talked to me at the Carmelite Monastery in Knock about her life as a contemplative nun and about the Carmelite foundation she helped found in Nigeria in 1974.

Born in Dublin in May 1926, she believes that she never had any doubt about what she wanted to do in life. "I had from a very early age a firm belief in the apostolic dimension of a life of prayer. I became interested in the Carmelite Order after reading the autobiography of St. Therèse of Lisieux. When I joined the congregation, I truly believed that God had called me to a way of life that would enable me to serve humanity. Looking back over the years, I am conscious that happiness has been dominant in my life. There has been suffering and some difficulties of course but that is to be expected in any walk of life. Our life as contemplative nuns is predominantly one of prayer. It has a hermetical spirit but it is a life that is also rooted in the outside community. We do not consider ourselves cut off or apart from the world. In fact we make it our business to stay in close touch with what is happening. We read newspapers and certain other publications. We listen to radio and we watch a selected number of television programmes.

"Prayer is the *raison d'etre* of every Carmelite Carmel (monastery) worldwide. It has its source and summit in the daily celebration by the community of the Eucharist. The daily chanting of prayer, the hours of personal prayer and the reading of scriptures and other suitable books all anticipate and prolong the great moment of the Eucharistic celebration.

"Our work which is an important part of the day in the monastery includes the usual chores of any household and the activities which earn us our living such as the making of altar breads, church vestments, crafts and print works. All this is carried out in a prayerful and silent atmosphere. Apart from two periods of daily recreation which take place after our midday meal and after supper, silence is largely observed. After compline each evening, we observe what we call *the great silence*. This is only broken in cases of absolute necessity.

"I think of our life of prayer as a ministry of the Church which bears fruit. My personal prayer as part of that fruit-bearing ministry. When people who come to us asking for prayers return at a later date to tell us that our prayers have been answered, we are conscious that it is not our own personal prayer which has born fruit but the combined ministry of prayer that it within the Church.

"It was around 1960 that a call to the missions presented itself to our congregation. Bishop Joseph Whelan, CSSp (Holy Ghost Fathers), first Bishop of Owerri, a flourishing diocese in the heartland of Igbo territory in Eastern Nigeria, wished to have a contemplative religious order in his diocese. He asked if we would be willing to establish such a foundation. Following considerable discussion and debate, the community voted in favour of the undertaking. While all this was taking place, God was making His own preparations as independently of the Bishop, three young Nigerian women were wishing for something in the nature of a cloistered convent. Their approach to Bishop Whelan must have appeared providential as shortly afterwards, arrangements were made for the three to travel to Ireland and enter our novitiate at Tranquilla in Rathmines, Dublin. Out of the three, two were professed as Carmelite nuns and the third went to Turin in Italy to join the Carthusians which is another contemplative order.

"Because of the Biafran war in the late 1960's, the two Nigerian nuns could not return to their country after their profession. In 1974 however, their ten-year period of exile ended and the two, accompanied by three Irish Carmelites – Sr. Magdalene Shaw, Sr. Josephine Joyce and myself set forth from Rathmines for Nigeria. The then Bishop of Owerri – Bishop Mark Unegbu heartily welcomed us. We arrived in the company of Fr. Denis Ononuju CSSp, on the evening of October 9 just as the Bishop and his household were saying the rosary. We crept quietly into the church and joined in the prayers. I still relish the memory of the Bishop's surprise when he turned around and caught sight of the new arrivals.

"The following days consisted of a round of visits and welcome celebrations. After a well-organized official welcome on October 13, our enclosed Carmelite way of life commenced – a way of life that is followed by every Carmel from Japan to Ireland.

"One might well ask what the point was of having an enclosed monastery in a place where there was so much work to be done on the ground and where the labourers in the vineyard were few. Understanding that it is only God who brings about His Kingdom on earth, the Church Fathers during Vatican II stressed the need for prayer and intercession and explicitly called on pastors of the young Churches such as the Church in Nigeria to establish contemplative orders in their dioceses 'as part of the fullness of the Church's presence.' The Mystical Body of Christ is composed of the different gifts and services that make up the Church. One of these services is the worship of the Lord directly through prayer. Some Christians are given the charism of attending single-mindedly to this kind of worship. Their contribution to life may not be visible but it is very real. Pope John Paul II once stated that the adoration of the Blessed Sacrament mysteriously contributes to the radical transformation of the whole world and to the sowing of the seeds of the Gospel. In stating this, the Holy Father was by no means just referring to contemplative religious orders.

"It was in January 1975 that young women began to join us in our newly established Owerri Carmel. Initially a big number came but many realized after a time that the life was not suited to them. They left and found alternative ways of serving the Lord. Those who stayed showed a genuine desire for a life of prayer and divine worship. They were eager to learn and it was a joy to impart to them whatever we knew. From the beginning, we noticed that most of the young women had a real gift for intercession and they took to heart, in a profound way, the needs of their people. Naturally, we had our teething problems and early set backs.

"Initially, the Nigerian young women found the whole notion of solitude difficult but as they gradually developed a taste for it, they took to it very easily and today their lives are lived in an identical way to those lived by the Carmelites here in Knock. It's a life of prayer, study and contemplation of the Truth. The Nigerians are very keen students of the Gospels and many can quote freely and extensively from them. In addition, they have a profound sense of the supernatural.

"The foundation has flourished and it now has about twenty members. In the year 2000, at the request of the Prior General of the Order of Discalced Carmelites, Father Camilo Macisse, the Owerri Carmel entered upon a new foundation in Malawi. That is now growing in size and strength."

Sister Mary spent sixteen years in Nigeria and by the time she and Sr. Máire Bourke who had joined the community in 1977 left in 1990, the Owerri foundation was well established and had grown in confidence. "By then, we were satisfied that the nuns would continue to flourish and we believed that it was the correct time for us to withdraw.

"My years in Nigeria were very fulfilling. I am thankful for the experience and thankful also to be now able to spend the rest of my life here in Knock as part of the Irish Church. The recent scandals in the Church are very disturbing but I believe that we are sincerely learning to understand and correct the human behaviour that has led to them. It would be easy also to be despondent about the crisis of faith we appear to be in right now. Many are worried that they are losing their faith or that they have lost it altogether but we should be conscious of the fact that faith needs to be purified constantly. The great Carmelite, Saint John of the Cross talks 'about the dark night of the soul' during which a person's faith is tested and ultimately purified. We should not forget that the Church is an institution which is both human and divine. It is in its humanity that it sometimes falters. The important thing is to endeavour to overcome these human failings and to be forgiving.

"In Ireland today, we are questioning every aspect of our faith and religion. I believe this to be a good thing as it shows that we are neither passive nor indifferent. We are struggling with our faith and we are having difficulty understanding many things such as the extreme poverty, suffering and violence that exist in the world. I myself understand these things from the point of view of the free will we have been given by our Maker – a free will that He will not interfere with."

Sr. Mary John, Prioress at Owerri Carmel

Congregation of
The Religious of Jesus and Mary

Lagos

Sr. Goretti McGowan - third from left, second row;
Sr. Regina Diamond - second from right back row

The Congregation of the Religious of Jesus and Mary owes its existence to Claudine Thevenet (Mother Mary Ignatius) who was born in Lyon, France in March 1744. Her youth was profoundly influenced by the violent repercussions of the French Revolution and especially by the brutal execution of her two brothers which she witnessed. Her heroic forgiveness however opened her heart to every form of human misery and led her into doing great works of mercy as a member of a pious association. She was helped by a number of companions who were attracted by her zeal. In July 1818, she formed a community which had as its objective the education of the children of the poorest of the poor.

Numerous establishments were opened throughout France and, over time, the congregation spread to every continent. Today, it has close to two thousand members. Their work is varied as it aims to provide education in the broadest sense.

In the early 1990's, the Irish province accepted an invitation by the Archbishop of Lagos, Anthony Okogie to establish a foundation in Nigeria. Four members set out for their unknown destination. Despite the difficulties of the early years, the foundation is thriving today.

Sister Goretti who was born Jo McGowan in Enniscrone, County Sligo in the 1940's, was among the pioneering sisters who arrived in Lagos. "The late Sr. Regina, Sisters Pauline, Anna and I arrived in 1992. The early days were very difficult as the heat was overwhelming, the food very different and there was little or no water or electricity. A military government was in power and life was tense and sometimes frightening. We quickly found out that Akoka where we were living was and is one of the poorest areas of Lagos.

"For health reasons, Sisters Pauline and Anna were unable to stay. We were then joined by Sister Maureen Dowley and later, Sisters Mary Barrett, Nancy and Eucharia joined us for short stays of a year or so. Currently, we have two sisters from our Indian province – Zelia and Gladys – working with us. From time to time, we have young women volunteers from both Ireland and Nigeria who come to help for short periods.

"We administer a very big school for the Archdiocese of Lagos which has won two awards for being the best school in Lagos. More than 1,000 children attend. Parents make huge sacrifices to educate their children as most of them never had an opportunity to receive an education themselves.

"Our parish is a vibrant one and the people are generous and caring. They also have a very strong faith. Sunday is their big social day and most of it is spent in the church – celebrating, rejoicing and renewing the Spirit for the week to come.

"In addition to the school, we run a vocational centre for young village girls who have never had the opportunity to attend school. They learn to read, write and sew and many pursue a secretarial

First Communion groups and parishioners at Akoka

course which includes computer skills. Sister Gladys and her team ensure they attain high standards and many find good employment as a result.

"In 1999, we were invited by the Archbishop of Benin to work in conjunction with the Irish Carmelite Fathers in Ekpoma in Edo State. Sisters Regina and Zelia were missioned there – Sr. Zelia to administer a new school – *Mount Carmel Nursery and Primary School* and Sister Regina to be director of *The Brother Roman Centre* – a renewal and pastoral centre for catechists. Unfortunately, just as their work was getting under way, Sr. Regina became very ill with a rare and rapidly advancing cancerous tumour. When she failed to respond to treatment in two Nigerian hospitals, she was air-ambulanced to Ireland where she died within a few weeks. She loved Africa and was dearly loved by all who knew and worked with her. We in our little community here in Nigeria miss her enormously.

"Sister Zelia was acutely affected by the loss. They had begun to form a wonderful team in Ekpoma and were extremely happy with their new life. Just as she was recovering from that trauma, she and two young Nigerian sisters came under attack at the *Brother Roman Centre* at 4:00 a.m. one morning by seven heavily armed robbers demanding money. At the point of a gun, Sister Zelia was made to hand over all school and community funds. It was providential that none of the sisters was harmed. The memory of that harsh experience remained with the sisters for some time. Thankfully their fear has now begun to fade.

"Mount Carmel school which opened in 2001 has now over 500 pupils and there is a growing demand for places. The school accepts children from all religious and ethnic backgrounds. A secondary school which has been under construction and almost completed has begun to take in a sizeable number of students.

"Sister Regina's catechetical programme is now administered by our Nigerian sisters. Because of the shortage of priests, catechists provide an important service in parishes by preparing people for sacraments, leading prayer services when mass in not available and translating prayers and homilies into local languages.

"Since coming to Nigeria, the Jesus and Mary Sisters have opened a formation house in Lagos for young women who have a desire to follow their life. After one year, the young women enter the sisters' international novitiate in Yaoundé in Cameroon. Presently, the congregation has four professed Nigerian sisters, six novices and three postulants."

I often enjoyed the hospitality of the Jesus and Mary Sisters in Lagos and in Ekpoma. On my first Christmas night in Nigeria my husband and I, as well as a number of Irish missionary priests and sisters from Lagos and the surrounding areas were treated to a very good Christmas supper by them. The evening then turned into an impromptu concert and many of the company excelled in singing a song or telling a story that showed above all their sense of fun and enjoyment. I began to see beneath the soutanes and the habits the ordinary everyday side of these missionaries. Sr. Regina simply shone through the evening as she happily waited on everybody. I can still see her smiling, radiant and almost childlike expression as she told me that it was she who had made the Christmas pudding.

A display of African dancing performed by the sisters' Nigerian staff was particularly enchanting to newcomers like myself. During the course of the evening, a number of the Irish were encouraged to drop inhibitions and take to the floor.

Sr. Zelia Fernandez

Monsignor Christopher Chukwumeh

Parish Priest, St. Joseph's Parish
Asaba, Delta State

Msgr. Christopher Chukwumeh

We arrive in Asaba, which is situated on the west bank of the Niger in Delta State, in the afternoon. French SMA Fathers founded a mission there in the 1890's. For most of the twentieth century they were followed by Irish SMA and Irish OLA Sisters. The cemetery adjacent to St. Joseph's Catholic Church bears testimony to their lives, some of which were tragically cut short. The week before our visit, the city was besieged by bands of armed robbers who ransacked most of the banks and left in their trail a great number of murdered, maimed and terrorized citizens. Though the story had made media headlines, we had not heard of it so we drive into this busy place with nothing on our minds but our meeting with Monsignor Christopher Chukwumeh, parish priest of St. Joseph's.

I am accompanied by Fr. Christopher Clarke and Fr. Mícheál Mac Laifeartaigh, two Irish Carmelite Fathers from the Carmelite monastery in Nsukka in Enugu State. We have driven that morning from Lagos via the Kiltegan Fathers' mission in Ijebu Ode, the former slave port of Badagry and Topo Island, scene of the ruins and graves of the once flourishing missions of the Irish SMA and the Irish OLA.

Asaba is a lively metropolis. When SMA Father, Carlo Zappa was reporting on it in 1897 to his superior in France, he described it as a little town with five or six thousand inhabitants and three hundred chiefs. 'It is the ambition of every man,' he wrote, 'to become a chief and to do this, he has to dip his hands in innocent blood by killing two slaves.' Today Asaba has a teeming population and a great number of chiefs who are no longer required to spill innocent blood to achieve their honours.

Monsignor is sitting on his verandah holding court with a number of people when we arrive. He is not expecting us so our arrival causes something of a stir. Fr. Christopher who is known to him makes the introductions. Septuagenarian Monsignor has a commanding presence. He introduces his own companions and invites us to seat ourselves around him. We have come to ask if he will agree to give me an interview. He is not a shy man so he has little trouble agreeing and even less when I ask permission to turn on my tape-recorder. He is full of jokes and humour and starts by telling us how disappointed he is about 'the recent trouble in heaven' which caused his namesake St. Christopher to be demoted from sainthood.

"My surname Chukwumeh means *God knows!* I was born and raised here in Asaba. I was educated in SMA schools. My education commenced in 1934 and I entered the junior seminary in 1944. My ordination was the last to take place in Benin City. After that they moved the seminary to Ibadan. There was once a seminary here in Asaba but that was a long time ago, going back as far as the twenties.

"Growing up, we were very familiar with the Irish priests and sisters. They came visiting to the houses and that is how I began to take an interest in priesthood. There was a story going around at the time about a young boy who was asked why he wanted to be a priest. His answer was that he would like to be able to eat chickens! Everyone knew that priests were able to eat a lot of chickens! When I told my father that I wanted to become a priest, he wouldn't hear of it. Priests don't marry and here in Africa, everyone is expected to propagate his own seed and continue the family line."

At this point Monsignor is interrupted by a man who approaches him for his blessing. "Apart from the priestly blessing which I will give him," he tells us, "I will give the blessing of the Diokba which is the blessing of the head of the clan which I now am. Becoming the Diokba is determined by inheritance and not by age. You become the Diokba when your time comes.

"Going back to my father, I remember having to steal away to Lagos by the transport car which carried the letters. Once inside the vehicle, I covered my head with baskets so that nobody could see my face. When I arrived in Lagos, I headed for the junior seminary in Okare in Ibadan. That was 1944."

We are interrupted again, this time by Chief Ikpokpo. "Oh you must meet this man," Monsignor calls. "He is a great educationist from the University of Nsukka." Introductions are made and since the two Carmelite Fathers are from Nsukka, mutual acquaintances are identified and Monsignor is delighted when he finds out that his late friend and classmate Victor was the actual person who was instrumental in finding the land on which the Carmelites built their monastery in Nsukka. He then turns to me and excuses himself for diverting.

"It was not only my father who was against me. My whole family was opposed. I am not sure what was pushing me. I just wanted to become a priest. I told you about the chickens! We had all these priests around us and they were so neat and organized. They rode from place to place on bicycles and each had his own bicycle, which in those days was really something! We watched them and the reverend sisters who were all immaculate in white. They covered up and we could only see their faces. Sometimes we wondered if they were real and if they ate or slept or anything. I think we were attracted to the neatness, the order and the learning. Most were very learned and some were even astronomers. We could see that they were able to do all sorts of things like coming out, looking for a shadow and then telling the *o'clock*. I remember one priest who could sing and play instruments really well and when he was teaching singing, he could point to the person who was singing a wrong note. He might say 'number two in the fourth row is out of tune!' He could sing in Latin, French and English. It was Father Carlo Zappa, who died in 1917 who made the first Igbo dictionary.

"We were all associating with the Irish missionaries before and after ordination so they had a great influence on us. I was ordained in 1957 and I worked and lived with some Irish priests here in Asaba until I was asked to go to Ireland for studies. When I went to Cork, I couldn't understand what they were saying! I spent four years doing my degree and my higher diploma in education. Then I went to Rome and while I was there, Nigeria had its first military coup. By then I was tired of being out of my own country and the turmoil following the coup made me anxious to get home. Three days before I left Europe, the Igbo General, Aguiyi Ironsi, Nigeria's first military ruler and instigator of the first coup was killed.

"It was not easy to travel to Nigeria at the time and halfway through the journey we were told that we would have to land in Ghana. There were three of us – Dr. Lambo, a very famous neurologist from Abeokuta, a Dr. Mbanefo from Onitsha, and myself. After three days in Ghana we were allowed to return to Nigeria. On arrival at the airport, we were all more or less arrested! They confused me with the Igbo Major, Chukwuma Kaduna Nzeogwu who was involved in the coup. His home is five miles from here. They took our passports and told us that we were under arrest. We were released a few days later.

"When I arrived home, Bishop Kelly, SMA, of Benin sent me to teach in Ubiaja. I started teaching but it was not easy because the civil war broke out in 1967 and Ubiaja was overrun very quickly by the Federal troops. All around Asaba was a war zone. It was a very brutal time. You could hardly believe or imagine the brutality. In war, man becomes very animalistic. The fact that I'm alive talking to you today is a miracle. Everywhere there were corpses and sometimes you had to watch the pigs and dogs feeding on human remains. When it ended, we had to start afresh and it was very difficult. Asaba has changed a lot since those days. It is now the capital of Delta State."

I ask Monsignor what his feelings were about the war.

"Well, in that I am an Igbo man, I am inclined towards the idea of an Igbo nation. I feel that we are a very intelligent people and if we had succeeded in the war, we might now be much more advanced. The British, the Americans and others were brought in on the Federal side and unfortunately everything went against us. Our leader, Colonel Ojukwu did not do very well and it was unfortunate that the war ended the way it did. When I now hear this man talking about re-entering politics, I say that he is foolish.

"Now, you want to know more about the Irish missionaries! Well, there is a cemetery over by the church with the graves of a great number of them. Many came here and died very young – some in their early twenties. West Africa was then known as the white man's grave. They were very enterprising young men and women. I do not know how they were able to work here because nothing was easy. Even today, the young Nigerian priests don't want to go out into the rural areas; they want to be in the cities. The early missionaries suffered and laboured. I think that they wanted adventure. They wanted to see another life. They wondered too if we were human beings! They worked against all odds. They had to deal with a strange climate, strange food, strange languages, strange customs. They worked and worked and had successes. What was the attraction? Was it religion? Was it adventure? Whatever it was, they were great men and women. You had rascals amongst them from time to time of course but on the whole they were very good.

"We have only one Irish missionary in the diocese now. Our own people are running things. They are doing a good job but there is great materialism creeping into our lives. We are not as dedicated as we were in the past. There is a similar problem in Ireland. I know because I go there almost every year. Can I tell you a story? I was in Dublin last year and there was an old reverend sister who wanted to take me out. I put on my coat, my hat and I had my walking stick.

I had everything but a crozier! The sister looked at me and said: 'take off the priest's collar.' I said: 'oh, you are ashamed to walk with me in this dress.' I put out my arm and hooked it into hers and said 'people are now going to see us walking through Ireland like this.' The other sisters were laughing so hard! We headed off down the street! I tell you Ireland is almost gone but God works in mysterious ways. There's still something there and it will come up again."

I enquire about Monsignor's hopes for the future of Nigeria are.

"The future does not look good. There is bound to be trouble. The recent elections were marred by rigging. The PDP (Peoples Democratic Party – the winning party) rigged too much. God is a wonderful God though and we cannot predict what will happen in the future. I pray that the people of Nigeria will continue to have the strong belief in God which we had in the past."

He now calls out to a very elderly man who is respectfully trying to catch his attention. The man approaches and lowers his head and shoulders for Monsignor to greet him in the traditional manner. Monsignor tells us that he does not like all this shaking of hands which the white man has brought to Africa. He is also opposed to it during the mass. "The custom of shaking hands is not in our culture. Our customs have not yet been inculturated into the African Church."

This brings us to the topic of inculturation which has been engaging the African Church for a long time. Monsignor is cautious. "It's not something that we can go overboard with. Essentially it is a fusing of the culture into Christianity. It's an effort to bring aspects of our own way of life into Christianity. You can only go so far with all of this and too much of anything is bad!"

Chief Ifpokpo who has been sitting on the verandah with us now wants to say something about Monsignor – his friend.

"I met him about six years ago and he appointed me as chairman of the laity council. We have been working hand-in-hand and I have come to know him as a practical man who has foresight. He is extremely well read and he is highly respected for his appreciation and knowledge of our culture. He has an excellent command of his own language and he reaches out to the people with proverbs and anecdotes. He has written quite a lot in the past about our customs, traditional ceremonies and rituals and even though he has a very strict attitude to liturgy, he is adept at choosing the specific aspects of these things that are suitable for inculturation into the Nigerian Catholic Church. Monsignor personifies the Church in Asaba and the young priests, who regard him as their father, are given a lot of practical training by him. He has an ability to mix with all ages and that teeming mind of his remembers every detail. Furthermore, he keeps abreast of all current developments."

I ask Chief Ifpokpo to tell us something about his own life.

"My chieftaincy has not come by way of dipping hands in the innocent blood! Neither was it inherited. It was given to me in recognition of my contribution to society. My title is 'Adozoji' which means 'crisis dowser' and to some extent, I would say that I am good at doing that. I am first and foremost an educationist and I have taught in many federal government colleges. I was also the co-ordinating inspector of education for the Federal Ministry of Education in Delta State for a period. I was in that position when I retired."

Before we go, Monsignor calls his house steward to check if he has been able to find any diesel for us in the town. Nigeria is in the middle of one of its frequent fuel shortages so when we arrived, we asked Monsignor if any of his people could procure the twenty litres of diesel which we needed to complete our journey to Nsukka. The steward comes quickly and whispers something. "Speak up" Monsignor tells him, "or they will think we are not speaking well of them." The steward who thinks that he has been asked to find forty litres tells that he could only find twenty. "Go find the driver and put the twenty litres into his car," Monsignor tells him. "We never promised forty."

Chief Ifpokpo

Congregation of the Sisters of Mercy

An Introduction

The Congregation of the Sisters of Mercy is a Catholic religious women's congregation which was founded by Catherine McAuley in Dublin in 1831. Her aim at the time was 'to care for the poor, sick and ignorant'. Today nearly 3,000 members follow in her footsteps in ten countries worldwide.

The first Mercy Foundation in Nigeria was established by the Mercy Sisters, Dungarvan, Co. Waterford in response to an invitation from the Bishop of Yola. In October 1969, four Sisters set out for Yola in Northern Nigeria. Initially, their work included secondary education, work with YCS (Young Catholic Students), charismatic renewal, catechist training, work with women and home, hospital and prison visitation.

In 1970, two of this pioneering group opened a clinic in a village fifty miles outside Yola but it closed in 1990 due to lack of personnel.

A second Nigerian foundation was opened by a group of Strabane Mercy Sisters in Minna in Niger State in 1975. As in Yola the Sisters were involved in education, catechetics and visitation.

In 1996, in response to an invitation from the Archbishop of Lagos, Anthony Okogie, Sisters from the Armagh Diocese arrived in Lagos to become involved in a wide range of ministries such as leadership training, development and parish work. One of these was Sister Carmel Loye. Sadly, once again the sisters had to withdraw from Lagos in 1998 due to lack of personnel.

Prior to that however, in 1994, the three groups agreed to become one unit in Nigeria and they subsequently voted to be attached to the Northern Province in Ireland.

The Sisters currently work in Minna and Yola.

Sister Carmel Loye

Mercy Convent, Minna, Niger State

L to R: Sr. Theresa McGilloway; Sr. Carmel Loye; Sr. Mary Geraghty

Gidan Rahama (House of Mercy) nestles cozily amidst tropical shrubs and fragrant trees at the edge of the Catholic cathedral compound in Minna, the capital of Niger State. The house resembles an English country cottage and is home to the small group of Irish Sisters of Mercy whom I have come to visit.

Sister Carmel Loye welcomes me warmly, introduces me to her colleagues Sisters Theresa McGilloway and Mary Geraghty over tea and then takes me for a peaceful walk in the adjacent cathedral grounds. It is late afternoon. The air is warm and heavy with the perfume of sweet-smelling frangipani. Some hundred metres outside the grounds, a throbbing Minna tumbles towards the evening of another day. I am conscious of a tide of people and traffic pushing its way down the town's broad main thoroughfare. The shouts and calls from street vendors and the many roadside eating places echo within the cathedral grounds. The people we meet are without exception friendly. Some stop to say a few words; others greet us warmly and hurry on their way.

Carmel Loye from Bessbrook, Co. Armagh arrived in Lagos in 1988. Her coming to Nigeria was totally unexpected. "Cardinal Tomás Ó Fiach asked our congregation if it would send sisters to Lagos to help with the teaching of catechetics. A number of us volunteered. After coming, I spent a short time teaching and then changed to pastoral work in St. Leo's Parish in the western outskirts of the city which was being run at the time by Vincentian Fathers, Fr. Paul Roche and Fr. Rod Crowley. I felt privileged to work with them as their sense of caring for the poor was outstanding.

"While I was there, an event happened in the Lecky neighbourhood of Lagos which traumatized whole communities. The Government gave orders that all buildings and homes in the area be demolished so as to make room for up-market development. No provision was made for the thousands of poor who lived in this largely slum place. They were just told to be out by a certain day. As a result, huge numbers of people became homeless. Those who could move in with already struggling relatives in other parts of the city did so; those who could not were left to wander around with nothing but the few belongings they could rescue. We were among those who moved in to try to help with food, clothes, medicine and small finance. Our mobile clinic was taken to where the majority of them were huddled and it was an overwhelming experience dealing with their shock and suffering. Nobody ever imagined that a government could be quite so ruthless with its own citizens. The trauma of that episode is etched deeply in the memory of the poor of Lagos and a high level of cynicism and hopelessness endures.

"In 1992, I moved to Yola, the capital of Adamawa State in north-eastern Nigeria. This was a huge change as the area is largely Muslim and completely different in culture, language, and climate to that of Lagos. The Mercy Sisters were already established there so I started working with their team in pastoral centres in different parishes. We focused on leadership training and catechetics. The catechetic programme there was highly organized and trainees often moved with their families into the cathedral compound in Yola to do full-time one or two-year courses. Their training was experiential and all teaching was related to their everyday lives, existing knowledge and wisdom. We found that the faith of the people was very strong and this was always a reminder to us that God was very much in this land before we came.

"After two years in Yola, I went to study at the *Institute of Formators* in Du near Jos in Plateau State. This was in preparation for my becoming a member of the formation team for our congregation in Nigeria. The training was a rich experience from the point of view of insight into many different African cultures.

"It wasn't until I came to Minna in 1998 however that I had the opportunity to work in the field. It's now my main work and I am committed to doing it here in Nigeria for the foreseeable future. As the work involves a fair amount of travel, I have to make sure that I don't get too tied into other projects. I travel a lot visiting the families of the young girls who are thinking of entering religious life and who come here to us for a period to experience our way of life.

"I also move around the churches within a number of dioceses to announce, for example, that I will be organizing a retreat for young women. The numbers who attend these retreats vary. Here in our own parish church recently, we had two hundred. With a number like that, I might introduce as a subject for discussion the whole area of life choices – marriage, single life, religious life. The objective would be to put forward thoughts of different options. Those who come to me later feeling that they are attracted to our way of life are sometimes invited to come and live with us or *journey with us* as we call it, for a while. When this happens, it is a privileged time for all of us. At the end of such a period, a young woman may find that she is called in another direction or it could also happen that we would advise another way of life for her. At the moment, we have two young women here with us in Minna who are considering a future with the congregation.

"Apart from my work in formation, there are a number of other activities I am involved in. I engage with the YCS (Young Catholic Student Groups). With these young people, I try to be sensitive to the difficulties they might be experiencing in their lives. At the moment, I am working on a theme which I call *The Journey of Love*. I use stories, drama and dance in my presentations. Dance is a very powerful cultural ingredient in Nigeria so I make it very present. Together we explore how loving oneself can be the first step to loving others; how love is the way forward and how negativity can drive energies down and create apathy and hopelessness. We explore stories of people in impossible situations and examine how they frequently come through in the end.

"From time to time, we do guided meditation. This can be very powerful because in the end, I bring them into a beautiful garden – into the presence of Jesus or Another, leave them there for a while and then bring them back. The feed back from this is usually very strong with many of the young people feeling that they experienced something profound. All of this work is a form of evangelization as I am introducing young people to Jesus and I am bringing them to know love.

"I like to visit the prison here in Minna. I go regularly to talk, listen and share. There are certain little things that I am able to do for them like phoning a relative, posting a letter or persuading a friend or family member to visit. Last Christmas, one particular young man was feeling acutely lonely for his estranged family. I went to visit them and the father ended up by coming to see his son and helping him a great deal."

During my visit to Minna, I visited this prison with Sr. Carmel. I had previously read about prisons in Nigeria, in Ireland, in America but I had never been to one. Prisons are supposed to be full of criminals, full blown or in the making but looking into the crowded cells of young men that day in Minna, I couldn't help thinking that many were innocent victims and could be counted among what one Nigerian writer, Chris Anyanwu referred to as – the rising population of men and women – wounded, broken and angry that was filling the prisons of Nigeria. We were left to make our rounds of the barred but glassless windows and doorways by a fatherly and jolly prison warder. Young and old, some weary, some confused, some venturing a smile – all in tattered clothing, vied calmly for viewing space against the bars. Since Carmel was known to some of them, communication was easy. The answers to my questions came with dignity and a certain sadness. A few spoke of the peace they received from reading the Bible or the Koran. Most were awaiting trial. This wait – I was told, can be for as long as two, five or ten years. Some can never hope to have that trial because they are too poor to afford a lawyer or have no connections with important people.

Being less self-conscious about touching than those of us raised in regions further north of the equator, many stretched out their hands to greet us. Some spoke with sadness about their conditions – their lack of space to lie, sit or sleep and of course their lack of hope. One very good-looking young man, known to Carmel from previous visits was relentless in his begging of her to contact a local 'big man' about his case. Another graciously presented me with a bath scrub which he had woven from nylon strings of many colours. It now hangs in my bathroom and is indeed a useful accoutrement.

We moved on to the women's section. They, deemed less dangerous than the men, were sitting around on mats in the courtyard adjacent to their quarters. Their subdued and indifferent mood contrasted overwhelmingly with that of groups of women you might encounter at any market or meeting place in any location in Nigeria. Nevertheless, they were enveloped in a subtle if uneasy camaraderie. An emaciated middle-aged lady – undoubtedly a *duine le Dia* kept close to the others – for protection perhaps. Even the woman who had allegedly killed her husband fitted easily. I wondered what hardship or cruelty drove her to such a desperate act. I ask Sr. Carmel if the allegation is true. "It's an accusation that can be directed against women from a small number of ethnic groups after the death of a husband," she tells me. "The woman can come under suspicion from some members of the extended family who might have designs on the dead husband's property. I am not privy to the details of the case of the woman in this prison." Unlike the men, most of the female prisoners were engaged in some activity – sifting grains, sewing, embroidering, drumming. One who was heavily pregnant was engrossed in an elaborate task of tailoring. It was her trade when she was *outside*.

We depart; Carmel promises to visit again. They know she is telling the truth. "You will come again from Abuja by the grace of God," they call after me.

Our next port of call is a home for destitute women – young women, wizened old crones, pregnant women. Misfortune of some kind or other had brought them to this sad place. Some inanimate faces light up when Carmel approaches. She chats, puts her arm around them, consoles, cajoles and brings forth the odd smile. In their misery, they are gracious, grateful, warmhearted. Our visit adds a spark of interest and breaks the monotony. I found the home to be a depressing place, despite the obvious efforts of a number of sincere hardworking staff to give comfort.

"Since coming to Nigeria" Carmel continues, when we arrive back at *Gidan Rahama*, "I was fortunate to have been able to have a short sabbatical in the United States in 1998. It's good to make a complete break from time to time. Otherwise the constant struggle all around you can cause you to lose perspective. I spent three months at *Genesis Farm* in New Jersey doing a course related to the care and spirituality of the earth. The earth goes back fifteen billion years and it has a powerful spiritual story. The *Farm* is run by an American Dominican Sister who studied with Thomas Berry, a Passionist priest who is author of *The Universal Story – The Dream of the Earth*. This Dominican as well as many of his other pupils are now guiding lights when it comes to promoting his teachings. Because of what I learned at that wonderful place, I am now able to incorporate some powerful aspects of the spirituality and the preciousness of our environment into my work. It's a subject that young people care about a great deal.

"My colleague Sister Mary Geraghty, who came to Nigeria for the first time in the late 1990's and who feels 'that she has come home' also works on the cases of prisoners through the justice and peace organization which she helped establish in Minna. In addition, she does a great deal of work with women's groups – helping them to build self-esteem and formulate strategies for bettering their lives on different levels. She liaises with the St. Vincent de Paul Society which helps to raise funds which are used for setting up small businesses for the women.

"Sister Theresa McGilloway, who was asked by our congregation to come to Nigeria in 1996 when she was in her mid-sixties, is currently principal of a primary school we run in the nearby village of Maikenkele. Her attitude to being here is that she thanks God every day for giving her the opportunity to extend her working life away past the normal age of retirement. She has developed the school from a three-classroom building with twenty-four pupils to one with nine classrooms and two hundred and forty-eight pupils who are either Christian, Muslim or traditional believers."

Sr. Theresa took me to visit the school some twenty minutes from Minna. There I was welcomed by an impressive performance of ethnic songs and dances by groups of beautiful children dressed in smart blue uniforms. Included in the repertoire were a number of Irish songs which, according to Sr. Theresa, the children learned very easily. Then came the dancing. Dance permeates the social life of Nigeria and Nigerians dance to express themselves, to express the life force or to show off manhood or feminine pulchritude. The beauty of most of the dances lies in their ability to celebrate communal life and to unite the dancer with the dance with a frank intensity. Nigerian dance is flourishing because it has enjoyed the freedom to develop without interference from European-style choreographers. Every ethnic group has its own repertoire and that morning in Maikunkele, groups of children performed Yoruba, Igbo and Gwari dances with joy and conviction. From a young age, the Nigerian child is encouraged to respond with his whole being – his soul and mind through the body – to the inescapable power of music.

This delightful interlude which took place under the shade of many mango trees was concluded with short speeches in different languages from pupils of varying ages and a longer one by Sr. Theresa herself – whose enthusiasm for all aspects of the work and activities of the school was infectious and inspiring.

The Little Sisters of the Poor

An Introduction

The Congregation of the Little Sisters of the Poor was founded in France in 1839 by the charismatic Frenchwoman, Jeanne Jugan. In the winter of that year, she received into her own home two sick elderly women whom she nursed, clothed and fed until their death. This was the humble beginning of a congregation of women who devote their lives solely to the care of the elderly poor.

Today the Little Sisters have 237 homes for the elderly poor in 33 countries.

The Sisters are professionally trained to care for their residents to assure personal and loving care in health and sickness. To provide for the upkeep of their homes, they depend totally on Divine Providence and charity.

The sisters established their *Home for the Elderly* in Enugu Nigeria in 1975.

Sister Anthony Devlin

Little Sisters of the Poor
Home for the Elderly, Enugu

Sr. Anthony Devlin

I met with Sister Anthony Devlin from Newcastle, County Down at the *Home for the Elderly* in Enugu which is run by her congregation – *The Little Sisters of the Poor*. Caring for the elderly poor of the world is the apostolate of the sisters. They currently do this work in thirty-two countries worldwide. The congregation was founded in France in 1839 by a charismatic lady called Jeanne Jugan. The sisters rely totally on charity to run their *Homes*. They themselves go out on the streets to collect the money they need. "This very act of begging on the streets," Sister Anthony explains, "is part of a double apostolate – caring for the elderly poor and at the same time letting our presence on the streets remind people that there are others in the world in great need. We have a policy of never accepting a fixed or a regular income from any source. Our absolute faith in Divine Providence since 1839 has never failed us because God inspires generous people to help us to help the poor.

"While growing up, I was greatly influenced by my mother who was full of charity. She could never turn a poor person away. She'd bring them in, sit them down and tend to them. Sometimes I used to get annoyed with her for inconveniencing us all or because the smell of some poor person was bad. 'Saying no to the poor is saying no to God,' she used to say. Then one winter's night when I was about eight or nine, I felt I had a vocation to devote my life to the poor. When the time came for me to do something about it, I thought of joining *The Missionary Sisters of the Holy Rosary* because I had a dream of going to Africa. A plan to take a retreat at their convent in Killeshandra, County Cavan fell through. Some short time afterwards, I heard of *The Little Sisters of the Poor* through an elderly lady who had a daughter in the congregation. She gave me all the information literature. I hid it under my bed and spoke to nobody about my thoughts. Then out of the blue, my older sister went off to join the *Little Sisters*. Neither of us had ever spoken to each other about our intentions. I was greatly taken aback as I felt that my own plans were scattering before my eyes.

"I waited a year before going to my confessor to tell him that I wanted to follow my sister. 'Get that idea out of your head,' he told me. 'One of you is enough.' I went away disconsolate but was back to him within a few months telling him that I had to go. When the day came for me to leave for the convent in Dublin, my Mom was crying and my Dad was heartbroken. My sister and brothers just couldn't believe that I wasn't coming back. I myself felt a deep joy. I was happy. I kept saying to my family – 'Why are you all crying? Don't you see that this is what I want to do?' The first night in the convent, I remember kneeling down and telling God that I hoped that I would be with the Little Sisters for ever. Since then there have been days that were hard but He was always by my side.

"I went to our mother-house in France in 1967 for my final profession and remained there for twenty years. My sister unfortunately died in France at the age of thirty-three of a massive heart-attack following flu. She had never had a day's illness in her life before that. It was a terrible shock for my parents and after that, my mother did not want me to go to Africa. When she died in 1985, God rest her soul, I told my family that I wanted to realize my dream.

"I first went to Algiers for a few months and then transferred to Kenya where I spent five years. It was beautiful. I settled in really well, learnt the Swahili language and was very fulfilled. After all, it was what I had wanted to do, so there was no looking back.

"In 1991, I was moved to Congo Brazzaville. I was there when the civil war broke out in 1997. From May of that year until the following November, it rained terror, rockets and uncertainty. All the French left and the French army came to our convent to evacuate expatriates. We refused to leave, saying that we couldn't leave the old people. They didn't insist but became very grave and left, wishing us *bon courage* and letting us know that things were going to be bad. The old people kept telling us, even as the rockets were falling on our house, that we would not be harmed. Our *Home* was located between the firing positions of the two armies so it was miraculous that we managed to stay alive and together. The old people who have wisdom and who are close to God were right. They knew that we would have God's protection. When the war was finally over in November, we all took turns at taking a break. I went to my family in County Down for six weeks and had a beautiful time.

"In 1999, I was posted to Nigeria. It took time to settle in. I am still struggling with the Igbo language which is the language spoken in our *Home* by most of the residents. In Congo Brazzaville, we spoke French which is almost my native language now."

"In all our *Homes*, we create a family and there is a very strong bond between the residents and the sisters. We are as one family with dignity. We take in people of every race, colour and creed. We try to provide good facilities and we make sure that they have daily exercise and sufficient activities to engage in. Our mother foundress was very strict about all these things. She particularly didn't want people sitting around all day doing nothing. She wished them to feel useful and fulfilled by being occupied in some suitable way. She was ahead of her time in this respect. Our *Homes* are also very clean and we work very hard to keep them that way.

"Generally the people who come to us have no family and before we take in a new resident, we visit them at their place to acquaint ourselves with their circumstances. If there is anyway that they can be cared for by family, we encourage that. Occasionally, we make an exception and take in, for example, an elderly, unwell person whom a young woman with lots of children and no husband is trying to look after. Recently we took in six who had absolutely no care available to them. Some are blind and one man is paralyzed from a stroke. His wife deserted him when she found that she could not look after him.

"The level of respect and compassion old people get varies from country to country. In Brazzaville, the old people were not wanted. In France, old people can often be made to feel a burden. Here in Nigeria, people are more caring and old people still get respect. Our service as sisters must always be *gratuite* and we must never ever give the impression that our residents are a burden. People often come to us and say 'Sister, your work is very hard.' We tell them that it is because of the old people that we have everything we need both spiritually and materially.

"Our own lives are lived in a simple, frugal and humble way. We aim to sustain a vibrant faith and a loyalty to the spirit and inspiration of our foundress. Our community togetherness or *lien* as we say in French is very strong. We pray together, eat together and recreate together. We rarely watch television but occasionally we might look at a video. Once a year, we do an eight-day retreat. That is extremely important. It's how we charge our batteries. We give time to the Lord and this helps us to be faithful and steadfast. The retreat is a strong prayer. Without God, we know that we can do nothing. We are always aware of that. We read the Bible. Mine is now in French. I have grown to love the language.

"The sisters retain strong links with their families when possible. My own family is very united. When I go home to the house where I was born and where my youngest brother Christopher lives with his wife and young family, it is beautiful. I have a niece who wants to come here for a while. She is a nurse. I tell her that she might have a vocation but she says, 'no, no, no, Auntie, I know that I could never leave my family!' I tell her that I used to say the same!

"I find that the young people in Ireland are generous and enthusiastic. They have their way and it is not our way. There is no rosary on their knees: it's more likely to be a *Hail Mary*. They are very open and they cannot do enough to help. It's true that there are no vocations to religious life. That may change in the future. There are many vocations in Africa and India.

"A sister in our congregation can be moved to any place in the globe. If she is told that she is needed in a particular place, she just goes. The number of our foundations and Homes keeps increasing so there is always a lot of work. Very shortly we will open in the Philippines and we are about to establish a second Home in Taipei."

Contributions
from three distinguished Nigerians
who were educated
by the Irish Missionaries

I made many good friends in Nigeria. Three who became very special to me during the period when I was preparing to present my first book *TREASURES OF OUR ELDERS* in Enugu in 2002 were Chief Joe Uka Idigo, Mrs. Elizabeth Ekechi Okaro and Dr. (Mrs.) Virginia Anohu. Despite my having to leave Nigeria, our friendship has endured. When I started compiling this book, I asked each of them for a contribution since all three were educated by Irish missionary priests and sisters.

Chief Joe Uka Idigo

Enugu
Academic, Businessman, Philanthropist

Chief Joe Uka Idigo

"I found it delightful to go down memory lane and recall my first contact with the Irish missionaries. In my very early years, we referred to them as *onye ocha* (white man). We knew that they came from the white man's land but were unaware that there were many countries in that land. Furthermore, white people looked all the same to us and we were unable initially to distinguish between Fr. Murphy and Fr. White.

"The first white priest I remember was Fr. James Mellet. This was in 1942 when I was about five years old. He was a towering, long-bearded, strong man who visited my home town of Aguleri not very far from Onitsha in present-day Anambra State. Much was being said at the time of how he wrestled with our traditional deities. It was thought that he was too daring and eventually he was beaten up by the witches at nearby Igbariam.

"His flowing beard held much fascination for us youngsters. His favourite dish was pounded yam and ocro soup. The slimy soup often glided down the long beard in tiny meandering ripples as the beard moved up and down with each swallow of each lump of pounded yam!

"My father recounted to me the advent of the French Holy Ghost missionaries (the precursors to the Irish), into Aguleri in 1885. They came from Onitsha where they had already established themselves, through a winding bush path. They were lead by Father Joseph Lutz, an Alsatian and leader of the pioneer missionaries to the area. The farmers who first saw them raced to the townspeople and raised the alarm. Word quickly went around that white witches were seen moving into the town in convoy. There was panic and people fled into the bush.

"My grandfather, Chief Ogbuanyiya Onyekomeli Idigo (sometimes called Eze, meaning king) who was reputed to be a strong juju priest was courageous enough to meet the missionaries. He harboured them in his house and tried to assure the people that the white men were friendly. The people were not convinced however, and after much debate, my grandfather was asked to send the missionaries away or leave town with them. He opted to leave. He was accompanied by his wives, children, relations and loyal subjects. They settled on a nearby plateau knows as Ugwu Ndiuka. Eventually a church and mission house was built in that area and they are both in existence to this very day.

"Gradually, people became attracted to the Ugwu Ndiuka settlement and it was there that the white missionaries presented

Christianity – not just as a set of rules outlined in the catechism book but as a way of life. The settlement grew rapidly and converts built houses near the church and mission house. Their proximity to the mission gave them protection from enemies. In 1892, the combined efforts of the missionaries and the people shielded Aguleri from being run over by the dreaded Adas – renowned and fierce warriors from Arochukwu to the south east. The great courage of the missionaries during that period drew thanks and admiration from the people and because of that more and more of them advanced towards the Christian ideal.

"My grandfather who was among the first converts was baptized on 3 December 1891 by Fr. Lutz and given the Christian name Joseph. He surrendered his idols and gave up seven of his eight wives. He wedded with one in the Catholic Church. All his children were baptized and the event was much celebrated. Traditional diviners and witch doctors accused Idigo of betraying his ancestral deities and predicted that he would die within the year. Idigo lived on until his death on 3 June 1900.

"My own next encounter with the white missionaries – this time with the SMA Fathers – was in Minna in northern Nigeria in 1943. I was enrolled as a mass server at St. Michael's Catholic Church where the priest in charge was Fr. Murphy. We were taught to recite prayers in Latin. When Father made the sign of the Cross in Latin, we answered 'Amen'. Whatever it was he said next, we responded, 'Ad Deum qui laetificat juventutem meam.' Then we recited the Confiteor. We carried the 'mass box' into Father's car and jumped into its open back to travel with him to the remote out-stations. The experience of riding in a car was very exciting. We were learning and we had fun. We copied every thing the priests did. We tried to speak as they spoke. Fr. Prior stammered so we thought it was fashionable to stammer. We even tried to walk as they did and we had nicknames for most of them. Fr. White was called 'speed and accuracy' as he constantly emphasized that combination in the mathematics classes!

"In 1952, I entered *St. John's College, Kaduna* which was also run and managed by the SMA Fathers. That year it suddenly dawned on me that Father Prior – another Fr. Murphy, and all his colleagues were Irish. The motto of our school was 'Lucerna Lucens'. We were taught many subjects which included singing and drama. Going on picnics was a feature of school life and much attention was devoted to sports. As a result, *St. John's* was unbeaten in inter-college sports. Our school was at the time the premier Catholic secondary school in northern Nigeria. It produced many eminent Nigerians which included radicals such as Nzeobgu, Nwobosi and others who organized the first military coup in post independence Nigeria in 1966. My own contemporaries included luminaries in every walk of life and eminent predecessors included Cardinal Francis Arinze, Cardinal Dominic Ekandem and Blessed Iwene Tansi.

"When I left *St. John's*, I entered the Holy Ghost-run *All Hallows Seminary* in Onitsha. The rector and all the priests were Irish. The first Nigerian priest to join the staff was Rev. Fr. Innocent Egbujie. Frs. Michael Eneja and Godfrey Okeye (educated by the Irish) became rectors after Independence in 1960. Both later became bishops of Enugu. Bishop Okoye died in 1977 and Bishop Eneja – now emeritus – lives in Holy Trinity Parish, Enugu.

"In 1958, I went to *Bigard Memorial Seminary* in Enugu where I read philosophy for three years. Again many of the priests were Irish and I remember our rector Fr. O'Neill and Frs. O'Sullivan, Peters and Berne. It was after that period that I decided not to pursue my calling to the priesthood. My subsequent professional career took me to the University of Nigeria at Nsukka as a researcher, to the Ministry of Rural Development of the then East Central Government and finally to work as an architectural consultant for a period of fifteen years. Today I administer the *Pax Christi Trust* which is an agency that concerns itself with destitute people in Enugu and districts beyond.

"Prior to the civil war (1967-1970), most Nigerian Catholic primary schools were run and managed by the Irish. They hired, sacked and paid the teachers. They were also principals and teachers in secondary schools. They did not show the same strong presence in our universities. They concentrated instead on grass root mass education. Towns and villages vied with each other to get missions to open schools. Land was freely and generously given for that purpose. In the Irish-run schools, discipline was strict and mission-educated pupils were eventually to be found in every walk of life in

Nigeria – politics, law, education, journalism, the military and in large numbers in the civil service.

"Nor did communities in remote parts of the country escape the attention of the missionaries. When I was in the seminary, I remember going to many out-stations in such places assisting Frs. Sweeney and O'Hara. These were often located on the small tributaries of the Anambra River which itself is a tributary of the Niger. We slept in open school and church halls where mass was said the following morning. The night before, a town crier was sent round to the villages and farms to announce that the white man

King Joseph Ogbuanyiya Onyekomeli Idigo of Aguleri, 1840-1900, grandfather to Chief Joe Idigo

would be having a meeting with the authorized spokespersons of the communities. These meetings were scheduled after breakfast and it was always a big task convincing the community to send their children to school. The elders after listening would often retire to confer and a reply would come in due course through the community orator. Arguments against attending schools were frequently advanced: 'Those of our children who do not go to school make a lot of money from fishing and farming. Their yam barns are full and they can build zinc-roofed houses. Their educated counterparts have often little to show for the time spent in school. They run after girls and corrupt the youth with their new and queer ideas.' Eventually education became accepted in most places.

"There is no doubt that the Irish priests had a tremendous influence on me and my fellow Nigerians and they played a significant role in shaping our lives and destinies. The faith they implanted instilled in us a life of discipline, honesty and hard work. These are among the cherished legacies of the Irish in Nigeria. We will forever remain indebted to them."

Mrs Elizabeth Ekechi Okaro, MFR

Enugu
Educator, Broadcaster, Writer, Business Woman

Right: Mrs Elizabeth Ekechi Okaro

Since I met Elizabeth, she has been my good friend and inspiration. Now 75 years old, she continues to give a life of service and is most happy when she is helping others.

Educated by the Irish OLA Sisters in Kaduna and later at St. Osyth's College, Claxton on Sea, Essex, England, she went on to raise a family of six and engage in a disciplined career in the fields of education, broadcasting, writing and business. She has held many high profile positions in federal and state agencies. For her services in many fields, she has received many honours which include that of MFR (Member of the Federal Republic of Nigeria). At the age of 71, she launched herself into the world of business but continues to be actively involved in many charitable organizations and is frequently in demand as 'matron of ceremonies' for many prestigious civil and church occasions. What follows is a description in her own words of her early years and her contact with Irish missionary sisters in Nigeria.

"As a child from a Catholic home in Bukuru in the now Plateau State, I recall that there was no building designated as a Catholic church. The school which was named *St. Garlathi's Catholic School* served as school during the week and as church on Sundays. The reverend fathers, who were Irish, lived in nearby Jos and drove down to Bukuru to celebrate mass. Because my mother, Magdalene Udenkwo Iwugoh was a leader among the catholic women, the officiating priest would, after mass, come to our home for breakfast. Preparing for this weekly event was quite exciting. I recall my mother preparing potato chips, omelettes and bread. We children looked forward to sharing whatever was not consumed by the priest! Of all the priests, the one that left an indelible mark on my mind was Fr. McCauley; he gave me my first *rosary beads* and often gave me sweets. My father always encouraged me to entertain the priests with songs if time was available. The Irish priests baptized all the children in my family. They were operating throughout Plateau State and beyond – building schools and churches and engaging in pastoral work.

"My father who attended mission schools in Southern Nigeria did not go beyond Primary 4. Despite this, he was a great believer in education and he put us all to shame with his beautiful hand-writing and impeccable oral and written English. He was a renowned motor mechanic who worked for *Amalgamated Tin Mines of Nigeria*. In 1943, while I was attending primary school, he learned from one of the priests in Jos about a new school for girls in Kaduna which was being run by Irish OLA Sisters. He seized on the opportunity to make further enquiries and as a result, my two sisters, Jane and Vic, and I received our secondary education at *Our Lady's High School*, Kaduna and *Queen of Apostles College* (now *Queen Amina College*), Kakuri, Kaduna. Both high school and college were melting pots for girls from all over Nigeria. Our teachers included, Sister Felim, Sister Peter, Reverend Mother Arcade, Sister Marciana and Sister Comhgall.

"During this time the Irish SMA Fathers established *St. John's Secondary College, Kaduna* and I remember meeting Fr. O'Hara, Fr. Morris, Fr. Murphy and Fr. Minihane. My brother Michael attended this school which today is called *Rimi College*.

"After completing my secondary education, I spent a short period at the OLA-run *St. Agnes Teacher Training College* in Ikeja, Lagos. There I met Sister Mary Alacoque, a great lady who influenced my attitude to work by always encouraging, always appreciating and always teasing! May her gentle soul rest in peace!

"Although my close contact was with the OLA Sisters, there were many other Irish congregations who played an important role in educating Nigerian girls. Among these were the *Missionary Sisters of the Holy Rosary* (MSHR), the *Holy Child Sisters*, the *Sisters of St. Louis* (SSL) and the Daughters of Charity. My friends who were raised and educated by them have many praising stories to tell. Most of us who were educated by the Irish Sisters have not only excelled in our various fields of endeavour but have also become mothers of well-educated children in leadership positions. Often during meetings of old students, we ask ourselves what would have happened to us if we had not had the privilege of being educated by these wonderful, selfless human beings who left their country and their loved ones to come and work under difficult conditions in order to give us a better future. Even at my present age and stage of life, I can still hear Sister Mary Alacoque's voice saying, 'Elizabeth, no half measures please.' The reverend sisters were very proud of us and we are prouder of them because they made us what we are today.

"Furthermore, those of us who were educated by them have insisted on Catholic education for our children so that we can share the same values. The work of the Irish sisters has continued because the Nigerian sisters and fathers who have gradually taken over from them are carrying on their work."

In his book *IN THE BOWELS OF BIAFRA*, Matthew N. Okonkwo describes Elizabeth Okaro's leadership qualities and humanitarian work during and after the Nigerian civil war. The following is a short excerpt from that description. "I must not fail to dwell on the sterling qualities and leadership activities of a lady who still stands out clear in my mind. She was simply known as Lizzi, but very fondly called Mummy by both the young and the old. She was a woman of many parts, of wonderful and almost unbelievable capabilities, a great organizer and administrator, the product and one of the gems of the most famous Catholic secondary school for girls in Northern Nigeria."

Dr. (Mrs) Virginia Anohu – née Okoli

Abuja
Academic, Writer, Banker

Dr. (Mrs) Virginia Okoli Anohu

Dr. Virginia Anohu who was educated by the Irish Sisters of St. Louis (SSL) also offered "to go down memory lane and produce some impressions and expressions of her school days with the Irish sisters in Nigeria."

Dr. Anohu is a distinguished academic, astute banker, author, poet and literary critic. Currently vice-president and chief executive officer of mortgage bank *Mortgage Guarantee Saving and Loans Ltd.*, her previous positions include senior lecturer in literary and language studies at the *University of Nigeria*, at Nsukka, senior branch manager *Diamond Bank Nigeria Ltd.*, vice-president *First City Monument Bank Ltd., Nigeria* and executive director *Guardian Express Bank Plc.*

Though born in Eastern Nigeria, Dr. Anohu had part of her primary and secondary education in Northern Nigeria. She attended *St. Louis Secondary School, Jos* and had the following to say about her experiences during the four years she spent there.

"I recall with nostalgia my schooldays in Jos. Our principal, Sister Patricia Maloney (then called Sr. Mary Derinella) was a woman of distinction. All her colleague sisters in the school at the time were Irish. Under the St. Louis Sisters, we received the best education that the times offered. The sisters were totally dedicated and believed in what they were doing. We had relentless grooming in morality, learning and discipline. In the end, most of us grew to cherish the values they instilled in us.

"It was from this group of selfless missionaries that we understood the true meaning and importance of humility, hard work, honesty and dogged dedication to work and calling. I personally left the school with so much.

"The reverend sisters encouraged us to aim for the best in everything we set out to do. They infused us with the capacity to distinguish between what matters and what only seems to matter. They taught us sophistication in simplicity and they taught us to dare.

"They planted the fear of God in us, led us to develop a sensitive conscience and showed us the beauty of selflessness. They taught us to sing and to appreciate music and to see music as a vehicle to connect us with our Maker. They were responsible for leading me personally into the world of poetry.

"My greatest love and gratitude go to Sr. Patricia whose intellectual and moral height dwarfed those of her peers. She has come to be my mentor, my role model, my mother and my best friend. Whenever I remember my schooldays in Jos, she stands tall. No student could ever forget her as she was and still is the embodiment of all that is good and noble. Now in her mid-eighties, she is retired in Ireland and it has been my privilege to pay her frequent visits.

"The Sisters of St. Louis who first came to Nigeria in 1948 contributed enormously to the education of young women all over the country in the 1950's and 1960's and they played their part in sustaining the high standard of education of the times. Though their number is now greatly diminished, the Nigerian SSL, along with some Irish colleagues continue the work in schools in a number of locations in Nigeria today.

"Nobody was surprised in 2003 when the President of the Federal Republic of Nigeria – General Olusegun Obasanjo conferred on Sr. Patricia Moloney the honour of OFR (Order of the Federal Republic of Nigeria) in recognition of her invaluable contribution to the Nigerian educational system.

"By the sheer coincidence of fate and destiny, the award was presented during my son's wedding ceremony in the Dorchester Hotel in London by Dr. (Mrs.) Obi Ezekwesili, currently the Honourable Federal Minister of Solid Minerals. It was a memorable occasion for Sr. Patricia and her family who flew to London for the occasion.

I take this opportunity to remember my godmother – who was also my teacher – Sr. Mary Galgani. May her soul rest in peace. I will one day lay a bouquet of flowers on her graveside.

"The SSL were saints of sorts. They taught us to rejoice and laugh and to cry only in the rains."